Sephardic Jews in America

Sephardic Jews in America

A Diasporic History

Aviva Ben-Ur

NEW YORK UNIVERSITY PRESS
New York and London

NEW YORK UNIVERSITY PRESS
New York and London
www.nyupress.org

© 2009 by New York University
All rights reserved

Library of Congress Cataloging-in-Publication Data

Ben-Ur, Aviva.
Sephardic Jews in America : a diasporic history / Aviva Ben-Ur.
p. cm.
Includes bibliographical references and index.
ISBN-13: 978-0-8147-9982-6 (cl : alk. paper)
ISBN-10: 0-8147-9982-5 (cl : alk. paper)
1. Sephardim—United States—Identity. 2. Jews—United States—Identity.
3. Sephardim—United States—History—20th century. 4. Sephardim—United States—
Social life and customs. 5. United States—Ethnic relations. I.Title.
E184.36.E84B46   2009
305.892'4073—dc22   2008038143

New York University Press books are printed on acid-free paper,
and their binding materials are chosen for strength and durability.
We strive to use environmentally responsible suppliers and materials
to the greatest extent possible in publishing our books.

Manufactured in the United States of America

10 9 8 7 6 5 4 3 2 1

Contents

	Acknowledgments	vii
	Introduction: The Jews Who Weren't There: Scholarly and Communal Exclusion	1
1	Immigration, Ethnicity, and Identity	23
2	Hebrew with a Sephardic Accent: A Test Case for Impact	51
3	East Meets West: Sephardic Strangers and Kin	81
4	Ashkenazic-Sephardic Encounters	108
5	The Hispanic Embrace	150
6	Conclusion: A View from the Margins	188
	Appendix: Population Statistics of Non-Ashkenazic Jews in the United States of America	193
	Abbreviations	197
	Notes	199
	Index	297
	About the Author	321

Acknowledgments

The Sephardic Home for the Aged, located in Brooklyn, New York, was the focus of a study in the late 1960s by Giselle Hendel-Sebestyen, a Ph.D. candidate of Eastern European Jewish descent. This young anthropologist was surprised that, instead of discomfort or defensiveness, residents and staff displayed "pride in being observed" and an eagerness to discuss their cultural heritage as Eastern Sephardim.[1] This approachability perfectly describes what I, too, encountered while conducting oral interviews on and off over the past fourteen years. It took me many years to fully understand the reason for this openness. Eastern Sephardic Jews have never been silent, but they have seldom been heard.

I am deeply grateful to the dozens of Sephardic Jews in Boston, Cincinnati, New York, Los Angeles, Portland (Oregon), and Seattle, who so freely gave of their time, knowledge, and reflections. They are the mainstay of many of my arguments, and they instilled within me an ardent drive to delve into this research. Many of these informants also shared with me precious materials from their personal archives. Over the years, this list of interviewees expanded to include many non-Sephardic Jews and non-Jews. I recognize all of these informants individually: Allan Abravanel; Magnolia Albalat; Edward Alcosser; David Fintz Altabé; Victor and Thiya Altchek; Fannie Israel Alvo; the late Albert J. Amateau and the late Edith M. Amateau; Micaela Amato; Sol Amon; Hy Arnesty; Gloria Ascher; Aaron Assael and Murray Farash of the Broome and Allen Street Boys Association; Isaac Azose; Louise Azose; Robert Bedford; David A. Behar; Elazar Behar; Norman Belmonte; Jack and Bernice Belur; Diego Benardete; José Benardete; Yilmaz Benadrete; Joe Benezra; Sarah Benezra; Art Benveniste; Victor R. Besso, Victor E. Besso, and the late Dorothy Besso, son, nephew, and widow, respectively, of the late Henry V. Besso; Rachel Amado Bortnick; Daniel Bouskila; Irma Cardozo; Jack and Sara Calderon; Barry Cohen; Stanton Cole; Howard Danon; Louise DeFez and Mathilda Turiel; the late Marco DeFunis; Lilly DeJaen; Máximo Dextre; Ricardo D'Jaen; Howard A. Droker; Joe

Elias; Morris Epstein; Susana Redondo de Feldman; Phil Flash; Johnny Franco; Nathan Franco; Robert Franco; Ralph Funes; David Gedalecia; Diana Galante Goldin; Dora Matarasso Green; Ceila and Dinah Hakim; Hank and Phyllis Halio; Joel Halio; Isaac and Mary Hanoka; Yaakov and Bina Hanoka; Michael Harrington; Hannah R. Hubbard; Esther Israel; Flory Jagoda; Isaac Jerusalmi; Chaim Kofinas; Richard Kostalanetz; Bess Kremens; Benjamin Lardizabal; Victor Laredo; Denah Lida; Lenny Lubitz; Dina Dahbany-Miraglia; Emilie de Vidas Levy; Joel N. Levy; Rachel Levy and Jean Akrish (daughters of *La Vara* editor Albert Levy); Rashel Levy; Rena Levy; Robert Levy; Shoshana Levin; Zachary Levy; Denah Lida; Otto Maduro; Isaac Maimon; Solomon Maimon; Daniel Matarasso; Richard Matsa; Jack and Suzanne Mayesh; Joanne Menasche; Sam Menasche; James Moché; Esther Morhaime; Asher Murciano; David Mushabac; Jane Mushabac; Beatrice Coralnik Papo; Al Passy; Caren and Rachel S. Pauley; Lenora (Leni) Peha La Marche; Ralph and Raye Policar; Diana Polichar; Gregory Rabassa; David Rabeeya; Joyce Rivkin; David Romey; Linda Ezratty Rosenberg; Daniel Santacruz; Marianne Sanua; Victor Sanua; Barry Dov Schwartz; Stella Altchek Shapiro; Katherine Scharhon; Barton Sholod; Benjamin Soulam; Charlene and Marlene Souriano; Linda Souriano Israeli; Stanley Sultan; Ralph Sutton; Morris Tarragano; Mathilde Touriel; Joseph Uzel; Laura Varon; and the "Sephardim for Yeshua" members of Congregation Adat Yeshua in Albuquerque, New Mexico.

Deep gratitude is due to the many institutions that supported this project during its years of development. I list them here in chronological order. The Woodrow Wilson National Fellowship Foundation named me a Mellon Fellow in the Humanities in 1990 and provided funding for three years of graduate school, including the crucial last year of the doctoral program. Temple University's Center for American Jewish History awarded me the 1995 Summer Fellowship to research the advice columns of Moise B. Soulam and also provided a 1998 dissertation grant. The Jewish Historical Society of New York named me the Malcolm H. Stern Memorial Fellow for my research on Moise B. Soulam (1995–1996). Brandeis University's Department of Near Eastern and Judaic Studies provided me with graduate fellowships that enabled me to complete my coursework and research (1995–1997). The American Jewish Archives of Cincinnati named me the Ethel Marcus Memorial Fellow in American Jewish Studies (1997–1998) to examine the papers of Joseph M. Papo. The Hispanic/Sephardic component of this study was supported by a fellowship from the National Endowment for the Humanities, an independent federal agency (Fellowship for College Teachers and Independent Scholars, 1999–2000, FB-35756). Concurrently, I held the Hazel D. Cole Fellowship in Jewish Studies at the University of Washington (1999–2000). Finally, the American Jewish Historical Society awarded me the Sid and Ruth Lapidus Fellowship (2007–2008).

Jane S. Gerber and Ruth Abram, founding president of the Lower East Side Tenement Museum, engaged me as researcher and historian for the "Komunidad Project" from 1994–1995, an endeavor that led me to my dissertation topic. I take this opportunity to express my profound thanks to my dissertation committee members: Joyce Antler, Sylvia Barack Fishman, Avigdor Levy, and especially Jonathan Sarna, the best adviser a graduate student could hope for. They and the many other scholars, teachers, and librarians who assisted me at Brandeis University are constant reminders of the intellectual haven I found there.

Many colleagues, friends, communal leaders, librarians, archivists, and family members pointed me to critical sources, supported this project, read early versions of this manuscript, offered assistance with arcane Ladino vocabulary, or offered helpful feedback, and I thank them here: David Fintz Altabé; Marc D. Angel; Sam Armistead; Sarah Bunin Benor; Judith B. Coffey; Charles Cutter; Dina Dahbany-Miraglia; Lev Hakak; Seth Jerchower; Denah Lida; Gerard Klooster; Wim Klooster; Shahanna McKinney-Baldon; James Moché; James Rosenbloom; Jonathan L. Roses; Lorraine E. Roses; Marianne Sanua; Shuly Rubin Schwartz; Susan Shapiro; Sarah Abrevaya Stein; Esther Toledo; James E. Young, Linda Zenner, and the late Walter Zenner. I would also like to thank the many archivists, librarians, administrators, and faculty members who assisted me at the following institutions (their names are included, where possible): American Jewish Archives; American Jewish Historical Society; American Sephardi Federation (Randall Belinfante); Hebrew Union College (Cincinnati, Ohio); the Hispanic Institute at Columbia University (Patricia Grieve and Patrick McMorrow); the Library of the Jewish Theological Seminary of America; the Grand Lodge Library in New York (Tom Savini); the New York Public Library and the Library's Jewish Division; the Sephardic Reading Room of Yeshiva University (Mitchell Serels); the Educational Alliance in New York (Scott Stein and Linda Mazer); the Judaica Division of Harvard College Library (Leah Orent and Elizabeth Vernon); Congregation Shearith Israel (Marc D. Angel and archivist Susan Tobin); Sephardic Temple Tifereth Israel in Los Angeles and YIVO Institute for Jewish Research. I would also like to thank two anonymous reviewers, one of whom turned out to be Zion Zohar, for their helpful corrections and feedback. I owe a debt of gratitude to Jennifer Hammer, senior editor at New York University Press, who has awed me with her unmatched alacrity and incisiveness. My debt to the pioneering works of Marc D. Angel and the late Joseph M. Papo and Joseph A. D. Sutton should become clear in the following chapters.

A special thanks are due to Luke Doubleday for his technical assistance with many of the illustrations that appear in this book, and to Ari Benveniste and his colleagues at Sephardic Temple Tifereth Israel, for their help in securing the cover image.

Prolonged archival and field research has made me ever more aware of my limited knowledge. Notice of corrections and omissions are welcome and should be communicated directly to the author.

Introduction
The Jews Who Weren't There:
Scholarly and Communal Exclusion

On a late summer day in 1910, twenty-one-year-old Albert J. Amateau, a Sephardic Jew from the Aegean town of Milas, arrived at Ellis Island.¹ His ship, the SS *Santa Maria,* had provided no cabin accommodations, obliging passengers to cross the frigid Atlantic on the open deck, lying on their own mattresses and consuming only the food they could bring with them. The passage dragged on for twenty days.² Similar hardships are conveyed in the diary of Alfred Ascher, a native of Izmir who left the Peloponnesian port of Patras for New York in November 1915. A ferocious nighttime storm during the one-month crossing thrust his ship back 350 miles. The sight of "men, women, children crying, screaming," some praying fervently with phylacteries and prayer shawls, others with icons of the Virgin Mary, reduced the stalwart Ascher to tears.³

These adversities prepared neither Amateau nor Ascher for the difficulties that lay ahead on land. For unlike most Jewish immigrants, Eastern Sephardim were not readily recognized as Jews by their established Ashkenazic coreligionists and could therefore not expect automatically to receive the assistance extended to Jewish immigrants, the vast majority of whom were Yiddish-speaking and of Eastern European origin. Toward the end of an amazingly long and varied life, which stretched nearly 107 years, Amateau still vividly recalled several incidents in which Ashkenazim either denied or doubted his Jewishness. Some of these Ashkenazim were boarding-house proprietors who had turned Amateau away, forcing him to seek out a hostel run under Sephardic auspices.⁴ Alfred Ascher must have also experienced similar frustrations. His niece Gloria Ascher, who grew up in the Bronx in the 1950s, recently testified that for some Ashkenazim, "people who spoke something like Spanish instead of Yiddish and ate grape leaves instead of gefilte fish were simply not Jews!"[5]

This denial of Jewishness was a defining experience for Eastern Sephardic immigrants (and, in some cases, for their native-born children and grandchildren as well). Perhaps not accidentally, in both the U.S. Jewish community and the academic study of its past, Jewishness has tacitly been assumed to be synonymous with Germanic or Eastern European descent.[6] What began at the turn of the twentieth century as denial of shared ethnicity and religion (whereby Ashkenazim failed to recognize Sephardim as fellow Jews) continues today in textbooks, articles, documentaries, films, and popular awareness. More often than not, Sephardic Jews are simply absent from any sort of portrayal of the American Jewish community.

This exclusion is deeply embedded within historiographical paradigms. The overwhelming majority of scholarly works devoted to the American Jewish past and present communicate unawareness of non-Ashkenazic communities.[7] Narratives stretching back to colonial times typically display a perfunctory mention of the pioneering Western Sephardim who arrived in 1654—the proverbial "first Jews on American soil"—and an equally mechanical reference to their rapid assimilation into majority cultures.[8] Studies of American Jewry focusing on the nineteenth and twentieth centuries reserve at best a one-sentence nod at Eastern Sephardim (Iberian-origin Jews transplanted to the Balkans and the Anatolian Peninsula) and Mizrahim (Jews indigenous to North Africa and the Middle East), who came to these shores from the disintegrating Ottoman Empire. The non-Ashkenazic Jew then plunges precipitously off the page into the abyss of historical oblivion.[9]

Significantly, works aiming to be temporally or thematically inclusive bear this trait of exclusion or marginalization no less than more specialized studies. Consider, for example, a diachronic history of American Jews (2003) and an award-winning history of American Judaism (2004), neither of which includes a single mention of Ladino-, Arabic-, or Greek-speaking Jewish immigrants.[10] The author of the first work also produced a 350-page history of American Jews (2004) that devotes a lone paragraph to "Jews from the Balkans, Turkey, and Greece," with no mention of the far more numerous Arabic- or Farsi-speaking Jews.[11] These examples from some of the leading American Jewish historians illustrate that an exclusionary narrative frames even the finest contemporary scholarship. These omissions do not reflect a failure to absorb trends from the broader field of U.S. history. The assumption that Jews are either Germanic or Eastern European prevails in American immigration historiography as well.[12]

Communal leaders and scholars of various disciplines have long recognized the neglect of Sephardi, Mizrahi, and Romaniote Jews in portraits of the American Jewish experience.[13] Pedagogues in both U.S. institutions of higher learning and Jewish religious schools have openly acknowledged this lacuna as a serious problem. Suggestions for integrating Sephardic studies into various curricula have appeared in dozens of articles and several volumes[14] and have been voiced at numerous Jewish studies conferences.[15]

The struggle against invisibility has produced laudable results in both the scholarly and lay communities. The ethnic revivalism of the 1960s and 1970s, epitomized in the film version of *Fiddler on the Roof* and Alex Haley's *Roots* and influenced by the growing consciousness of the Holocaust's destructive impact,[16] witnessed an efflorescence of higher learning and research about neglected Jewish minority groups. The founding of the Sephardic Studies Program at Yeshiva University in 1964 not only helped to develop the field intellectually but also spawned dozens of rabbis, teachers, cantors, and community leaders, trained to enrich popular awareness.[17] Following quickly in Yeshiva University's footsteps was the establishment of the American Society of Sephardic Studies (1967) and its journal, the *Sephardic Scholar* (later incorporated as the journal of Yeshiva University's Sephardic Studies Program), the American Sephardi Federation (ASF, 1973), and Sephardic House (1978), now part of the ASF.[18] Recently, Sephardic studies programming officially integrated into Jewish studies or Jewish history has developed at Brandeis University, Florida International University, Stanford University, the University of California at Los Angeles, and the University of Washington, to name the most prominent examples. These innovations and developments, alas, have done little to draw Sephardi and Mizrahi Jews out of public obscurity and still less to reshape the paradigm of American Jewish history.

If non-Ashkenazic Jews are generally not part of the recognized portrait of contemporary Jewry, or of American and U.S. Jewish history, one might wonder if this anonymity is deserved. Why focus on a segment of the American Jewish community that has probably never risen above 3 or 4 percent since colonial times?[19] Sephardi and Mizrahi studies scholars and communal leaders have offered some suggestive responses to this question. In the context of neglected Jewish belles-lettres, Norman Roth has observed, "we are missing a tremendous opportunity in field research."[20] Author and activist David Shasha argues that Sephardic civilization, with its "religious humanism," can speak to many of the crises that confront American Jews, including assimilation and cultural alienation.[21] Joel Marcus, a member of the ASF board of directors, stresses that non-Ashkenazic Jews, to whom the Orthodox, Conservative, and Reform movements are not indigenous, can serve as leading examples of "religious pluralism," "great tolerance and mutual respect."[22] Sociologist Abraham Lavender has argued that since Sephardic Jews constitute a separate group, they should be granted the same attention bestowed on other ethnic groups. He also points out that outside the United States, and particularly in the State of Israel, non-Ashkenazic Jews constitute a sizeable segment of the general Jewish population, and thus these Jews are "consequential to the future of Jewry." Finally, Lavender affirms that Sephardic history offers rich lessons for "the relations between the dominant society and minority groups."[23]

It is tempting to contend that *despite* their small number, non-Ashkenazic Jews are indeed worthy of study or consideration. This book, however, argues for a focus on Sephardi and Mizrahi Jews precisely *because* they constitute the periphery of America's Jewish community. The inspiration for this approach comes from the study of the margins as a tool for shedding light on broader society. In an examination of newly Orthodox Jewish women, sociologist Lynn Davidman has explored in detail a very small and unusual group as a way of understanding "more general social trends." Though Orthodox Jews constitute only about 10 percent of the U.S. Jewish population, the adoption of that denomination by mostly young, Jewish women and their explanations for this radical choice may shed light on dilemmas of women from broader society whose concerns are seldom articulated.[24] Similarly, Jill Matthews has studied the case records of women living in mental institutions "as a way of uncovering the normative definitions of femininity in Australian culture." By examining the women who "'broke the rules' of femininity," Matthews was able to "tease out the underlying, implicit rules for what it means to be a woman."[25] Sociologist Charles Selengut and poet-professor Bruce Kamenetz, in their interviews with Jews who have adopted Buddhism or joined a wide variety of so-called cults, both discovered that defection from the Jewish community reveals dissatisfaction with the various denominations of Judaism or with broader Anglo-American society.[26] These observations suggest that the exception is well deserving of scrutiny, for it illuminates what is otherwise imperceptible in mainstream society. A focus on the Jewish community's ethnic margins may help recast understanding of the country's majority Ashkenazic community and, more generally, the broader theme of U.S. intraethnic relations.

The secondary, and related, concern of this book is the image of excluded Jews on those rare occasions when they do make an appearance on the U.S. stage. As M. Mitchell Serels observed in the 1980s, "The Sephardim have often been viewed as exotica, curiosities which have shot off from the mainstream of Jewry, shunted into an isolation from the flow of Jewish ideas, and fossilized into an unsophisticated backwardness. This inaccuracy has permeated the entirety of the body of Jewish history."[27] Author and religious leader David Rabeeya described as racist the "distortions" and "falsehoods" about Sephardic Jewry perpetuated in the field of American Jewish education.[28] Anthropologists Walter P. Zenner and Shlomo Deshen observe that in the United States scholars and laymen "concerned with matters of Jewry and Jewish culture" see non-Ashkenazic Jews as requiring "either justification or improvement, but they are not perceived for what they are, simply traditional manifestations of Jewry."[29] At the opposite extreme are depictions of Eastern Sephardim and Mizrahim as "more Jewish" than Ashkenazim, either because of purported ancestral "purity" or closer geographical association with the Land of Israel. An assessment of recurring images at both ends of the spectrum is crucial to a paradigm shift in American Jewish historiography.[30]

The phenomenon of scholarly and communal exclusion raises sensitive questions. Why are non-Ashkenazic Jews often overlooked in the broader field of Jewish studies and in the mainstream Jewish community's portrayal of itself both privately and to the outside world? The simplest explanation is that Sephardi and Mizrahi Jews are not situated at the geographic or ethnic centers of the contemporary Jewish world. The vast majority of Jews, both globally and in the United States, is of Ashkenazic descent, with roots in Western and Eastern Europe. Moreover, the traditional periodization of American Jewish history, which divides the past into the Sephardic, Germanic, Eastern European, and American phases, does not account for Eastern Sephardim and Mizrahim.[31] But in an age in which the study of minority groups is often privileged, one wonders what other factors might be involved. Academics and community members have offered various suggestions likely to generate heated debate. In a broader Jewish history context, historians Marina Rustow and Sarah Abrevaya Stein have pointed to the force of Eurocentrism, "laziness," and "a profound resistance to reconceptualize."[32] In an analysis of the neglect of Sephardi- and Mizrahi-authored fiction, Edouard Roditi suggests that "guilt-feelings about their own cultural assimilation or nostalgia for their own ancestral past" are what gravitate most American Jewish readers to Ashkenazi writers, such as Bernard Malamud, Chaim Potok, and Philip Roth.[33] Roditi seems to imply that American Jewish readers—who are largely of Eastern European Ashkenazic origin—are most interested in reading about their own cultural group. Rachel Wahba, a writer and therapist based in Los Angeles, trenchantly argues that the failure to conceptually incorporate Mizrahi Jews into the American Jewish community represents not "benign ignorance" but rather an "unconscious and deep-rooted need to identify as European, . . . wanting to identify with the West, not wanting to be seen as 'other.'"[34] Whether or not one accepts these explanations, the ongoing exclusion of non-Ashkenazic Jews from American Jewish historiography and communal self-representation should be of great concern.

American Jewish History from the Margins

Sephardic Jews in America considers a "minority within a minority," the 4 percent of the U.S. Jewish community that is not of Germanic or Eastern European Ashkenazic descent.[35] Though the diversity of this group defies easy categorization, its main overarching ethnic classifications are Sephardi, Mizrahi, and Romaniote Jews. Sephardic Jews are here defined as Spanish- and Portuguese-speaking Jews of Western Europe and Ladino-speaking Jews of the Ottoman Empire. Mizrahi Jews encompass predominantly (Judeo-)Arabic-speaking Jews who are native to the Middle East and western Asia, and Romaniotes are Greek-speaking Jews native to the former Byzantine Empire.[36] This book acknowledges these three groups as constituting the principal non-Ashkenazic populations in the United States. But the emphasis in these pages is on communities of Iberian Jewish descent, which formed the majority of the non-Ashkenazic community through the first half of the twentieth century. Since then, Mizrahi Jews have vastly outnumbered both Iberian- and Greek-origin Jews. Their history and rich multilingual archives, considered only briefly in this book, deserve a separate monograph.

Readers familiar with American Jewish history will not find in these pages the traditional narrative of immigration, adversity, achievement, and impact on broader U.S. society.³⁷ Nor will they read of American Jewry as more or less a conglomerate whole that rarely interacts with other ethnic groups.³⁸ These paradigms are generally not meaningful for the history of non-Ashkenazic Jews. Rather, the focus here is on the experiences of Sephardi and Mizrahi Jews with the dominant Ashkenazic community and with non-Jewish subgroups with whom they shared varying degrees of cultural and linguistic affinity. These experiences illuminate hitherto unknown phenomena in ethnoreligious identity and intra- and interethnic relations. Through an investigation of these relations, this book ponders the elements that drew Sephardi and Mizrahi immigrants apart from their new neighbors in the United States, the factors that encouraged productive encounters and rapprochement, and the ways in which they were forced to reassess and remake their ethnic identities as a result of these interactions. The ties these multiethnic Jews forged among themselves and with neighboring communities broadened—and sometimes disrupted—the panoply of Jewish, Hispanic, and Arab identities.

Because most of the immigrants landed and remained in the city of New York, Eastern Sephardi and Mizrahi history in the United States is very much a New York story. A focus on this metropolis is more broadly justified by its global significance as home to the largest Jewish population in history, with over 1.5 million residents by 1920.³⁹ Eastern Sephardim and Mizrahim established much smaller communities in Los Angeles, Seattle, Atlanta, Cincinnati, Montgomery (Alabama), Indianapolis, Chicago, New Brunswick (New Jersey), San Francisco, and later in Miami.⁴⁰ These settlements are not extensively considered in this book but should be examined in greater depth as a way to appreciate New York's national impact and, conversely, the distinctive traits of smaller communities.⁴¹

As the first full-length, academic study of non-Ashkenazic Jews in the United States, this book is meant to be suggestive rather than definitive and will hopefully stimulate many additional forays into the archives.⁴² This book is written within the framework of American Jewish history, by a scholar of the Jewish past, but its relevance will hopefully be farther reaching. This prospect may be bolstered by recent demographic shifts and political developments, including the status of Hispanics as the fastest-growing minority group in the United States and the current national focus on the Middle East and its immigrant descendants.⁴³ In light of these trends, this book offers fresh perspectives on an earlier Hispanic and Arabic presence in the country, rarely considered through the lenses of Jewish history.

Scholars and students of U.S. Jewish and ethnic history, and the lay community alike, have yet another reason to grant serious consideration to the country's non-Ashkenazic population. In a survey conducted in 2002, the Los Angeles–based Institute for Jewish and Community Research found that at least 20 percent of the country's six million Jews are "diverse Jews." This recently coined term refers to "racially and ethnically diverse" individuals who identify as "African, African American, Latino (Hispanic), Asian, Native American, Sephardic, Mizrahi and mixed-race Jews by heritage, adoption, and [sic] marriage." The institute's broad definition of Jewishness, as well as interview methods sensitive to the idiosyncrasies of non-Ashkenazic Jews, resulted in a population estimate significantly higher than the latest conventional figure of 5.2 million, offered by the National Jewish Population Survey in the year 2000.⁴⁴ The institute's findings suggest that the population of non-Ashkenazic Jews will exponentially increase in the coming decades. Perhaps with it will increase the awareness of the intrinsic significance of Sephardi and Mizrahi Jews to the broader Jewish community and to various non-Jewish subethnic groups throughout the United States. This demographic trend may help underscore the present book's thesis, that the acknowledged portrait of American Jewish history and society remains incomplete without the integration of non-Ashkenazic Jews. The contemporary American Jewish community emerged from the interaction of its subethnic groups and cannot adequately be understood without considering its Sephardi, Mizrahi, and Romaniote legacies.

Finally, it is important to state what this study is not. The aim here is not to compose a linear history of the Sephardic community in the first half of the twentieth century or of the various institutions that Sephardi and Mizrahi Jews founded over the years. Rather, this study has the thematic aim of exploring intra- and interethnic relations between the various groups that Eastern Sephardim and, to a lesser extent, Mizrahi Jews encountered in the United States. This book is also not a call for social justice in the American Jewish community. This fact is especially important to underscore given recent studies authored by socially conscious authors who deal with Jewish multiculturalism.⁴⁵ If this book contains any plea, it is that scholars of American Jews no longer ignore the sources documenting the experiences of non-Ashkenazim in the United States.

Sources Used for This Study

Among the central aims of this book is to turn attention to heretofore-untapped primary sources. Perhaps the richest of these sources for the first half of the twentieth century is the Ladino (Judeo-Spanish) press, a prodigious subethnic goldmine that has rarely informed any study on American Jewish immigration. The first enduring American Ladino newspaper, *La America* ("America," 1910–1925), was joined by at least eighteen others of varying lifespans, until the complete demise of the American Ladino press in 1948. With two minor exceptions, all known Judeo-Spanish tabloids in the United States were published in New York.[46] Ladino newspapers in the United States varied politically and religiously, and they reflected the ideological diversity of their editors and readership.

Other sources that shaped this book are multilingual letters, circulars, minutes, memoirs, vintage audiotapes, documents, dramatic scripts, and photographs, gathered from archives and interviewees in Boston, Los Angeles, Miami, New York, Portland (Oregon), and Seattle. I have also drawn on articles from the Anglo-American, Anglo-Jewish, and, to a lesser extent, the American Hebrew and Yiddish press. Aside from the Ladino press, the most precious source is oral testimony. Since the mid-1990s, I have conducted interviews with dozens of Eastern Sephardic immigrants and their descendants and with what has become a sizeable group of Ashkenazim, Mizrahim, and non-Jews. These qualitative interviews have, in some cases, confirmed or embellished my archival findings and, in other cases, provided information unavailable in written sources.

Because some of my interviewees were "Mizrahi" and "Romaniote" Jews, it seems appropriate to offer a brief comment about their distinctive legacies in the United States. The country's Arabic-speaking Jews are the focus of only one book, by Joseph A. D. Sutton, whose work deals with the Syrian community of Flatbush.[47] To date, no other book on Arabic Jewish communities has appeared, though Dina Dahbany-Miraglia is currently writing a study on Yemeni Jews.[48] The Greek-speaking

Jews of New York still await their own historian.[49] My intention during recent years has been to visit archives pertaining to Brooklyn's Syrian Jewish community, in the hope of tapping previously unknown sources pertaining to Mizrahim. There is some indirect evidence, for example, that Mizrahi Jews may have produced their own newspapers or newsletters in their native languages,[50] but the archives I have examined do not preserve any of them.[51] That archival visit did not materialize. Time constraints also prevented me from giving due attention to Greek-speaking Jews. I hope the many gaps in this study will serve as incentive for future scholars, particularly those better linguistically equipped than I, to research these non-Ashkenazic communities, which were smaller, though collectively no less significant, in the twentieth century's first half.

The "Other" Jews: A Historical Overview

Jews in the Iberian Peninsula

In the autumn of 1922, José M. Estrugo set sail for Spain, the land of his medieval ancestors. Born in the Ottoman Empire, Estrugo had arrived in the United States in his youth and in 1920 became a founding member of the Sephardic community of Los Angeles. But Estrugo could find no peace in the United States, and since he was not a Zionist, Jerusalem held no allure for him. Only in Spain could he feel like "the Indian in America."[52] In the early 1930s he reminisced, "For the first time in my life I felt truly aboriginal, native. Here I was not, I could not be an intruder! For the first time I felt very much at home, much more than in the Jewish quarter where I was born! I am not ashamed to confess that I bent down, in an outburst of indescribable emotion, and kissed the ground upon which I tread for the first time, nearly a century after the end of the Inquisition."[53]

José M. Estrugo is a modern manifestation of the deep connections that many Sephardic Jews have felt to Spain through the ages, even centuries after their exile. This sense of belonging is anchored in historical memories that stretch back to antiquity. Not every Sephardic Jew in the twentieth century would have shared Estrugo's nostalgia or his exoneration of Spanish Catholic society for centuries of religious and racial persecution. But none could deny the formative power of a millennial sojourn in the Iberian Peninsula.

According to one Sephardic tradition, Jews settled in the Iberian Peninsula after the Babylonian monarch Nebuchadnezzar undertook an expedition to Spain in the sixth century B.C.E., bringing in his wake "many families of the tribe of Judah, and the house of David." This legend was particularly popular among Sephardim in Christian lands, for it demonstrated that their ancestors were guiltless of Christ's crucifixion in first-century Jerusalem.[54] These legends were evoked particularly during times of crisis, for example, in the months before the Jews were expelled from Spain. Muslims in Spain, who faced expulsion at the end of the sixteenth century, attempted to demonstrate their own longevity in the peninsula for similar reasons.[55]

The peninsula's first Jewish immigrants supposedly constructed cities they named after Hebrew words or toponyms of the Land of Israel. The false Hebrew etymologies that this legend attributes to Iberian place names since at least the fourteenth century underscores the ties that Sephardic Jews felt to their diasporic homeland. "Yepes," south of Madrid, was allegedly named after Joppa (Israel's modern-day Jaffa), and "Távora" (from the Távora river in what is today Portugal) was said to derive from Mount Tabor in the Lower Galilee.[56] "Toledo" supposedly represented the word *Toledoth*, Hebrew for "generations."[57] Daniel Levi de Barrios, a Spanish-born *converso* who returned to Judaism in Leghorn in the seventeenth century, pushed the Hebrew precedence further back in time when he affirmed that the Garden of Eden had been located in his native Spain. The peninsula was not named "Celtiberia" after the Celts and the Iberians, he explained, but rather after the Hebrew word for ribs (*tseluot*), recalling the biblical account in which God extracted one of Adam's ribs during his sleep.[58] These etymologically and historically baseless legends underscore Sephardic Jews' strong sense of belonging in the Iberian Peninsula. Naming, as one historian has argued in the context of Europe's conquests in the New World, can be understood as an act of possession.[59] Even as they faced toward Jerusalem in their daily prayers, very few Sephardim abandoned their birthplace for Palestine; the Iberian Peninsula was their home.[60]

A more widespread Sephardic legend, however, explains that Jews from the southern kingdom of Judah settled in the peninsula only after the destruction of the Second Temple in 70 C.E. The classical Hebrew word for Spain is *Sefarad*, a toponym derived from the verse "The exiled of Jerusalem who are in Sefarad" (Book of Obadiah 1:20).[61] Although the biblical source does not specify the location of this toponym, Jewish exegetes since the first century C.E. have identified it with Hispania, the Roman name for the Iberian Peninsula.[62] Most of these biblical interpreters also identified the founding of the peninsula's Jewish community with the Judeans exiled by the Romans in 70 C.E.[63] Jews with origins in the Iberian Peninsula are known in Hebrew as SefaraDIM, which, under the influence of Ashkenazic usage, is usually pronounced SeFARdim.

There is some historical evidence that Jews settled in the peninsula during the first centuries of the Common Era. In his *Letter to the Romans* (15:24, 28), Paul expresses his intention to go to Spain to spread the gospel, which suggests a Jewish presence there by the mid-first century C.E.[64] The earliest extrabiblical evidence for a Jewish presence in the peninsula comes from archeological ruins. A tombstone excavated in the nineteenth century and now lost bore a Latin epitaph of a Jewish toddler. Particularly because the decedent was a child (as opposed to an adult man, who could have been traveling there alone as an itinerant merchant), this epitaph is irrefutable proof that a Jewish community had developed on the peninsula by around 200 C.E.[65] An epigraph subsequently unearthed has pushed back that date a century or two earlier.[66]

The history of Jews in the Iberian Peninsula under various pagan, Christian, and Muslim rulers has been oft recounted and need not be repeated here.[67] Two periods, however, deserve mention, as they played a central role in shaping the images and self-representation of Sephardic Jews in the United States: the periods under Muslim and Christian rule.

The period under Muslim rule, particularly from the tenth through twelfth centuries, is among the best known in popular Jewish consciousness. That era—the so-called Spanish Golden Age—refers to the intellectual, literary, and cultural heights that prominent Sephardim achieved in Muslim Iberia.[68] The community produced courtiers, Hebrew poets and grammarians, philosophers, military leaders, and exceptional rabbinic leaders, including the legalist Moses Maimonides and Judah Halevi, sometimes called the national poet of the Jewish people.

The memory of Iberia's Christian period also played an important role in the ascribed- and self-identity of U.S. Sephardic Jews. Under Christian rule, dating from the conquest of Toledo in 1086, Jewish religious and legal status steadily declined. In 1391, wide-scale mob violence broke out, instigated by a fervent preacher and resulting in the forced conversion of tens of thousands of Jews across the whole of Spain, including the islands of Mallorca and Minorca. In Hebrew historiography, this year is known as *shenat hashemad*, or "the year of apostasy." Many of these new converts continued to practice Judaism or secretly to identify as Jews. They were popularly known as *marranos*, the Castilian word for "swine," and in legal terms as New Christians (*cristianos nuevos*) or converts (*conversos*).

According to Catholic doctrine, converts to Christianity who strayed back to their ancestral faith were guilty of heresy. That many new converts to Catholicism continued to practice their former faith sub rosa was a public secret. In response to rampant secret Judaism in Spain, the Inquisition was established in 1478. The Catholic monarchs, convinced that unconverted Jews were a major factor in encouraging New Christians to practice secret Judaism, decided that the only solution was to remove the open Jewish community from Spain. In 1492, King Ferdinand and Queen Isabella expelled the Jews from Spain and its provinces, including Sicily and Sardinia. In the absence of reliable archival records, modern historians have radically disagreed on the number of Jews exiled from Spain, but the figure of two hundred thousand seems reasonable.[69]

In 1492, possibly half of the Spanish Jewish exiles migrated to the kingdom of Portugal,[70] where, in 1497, the entire Jewish community was forcibly converted to Catholicism. Though initially lenient toward new converts and their children, the Portuguese rulers eventually exhibited a harshness exceeding that of Spain. The Portuguese Inquisition was established in 1536 in order to uproot the Judaizing "heresy." So brutal was its punishment that the public ceremony, in which recalcitrant Judaizers and other offenders were burnt alive, became widely known by its Portuguese name, "auto-da-fe." Perhaps paradoxically, the emotional tie of Sephardic Jews to Portugal was even stronger than their attachment to Spain. After Portugal regained its independence in 1640 (having been forcibly united with Spain in 1580), many in the Western Sephardic Diaspora yearned to return to their native land and hoped that the monarchs would put an end to social and Inquisitorial discrimination against New Christians.[71]

The Iberian-Jewish Diaspora:
Western Europe and the Ottoman Empire

In 1492 and 1497, open Jewish life in Spain and Portugal, respectively, came to an end.[72] The forced converts to Catholicism who remained in the Iberian Peninsula are considered to be part of Jewish history, since many continued to practice Judaism or to identify as Jews, or were sincere

Catholics who were discriminated against for their Jewish ancestry. Some of these forced converts and their descendants managed to leave the peninsula for other locations in Western and Northwestern Europe where they could openly embrace Judaism; others left with no firm religious convictions, in search of economic and spiritual stability.[73] The largest communities of former secret Jews developed in Amsterdam, Antwerp, Bordeaux, and London. Having lived and participated in Catholic, and later Protestant, Christian society, these individuals represent the first Jewish encounter with modernity. Leaders from these communities took a leading role in advocating Jewish emancipation and often argued that Sephardim were more deserving of this legal privilege than Ashkenazim. France was the first country to emancipate its Jews: the Sephardim in 1790 and then a year later the Ashkenazim.[74]

The Sephardim of Western Europe, most of them descended from crypto-Jews, were instrumental in the development of Jewish communities in the New World. A group of these Jews fleeing the Portuguese takeover of northern Brazil arrived in 1654 in Nieuw Amsterdam, present-day New York. Their arrival is usually marked as the founding of North America's first Jewish community.[75] The oldest Jewish congregation in the United States, Congregation Shearith Israel, traces its founding to that year.[76]

Another branch of the Sephardic Diaspora developed in the "Orient," primarily in North Africa, the Balkans, and the Anatolian Peninsula. Scholars disagree as to the number of Spanish Jewish refugees who settled there after 1492, but within two or three decades tens of thousands of them had settled in Ottoman cities and towns.[77] According to Jewish chronicles, Sultan Bayezid II (1481–1512) welcomed the Jewish refugees with open arms, hoping to strengthen his empire economically. In the words of Imanuel Aboab, the Ottoman sultans allowed the Jewish refugees into their territories, "marveling that the Spaniards, who profess to be prudent and wise, would eject such a people from their realms."[78] Although these statements are not found in Ottoman documents of the era, scholars including Aron Rodrigue affirm that the empire's rulers viewed Sephardim "as a useful addition to the population."[79]

The refugees encountered other Jewish communities already established in the Ottoman Empire, communities that they largely absorbed by the late sixteenth and early seventeenth centuries.[80] Most of these established communities were composed of *Benei Romania* (*b'nai Roma*), or Romaniote Jews, who traced their origins to Byzantine times. A minority were German Jews, or Ashkenazim, who had settled in the empire during the fifteenth century.[81]

The number of Iberian Jewish exiles who braved the perils and bore the expense of sea voyages to the Ottoman Empire was small in comparison to the number of those who fled by land to Portugal, the kingdom of Navarre, and the French region of Provence. But by the sixteenth century, Ottoman Jewry came to represent the largest Jewish community in the world. Through most of the seventeenth century, more Jews resided in the Ottoman Empire than in any other state. According to Avigdor Levy, Ottoman Jewish communities "emerged as the foremost Jewish centers in the world, rivaled, perhaps, only by those of Poland and Lithuania."[82]

The first century of Iberian Jewish settlement in the Ottoman Empire constituted another "golden age" for Sephardim, concomitant with the flourishing of the Ottoman Empire.[83] Iberian Jewish refugees and their descendants were key to the development of commerce, due in part to their multilingualism and extensive trade connections with Jewish and crypto-Jewish communities throughout the Mediterranean and Western Europe. Rabbinic learning flourished; many Ottoman cities, especially Salonika, became centers for Talmudic study, attracting students from all over the world. Jews also contributed in significant ways to science, technology, and entertainment.[84]

By the late sixteenth century, the Ottoman Empire began to decline, and its social and political fabric began to disintegrate. The principal cause for this deterioration was the expansion of the empire through territorial and military conquests. With this expansion, it became more difficult and costly for Ottoman rulers to maintain control over their numerous, often far-flung, territories. These challenges increased as the empire gained political enemies, such as Austria, Poland, Russia, Spain, Venice, Portugal, and Persia, and economic competitors from European industries.[85] Nevertheless, it would be a mistake to view the period from the late sixteenth to the early nineteenth centuries as a continual process of disintegration. Rather, this time should be seen as a "general curve of decline ... punctuated by extended periods of stability, recovery, and even temporary ascent."[86] In general, Ottoman Jewish communities suffered along with the rest of the population but were "more susceptible than others" to economic, political, and cultural upheavals.[87]

The period from the early nineteenth to the early twentieth centuries represents the era of Ottoman reform and modernization. The years stretching from 1839 to 1876, known as the *Tanzimat* (reorganization), witnessed the improvement of roads, transportation, public health, and education. Reflecting rising rates of literacy, the empire saw an efflorescence of its printing presses, with prolific consequences for the Ladino press. An extensive bibliography of the Ladino press worldwide, published in the 1960s, identified 296 separate publications, with the bulk of these titles emanating from Salonika and Istanbul.[88]

This efflorescence could not deter the final collapse of the empire. Although the direct military menace of Europe had largely subsided by the nineteenth century, the Ottoman Empire was now threatened by internal nationalistic separatism. Various Ottoman regions, including Greece in 1832, became sovereign states. This breakup continued through the early twentieth century. Progressive territorial disintegration, coupled with wars and natural disasters, contributed to an unprecedented Jewish exodus from the Ottoman Empire and its former regions.

By 1900, the eve of mass immigration of Ladino-speaking Jews to the United States, the now largely dismembered Ottoman Empire was home to approximately four hundred thousand Jews,[89] representing 4 percent of the world Jewish population[90] and the fifth-largest Jewish community in the world, following Russia, Austria-Hungary, the United States, and Germany.[91] The *kolonia* ("colony") that Ladino-speaking Jews established in the United States became the most important Sephardic community from the former Ottoman Empire.[92]

The Languages of Sephardic Jews

Language, notes Hispanic studies scholar Maír José Benardete, was "the most precious possession . . . [the Jews of Spain] took with them in their exile."[93] Ladino, known by scholars as Judeo-Spanish, is the language developed by Iberian Jews after their exile from the Iberian Peninsula and resettlement in the former Ottoman Empire (western Anatolia and the Balkans).[94] Based on late medieval or early modern Castilian, Ladino includes admixtures of Hebrew, Turkish, Portuguese, Aramaic, Italian, French, Greek, Arabic, and other languages spoken in the various lands where Eastern Sephardim resided. Ladino was traditionally written in Hebrew letters but gradually gave way to Romanized script with rising forces of secularization and after the revolutionary Turkish government outlawed the use of non-Roman alphabetical systems in 1928.[95]

In its calque form,⁹⁶ Judeo-Spanish (in this context usually called Ladino) was used to translate sacred texts from the Hebrew, a tradition known as *ladinar*.⁹⁷ In its vernacular form, Judeo-Spanish appeared in both religious and secular literature from the sixteenth century on. From the 1540s to the early twentieth century, some three thousand Ladino books, journals, and broadsides were published on the five continents of Europe, North America, South America, Africa, and Asia.⁹⁸

One of twenty-one Jewish languages worldwide, Ladino represents the most direct parallel to the best-known Jewish diasporic language, Yiddish. Both Yiddish and Ladino are the only two major Jewish languages that did not establish as their foundations the language of their respective host countries. In other words, Jews developed not a Judeo-Russian or Judeo-Turkish, but rather a Judeo-German in Slavic lands and a Judeo-Spanish in the land of the Turks. A transported, fusion language, Ladino, like Eastern European Yiddish, is in essence a medieval European language carried from the west eastward.

There are, however, important differences. According to Uriel Weinreich, Yiddish began to develop around 1000 C.E., when French and Italian Jews began to migrate to the Rhineland.⁹⁹ Ladino, whose genesis can be traced to 1492, had a much shorter time to develop linguistically and literarily. Also, Ladino never achieved the linguistic hegemony of Yiddish. Greek Jews of Ioannina generally continued to speak Greek, while Jewish communities in Arab countries—even those that had absorbed Sephardic Jewish exiles—by and large still spoke Arabic.¹⁰⁰ The most dramatic difference is numerical and proportional. The Ladino-speaking population of the world never came close to rivaling the Yiddish-speaking masses. According to estimates from the 1930s, only 350,000 Jews worldwide spoke Ladino in the years 1900 and 1925, representing 3 percent and 2.3 percent of world Jewry, respectively. In comparison, the world's Yiddish-speaking population in those years was 7 million and 8.2 million, representing 60.6 percent and 54.7 percent of world Jewry.¹⁰¹ Immediately prior to the Nazi Holocaust, 75 percent of world Jewry spoke Yiddish.¹⁰²

Despite these small numbers and proportions, Sephardic Jews left an enduring imprint on modern Ashkenazic civilization. Perhaps the best example is the myth of Sephardic supremacy, which imagines Sephardic Jews as culturally, religiously, linguistically, and in certain contexts racially superior to their Ashkenazic brethren. First cultivated by Sephardim themselves in the Middle Ages, the myth of Sephardic supremacy was then adopted and developed by German-speaking Ashkenazim during the age of Enlightenment. Sephardic Jews of Golden Age (Muslim) Spain, many Ashkenazic leaders maintained, were to be emulated for their integration into and contributions to non-Jewish society. Their aesthetic taste in architecture, liturgy, language, and dress was to serve as a model for an emancipated Ashkenazic Jewry.[103]

Ashkenazic scholars influenced by the *Wissenschaft des Judentums* ("Science of Judaism") movement inherited these attitudes, particularly with respect to language. For many of these historians, the catchword was "grandezza," a misplaced Italian word referring to the innate grandeur or nobility of Sephardic Jews.[104] According to German rabbi and historian Moritz Kayserling (1829–1905), Eastern Sephardim "preserved not only the Spanish dignity, but the Spanish idiom also; and they preserved the latter with so much love and with so much tenacity that it has remained surprisingly pure up to the present day. It must be remembered that Judaeo-Spanish, or Ladino, is no wise as corrupt a language as is the Judaeo-German."[105] Similar ideas found their way into the scholarship of American Jews. New York City Reform rabbi Maurice Henry Harris (1859–1930) stated in his 1907 history of medieval Jewry that the Iberian exiles preserved "their Spanish and Portuguese languages which they spoke with purity, as half sacred tongues."[106] As Harris correctly understood, Western Sephardic Jews spoke not Ladino but rather modern Portuguese and Spanish.

Eastern Sephardi and Mizrahi Jews: Defining the Terms

Ethnic terminology is a complicated and often heated issue in the historiography of non-Ashkenazic Jews. What term or terms should be used to designate non-Ashkenazic Jews from the Anatolian Peninsula, the Balkans, North Africa, the Middle East, and Central Asia? The prevailing tendency is to group all of them together under the rubric "Sephardic Jews."

The trend to group together widely variant Jewish communities can be traced, in part, to the nineteenth-century scholarly paradigm that subclassified the Jewish people into two distinct races, the Jews of the "North," in Central and Eastern Europe, and the Jews native to the "Orient" and the Mediterranean basin.[107] There are various ways to explain the triumph of the word "Sephardic" as the designator of Jews from these last two regions. Judith Laikin Elkin attributes the widespread adoption of the term "Sephardic" to the "aristocratic cachet" of a Hispanic origin, "more desirable than a connection to Moslem culture."[108] Similarly, Haim Vidal Sephiha points out that some of the alternative terms, such as "Arab" or "North African," bear pejorative connotations.[109] Mark R. Cohen argues that lumping Iberian-origin Jews together with non-Ashkenazim indigenous to the Middle East and Central Asia indicates, in part, the "overwhelming historical influence that Jews from Spain had on Jewry in the Ottoman Empire and in Morocco."[110]

In the context of American Jewish history, a stronger motivation was probably terminological convenience. Communal leaders in the United States, whether Western or Eastern Sephardic, needed a compact designation that would encompass all recently immigrated non-Ashkenazi Jews, the majority of whom were of remote Iberian origin. This need became evident with the mass immigration of non-Ashkenazi Jews in the 1910s.[111]

However, these leaders also realized the importance of distinguishing the long-established Western Sephardim from the recent non-Western immigrants. Ultimately, the prevailing terms among both Jews and non-Jews during the first half of the twentieth century were "Oriental Jews" or "Levantine Jews."[112] These new labels not only preserved the elite status of Western Sephardim but also more accurately described Arabic- and Greek-speaking Jews bereft of any Iberian ancestry.[113] Concurrently, various additional terms were invented to distinguish the majority Eastern Sephardic population from the smaller numbers of other non-Ashkenazic Jewries: "Oriental" or "Levantine Sephardim," "Spanish Jews," "Spagnuali," "Ladinos," "Turkish Jews," "Turkish Sephardim," and "Turkinos." Romaniote Jews were sometimes identified as Greek-speaking Jews, while Jews of Arab lands often fell under the rubric of "Arabic-speaking Jews," "Syrian," or "Arabian." Western Sephardim—descendants of Spanish- and Portuguese-speaking Jews whose ancestors left the Iberian Peninsula for other locations in Western and Northern Europe and the Americas but never migrated to the Ottoman Empire—were sometimes termed "Old Sephardim" to distinguish them from Ladino-speaking "New Sephardim."

Over the past few decades, scholars and lay people have continued to debate the terms "Sephardim," "Eastern" or "Levantine Jews," and "Eastern" or "Levantine Sephardim." The controversy generally lies between those who insist that Eastern Sephardi and Mizrahi Jews should collectively be categorized as "Sephardim"[114] and those who argue that the term as a blanket categorization overlooks vastly divergent linguistic, cultural, ancestral, and historical legacies.[115] Aside from this debate, there is an unfortunate tendency, borne of ignorance or intellectual sloppiness, to lump all non-Ashkenazic Jews together as constituents of one homogeneous subethnic group.[116] Finally, the political exigency of uniting all non-Ashkenazic Jews has led many scholars to force square pegs into round holes. They argue that even though non-Ashkenazic Jews are often not Iberian in origin, their culture and religious traditions *must* be the same or similar to Sephardic ritual.[117] This argument is a classic example of a contemporary assumption (that all these diverse Jews are Sephardic) being awkwardly imposed on the past. As I will argue in the next chapter, it is far more useful to conceptualize non-Ashkenazim in the United States as a *social* rather than an *ethnic* group.

Perhaps the most important point is that non-Ashkenazic Jews in the immigrant era saw themselves as distinct subgroups and organized accordingly. Language (Ladino, Arabic, Greek) was central to both communication and identity and informed their workaday, social, organizational, and romantic lives. Even as many of them clung to microidentities, naming their synagogues and societies after natal cities and towns, language was an overarching unifying force.[118] A consideration of ethnic terminology in the Ottoman Empire also supports the case for upholding subethnic distinctions. Jews indigenous to North Africa and the Middle East were sometimes denoted as *toshavim* (Hebrew for "settlers") to distinguish them from the Jews expelled from Spain in 1492 (*megorashim*). Jews in the Ottoman Empire's Arab provinces were subdivided into ethnic enclaves that distinguished between Arabic-speaking Jews (*musta'rabim*, *mustarabi*, or *mista'arvim*, all meaning "like Arabs," or *Moreschi*, denoting "Moors"), Sephardim, Maghrebis, Italians, and Ashkenazim.[119]

The two Sephardic groups that are the focus of this study are Ladino-speaking Sephardim, also identified as Eastern Sephardim, and Spanish- and Portuguese-speaking Sephardim, referred to as Western Sephardim. Both of these groups trace their remote ancestry to the Iberian Peninsula, and more recently to the Ottoman Empire (in the case of Eastern Sephardim), and Western and Northern Europe and the Americas (in the case of Western Sephardim). Arabic- and Judeo-Arabic-speaking Jews, most of them indigenous to North Africa and the Middle East, are referred to in this study as Mizrahim, the Hebrew word for "Eastern," which gained currency in Israel during the early 1990s, primarily in reference to Jews

Cover of the annual publication of the Sepharadic Brotherhood of America, 1923, originally founded in 1915 as a mutual-aid society to benefit Eastern Sephardim of primarily Salonikan origin. The organization later anglicized the first word of its name to "Sephardic."

from Arab lands.[120] Greek-speaking Jews native to Ioannina and other cities of the former Eastern Roman Empire are identified as Romaniote Jews.[121] Where appropriate, following the example of most communal leaders of the time, all non-Ashkenazic Jews, with the exception of Western Sephardim, are sometimes collectively identified as Eastern or Levantine Jews. For reasons explained in the following chapters, Ashkenazic Jews born in the Ottoman Empire sometimes fall under this rubric as well.

The deficiency of all these terms has been widely recognized in both scholarly and communal circles since the beginning of the twentieth century.[122] First is the question of actual descent. The historical intermingling of various Jewish populations means that some Ladino-speaking Jews had Romaniote or Ashkenazic ancestry, or that Arabic-speaking Jews might have traced some of their genealogy to the Iberian Peninsula. The case of modern-day Syrian Jews is emblematic. The first Jews in

Syria were indigenous to the Middle East and were joined by significant numbers of Iberian Jewish exiles only after the Expulsion of 1492. Spanish Jewish settlers there quickly gained ascendancy and imposed their prayer rite and language on the native Jews. Thus, some Syrian Jews have ancestry indigenous to the Middle East, others trace their origins to the Iberian Peninsula, and still others are a combination of both. So too, Jews of Ioannina in northwestern Greece trace their origins to the thirteenth century, if not before, and are therefore indigenous to the region. But linguistic traces, names, and religious traditions suggest that some Sephardic exiles intermingled with the historically Greek-speaking Jewish community after 1492.[123] Examples such as these may explain why some modern-day descendants are inconsistent when describing their own geographical origins.[124]

It is also important to point out that "Mizrahim" is especially problematic. This term seeks to collectively designate populations that are culturally, linguistically, and geographically much more diverse than either Ashkenazic or Sephardic Jews. Michael Pollack, a historian of China's Jews, correctly observes that this blanket term deprives these populations "of their unique histories and their own rich diversity of customs and practices."[125] Moreover, the terms "Eastern" and "Levantine," as well as their Hebrew translation, "Mizrahi," are laden with geographical ethnocentricism. Only some of these populations are eastern from the perspective of certain places in Europe. In point of fact, North African Jewry has historically defined itself as part of the West (*Maghreb* in Arabic).[126] As a rejection of similar geographical ethnocentricism, the field of South Asian studies abandoned the term "Oriental" decades ago.[127]

This study also briefly considers Hispanics of the U.S. Southwest who have in recent decades claimed crypto-Jewish ancestry; some have joined the "mainstream" Jewish community. Here, too, the question of terminology is delicate. Janet Liebman Jacobson, in her recent research on this population, found that her informants identified variably as "Chicano/a (Mexican American)" and "Hispanic (having Spanish ancestry)." In her published analysis, Jacobson chose to use the term "Latina/o" to encompass both categories.[128] Stanley Hordes, in his study of crypto-Judaism in the American Southwest, favors the term "Hispanos," which he defines as descendants of Spanish colonists.[129] In the context of these modern-day individuals who claim crypto-Jewish descent, the present study employs the term "Hispanic," indicating a person of Iberian descent.

1

Immigration, Ethnicity, and Identity

America Is Mine!

In the spring of 1915, twenty-four-year-old Isaac Azriel, a native of Salonika, arrived at Ellis Island aboard the SS *Vasilefs Constantinos*. The owner of a carpet business, Azriel was conversant in Hebrew, French, German, and Turkish. Unexpectedly, Azriel was detained after a medical official diagnosed him with a deformity of the spine.[1] Immigration officials then promised to release him on condition that he procure a sponsor closely related to him. After ten days in limbo, he was informed that he would be deported, though no one could tell him the precise reason. An Ashkenazic official from the Hebrew Immigrant Aid Society (HIAS) had taken down his name and tried to hearten him with daily visits, but the decision to deport Azriel had already been made, and not much was formally done on his behalf.

Then, Azriel noticed in a trash can a copy of the Ladino newspaper *La America*. He wrote a letter to the journal appealing for help, and within two days Aharón Pardo, a young man dispatched by the editorial office, came to his aid. Only then did HIAS take Azriel's case seriously and successfully petitioned Washington. Had Pardo not intervened, Azriel would have been returned to his native city depleted of all his savings, which he described as "a sizeable fortune."[2]

The case of Sarah Baruh Kamhi also illustrates the ongoing indispensability of Eastern Sephardic mediators in deportation cases. Kamhi, a native of Monastir (the present-day city of Bitola in the Republic of Macedonia), who had had most recently resided in Skopje (Serbia), arrived at Ellis Island aboard the SS *Majestic* in January 1923. Although she presented the address of her guarantor in Rochester, New York, her brother-in-law Ya'akov Alva, Kamhi was also slated for deportation. This time the reason was illiteracy.[3] Alva contacted the Sephardic Brotherhood

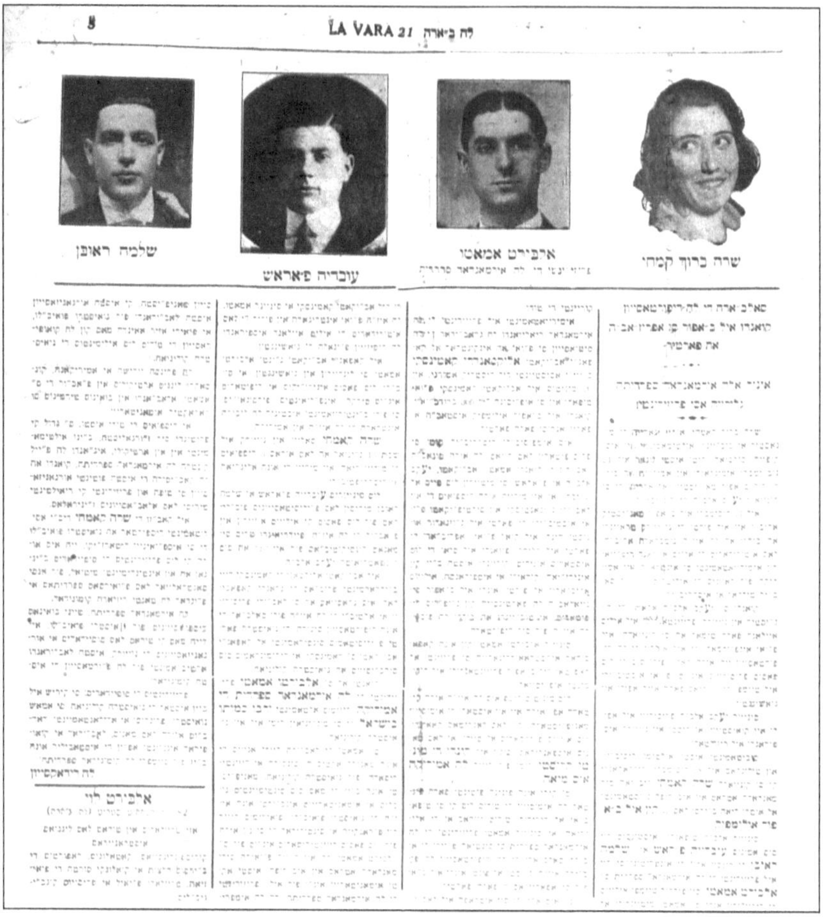

"Saved from deportation just as the ship was about to leave," La Vara
(January 19, 1923): 5. From right to left: *Sarah Baruh Kamhi,
Alberto Amateau, Ovadiah Farash, Shlomo Reuben.*

of America, a mutual-aid society, for assistance and was able to enlist the efforts of its president, Albert J. Amateau, as well as a prominent Ashkenazic lawyer who successfully petitioned Washington. The "rescue" scene, as described in the Ladino periodical *La Vara*, evoked the melodrama of a serialized novel. Just before the ship embarked for Europe, a weeping Kamhi was delivered, with her "eyes fixed toward heaven and her hands spread outwards," as if to say, "America is mine!"[4]

These anecdotes provide a hint of some of the challenges that Eastern Sephardim faced in the initial years during which they arrived in large numbers and initiated a long process of community formation and adaptation to the United States. As these vignettes suggest, the difficulties emblematic of later struggles were already evident at Ellis Island. Ladino speakers who arrived in the New York port of entry often likened Ellis Island to a prison cell or torture chamber. One *kolonia* leader, addressing his cohorts at a public lecture in the 1960s, remembered the ordeal at Ellis Island as an incarceration.[5] In the Ladino lingo of the Lower East Side a common nickname for that immigration station was "the island of suffering" (*la izla de las sufriensas*) or "the scourge" (*el kastigar*).[6] Insufficient funds, lack of a personal guarantor, and disease were among the most common reasons for detention and deportation.[7] But the more formidable barrier that Eastern Sephardic travelers encountered was linguistic.[8] As both Azriel and Kamhi learned, if the necessary interpreters were not present at Ellis Island and difficulties arose, there were few chances for redemption.

The detention of Levantine and Eastern Sephardic Jews was a distinct possibility because their arrival in significant numbers coincided with the rise of the restrictive immigration era. Beginning in the 1890s, about 20 percent of immigrants processed at Ellis Island—the majority of them of Southern and Eastern European origin—were confined to custody either for medical reasons or for further questioning.[9] The first law to regulate immigration had been passed in 1875, but not until 1907 did legislation begin to seriously menace the Jewish immigrant masses.[10] That year, Congress established the Joint Commission on Immigration, informally known as the Dillingham Commission. Its officers based their anti-immigration sentiment on the conviction, backed by contemporary science, that Southern and Eastern European immigrants were innately inferior to those of Northern and Western Europe, who had constituted the majority of newcomers until the last two decades of the nineteenth century.

The Quota Law of 1921 was the first to establish numerical limits to immigration. This law limited annual immigration to approximately 350,000 people. More importantly, the influx from any one nation was reduced to 3 "percent of the number of foreign-born persons from that country living in America in 1910."[11] The Reed-Johnson Act of 1924, finally implemented under Herbert Hoover on March 22, 1929, further limited immigration to 2 percent of the number of foreign born who, according to the 1890 census, were living in America.[12] The attempt to reduce the number of "innately inferior" immigrants was cleverly disguised behind seemingly arbitrary years. In reality, 1910 and 1890 reflect deliberate calculations to favor the influx of Northern and Western Europeans, who dominated America's population in precisely those years. The 1921 quota permitted Southern and Eastern European immigrants to constitute at most 45 percent of all newcomers; that ratio was reduced to less than 14 percent under the 1924 law.[13] For non-Ashkenazic Jews this meant that in 1924 the quota from the principal lands of Eastern Sephardi and Mizrahi immigration was reduced to between about one hundred and three hundred individuals per country.[14]

Established in 1892 as the country's leading immigration station, Ellis Island received over twelve million immigrants until its doors closed in 1954.[15] Detainees were housed in what one journalist described in 1912 as "iron-barred rooms, hallways, and endless corridors" leading to "the labyrinth of madness, of hopelessness, despair, and suicide."[16] HIAS—which had attempted to intercede for Isaac Azriel in 1915—was founded in 1902 to assist Jewish newcomers, most of whom at that time were streaming in from Eastern Europe. This immigration aid society was founded as a result of the dissatisfaction of Jews of Eastern European origin with the United Hebrew Charities (UHC), whose leadership was dominated by Germanic Jews. Eastern European Jewish leaders had complained that the UHC was denigrating and insensitive to the needs of its largely Yiddish-speaking immigrant constituents. Moreover, they claimed, the representative stationed at Ellis Island was ignorant of Yiddish, and deportation decisions were rarely appealed.[17] By the next year, HIAS had installed its own Yiddish-speaking representative. This official worked with the organization to appeal deportation cases, provide translators, monitor conditions aboard ships, and help unite newcomers with relatives.[18]

Ironically, HIAS was soon reprimanded for the same behavior that its officials had protested in 1902, this time in relation to non-Ashkenazic Jews. In the early 1910s, as immigration from the Balkans and Middle East became noticeable, Levantine Jews began to complain that HIAS was not linguistically and culturally equipped to handle these newcomers. Officials were unable to communicate with Eastern Sephardim and Mizrahim and sometimes did not recognize them as Jews because of their last names. Ailing immigrants, if fortunate enough to be admitted as patients by local Jewish hospitals, were often not considered Jews because of their languages.[19] Prodded by *kolonia* leaders, HIAS officials agreed to found the Oriental Bureau (sometimes also called the Committee on Oriental Hebrews) in December 1911. The bureau, staffed largely by Eastern Sephardi and Mizrahi volunteers, proved crucial. Joshua Cohen, director of the Oriental Bureau, reported in 1917 that many Mizrahim and Eastern Sephardim were so grateful to both HIAS and its Oriental committee that they contributed "their last savings in order to enable us to continue our noble work."[20]

The unpaid labor that Eastern Sephardic volunteers offered their immigrating cohorts was all the more admirable considering the financial straits the community experienced as a whole. During the first three decades of the twentieth century, economic hardship was widespread among New York's Sephardic community. In 1910, *La America* reported that the majority of Sephardim in the United States were living in poverty.[21] Consequently, many leaders actively encouraged Sephardim to remain in their native lands. These exhortations continued through the 1920s and '30s, when many upwardly mobile Eastern Sephardim of the Lower East Side had migrated to Harlem. In 1924 the Ladino newspaper *La Vara*, addressing those contemplating immigration from Turkey and Greece, cautioned that there were no jobs in the United States, the cost of living was high, and there were no factories to which one could "rent out one's arms." One could observe "young men wandering around looking for work to earn a bite of bread and immigrant families with children and no money."[22] Moise Soulam, an editor of that newspaper who had fled Salonika in 1913, admitted that he once dreamed that trees in America sprouted money. In rhymed Ladino prose, Soulam reflected, "Now I see you labor night and day and the first of the month comes all too soon, the landlord demanding rent. Immigrants arrive and after years find themselves in the same economic position. Jews in Turkey think that money grows on trees here, but the truth is that this country yields not only dollars (*dolares*) but also pain (*dolores*)."[23]

Alongside these exhortations appeared useful advice on how to immigrate to the United States and procure ship tickets, a paradox suggesting that living in dire poverty in the United States was seen as preferable to remaining in the Old Country.[24] The year 1917 proved especially trying for prospective Eastern Sephardic immigrants of the Anatolian Peninsula and Greece who were fleeing "famine and unspeakable catastrophes" in the midst of World War I.[25] The Oriental Bureau's director, Joshua Cohen, reported having assisted 357 immigrants that year, most of them prospective immigrants from Greece. The majority arrived without funds and stricken with physical disabilities, which almost automatically slated them for deportation. The bureau, in cooperation with HIAS, provided bonds guaranteeing that the new arrivals would not become public charges. In cases of contagious diseases, the bureau often successfully appealed to Washington to procure medical treatment in local Jewish hospitals. Once the immigrants' entry was secured, the bureau provided clothing and helped secure employment and lodging, often dispatching an interpreter to hospitals and the place of employment.[26]

Many cases processed by the Oriental Bureau were at once redemptive and tragic. Representative is the story of Isaac Nachmi, a twenty-three-year-old immigrant who arrived with his wife, Sultana, and child in January 1917. Nachmi was detained at Ellis Island with valvular disease of the heart and dispatched to a hospital, where he was also diagnosed with trachoma, the most common disease detected among detainees. The family was ordered deported, but HIAS successfully appealed to Washington, citing the dangers of submarine bombings.[27] HIAS then arranged to have Isaac transferred to Beth Israel Hospital, while his wife and child remained in the society's care. Sadly, during Nachmi's eight-month convalescence, his child became seriously ill. The Oriental Bureau's representative contacted a physician and arranged for the child's transportation to a local hospital, but two weeks later the child succumbed to scarlet fever.[28]

Not all Sephardim, of course, were so impoverished that they had to rely on the charitable endeavors of HIAS. At the other extreme are the success stories of immigrants who arrived in the late 1890s and early 1900s. The Schinasi or Schinazi brothers (their name is derived from "Eskenazi") came to New York in 1891 from Manisa in western Turkey via Alexandria, Egypt, with no means of employment. By 1911, they owned two cigar factories and were millionaires.[29] The home of one of the Schinasi brothers, as richly described by a *kolonia* member who knew them well, reflects a harmonious mélange of Middle Eastern elegance and American sophistication. The large den was furnished with "heavy ornately carved furniture and thick wall hangings," a plush oriental rug on the floor, an ornamental lamp, a piano, and a Victrola that played jazz music. The family's dwelling in Larchmont, a resort community for wealthy New Yorkers, sported private tennis courts.[30] For all their opulence, the Schinasis remained loyal to their community and became generous philanthropists. They made particular efforts to hire their own people to labor in their factories and, as *La America* reported approvingly in 1911, made "sacrifices for their workers."[31] They also did not forget their native lands. Upon his death in 1928, Mussa (Morris) Schinasi made a million-dollar bequest to found a hospital in Magnesia (central Greece).[32]

The Eastern Sephardic community could point to other success stories as well. Capitalizing on their mercantile connections with the Middle East, Ben Guiat, Samuel Coen, and the Mayorkas brothers succeeded in building large establishments in the Oriental rug and antique businesses. The Valensi brothers made their fortune in the amusement and recreation industry.[33] Turkish-born Albert J. Bonomo (1872–1933), known for several years as the "Ice Cream King" of Coney Island, arrived in the United States around 1893 and gradually developed a lucrative confectionary business.[34] Hadji Ephraim Benguiat, a native of Izmir, in what is today Turkey, who settled in the United States most probably in the 1890s, became a famous art dealer and collector.[35] Many of these Eastern Sephardim—including, apparently, the Schinasis—had first arrived at the turn of the century as exhibitors in the World's Fair.[36]

The Schinasis and their successful cohorts represent the trickle of Levantine Jewish immigrants barely detectable before the turn of the twentieth century. Only a few hundred Eastern Sephardim arrived from the Ottoman Empire in New York before 1900, partly because emigration was prohibited until 1896.[37] Travel in general, even within the Ottoman Empire, was difficult before the revolution of 1908.[38] These newcomers, who earned their living as merchants, hailed mostly from Istanbul and immigrated to America in search of economic opportunities.[39]

Those who immigrated during the late nineteenth and turn of the twentieth centuries apparently acclimated quickly both economically and communally. In 1912, their main social and religious organization, the Society of Union and Peace (*La Sosieté Unión i Pas*), listed almost two hundred members, hailing from Morocco, Spain, and Turkey. The official language of the organization, which counted among its members the Schinasi brothers, was English. This group apparently felt at home with Western Sephardim, the country's founding Jewish elite. As the *Sosieté* did not have a synagogue, members worshiped during the High Holy Days at Congregation Shearith Israel.[40] Another well-adjusted Levantine Jewish society was the Oriental Progressive Society (*La Sosietá Progresiva Oriental*), founded in 1904. Its members spoke Yiddish and English, and almost all were Ashkenazim from Turkey. Moise Gadol, editor of the Ladino weekly *La America*, considered this the best organized and most

Americanized society of Levantine Jews. Among its members were the controversial *kolonia* leaders Joseph Gedalecia and Samuel Auerbach.[41]

The profile of this newest Jewish immigrant group, the Levantine Jews, was to change in the 1910s, most directly due to the 1908 Young Turk revolution, which visibly increased their influx, drawing to them national attention.[42] Many or most of these newcomers lacked a formal education and vocational skills.[43] Evasion of military conscription was among the most commonly cited motivations for departure in both reportage and immigrant testimonies.[44] The new Turkish government's constitution now mandated compulsory service not only for Muslims but also for Christians and Jews.[45] Moise Gadol explained that under this new policy, which targeted men between the ages of twenty and forty-five, Turkish citizens could pay an exemption each time they were called up for maneuvers or war, which could occur frequently. The exemption lasted only for three months and was costly (in 1911, about two hundred dollars).[46] Joseph A. D. Sutton affirms that mandatory conscription and the repeal of the (former, one-time) tax demanded in exchange for military exemption was an "intolerable prospect," as there was general dislike of the military among Jews and the fear that their dietary restrictions and Sabbath observance would be threatened.[47] These testimonies, though perhaps reductionist, would partly explain why most of the early immigrants were young, unmarried men.

Perhaps more common was the desire for economic betterment. As Ottoman-born businessman Ezra Sitt noted in 1913, "business over there is becoming worse every day and . . . every city in the world now hears about the prosperity in America." According to Sitt, who had arrived in New York in 1892, Syrian Jews immigrated as birds of passage, intending to return to the Old Country with new fortunes, but ended up remaining and sending for their wives and children.[48] Even Albert J. Amateau, who elsewhere stated he had left his native land to escape army service, affirmed in 1991 that his "fellow Sephardic and Muslim Turks came to seek better economic and educational opportunities."[49] Famine, war (particularly the Italo-Turkish War of 1911 and the Balkan Wars of 1913–1914), family reunification, the quest for adventure (especially among young bachelors), and the dearth of marriage-eligible males[50] induced others to abandon their native lands.

In some cases, immigrants had distinctive regional reasons for leaving their homelands. The loss of Ottoman Salonika to Greece and the rise of Greek nationalist anti-Semitism stimulated a massive Jewish exodus beginning in 1912.⁵¹ Shortly after Moise Soulam fled from his native Salonika, he published a nostalgic and bitter poem chronicling his own refugee experience. In "A Final Farewell to My Native City," which appeared in a September 1913 edition of *La America*, Soulam explained that nationalist fervor incited many Christian Greeks to wreak havoc on the Jewish community and its quarter. His Ladino poem, evocative of the Book of Lamentations, is representative of Eastern Sephardim who from the start intended to remain in their adoptive land.

> Like those who flee a house in flames,
> So flee thousands of souls from a bygone Turkey . . .
>
> Only to escape those barbarian Greeks,
> The Salonikan Jews flee like blindmen,
> And arrive in America with the sole intention,
> Of seeking a quick salvation.
>
> . . . And so, I bid farewell to the city of my birth,
> To the site of my childhood and my youth.
> Farewell, Salonika, farewell forever . . .
> . . . Salonika, the city populated by Jews,
> Today remains almost deserted.
> A city which yesterday was filled with beauty,
> Today fills me with bitterness.
>
> Farewell, city of faded beauty . . .
> The city from which yesterday flowed milk and honey.
> Today gushes out anguish and bile.
>
> Farewell, Salonika, the seat of great sages.
> Today, even your students abandon you.
> A city only yesterday filled with Judaism,
> Today seethes with anti-Jewish hatred.⁵²

Details from Soulam's poetic testimony are confirmed in the same issue in a news article describing the destruction of Jewish property and recurring blood libels perpetuated by Greek Christians.⁵³

Another distinctive reason for leaving Salonika was the great fire of 1917, which consumed most of the homes and businesses of the city's Jews. The Oriental Bureau of HIAS reported in 1917 that most of its 357 beneficiaries were from Greece, and most of these were fleeing the conflagration, which left eighty thousand Jews homeless in the midst of winter. These newcomers were usually held at Ellis Island for special inquiry because they arrived with neither money nor addresses and thus could not prove to officials that they would not become public charges. An additional reason for their detention at Ellis Island was, ironically, physical defects, which had exempted them from military service and permitted them to leave Greece in the first place.[54]

The immigration of Jews from Arab lands, slight in comparison to Eastern Sephardim, was sometimes also stimulated by distinctive factors. For example, unmarried Yemeni Jewish minors orphaned of their father were vulnerable to a local Muslim law that mandated their conversion to Islam.[55] Many of these fatherless Jews arrived between 1905 and 1907.[56]

These examples suggest that many Eastern Sephardim and Mizrahim probably did not intend to eventually return to their native lands. If true, the nature of their immigration would be similar to that of Eastern European Jews, distinctive among Eastern and Southern European immigrants of the time for having the lowest rate of reverse migration. Between 1908 and 1923, five out of one hundred Eastern European Jews returned to their native lands. By contrast, southern (gentile) Italians, Russians, Slovaks, and various Balkan peoples returned at a rate of fifty or more per hundred immigrants.[57] Comparable statistical calculations do not exist to the same extent for Sephardi and Mizrahi Jews in the United States, but the few figures available suggest that most non-Ashkenazic Jews also came to stay.

In 1914, for example, 17 percent of all immigrants who *arrived* that year from European Turkey were Jews, but only 2.7 percent of all European Turkish immigrants who *left* the United States that year were Jews. That same year, nearly 4 percent of all immigrants who *arrived* from Asian Turkey were Jews, but only a tiny fraction of 1 percent of all Asian Turkish immigrants who *left* the United States were Jews.[58] These statistics may not be representative of previous years, before the outbreak of World War I. But they do suggest that gentiles from European and Asian Turkey were more likely to be birds of passage than their Jewish landsmen were. Figures from 1921–1922 confirm this pattern. During that period, some 4 percent of the total number of persons *admitted* from Greece were Jews, but only a fraction of 1 percent of those *departing* were Jews. A similar tendency applies to European and Asian Turkey.[59] These samples suggest that while Jews formed a significant proportion of immigrants from Turkey and Greece, their return rate was significantly lower in both real numbers and percentages than their non-Jewish landsmen. Like Eastern European Ashkenazim, Sephardi and Mizrahi Jews on the whole came to stay and did so relatively more frequently than their non-Jewish cohorts.[60] These statistics confirm Simon S. Nessim's straightforward statement in 1921 that most Eastern Sephardim "have resolved to stay here."[61]

Quantifying the Community

It is difficult to estimate the total number of Eastern Sephardi and Mizrahi Jews who entered the United States beginning in the 1880s. One challenge, true for Jewish immigration statistics in general, is that U.S. government figures before 1899 classified immigrants based on country of birth or residence, rather than "race" or nationality.[62] The problem was partly mitigated in 1899, when the Bureau of Immigration began to apply the term "Hebrew" to all Jewish newcomers. But many Levantine Jewish immigrants were not being processed as Jews. For example, federal records for the period between 1909 and 1912 estimated the number of Levantine Jewish immigrants at 1,854, while HIAS recorded 2,865. This difference of only one thousand would presumably result in cumulative inaccuracies over the years. The immigration statistics of the Oriental Bureau, David de Sola Pool asserted, were far more reliable.[63] Unfortunately, as we will see, the Oriental Bureau functioned only intermittently.

Moreover, federal forms employed to quantify ethnic populations took Eastern European Ashkenazic heritage as the norm for Jewish immigration. In 1910, for example, the U.S. census began to include mother tongue for "foreign white stock." The rubric for Jews was "Yiddish and Hebrew." This, of course, overlooked Jews who were ignorant of Yiddish and spoke Ladino or a variety of non-Jewish European languages.[64] This lack of sensitivity led many non-Ashkenazic Jews to slip through the cracks. David de Sola Pool remarked that many Eastern Sephardim and Mizrahim had not been included in Jewish immigration statistics "because they have been passed as Turks or Greeks, not being easily recognizable as Jews, either in name, language or physical appearance."[65]

Likewise, statistics gathered by Ashkenazic-dominant immigrant societies were generally oriented toward their constituents and were thus seldom if at all concerned with the immigration of non-Ashkenazic Jews or with the question of subethnic identity.[66] The influx from countries whose populations were predominantly Eastern Sephardi and Mizrahi paled in comparison to the droves from Eastern Europe, who represented more than 95 percent of all Jewish immigrants between 1881 and 1910.[67] Between 1881 and 1910, according to one calculation, immigration from Turkey to the United States represented only half of 1 percent of all Jewish immigration during that period.[68]

The figures of the United Hebrew Charities in New York, the Association for the Protection of Jewish Immigrants in Philadelphia, and the Hebrew Benevolent Society of Baltimore, for example, all classified Jewish immigrants according to country, rather than Jewish ethnicity. In the case of Turkey, one may assume that many or even perhaps the majority of immigrants are Eastern Sephardim. But Eastern Sephardim and Mizrahim who may have immigrated from or through countries such as Romania and France or from "all other" countries—which in theory could amount to hundreds or even thousands of newcomers—are not accounted for.[69]

The question of language also highlights the fact that many Jewish immigrants from Turkey were in fact Ashkenazic. The 1910 census, for example, reported the presence of 1,616 Yiddish-speaking, foreign-born Jews from European and Asian Turkey. Together with their progeny, they amounted to 2,039 persons.[70] If this calculation is accurate, it provides broader context for the rise to leadership of "Levantine Jewish" leaders in New York who were actually Ashkenazic, as were most of the city's Jewish elite. Members of this new population living in New York founded the aforementioned Oriental Progressive Society, whose membership stood at around sixty by 1912.[71] These Ashkenazic Ottoman Jews were considered part of New York's "Levantine Jewish" community in the first decades of the twentieth century, but they probably would not be included today.

Another factor making it difficult to estimate the size of the non-Ashkenazic population is the multiple national identities that Eastern Sephardim and Mizrahim carried with them to the United States. Joseph Gedalecia confessed in 1914 that since he immigrated to the United States via Paris, he came as "a Frenchman." Similarly, he noted that Jews who had been educated in Alliance Israélite Universelle schools in Greece or other countries often passed as non-Jewish upon immigration to the United States. Gedalecia blamed the secularizing influences of the Alliance for exacerbating the tendency of "Levantine Jews" to "hide their Jewishness."[72]

Facing this dearth of statistical information, communal leaders and outside observers over the years have offered varying estimates of the number of immigrants and the size of the country's Sephardi and Mizrahi population. Taking into account the failure of immigration officials to recognize Sephardim and Mizrahim as Jews, as well as the general disinterest of Ashkenazic organizations and the U.S. government in monitoring their influx, the figure of fifty to sixty thousand immigrants arriving between 1880 to 1924 seems reasonable. But since this estimate relies on previously published sources, the need for more studied calculations remains.

Even without reliable statistics, it is clear that Arabic- and Greek-speaking Jewish immigrants formed a small minority of Levantine Jews. This disproportion was evident from the first years of their immigration. In 1913, the total Levantine Jewish population of the United States was around ten thousand.[73] Of this figure, the Greek-speaking Jews in New York numbered "several hundreds," while the city's Arabic-speaking Jews counted not less than one thousand.[74] This would leave the Ladino-speaking community in the early teens with well over eight thousand members. Even as the Judeo-Arabic community in Brooklyn burgeoned, stabilizing at approximately fifteen thousand by 1950,[75] Ladino-speaking Jews remained the majority of the Levantine Jewish population in both New York and the United States throughout the first half of the twentieth century. In 1923, *La Vara* estimated the Ladino-speaking population of New York and the United States at thirty-five thousand and fifty thousand, respectively.[76] In 1934, the American Sephardic population was estimated at seventy-five thousand.[77] The numerical preponderance of Eastern Sephardim continued until the third generation, when intramarriage with Ashkenazim and intermarriage with non-Jews diluted the distinct identity and characteristics of most Ladino-speaking Jewish communities.[78] Today, the large majority of non-Ashkenazic Jews are Mizrahim, Jews of Arab lands and Persian Jews.[79]

Estimating the Sephardi and Mizrahi population of the country today continues to challenge communal leaders and historians alike. No reliable statistics exist. Over the past two decades, leaders of the New York–based American Sephardi Federation, representative of the country's non-Ashkenazic Jews, have alternately suggested 250,000 and 400,000 as official figures, but it is clear that these are both rough estimates. Likewise, the country's discrete, non-Ashkenazic subgroups have no authoritative statistics for their individual communities and have also offered only approximations. Combined, these educated guesses approach 250,000 but only reflect the country's largest non-Ashkenazic communities, such as Iranian and Syrian Jews.[80]

New York as a Sephardic Center

By the 1910s, communal leaders in New York realized that their city was becoming the country's hub for Eastern Sephardic immigrants. The community became not only the largest and most ethnically diverse in the country but also the most influential.[81] Aside from Levantine Jewish mutual-aid societies and organizations of various political and cultural leanings, which proliferated in the 1910s and 1920s, the Ladino press is the best indication of the community's centrality among the country's non-Ashkenazic Jews. All but two of the nineteen known American Judeo-Spanish periodicals appeared in New York City. Moreover, the city attracted Jewish intellectual elites of the former Ottoman Empire, particularly the young male leaders of Salonika who, imbued with socialist and humanitarian ideals, dedicated their lives to improving the economic and educational lot of their immigrant brethren.

One explanation for the ascendancy of Eastern Sephardim in New York is the size and consequent diversity of the city's broader Jewish community. New York Jews were the world's largest Jewish community at the time and also constituted a significant proportion of the city's general population. By 1910, over a million Jews dwelled in the Big Apple, representing 23 percent of the city's total population.[82] The city's general ethnic diversity stimulated the literary and cultural efflorescence evident among the city's Sephardic inhabitants. Seattle resident Albert Adatto offers another explanation. He noted in 1939 that most Sephardic immigrants in Seattle were from Rodosto and the islands of Rhodes and Marmara, none of which were "centers of Sephardic culture." Life in these places "was peaceful, provincial, and un-intellectual."[83] New York, on the other hand, attracted Eastern Sephardim from both rural and urban settings.

The first sizeable neighborhood of the country's Ladino-speaking Jews developed on New York's Lower East Side, primarily on Christie, Forsyth, Eldridge, Allen, Orchard, and Essex streets. The Lower East Side was more often than not their first destination, as it was for the majority of Jewish immigrants until the 1910s, when the predominantly Yiddish-speaking population there reached its peak. Upwardly mobile Sephardim began to settle in the city's outskirts by the 1920s. One of their largest neighborhoods was in Harlem, from 110th to 125th streets and between Fifth and First avenues. By that decade they had already branched out into Brooklyn as well.[84] Perhaps their most public display of economic achievement came in the early 1950s, with the founding of the Sephardic Home for the Aged, financed largely by the munificent contributions of native-born Eastern Sephardim.[85]

Communities that Ladino-speaking Jews founded in other parts of the country are notable for their economic and communal distinctiveness. Seattle's Eastern Sephardic pioneers were known for their important role in the fishing industry. They and their descendants also established an impressive religious educational system for their children and an influential rabbinical leadership, arguably qualifying Seattle as the strongest religious center of Eastern Sephardim in the United States.[86] The Ladino language preserved there has long served as a magnet for scholars of Sephardic linguistics, folklore, and history.[87] Members of the Eastern Sephardic community of Los Angeles produced *El Mesajero*, the only known Ladino organ of the West Coast, published from 1933 until at least 1934. Unlike New York's Ladino periodicals, produced on modern printing presses, the Los Angeles journal was first handwritten and then later typewritten.[88] Future historians of these and other modestly sized Sephardic communities in the United States will doubtlessly highlight other distinctions as well.

Acculturation to Anglo-American society, intramarriage with Ashkenazim, and World War II, which effectively ended the isolation of Jewish subgroups, largely succeeded in attenuating the distinctiveness and viability of the country's Ladino-speaking community. Nearly all Sephardim who immigrated in the early twentieth century married fellow Sephardim; but by the third generation, intramarriage "had become the rule, rather than the exception."[89] Hayyim Cohen found in the early 1970s that 72 percent of second-generation Sephardim had married non-Sephardic women, while that figure jumped to 90 percent in the third and fourth generations.[90] The demographic and communal decline of the country's Eastern Sephardim qualifies the first half of the twentieth century as the most historically interesting period for that community in terms of both communal vitality and primary sources. For Mizrahi

Jews, that distinction generally does not apply until the second half of the century.

Ethnic Identity in the Kolonia: Before the Sephardic Melting Pot

In 1914, violence broke out in an Eastern Sephardic restaurant on the Lower East Side. Avraham Nessim Levi, born in Dardanelles, struck Behor Algranate, a native of Izmir, wounding him in the nose. The injured man had Levi thrown in prison under a thousand-dollar bail. The following year, while planning their revenge, Levi's friends became involved in a feud with the opposing Izmir faction, resulting in further bloodshed. Moise Gadol noted with chagrin that the Dardanelles-Izmir confrontation had been picked up by the New York Anglo and Yiddish press, "discrediting our entire colony."[91] By the end of the year, Gadol was himself accused of subethnic prejudice, when a reader residing on the Lower East Side protested comments published in *La America* about Salonikan-born Sephardim and maintained that certain references "might have inspired some sentiment against native Salonikans in general." Bulgarian-born Gadol assured his reader that it had never occurred to him to specifically target this subethnic group and emphasized that "on the contrary, we have often written articles of merit describing them as the most progressive element of all the Sephardim."[92]

As these anecdotes suggest, many Eastern Sephardim in the United States self-identified according to hometown or natal city, especially in the early years of their immigration. Simultaneously, these newcomers were also constructing a meta-identity that would include all Eastern Sephardim (and sometimes also Mizrahim and Ottoman-born Ashkenazim), regardless of specific origin in the Balkans, the Middle East, or North Africa. This conglomerate identity—note Gadol's references to "colony" and "all the Sephardim"— was in part stimulated by outsiders, who could not easily comprehend the linguistic and cultural diversity of Levantine Jewish immigrants. As British historian Eric Hobsbawm has noted, immigrants who arrive in a new land "can no longer take themselves for granted as people who do not require definition."[93]

Since this book deals mainly with intergroup relations, it is important to address these issues of self- and ascriptive identity. The terms "ethnicity" and "race" are those most often used to designate immigrant groups in the United States. Both of these terms have been exhaustively debated by successive generations of scholars of American ethnic history, raising interesting questions. How are ethnic groups created? What are the differences, if any, between ethnicity and race?[94] As Jason McDonald has pointed out, it is probably impossible to precisely define ethnicity. Moreover, Eastern Sephardi and Mizrahi Jews during the first half of the twentieth century would not have been familiar with the term "ethnicity," which in the 1940s superseded "race" as a descriptive of distinctive cultural groups, largely in reaction against Nazism.[95] Race is even more problematic. McDonald points out that many scholars of American ethnic history understand this term as "a form of ethnicity which attaches greater social significance to physiological differences between humans and thus results in more rigid group boundaries."[96] But both scientists and serious historians now refute the biological basis of race.[97] Moreover, as Gerda Lerner has pointed out, the term is itself a "racist construct" that suggests "'purity' of hereditary characteristics."[98] With a few exceptions (e.g., some Yemenite Jews who passed as African American), the experience of race as a sociological reality generally did not inform the intergroup relations explored in this book. "Race," therefore, is used in this book only in reference to the pseudoscientific approach of immigrant officials in the late nineteenth and early twentieth centuries or to contemporary government categories that define population groups in the United States today.

For all its intrinsic problems, the term "ethnicity" is preferable in the context of Eastern Sephardi and Mizrahi immigration. "Ethnicity" in this book is defined as a shared identity or sense of peoplehood based on often overlapping characteristics of language, geographical origins, ritual, and historical consciousness.[99] Like many immigrant communities, the Ladino-speaking *kolonia* was a social construct with at times flexible borders, but it was a reality for people bound together by ancestral religion, language, common geographical origins (remotely Iberian and more recently Ottoman), and experiences as a displaced minority within broader American Jewish society.

Mizrahi Jews and Ottoman-born Ashkenazim shared the unifying elements of ancestral religion and displacement, though the latter group was more easily integrated into existing Ashkenazic communities in the United States. Generally, neither Mizrahim nor Ottoman Ashkenazim shared with Eastern Sephardim a common language or remote Iberian origins. Nevertheless, Eastern Sephardim, Mizrahim, and to some extent Ottoman-born Ashkenazim were often grouped together as Levantine

Jews. In this light it makes more sense to conceptualize Levantine Jews as a social rather than an ethnic group. Unlike members of an ethnic group, those affiliated with a social group do not have a common language, history, culture, traditions, or geographical origin. Rather, social groups share a common cause that binds them together and are seen by outsiders as a cohesive group.[100] In the first years of immigration, this "common cause" included integration into the broader American Jewish community and Anglo-American society and commitment to what was viewed as social and economic progress.

Regional Identity

The tendency of Ladino speakers to self-classify regionally had already existed in the Old Country. In Istanbul, for example, the Jewish quarter was subdivided into various communities based on geographical origins in the Iberian Peninsula or elsewhere in Europe. Each of these subcommunities possessed its own synagogue.[101] In 1603, Istanbul was home to roughly five thousand male adults affiliated with some forty separate synagogues. Divisions based on geographical origins were transplanted to the immigrant neighborhoods of Tel Aviv, Paris, and New York, but in those neighborhoods Eastern Sephardim paid tribute to Ottoman, rather than Iberian, place names.[102]

Dialect often varied according to geographical origin. Max A. Luria, a philologist and professor at the City College of New York, completed a study on New York Judeo-Spanish dialects in 1929 in which he identified no less than twenty-two distinct variants of the language.[103] On the Sephardic Lower East Side, this linguistic diversity could lead to embarrassing misunderstandings. In 1922, a contributor to *La Vara* recounted an anecdote in which a Monastir-born girl working in a skirt factory was asked by the owner, a native of Kastoria, to hand her the "chokaliko." The girl blushed, not knowing how to respond. Her employer then asked her to hand him the "chokaliko" in his desk. Upon opening the drawer, the girl understood that he was referring not to a chamber pot but rather to what she would have called a "martiyiko," or hammer.[104]

These examples help to explain why microcosmic identities based on geographical origins were sociologically meaningful, particularly for the first immigrant generation. In the earliest years, newcomers from a specific town tended to cluster together on a certain street, and later they transplanted themselves as a group to other neighborhoods. These distinctive identities endured, to varying degrees, through the century. In 1950, an accounting of Sephardic High Holy Day services in Brooklyn, the Bronx, Manhattan, and Long Island included twenty-nine separate listings, including the Manhattan congregations of Monastir, Rhodes, and Janina (Ioannina).[105] Through at least the late 1970s, residents of New York's Sephardic Home for the Aged tended to socialize with others of the same natal village or town. Arguments sometimes erupted over subethnic fault lines. Officers serving on the board of directors in a given cycle tended to be of the same regional origin, and financial contributions to the home stimulated intraethnic competition.[106] Oral interviews suggest that some native-born Eastern Sephardim still preserve their discrete regional identities.

Salonikan historian Joseph Néhama (1880–1971) identified the atomized behavior of Sephardim as an "ethnic psychological trait." According to him, wherever the "Spanish Jew" settled, he "hastened to reconstruct the neighborhood of his native city, and transferred [to his new home] his languages, mores, cuisine, preoccupations, and quarrels."[107] Like Néhama, Maír José Benardete attributed Eastern Sephardic factionalism to ethnic characteristics. The failure of Eastern Sephardim to unite in the United States and their tendency to cling to regional organizations demonstrated "semitic [sic] tribalism combined with Iberic [sic] temperament." He further explained, "it is in the Oriental temperament to be suspicious even of the slightly unfamiliar, with the result that because of a localism that was the development of centuries[,] men from towns only thirty miles apart were prone to regard one another with distrust."[108]

A comparative perspective, however, reveals that lingering regional identity was not specific to Iberian-origin Jews. New York's Eastern European Ashkenazic immigrants also tended to organize according to *landsmanschaften*.[109] In 1938, the Works Progress Administration documented the existence of some three thousand of these organizations, the majority founded by Eastern European Jews between 1890 and 1914.[110] Perhaps the ultimate symbol of Ashkenazic factionalism is the demise of New York's Kehilla organization, attributed to the inability of Eastern European Jews to relinquish Old Country regional ties.[111]

Max Raisin argued that this type of factionalism was an Eastern, as opposed to Central, European Jewish trait. According to him, "The idea of federation and union is distinctively German; it originated with the Temple Jew at an early stage in the life of American reform, and is today the greatest source of strength of the reform contingent. The Polish and Russian Jews, on the other hand, have from the very first shown a tendency toward individualism and decentralization."[112] Raisin, too, was misinformed. In fact, many of the umbrella organizations established by Germanic Jews, such as the Board of Delegates of American Israelites (founded in 1859) and the Union of American Hebrew Congregations (1878), were not indicative of true union, since they were narrowly conceived as representative of religious bodies.[113] Moreover, attempts at uniting some of these religious bodies failed, including the campaign in 1926 to merge the (Conservative) Jewish Theological Seminary with the (Orthodox) Isaac Elchanan Theological Seminary in New York.[114] Nor are provincial loyalties exclusive to Jews. Salo Wittmayer Baron suggests that in their tendency to organize according to place of origin, Jews in the United States "were, perhaps, only slightly more gregarious than other Americans."[115] The proliferation of such organizations, he argues, may have been a reaction to the "free competitive system" of U.S. society.[116]

Moreover, the proliferation of subethnic organizations is deceptive as an indicator of Eastern Sephardic factionalism. Many region-specific mutual-aid societies admitted members of other geographical origins, the result of either ties of friendship and benevolence or intramarriage.[117] In this way, immigrant associations actually fostered unity among various Jewish groups. Social-action programs sponsored by regionally specific societies could also break down subethnic divisions. The Rhodes mutual-aid society raised a great sum of money in 1922 to aid the Jews of Izmir suffering during the war between Turkey and Greece.[118] A further example of these intracommunal ties came three years later, when this society decided to welcome "outsiders" (i.e., not only members of the society) to its religious services.[119]

"Umbrella" Identity

Even as their regional-based societies proliferated, the various Eastern Sephardi and Mizrahi subcultures were rapidly undergoing what Jonathan D. Sarna has called a "process of ethnicization." This sociological phenomenon may be defined as the amalgamation of petty identities into an overarching identity. In the Old Country, Ladino-, Arabic-, and Greek-speaking Jews had identified according to religion (vis-à-vis their gentile neighbors) and according to language, city, or region (vis-à-vis other Jewish groups in the area).[120] In their early years of immigration to the United States, as we have seen, these newcomers self-ascribed or were ascribed a variety of overarching ethnic labels such as "Oriental" or "Levantine Jews," and "Oriental" or "Levantine Sephardim." Ladino-speaking immigrants often referred to themselves internally as "Turkinos" to distinguish themselves from both Greek- and Arabic-speaking Jews, as well as from "Turkos" or "Turkitos," the Ladino terms for Ottoman Muslims.[121] This conglomerate ascription is already apparent in the earliest reports on intraethnic tensions, which stressed that the reputation of all Eastern Sephardim—not the image of their subgroups—was what was really at stake.

Some Jewish immigrants from Arab lands referred to themselves in the first decades of the twentieth century as Arabian Jews. A portion of the core leadership of the Federation of Oriental Jews, in fact, was composed not of Eastern Sephardim but rather of Arabic-speaking Jews. Asher Levy, an immigrant from an unspecified Arab land, headed the Agudath Achim Oriental Society of New York. In June 1912, Joseph Gedalecia, a Jew of ambiguous subethnic heritage born in Istanbul, invited Levy to unite with his own organization of Levantine Jews. Asher agreed, and the united society became the Federation of Oriental Jews.[122] Another early attempt at overarching classification came from E. Silvera, a Jewish businessman based in New York and possibly a native of Aleppo. Silvera divided what he called "Arabic-speaking Oriental Jews" into two principal groups. He classified the first, originating from Syria, Palestine, Mesopotamia, and all of Asian Turkey, as "Asiatic Jews." The second group, designated as "African Jews," originated from Egypt, Morocco, Algeria, Tunisia, and Tripoli.[123]

The emerging conglomerate identity of Eastern Sephardi and Mizrahi Jews in the United States was a process shared by all immigrant groups. In the Old Country, identification had been based on region, city, or religion. In the United States, self- and ascribed identity among immigrants gradually broadened into categories based on emerging nation-statehood (e.g., "Italian," as opposed to "Sicilian" or "Roman") or overarching ethnolinguistic groups (e.g., "Chinese," as opposed to "Cantonese" or "Mandarin").[124]

This process was especially complex for Jews from the former Ottoman Empire because they included three major language groups (Ladino, Arabic, and Greek) and a minority of Yiddish-speaking Ashkenazim. Perhaps the earliest attempt in the United States to forge a union between these groups was the Oriental Progressive Society, which, as we have seen, was in existence since 1904. The only organization of its kind in the city, the society extended membership to Jews from the Levant who identified as "Germans," "Spaniards," "Greeks," and "Arabs."[125] Once the influx of Levantine Jews accelerated after 1908, with Ladino speakers numerically dominating, language became a stronger unifying factor. Eastern Sephardic Hispanist Maír José Benardete argued that Ladino-speaking Eastern Sephardim "in psychology, ethnology, and culture" formed "a sociological unity."[126] Historians, too, consider the "Judeo-Spanish community" a useful category for analysis.[127]

The "Salonician [Salonikan] Brotherhood," founded as a mutual-aid society in 1915, was probably the first Eastern Sephardic society in New York to explicitly broaden itself subethnically. In 1921 the brotherhood officially changed its name to the more ethnically inclusive "Sepharadic [sic] Brotherhood of America."[128] But twenty years later many other societies had not yet followed suit. In response to this lingering atomization, the editors of the Ladino weekly *La Vara* adopted a new masthead in 1935 featuring two hands clasped in a handshake, communicating the newspaper's advocacy of solidarity and the "centralization of the small groups of Sephardim in America."[129] In smaller Eastern Sephardic communities, where populations from specific cities or regions were not sufficiently large to justify separate societies, the process of "ethnicization" was often swifter.[130]

But the most enduring form of federation harked back to the early tendency to include all Jews of the Levant, whether Sephardi, Mizrahi, or Ashkenazi. By the year of its incorporation in 1912, New York's Federation of Oriental Jews had successfully affiliated various Ladino-speaking groups and, by 1916, the city's Arabic- and Greek-speaking societies.[131] Significantly, one of the federation's founders, the aforementioned Joseph Gedalecia, did not explicitly identify as a Sephardic Jew. The federation's stated purpose was "to improve the material, intellectual, and civic status of the Levantine Jews in America and to better their religious conditions by the establishment of Talmud Torahs."[132] The hope was that the federation would ensure that no Levantine Jewish immigrant would be abandoned and that no community member would lack medicine, doctors, English and music classes, and access to a bureau of employment.[133] Although the federation crumbled in 1917, the numerous leaders who subsequently attempted to create communal unity embraced the inclusive definition of Levantine Jew.[134]

Many factors reinforced the need for a new, overarching category. First, as Sarna has noted, the myriad regional, dialectical, and cultural classifications with which new arrivals identified were too complicated for outsiders to process and comprehend. Conglomerate ethnic identity also served as a means of self-defense against nativism and discrimination. A third factor was organizational pragmatism.[135] It was far more politically and economically strategic to organize an overarching "Oriental" Jewish organization in the United States than to rely on smaller organizations divided according to city of origin. Organizations based on regional identity were often financially untenable, and most sooner or later collapsed. Subethnic unity would allow them to purchase a synagogue building (avoiding the need to periodically rent halls for religious services), hire a spiritual leader, and found a religious school. A fourth stimulant to the process of ethnicization was the achievement of recognition within New York's organized Jewish community, a way to combat incredulous Ashkenazim who doubted the Jewishness of Eastern Sephardim and Mizrahim.

One result of ethnicization, hastened by intramarriage among the various Eastern Sephardic groups, was the gradual standardization of the Ladino language. By the early 1950s, Maír José Benardete recognized that the various dialects of Ladino had succumbed to the Sephardic melting pot, resulting in "the Judeo-Spanish common dialect evolved in New York . . . [and] written and spoken by all."[136] The American Ladino press also played an important role in creating a standardized Ladino. The language printed in its pages is often simpler than its Ottoman counterpart, contains fewer words of Turkish derivation, and is replete with Gallicisms and Anglicized words. In this sense, the American Ladino press parallels the Yiddish press in America, which also developed a simplified and popularized Yiddish.[137]

One Levantine Jewish group that long resisted broad ethnicization was the Syrian community of Brooklyn, which has by and large successfully repelled the tendency to merge with the broader non-Ashkenazic community.[138] The community's wartime organ, the *Victory Bulletin*, never evoked the term "Sephardic" as a self-descriptive. Instead, organizations active during World War II employed such phrases as "Syrian Jewish Blood Donors Day"[139] and "Syrian Donors Day."[140] Community members referred to their ethnic neighborhood as "our Syrian colony."[141] The Syrian Division of the Zionist Organization of America (formerly the FAZ) was active by at least the mid-1940s.[142] The self-applied nickname "S.Y.," in use by at least the 1940s, is still current in this community.¹⁴³ Syrian Jews' separate self-identity, however, did not dissuade some outsiders in the 1940s from referring to Syrian Jews as "Sephardic," especially in the context of the community's association with the broader Eastern Sephardic community.¹⁴⁴ One possible reason for Syrian Jews' resistance to broad ethnicization is their ambiguous ethnic background. While some Syrian Jews could trace their ancestry back to the Iberian Peninsula, as we have seen, others were indigenous to the Middle East, and still others were a combination of both.¹⁴⁵ Another reason is that, unlike the masses of Eastern Sephardim, Syrian Jews hailed from an Arab land.

The subethnic makeup of the Syrian Jewish community diversified after the founding of the State of Israel. The wars of 1956 and 1967 brought ten thousand Jews from Egypt to the United States, most of whom settled in the Syrian community of Brooklyn. In time, these new arrivals became an inseparable part of the Syrian Jewish community. This absorption was facilitated by the fact that many Alexandrian and Cairene Jews were originally from Syria and Lebanon.¹⁴⁶

Language (or ancestral language) arguably played the largest role in preserving the identity of Syrian Jews separate from that of Eastern Sephardim. David Sitton, a Jerusalem-born Sephardic Jew who visited the United States in the early 1960s, observed that "Arab" Jews and "Balkan" Jews in New York "do not maintain any inter-communal contact."¹⁴⁷ This division perseveres in many non-Ashkenazic communities formed after 1948 throughout the United States.¹⁴⁸ It is a reminder of the limitations of an umbrella term that was conceived more out of pragmatism than collective identity.

The communal distinctiveness of Syrian Jews has not barred them from inclusion in the premier organization of non-Ashkenazic Jews in the United States. Under the umbrella of the American Sephardi Federation, non-Ashkenazim with origins as varied as Bukhara, Ethiopia, India, Iran, Morocco, Sudan, Syria, Turkey, and Yemen are organizationally united and collectively refer to themselves as Sephardim. Sephardim, Mizrahim, and Romaniote Jews, and other non-Ashkenazic groups, some 4 percent of American Jewry, have fulfilled their communal aspiration to organizationally empower a "minority within a minority." The incorporation of the American Sephardi Federation in New York's Center for Jewish History in 1998 has enhanced their quest for unity and visibility in the broader Jewish community.

Levantine Jews and Race

For many years, Jewish immigrants, whether they disembarked at Castle Garden, Ellis Island, Philadelphia, Baltimore, or Boston, were designated according to nativity, not ethnicity or religion. But in 1899, the term "Hebrew" was applied to all Jewish newcomers, as evident in the Bureau of Immigration's annual reports. Evidence suggests that Jews from Turkey were also subject to this classification. In 1921, the quota for Turkey was about 2,500, which included 417 "Hebrews."[149]

Jews were the only ethnic group to object to governmental racial classification. Among them was Simon Wolf, who protested the new classification in 1901 at a meeting of the Industrial Commission on Immigration. Wolf's objection was emblematic of the Germanic classical Reform conception of Jews as a religious group rather than a people or "race." His objections were also pragmatic: the "Hebrew designation," he feared, "would stimulate anti-Semitism and restrictionist reactions."[150] He and his Central European Jewish associates in the United States argued that this distinction represented "unconstitutional classification and discrimination" that violated the First and Fifth Amendments.[151] Their battle was ultimately successful, but not until 1943, when government officials agreed that "Hebrew" was scientifically baseless and implicitly anti-Semitic, particularly in light of Nazi propaganda.[152]

Perhaps a greater concern for Eastern Sephardim and Mizrahim was the umbrella terms used to designate their immigrant community, particularly "Levantine" and "Oriental." These terms positioned non-Ashkenazic Jews in close association with other groups whose racial identity was not clearly "Caucasoid." One example are immigrants from Syria, whose in-between racial status during the late nineteenth and early twentieth centuries put into question their right to immigration and citizenship. The national-origins quota system divided the world into Europe and non-European areas and also identified five "colored races" including black, mulatto, Chinese, Japanese, and Indian.[153] Where did Syrians belong in this panoply of races? Syrian Jews might have shuddered upon learning of George Najour, a Syrian non-Jew who was declared eligible for citizenship in 1909 only after his case reached a federal court in Georgia. The decision was based not on the shade of Najour's complexion but rather on A. H. Keane's *The World's People* (1908), which classified humans into four groups. Keane categorized Syrians in the "Caucasian or white" division. Seven other cases between 1909 and 1923 were ruled in favor of Syrian, Armenian, and Asian Indian immigrants using similar justification.[154]

Another reason for objecting to the terms "Oriental" and, to a lesser extent, "Levantine" was their association with immigrants from East Asia, whom the U.S. government deemed undesirable.[155] Moise Gadol fretted in 1915 that the term "Oriental" would cause immigrant officials to confuse Eastern Sephardim with Asians, "against whom America manifests its most intense hatred."[156] Hostilities against these immigrants in America had been particularly virulent beginning in the late nineteenth century, coinciding with the mass immigration of Levantine Jews. Anti-Asian legislation, including the Chinese Exclusion Act of 1882, prohibited the immigration of Chinese workers into the United States until the early twentieth century.[157] The quota system, finally enacted in 1929, excluded native citizens of East Asia from immigration because they were racially disqualified from U.S. citizenship.[158] Chinese immigrants also witnessed the pillaging and demolition of their shops and industries and the burning of their ghettos, and they were stereotyped as opium and gambling addicts.[159] The word "Oriental" had come to connote "shiftiness and shyster tactics."[160]

This hostility implicitly informed a furious taxonomical debate in the non-Ashkenazic community. In 1916, J. de A. Benyunes proposed the term "Oriental-Sephardim," since "it accurately describes the real characteristics of this people both physically [!] and spiritually."[161] Another Sephardic Jew wondered why his community should use the designation "Oriental Jews"—did Ashkenazim call themselves "Occidental Jews?"[162] Only Joseph Gedalecia, a Jew of mixed Sephardic and Ashkenazic ancestry born in Istanbul, dared to challenge America's deprecation of East Asians. As he affirmed in 1914, "I feel proud to be classed with Hindus and Chinese and Japanese and other Asiatics."[163]

The issue of nomenclature was complicated by the multicultural nature of Eastern Sephardim. Their identity was linked with a broad array of ethnic, geographical, and linguistic dimensions that outsiders often found difficult to process. A 1914 article in *The World* identified these immigrants, who "come from Turkey, speak a mixture of Turkish and Spanish, and are Hebrews," as "a very mixed type of Jew."[164] To many interlopers, Eastern Sephardi and Mizrahi Jews were a puzzling component of New York immigrant society. One author in 1916 attempted to capture this confusion by reconstructing a stroll past the Sephardic cafés of the Lower East Side:

See the signs on these institutions. They read: "Cafe Constantinople," "Cafe Oriental," "Cafe Smyrna," and there are other signs in Hebrew characters that you perhaps cannot read. Are they Jews? No, it cannot be; they do not look like Jews; they do not speak Yiddish. Listen: what is that strange tongue they are using? It sounds like Spanish or Mexican. Are they Spaniards or Mexicans? If so, where did they get the coffee-houses, an importation from Greece and Turkey? . . . On your way home you think and wonder who these alien people can be who speak Spanish, yet are not Spaniards; speak Greek, yet are not Greeks; have Turkish as their mother-tongue and wear turbans, yet are not Moslems.[165]

Significantly, the author of this quotation is Istanbul-born Samuel M. Auerbach, whose Levantine Ashkenaziut further confounded easy understanding of Ottoman Jewish "ethnicity."

The aforementioned phenomenon of "passing"—whereby Eastern Sephardim were (sometimes with complicity) mistaken for non-Jewish French, Greek, Italian, or Hispanic immigrants—further highlights the plasticity of group identity.[166] Joseph Gedalecia, who had himself immigrated to the United States via Paris as "a Frenchman," noted in 1914 that many Mediterranean Jewish immigrants native to Greece and other countries intentionally passed as non-Jewish.[167] Reminiscing on Sephardic communal affairs from his Los Angeles home in 1976, Albert J. Amateau claimed he knew "fifty or more" Sephardim who "changed their names and pretended they were anything but Jews," one passing for a Christian Italo-Frenchman.[168] Many Eastern Sephardim allegedly succumbed to the temptation to "pass" for business reasons, Amateau alleged, including the Schinasi brothers of tobacco factory fame. This, however, did not prevent them from later embracing the community as prominent leaders and philanthropists.[169]

The relationship of Eastern Sephardim to the Hispanic thread of their heritage has positioned them somewhat awkwardly in relation to the modern concept of race and racial minorities. Marco DeFunis, a Seattle native who in the early 1970s sued the University of Washington Law School for refusing to admit him, did not once consider arguing that because of his Hispanic roots he, too, should have been considered for admission under the affirmative-action policy. When I spoke to DeFunis in the summer of 2000, he indicated that the idea had not occurred to him because he did not self-identify as Hispanic, nor did other Sephardim whom he knew.[170] Interestingly, a friend who delivered a eulogy upon

DeFunis's unexpected death in 2002 maintained that DeFunis refused to "portray himself as Hispanic" because he "had a sense of confidence in the American justice system."[171] In the early 1990s, however, the legacy of Spain did prove central to another lawsuit involving alleged discrimination. That case is especially noteworthy because the U.S. government now defines "Hispanic" as an ethnic group rather than as a racial group. The case involved one Alfred Bennun, a Rutgers State University biochemist who was denied tenure, he claimed, because his father was Sephardic. The judge allowed Bennun to sue even though his mother was born in Romania and his father in Israel. Bennun, the judge surmised, was Hispanic because his father was a Sephardic Jew whose ancestors had been expelled from Spain in 1492. In 1992, a U.S. Federal Court of Appeals ruled that Sephardim are entitled to the discrimination protection offered Hispanics in the U.S. Civil Rights Act of 1964.[172]

As this brief overview has shown, ethnic identity—and its more recent intensification into implicit racial identity—is shaped by numerous internal and external factors, some imported from the Old Country, others forged on American soil. The array of terminology that Eastern Sephardim, Mizrahim, and Ottoman Ashkenazim used and debated (Turkinos, Levantine Jews, Sefaradím, Sephardic Jews, Levantine Sephardim, Oriental Jews, Oriental Sephardim, Hispanic Jews, etc.) is evidence that their group identity, like that of so many other immigrants, was unstable. The files brought to court by DeFunis and Bennun are sure indicators that the identities of non-Ashkenazic Jews in America continue to fluctuate.

2

Hebrew with a Sephardic Accent
A Test Case for Impact

In 2004, sociolinguist Sarah Bunin Benor dispatched a query to the H-Judaic electronic listserv. When and why, she asked, did American Hebrew schools shift from the Ashkenazic to the Sephardic pronunciation?[1] A few years earlier, while researching and writing my doctoral dissertation on American Sephardim, I had grappled with the same question. In the context of the New York *kolonia*, I had come across a number of references to the "Sephardic" or "Land of Israel" pronunciation of Hebrew in the 1910s and its gradual acceptance among American Ashkenazic Jews. Could these findings, I wondered, demonstrate the impact of U.S. Sephardim on broader American Jewish society?

This question reflected the scholarly approach I embraced early in my academic career. I was trained as a graduate student to seek not the *influence* but, rather, the *impact* of the Jews on broader society. The paradigms of influence, and later impact, displaced the earlier historiographical quest for the "accomplishments" of American Jews, which smacked of apologia. I wholeheartedly adopted the paradigm of impact. Demonstrating the incontrovertible imprint of American Sephardim on broader Jewish society (their immediate reference group), I reasoned, would justify the worthiness of my investigation. In the ensuing years, my continued search for linguistic impact led to unexpected conclusions and, ultimately, to an entirely different historical paradigm.

The near-universal adoption of Sephardic-accented Hebrew in the Jewish world remains one of the most visible markers of the impact of a minority on a majority culture. In the early 1950s, for example, less than 30 percent of Israel's Jewish population was of Iberian origin.[2] But the Sephardic intonation of Hebrew was already standard in the newly founded state and was rapidly gaining acceptance abroad. As we will see, this impact was largely due to a preexisting receptivity among Ashkenazic majority populations.

The "Correct" Pronunciation of Hebrew

In the ancient Land of Israel, various pronunciations of Hebrew existed among the predecessors of the Jewish people. One source that suggests dialectical variation is the Book of Judges 12:5–6, in which the biblical Gileadites chose the word *shibboleth* (an ear of corn) as a password, fully knowing that Ephraimites could not pronounce the "sh" sound and would therefore not be able to slip through enemy lines. This story is early evidence that the language in the northern kingdom of Israel was spoken differently than in the southern kingdom of Judah.[3]

This linguistic diversity proliferated in exile. The Hebrew spoken in the Land of Israel during the Second Temple period could be distinguished from the Aramaic-influenced inflection of the Babylonian exiles.[4] The Talmud (tractate *Megilla* 24b) and the *Shulhan Arukh* (*Orah Hayim* 53), by deeming pronunciation changes as violations, point to coexisting ancient variations that have since been forgotten. Iberian Jewish legalist Maimonides (1138–1204) declared that pronunciation changes in prayer rendered worship unacceptable, which also hints at multiple traditions of diction. In medieval Iberia, three distinct inflections existed through the end of the fifteenth century, representing Muslim Spain, Christian Spain, and Catalonia, each influenced by the respective local languages (Arabic, Spanish, and Catalan and its cognate dialects).[5] In the modern period, no less than nine variations of Hebrew intonation have been documented.[6]

This multiplicity gave rise to debates about authenticity and aesthetics. Perhaps the earliest polemic concerning Hebrew pronunciation emerged among Europe's enlightened Ashkenazim (*maskilim*) in the late eighteenth century.[7] These leaders glorified the civilization of medieval Iberian Jewry for achieving what they perceived as a harmonious balance between commitment to Judaism and contributions to general society. Consequently, they strove to emulate several aspects of medieval Sephardic culture, including linguistic traditions. Philologist and educator Naftali Herz Wessely (1725–1805), a disciple of Moses Mendelssohn who was born in Hamburg, advocated in his manifesto *Words of Peace and Truth* (1782) that his Ashkenazic brethren adopt the Sephardic inflection.[8] Wessely and likeminded *maskilim* appreciated the perceived linguistic beauty and accuracy of this intonation. They were also motivated by an aversion to Yiddish, a language that epitomized for them the decline of Jewish culture.[9] Citing "the consensus of scholarly opinion,"

Parisian Jewry adopted the Sephardic intonation shortly after the establishment of the city's Jewish elementary school in 1818. By 1850, the majority of Jewish authorities in Paris had embraced the Sephardic intonation. They, too, had been influenced by the *maskilic* glorification of medieval Spanish Jewry and its related aversion to Ashkenazic culture.[10] By at least the 1880s, Germany's universities and other non-Jewish academies and theological schools employed the Sephardic pronunciation. As a result, Jewish historian Heinrich Graetz, who taught during that decade at the University of Breslau, felt duty bound to use this accent when reading or quoting biblical texts. In his classes at the city's Jewish Theological Seminary, however, he stuck to his native *ashkenazis*.[11]

Yemenite Hebrew was also greatly admired by Ashkenazic Jews. Yaakov Saphir (1822–1885), a Lithuanian Jew who visited the Jewish community in Yemen in 1859, proposed that its pronunciation of Hebrew could be directly linked to the Hebrew spoken in antiquity. Because of the influence of the local Arabic language and their long, uninterrupted sojourn in their exilic land, he argued, Yemeni Jews preserved an accent more authentic than either the Sephardic or the Ashkenazic.[12] Saphir compared this intonation favorably to the "broken-tongue of the Sephardic Jews" and the "hair strum of a language spoken by the Ashkenazi Jews."[13]

But the more widespread and enduring dispute concerned Sephardic versus Ashkenazic inflection. At the turn of the century, Hungarian rabbi and scholar Meyer (Moritz) Kayserling remarked in a widely quoted encyclopedia article that Sephardim "speak a purer Hebrew than do the Ashkenazim."[14] This view resonated with American Jewish educators and communal leaders. In New York, Board of Jewish Education superintendent Alexander M. Dushkin noted in 1918 that the Sephardic pronunciation of Hebrew "is purer and more correct than the pronunciation prevalent among the German-Polish Jews."[15] After Seattle's Ashkenazic community rejected Sephardic immigrants from the island of Rhodes as fellow Jews, a local Reform rabbi tried to convince his congregation that these newcomers "were even better Jews, spoke a purer Hebrew, than the Ashkenazim themselves."[16]

The Sephardic accent as spoken in Palestine and the early State of Israel was especially esteemed. One author in 1920 highlighted its "crispness and beauty and rhythm."[17] Observers often equated the Ashkenazic mode of speech with a harsh sound, whereas the Sephardic accent was referred to as "soft."[18] In comparison to its Eastern European cousin, Sephardic-accented Hebrew was "smoother, less harsh, and more melodious."[19] If the Sephardic dialect was ever characterized as "harsh," it was often in a positive context, for example, to highlight the heartiness of Jewish pioneers.[20] Many immigrants to Palestine disparaged the Ashkenazic dialect of Hebrew for its frequent use of diphthongs, which was evocative of the suffering "oy" emitted by Yiddish-speaking Jews in the diaspora.[21]

Scholars who have studied the use of Hebrew in ancient Palestine and throughout the diaspora agree that there is no "correct" tradition of Hebrew pronunciation.[22] Moreover, aesthetics is a matter of taste. But this knowledge seldom vitiated the idea of an authentic and beautiful Hebrew intonation.

Until the emergence of Jewish nationalism, the preference for Sephardic-accented Hebrew was largely confined to the realm of ideological debate. The question of Hebrew pronunciation only became critical during the late nineteenth century with the rise of modern Hebrew schools and the concomitant movement to transform Hebrew into a secular language of daily speech. Modern Hebrew schools were the first to adopt the "natural method" (*ha-shitah ha-tivit*) of Hebrew language instruction. This mode of instruction, also known as Hebrew-in-Hebrew (*ivrit be-ivrit*),[23] stressed spontaneous conversation over translation by rote. This method was a break with traditional instruction, in which the Hebrew language and sacred Jewish texts were studied through translation from Jewish vernaculars, such as Yiddish, Judeo-Arabic, and Ladino. In this time-honored mode, the Hebrew language was taught not as a living, spoken language but, rather, solely as an instrument for reading the Bible and other traditional Jewish sources.

The modern religious school (*heder hametukan*) of Eastern European Jews, and especially in Russia, first adopted the natural method in the beginning of the twentieth century, but they employed the Ashkenazic accent.[24] So, too, in the United States the first attempt at religious instruction in Hebrew, launched by Sundel Hirsch Neumann (1860–1934) of Brooklyn in 1893, was in "*ashkenazis.*"[25] Modern Hebrew pedagogues outside New York City likewise clung tenaciously to their native Ashkenazic accent. Louis Hurwich, a Lithuanian-born Hebrew teacher and principal who spent time in New York, Indianapolis, and Boston, taught the language in the Ashkenazic accent until at least the 1930s.[26] From its founding in 1911, the Talmud Torah (Jewish religious school) of Minneapolis employed the natural method under the direction of Elijah Avin, a Litvak and pioneer Hebrew educator who emphasized the enunciation of the prayers "in proper Hebrew, the classical Ashkenazic developed in Eastern Europe at that time."[27] His successors still retained the Ashkenazic intonation by the late 1930s, as did the Hebrew-in-Hebrew teachers of Detroit, Michigan.[28]

The question of an alternative Hebrew accent was rarely discussed in Eastern Europe and the United States, where Ashkenazim were both politically and numerically dominant.[29] But Palestine was another story. Because its Jewish population was much more subethnically diverse than either Eastern Europe or the United States, Palestine provided fertile ground for a linguistic shift. There, ethnically variant Jewish populations lived side by side, and Jews of Iberian and Middle Eastern origins had been numerically and politically dominant for centuries. This Palestine is the one that Eliezer Ben-Yehuda encountered upon his arrival from northwest Russia in 1881. Born to a pious Jewish family, Ben-Yehuda is often regarded as the reviver of Hebrew as a modern language.[30] His main activities toward that goal included writing a colossal, seventeen-volume dictionary of the Hebrew language,[31] maintaining a Hebrew newspaper (*Hatzvi*, founded in 1884), and raising the first exclusively Hebrew-speaking child in modern times.

The question of Hebrew intonation had occupied Ben-Yehuda even before his arrival in Palestine. Ironically, he had learned the exalted accent not from a Sephardic Jew but from an Ashkenazic Jew he had encountered in Paris. This acquaintance had spent time among North African Jews in Tunisia and Morocco and had communicated with the local Jewish community in Hebrew until he learned Arabic. Thus, it was in Paris that Ben-Yehuda first heard the "Sephardic" pronunciation and first attempted to speak Hebrew. To his delight, he found he could carry on simple conversations with his coreligionist.[32] Ben-Yehuda next encountered the accent in Algiers, where he spent the winter of 1881 to recuperate from tuberculosis. This time his partners in conversation were Maghrebi Jews themselves. Their inflection "captured his heart" and convinced him that this would be the accent for revived spoken Hebrew in the Land of Israel.[33]

The accent that Ben-Yehuda heard among Sephardic Jews in Palestine reinforced his resolve. After his arrival, his first business transaction conducted entirely in Hebrew was with a Sephardic Jew. As he exchanged his French gold coins for local currency, Ben-Yehuda noted that the money-changer's Hebrew intonation was "oriental, soft, and fluent."[34] Sephardic Jews, he observed, conversed "fluently and naturally" in a Hebrew characterized by "a wealth of vocabulary and idiom." Their pronunciation was "so original, so wonderfully oriental!"³⁵ His aesthetic appreciation was no doubt influenced by the prestige of local Sephardim. Palestine's Sephardic community not only boasted longevity in the region but also enjoyed a social and economic status higher than that of Ashkenazim. The few relatively rich Jewish residents of the land were mostly Sephardim. Besides, Ben-Yehuda noted that in the early 1880s, most Ashkenazim were not "normal human beings" who lived "normal lives" but were rather mainly full-time Torah scholars who worked only occasionally and were supported by the charitable fund (*halukkah*). By contrast, the Sephardic community, about seven thousand strong, "was more or less a normal group, because most of them were ordinary people making a living as craftsmen or laborers."³⁶ Of all Jerusalem's inhabitants, Sephardim most impressed Ben-Yehuda. "Most of them were handsome, all were elegant in their oriental apparel, and their manners were impeccable," he reminisced. Some Ashkenazim had acculturated to Sephardim in dress, manners, and pronunciation, he noted, but "one could easily tell that it was not a Sephardi speaking."³⁷

One of the Sephardim whom Ben-Yehuda especially admired was Nessim Behar (1848–1931). Behar, a Jerusalem native and scion of an eminent Sephardic rabbinical family, is best known for his activities on behalf of the Alliance Israélite Universelle, an organization founded by French Jews in 1860 to ameliorate the economic and social condition of Jews in the Levant and to introduce a francophone education. Behar founded or directed a series of Alliance schools, first in Aleppo at the age of twenty-one, then in Istanbul and Bulgaria, and finally in Jerusalem, where he was appointed in 1881 to direct *HaTorah VeHaMelakha*, informally known as *la skola* (Ladino for "the school"). Before his return to Palestine in 1881, Behar had once served as a French instructor according to the "natural method," also known as the "Berlitz method" or "French-in-French." It was in Istanbul that Behar first thought of applying this method to Hebrew language instruction. This idea was tantamount to a revolution in Jewish pedagogy, for in traditional Ashkenazi, Mizrahi, and Eastern Sephardi schools, as noted earlier, Hebrew was taught through translations of the Bible and rabbinical literature to the Yiddish, Judeo-Arabic, or Ladino.

Both Ben-Yehuda and Behar envisioned a rebirth of the Hebrew language, and they became close friends.³⁸ Soon, they would also become close colleagues. Students in the *HaTorah VeHaMelakha* school, which

Behar directed, were all Sephardim. In 1883, Behar decided to admit Ashkenazic students but fretted that the various domestic languages of the pupils would present pedagogical complications. His solution was to instruct Ben-Yehuda in the Hebrew-in-Hebrew technique and to hire him as a language teacher in the school.[39] Though sources are silent on the question of accent, it is unthinkable that Behar would have taught Hebrew in anything but the Sephardic intonation. An Anglo-Jewish visitor in 1888 observed admiringly of Behar's pupils, "the average European Rabbi would be put to the blush by these little scholars of Jerusalem, whose fluency and elegance of diction make us unable to realize that Hebrew is not a living language."[40]

Though deteriorating health prevented Ben-Yehuda from retaining his position in Behar's school for very long, two young adults observing his class—David Yellin and Yosef Meyuhas—were inspired to integrate his teaching methods into their own classrooms. Through these two men, Ashkenazic and Sephardic, respectively, the "natural method" rapidly spread to the rest of the country and then throughout the diaspora.[41] Especially key to this propagation were the numerous teachers working in isolated agricultural settlements in Palestine founded by Eastern European Jews after 1882. By perfecting the Hebrew-in-Hebrew method, Jack Fellman argues, these visionaries were ultimately responsible for making the "true revival of the Hebrew language in the mouths of the new younger generation."[42]

Given that most of the settlers at the turn of the century were Ashkenazim, many of whom habitually employed their ancestral Hebrew accent, one wonders how the Sephardic intonation came to prevail among them. As hinted earlier, Hebrew had existed as an intracommunal language in Palestine long before Ben-Yehuda's arrival.[43] Sephardim, Ashkenazim, Maghrebis, Georgians, and other Jews spoke their own languages among themselves, but among one another they were compelled to use Hebrew. In these conversations, everyone, even Ashkenazim, employed the Sephardic accent.[44] The antagonism that Ben-Yehuda's revivalist efforts created among Jerusalem's ultraorthodox Ashkenazic Jews may have had unintended consequences in favor of the Sephardic intonation. In opposition to the campaign for modern spoken Hebrew, Tudor V. Parfitt argues, most Ashkenazic Jews of the old *yishuv* (the Jewish community of pre-state Palestine) were by 1918 "adverse to using the Holy Language in daily secular intercourse" and were "almost completely closed to the Hebrew Revival."[45] The apparent abandonment of spoken Hebrew by the Ashkenazic old *yishuv* may have strengthened the position of the Sephardic accent throughout Palestine.

The gradual proliferation of Sephardic-inflected Hebrew was evident in both communal and institutional spheres. Ephraim Cohen, the director of the Von Laemmel School in Palestine and a Jerusalem native who had studied at Jews' College in London, decided in 1891 to adopt the Sephardic pronunciation. The language and some classes were taught in that accent.[46] By around 1900, the Sephardic pronunciation prevailed in almost all Jewish settlements.[47] In 1903, Palestine's Teachers' Association decided that the accent of instruction for all courses would be Sephardic. Tentatively, however, *ashkenazis* would be employed in the Ashkenazic schools in the first years, and thereafter the Sephardic pronunciation would be used. Ashkenazic variants would be preserved for prayers.[48] That same year the central committee of the Lovers of Zion organization of Odessa, which sought to strengthen Hebrew institutions in Palestine, generally concluded that the Sephardic accent should be used in all schools.[49] A modern school (*heder metukan*), founded in Jaffa in 1904, adopted the Sephardic pronunciation in 1909.[50]

The debate over accent in Palestine was officially resolved in the second decade of the twentieth century. This resolution was due largely to the Hebrew Language Council (*Va'ad HaLashon HaIvrit*), founded in 1890 by Ben-Yehuda, and the harbinger of today's Hebrew Language Academy (*Akademiya LaLashon HaIvrit*). In 1913, council members debated and ultimately affirmed the Sephardic accent's authenticity. Two years later, the council decided that all Palestinian high schools would be required to appoint a special teacher for the instruction of proper intonation.[51]

The precise name of this intonation, and what it actually sounded like, is a complex matter. Sources from the mid-nineteenth century refer to speaking Hebrew "in the Spanish way."[52] Eliezer Ben-Yehuda preferred the term "oriental" (*mizrahi*), which for him denoted Arabic-inflected Hebrew.[53] Likewise, in 1912 the Hebrew Language Council cited as one of its main tasks the preservation of "the Oriental quality of the language." Its officials advocated the study of this pronunciation in special classes offered by a teacher of the Arabic language.[54] By contrast, during the 1910s, the accent was commonly referred to in the American Ladino press as the "Sephardic" or "Palestinian" accent or dialect of Hebrew. In the mid-1930s, Eliezer Ben-Yehuda's son Ittamar Ben-Avi used the terms "'Sephardic' (Spanish) or Palestinian Hebrew."[55]

Collectively, this evidence suggests that the "Sephardic" intonation of Hebrew denoted a variety of different accents, depending on place and time. Modern spoken Hebrew underwent a process of development since the start of its dissemination in the late nineteenth century and was never uniform among the Jews who spoke and propagated it. Thus, the term "Sephardic accent" (*havarah sefaradit*) is in fact a misnomer, since there was never any single Sephardic intonation. Moreover, the Hebrew inflection of predominantly Ladino-speaking Eastern Sephardim differed markedly from historically Portuguese-speaking Western Sephardim, as readily evident in the way each group transliterated Hebrew words into Latin letters in their respective prayer books.[56]

The triumph of the term "Sephardic" to designate this accent is an outcome of a process of ethnicization similar to the concurrent one that divided the Jewish people into two groups: Sephardim and Ashkenazim. This false dichotomy of accent meant that there were purportedly "two basic forms of pronunciation, the Ashkenazic and Sephardic." A Hebrew primer published in 1940s New York explained the simplification in this way: "The Ashkenazic is the accent formerly used by the Jews of Germany and Eastern Europe. The Sephardic is used by the Jews of Israel and of the eastern countries."[57] The problem was, what exactly was a Sephardic Jew? Did the term refer to an Arabic-speaking Jew? If so, a speaker of which dialect?[58] A Ladino-speaking Jew of Iberian origin? Certainly not a Yemenite Jew, whose accent was in many ways more similar to Ashkenazic dialects.[59]

In light of these many variations, it is likely that contemporary Jews defined Sephardic Hebrew by what it was not. In all its diverse intonations, this Hebrew pronunciation was unmistakably distinctive from all Ashkenazic dialects. In the "Palestinian Sephardic" dialect, the Hebrew letter *taf* was always pronounced like a "t" and never like the "s," as in *ashkenazis*. In "Palestinian Sephardic" Hebrew, the emphasis was generally placed on the last syllable, whereas in the Ashkenazic intonation the penultimate syllable always bore the emphasis.[60] Thus, the "Palestinian Sephardic" Hebrew word for "Sabbath" could be pronounced "SaBAT" or "ShaBAT" but never like the Ashkenazic "SHObbes."[61] Jews raised with the so-called Palestinian dialect found that these differences could make conversation a rather arduous undertaking. This applied equally to Ashkenazic Jews. During his sojourn in Germany in 1907, Ittamar Ben-Avi spent much time in cafés conversing with Russian Jews, who spoke to him in a Hebrew he could barely comprehend, as it was the

Polish-Ashkenazic pronunciation.[62] The battle for Sephardic Hebrew in the diaspora had only just begun.

The Proliferation of Sephardic Hebrew in the Diaspora

Linguistic developments in Palestine, particularly the decisions of the Hebrew Language Council, gradually and decisively influenced spoken Hebrew abroad. The steady dissemination and ultimate triumph of the so-called Sephardic accent in the field of education is one of the few examples in Jewish history of children being key to ideological dissemination. As Eliezer Ben-Yehuda understood since at least 1880, the language's resurrection depended on the younger generation.[63] It is important to articulate the reasons why children were so instrumental to linguistic transformation. They were expected, ideally, not to earn a living but rather to receive an education. Moreover, their relatively unformed minds were more receptive than the minds of adults. Finally, since modern, spoken Hebrew was in part an invented language, it was arguably easier for parents of schoolchildren to accept because it did not displace a time-honored tradition. By contrast, other Jewish nationalist innovations, such as the adoption of a single system of handwriting or employing the Sephardic accent in Hebrew *prayer*, were more threatening because they did in fact displace age-old practices.[64] Thus, the most important locus for the dissemination of Sephardic Hebrew was not the social or political organization, or the synagogue, but rather elementary and high schools. As in Palestine, schools played a central role in the proliferation of the Sephardic intonation. In fact, as one American Hebrew educator commented in 1938, Hebrew language instruction in high schools represents "the first successful attempt to introduce the Sephardic accent on a large scale into America."[65]

New York's Jewish religious schools collectively enrolled the highest number of students in the country. These schools, largely under the auspices of Eastern European Ashkenazim, were initially designed after the *cheder*, the traditional elementary school regarded by modernizing Jewish immigrants as antiquated and ineffectual. As in Eastern Europe, the American *cheder*, with its by-rote teaching method, began to give way to Hebrew-in-Hebrew around the turn of the century. Soon after 1903, this modern pedagogy was adopted in the third and highest level in religious classes in Harlem's Uptown Talmud Torah,[66] which qualified as the country's largest Talmud Torah by around 1911, enrolling fifteen hundred students.[67] Another religious school that adopted the Hebrew-in-Hebrew method was the Rabbi Israel Salanter Talmud Torah, also of Harlem, founded in December 1909. Unlike the Uptown Talmud Torah, the "natural method" was employed in all class levels, from the basic alphabet to advanced Talmud studies.[68] At a convention of New York's Talmudei Torah principals in 1912, educators agreed to adopt the Hebrew-in-Hebrew method because it "lightens and considerably shortens the difficult road to the understanding of Hebrew as the medium of the Jewish religion." By the next year this method was employed by all schools affiliated with the Jewish Bureau of Education in New York and formed the basis of its textbooks.[69] This methodological innovation was remarkable for Jewish religious schools, because at this time they represented the most traditional of Jewish institutions, aside from orthodox synagogues.

The Hebrew-in-Hebrew method also made inroads in New York's public schools. By the first decade of the twentieth century, the student body in many Lower East Side public schools was as high as 80 to 90 percent Jewish. Hebrew methodological innovation therefore had an unusual impact in New York City. In 1930, Hebrew was introduced into the curricula of both the Abraham Lincoln and the Thomas Jefferson high schools, where Jews constituted as much as 80 percent of the student body. Enrollment in New York's high school Hebrew classes climbed from sixty to two thousand by February 1938.[70] By that year Hebrew-language high school instruction had also spread to Chelsea, Massachusetts; Schenectady, New York; Chicago; and St. Louis.[71] By 1938 the pedagogues in these schools all employed the "modified 'natural method,'" commonly known as *ivrit-be-ivrit*, with translation from the vernacular "used only infrequently as a supplementary exercise."[72]

Even though it was probably *ashkenazis* that prevailed in all these early examples, the acceptance of a modern teaching method opened the doors to yet another innovation: the Sephardic accent. Indeed, modern educators came to associate the traditional (or, according to others, "archaic") learning-by-rote method with the "tedious ashkenazic [sic] pronunciation."[73] Once Hebrew, rather than Yiddish or English, was used as the language of instruction, pedagogues became increasingly self-conscious of their own intonation in comparison to the Hebrew current in Palestine. Moreover, some of the most popular Hebrew-in-Hebrew textbooks then available in the United States were published in Palestine by authors who employed the Sephardic accent.[74] Finally, a Palestinian orientation became pronounced among American Jews during the post–World War I period, when American Jews increasingly embraced Labor Zionism, the dominant political movement in Jewish Palestine.[75] American Jewry's support of Labor Zionism was an expression of its increasing attunement to Palestine for cultural and political cues. Also significant was the Anglicization of American Jewry during the interwar period, which saw the decline of Yiddish and consequently opened the door wider to the influence of Palestinian Hebrew. By this decade, American Zionism increasingly relinquished its Yiddishist profile for a "Palestinocentric orientation."[76]

A string of anecdotes confirms the role of Palestine in spreading the Sephardic accent among American Jews. Louis Hurwich, the aforementioned Hebrew educator based for many years in Boston, employed the Sephardic accent when speaking to his two children, born in the late 1920s and early '30s. He had adopted the intonation from his Ashkenazic wife, who had learned to speak Hebrew during a sojourn in the Land of Israel from 1921 to 1922.[77] Likewise, it was an Ashkenazic Jew—this time from Palestine—who introduced the Sephardic accent to America's first Hebrew-speaking camp, located in Arverne, Long Island. In 1927, the visit of the Habimah Theater from Palestine, whose founding members had embraced Sephardic Hebrew in 1901, convinced Samson Benderly (1876–1944) to introduce the Sephardic intonation to his new camp.[78] Irving White, an American Jewish psychologist who came of age in Chicago, adopted the Sephardic accent after a Palestinian member of the *Irgun*, seeking refuge in the United States, began to teach Hebrew Bible in the 1940s at White's yeshiva.[79]

Here, it is important to note that the renowned New York–based pedagogue Samson Benderly taught and spoke Hebrew in his native Ashkenazic accent. This accent made Benderly something of a laughing stock among Hebrew-speaking Palestinian youth during a visit to Eretz Yisrael in 1920–1921.[80] When he decided to adopt the Sephardic accent in his new camp on Long Island in 1927, it "was quite a hardship upon Dr. Benderly himself who spoke Sephardit [Sephardic-accented Hebrew] with a strong Ashkenazic accent."[81] Benderly's family had resided in Palestine since the seventeenth century, but he had left his native land soon after 1889,[82] about a decade before the Sephardic accent prevailed in most Jewish settlements. The decision of Benderly and some of his disciples, the so-called Benderly boys, to adopt the Sephardic accent was an expression of the deepening relationship between American and Palestinian Jewry.[83] Moreover, Benderly's linguistic struggles demonstrate the difficulty with which even the most committed modernists adopted the Sephardic accent. The onerous burden of Sephardic inflection among many Ashkenazic Jews, including those born and reared in Palestine, was apparently not uncommon.[84]

In the diaspora outside the United States, Palestinian Jews also functioned as advocates of Sephardic-inflected Hebrew, sometimes indirectly or unwittingly. In the early 1920s, Hungarian-born ethnographer Raphael Patai (1910–1996) received training for his bar-mitzvah in the Sephardic intonation. The bar-mitzvah teacher would have normally offered instruction in the Ashkenazic accent, then the norm in Hungarian synagogues and Jewish schools, had not Patai's father intervened: "The reason Father insisted on Sephardic was that it was the Hebrew pronunciation of the yishuv of Palestine, that is, the pronunciation of Hebrew as a living language, and that is what Father wanted Hebrew to be for me."[85] Sephardic Hebrew was apparently not introduced into the Jewish schools of Pest and Győr until 1939.[86] In a small town in Poland in 1927, sixteen-year-old A. Greyno learned the Sephardic accent from a cousin visiting from Palestine. After his cousin's return to the Land of Israel, Greyno and his brother "worked diligently to learn the language with the same accent."[87] In Zagreb, the Jewish elementary school, founded in 1841, introduced the teaching of modern Hebrew in the Sephardic pronunciation sometime in the 1920s, as the community's executive board came under Zionist control. Like the early experiments in language shift among Palestine's Eastern European Ashkenazic populations, prayers (as opposed to Hebrew as a living language) in this Yugoslavian school were still conducted in the traditional accent.[88] Aron Horowitz, a rabbi who was raised in a Palestinian Hasidic family, arrived in Calgary, Canada, in 1942 to assume the position of principal in the local Hebrew school. Not without opposition, Horowitz successfully introduced "the living pronunciation" into the kindergarten and all eight grades.[89]

Of course, the Sephardic accent could not have spread abroad without some preexisting receptivity among diasporic Jews. A feeling of awe for Palestine as well as the need for modern Jewish role models deeply informed this openness. The romantic or sexual overtones of admiration for Sephardic Hebrew is noteworthy. A. Greyno recalled that his Palestinian cousin was a "beautiful, tall, healthy, normally developed woman" who "awakened boyish feelings of love and respect in me."[90] For Irving White, switching to the Sephardic inflection qualified him as "a potential Zionist hero to myself rather than a scared, compliant ghetto yeshiva *bochur*." White recalls, "It was in those ambivalent, often oppressive years that I became aware of my need for masculine Jewish 'heroes' with whom I could identify, the most potent of whom were the Palestinian Jews . . . as well as those young Jews who were preparing for aliyah and to fight for their people."[91]

Zionism on an institutional level also played an important role in dissemination. In 1909, Warsaw's Hovevei Sfat Ever (Lovers of Hebrew) organization required speakers to address their audiences in the Ashkenazic (as opposed to the Sephardic) accent so that they would be understood. As Arieh Bruce Saposnik notes, this resistance speaks to the power of the *yishuv* and its insistence on the so-called Sephardic accent.[92] But in Sholem Aleichem's epistolary novel *The Further Adventures of Menachem-Mendl*, organizers of the Eleventh Zionist Congress in Vienna (1913) instituted a policy that delegates address their audiences either in Russian or Sephardic-inflected Hebrew.[93] Though the meetings of the Zionist Congress were officially conducted in German until 1933,[94] some speakers before then did address their audiences in Hebrew, and Sholem Aleichem's fictional account is probably reflective of an actual linguistic shift.[95] Zionism was evidently also the driving force in South Africa, where in 1933 the Johannesburg Jewish Reform Congregation became the first in the country to embrace Sephardic Hebrew in both its synagogue and Hebrew school. Following its example, all constituents of the South African Union for Progressive Judaism in that city, as well as in Cape Town, Springs, and Durban, included in their constitutions a clause that the Hebrew accent in both religious services and pedagogy must be "Sefardi."[96]

The establishment of the State of Israel proved pivotal to Hebrew language pedagogy and accent in both Canada and the United States. Shortly after the founding of Israel, an Ashkenazic educator influenced by Aron Horowitz introduced the Sephardic intonation to Montreal's Jewish schools.[97] A Hebrew syllabus, in force in New York State high schools since 1930, was replaced in 1948 by a Sephardic Hebrew-in-Hebrew curriculum, with translation from English almost completely abandoned.[98] In June 1948 administrators and teachers convened to update the Hebrew syllabus, approaching Hebrew as a modern, spoken language.[99] The committee declared that the Sephardic intonation had been adopted in the high schools for the following four reasons: "it is the classic pronunciation of Hebrew; it is the pronunciation of Israel; it is the pronunciation of Hebrew used in all colleges and universities; it is more in harmony with its cognate Semitic languages." Echoing the conviction of Eliezer Ben-Yehuda, the committee made several references to this inflection as the "correct pronunciation of Hebrew" and "correct Sephardic pronunciation." Teachers instructing at various levels were to pay "continuous attention" to proper intonation.[100] By the following year, thirty-five hundred students in New York, most of them Jewish, were studying Hebrew in the Sephardic intonation.[101] By the late 1950s, one observer remarked that the Palestinian Sephardic accent of Hebrew "is constantly gaining vogue" and that the founding of the State of Israel "bids fair to make this the predominant pronunciation all over the Diaspora."[102]

So, too, in Great Britain and South Africa. At the "All-Hebrew Conference" organized in London in May 1948, a resolution was unanimously passed that the Jewish community should adopt the Sephardic pronunciation. The resolution evidently represented "the overwhelming backing of informed public opinion" of the country.[103] Among the apparently few detractors was the Glasgow Board of Jewish Education, which still debated the advisability of adopting "Sefardi" in Hebrew classes in 1950.[104] That same year, Johannesburg's chief rabbi noted happily that "this modern pronunciation was simultaneously introduced into all the synagogues of the United Hebrew Congregations" and the United Hebrew Schools of Johannesburg. The latter was at the time "the largest Jewish teaching institution" in the country, comprising nineteen schools that enrolled over one thousand pupils. The accent was first heard in the city's Great Synagogue during the dedication service for the proclamation of the State of Israel on May 16.[105]

The Impact of Eastern Sephardim on U.S. Hebrew Intonation

The foregoing discussion suggests that Sephardic-inflected Hebrew was imported to the Diaspora via Palestine and, later, via the State of Israel. Among Ashkenazim, Zionist-oriented institutions (i.e., Zionist Ashkenazim) were most receptive to this linguistic change. One still wonders, however, if the Sephardic community in the United States had any influence on the local acceptance of Sephardic-inflected Hebrew. This question is especially interesting for the United States, for as in Palestine, the founding elites of the Jewish community there were Sephardic Jews.

Whereas Palestine's Sephardim had lived for centuries in the Ottoman Empire, the first Jews in what would become the United States were Western Sephardim who first arrived in 1654. These immigrants did not establish a continuous settlement, but most of the Jewish newcomers in the decades immediately following were also Sephardim from the Western Hemisphere. By 1720, Ashkenazim of Central and Eastern European descent outnumbered Western Sephardim. But in most locations, Sephardic Jews did not relinquish their hegemony over the American Jewish community until the early 1800s. Even then, many Ashkenazim continued to associate themselves with Western Sephardic synagogues because of their prestige.

Through the first decades of the twentieth century, Western Sephardim in America provided the model for the Sephardic dialect of Hebrew. Their elite status predisposed many local Ashkenazim toward the Sephardic accent. Since colonial days, Germanic and Eastern European Jews who worshiped in Western Sephardic congregations adopted the Sephardic pronunciation and cantillation of Hebrew in place of their own ancestral tradition and even gave up their own traditional prayer for the dead (the mourner's *kadish*), in favor of the Western Sephardic tradition.[106] Judah Monis (1683–1764), an Algerian- or Italian-born Sephardic convert to Christianity who taught Hebrew at Harvard University for forty years, employed what is apparently the Western Sephardic accent in his writing and teaching, as suggested in the Roman-scripted transliterations in his Hebrew grammar primer, published in 1735.[107] Isaac Leeser, a Central European–born Jew who affiliated with the Sephardic communities of Richmond, Virginia, and Philadelphia, employed this accent in the Hebrew-language textbooks he published for American children beginning in the 1830s. These became the first primers for Jewish schools in the United States.[108] A Hebrew textbook published in 1834 by an American Jew, probably of Germanic or Eastern European origin, also employed the Western Sephardic transliteration system then in vogue among many American Jews.[109]

Another individual who adopted the Sephardic accent was Cyrus Adler (1863–1940). A native-born Jew of Central European origin, Adler was raised in Philadelphia's Sephardic congregation and demonstrated mastery of its Hebrew intonation. Israel Goldstein (b. 1896), a Philadelphia native of Eastern European origin who later became rabbi of New York's

B'nai Jeshurun congregation, enjoyed his first exposure to the Sephardic accent while a pupil at Gratz College in Philadelphia, where he enrolled in 1909. There, one Dr. Isaac Husik taught Hebrew in the Sephardic intonation "partly because Gratz College had been founded by leaders of the Spanish and Portuguese mother congregation of Philadelphia Jewry." This accent, Goldstein reminisced in 1984, was "a helpful anticipation of Israeli Hebrew."[110] Western Sephardic Hebrew was no doubt also the model for Hirsch Genss, the Reform rabbi in Seattle, who in the early 1900s tried to convince his Ashkenazic congregants that Sephardic Jews "spoke a purer Hebrew, than the Ashkenazim themselves."[111]

Somewhat unusual was Henry Iliowizi (1850–1911). Born into a Hasidic community near Minsk, Rabbi Iliowizi presided over the Ashkenazic congregation of Minneapolis (Shaarai Tov) as it began to embrace Reform. Iliowizi, then thirty years old, had lived in Morocco in 1877 as a teacher in Tetuan's Alliance Israélite Universelle school. It was there that he probably adopted the "Sephardic" accent, which was likely closer to what Ben-Yehuda would have defined as *mizrahi*. Iliowizi employed this intonation as a congregational rabbi in the United States, and he once lost an opportunity for a pulpit because of his distinct Hebrew accent. Iliowizi probably continued to use Sephardic Hebrew when he assumed leadership of Adath Jeshurun in Philadelphia, where he presided for twelve years.[112]

But ultimately, it was the Hebrew spoken in the Land of Israel that exerted the enduring influence on America's Jews. Cyrus Adler, when he visited Palestine in 1891, became convinced of the leading role this Sephardic accent would play in the revival of modern Hebrew. In Palestine, he met a Jerusalem-born Ashkenazic Jewish educator who had adopted the "Sephardic" or "Spanish pronunciation." Adler commented in his journal that "if Hebrew ever becomes the language of Palestine, it will be with the Sephardic pronunciation."[113] Years later, in 1923, Adler suggested that Ashkenazic Jews in the United States adopt the Sephardic pronunciation for the sake of Jewish unity. Ashkenazim in the Land of Israel, he pointed out, had already done so. Adler advised, "If Palestine is going to help us in a religious way at all, it ought point the way to a union, and one of the first steps toward this would be the adoption of the Sephardic pronunciation. If the Ashkenazim would adopt in their synagogues the Sephardic pronunciation, which they seem entirely willing to adopt in the use of Hebrew as a spoken language, we would take an immense step forward toward union."[114]

The rise of the American Ladino press in the 1910s allows us to explore the possible influence of local Eastern Sephardim in the proliferation of Hebrew as commonly spoken in the Land of Israel. Interestingly, *kolonia* members identified their native Hebrew pronunciation as identical to the Palestinian Sephardic intonation. Just a year after Palestinian Jewry's *de jure* adoption of the Sephardic inflection in 1913, Bulgarian-born Moise Gadol declared with some exaggeration that "the Sephardic dialect we speak is even recognized by all the Ashkenazim of America as the true [pronunciation of Hebrew]."[115] A year later, Ben-Sion Behar remarked with equal hyperbole that "in the entire Hebrew world, the Sephardic pronunciation of Hebrew ... has been accepted, [and] is practiced today in all of the schools and modern Hebrew seminaries."[116] But neither Gadol nor Ben-Sion Behar (nor any other member of the *kolonia*, to my knowledge) ever attributed this linguistic proliferation in the United States to American Sephardim. Rather, these overstatements probably speak to the Palestinian-oriented circles in which these Eastern Sephardim socialized, as is evident in the terms that *kolonia* leaders used to designate this inflection: the "Palestinian pronunciation"[117] and the "Land of Israel (Sephardic) dialect."[118]

Of course, the process of acceptance was much more uneven than these hyperboles would have us believe, even in Palestinian-oriented circles. In 1914, Moise Gadol cited the Zionist Sepharadim Society of New York (*Aguda Sionít Sefaradít*) as "the only American Zionist organization which speaks Hebrew in the correct dialect."[119] A year later, this society felt compelled officially to adopt a ruling that its propaganda in the Hebrew language would be "in the (Sephardic) dialect of the land of Israel."[120] This resolution was accomplished only after a prolonged debate over a new constitution, at a meeting attended by Federation of American Zionists president Louis Lipsky.[121] Evidently, some Eastern Sephardim were concerned that officially embracing Sephardic Hebrew would reinforce their exclusion from Ashkenazic Zionist circles. Eastern Sephardim suffered the consequences of the Ashkenazic accent more than any other Zionist-oriented community in the country. In 1915, Sephardic activists, frustrated by the incomprehensible Hebrew accent they encountered in Ashkenazic-dominant Zionist organizations, founded the *Ivriya* (the feminine form of the Hebrew adjective for "Hebrew"), a society whose goal was to "cultivate and propagate Palestinian Hebrew among the younger generation."[122]

These challenges were somewhat mitigated during World War I, when several linguist-patriots temporarily relocated to New York from Palestine. The idea to include Hebrew in public schools in New York areas heavily populated by Jews was reintroduced in 1916 by David Ben-Gurion and Yitshak Ben-Zvi, who were expelled from Palestine by Ottoman authorities and organized a base for labor Zionism while in New York exile from 1915 to 1918.[123] Though both leaders were Ashkenazim, they were undoubtedly conversant in Sephardic Hebrew and may have advocated this intonation in the United States. Two other transplanted Palestinians most definitely did: Eliezer Ben-Yehuda and his son Ittamar Ben-Avi, who arrived in 1915.[124]

In honor of the arrival of Eliezer Ben-Yehuda in June of that year, the Federation of American Zionists, the Bnei Zion Order, and the Zionist Council of New York jointly organized a reception held at the Educational Alliance on the Lower East Side. Perhaps in anticipation of this visit, Louis Lipsky had invited the Zionist Sepharadim Society of New York to join the FAZ the month before.[125] Encouraging his readers to attend, Moise Gadol remarked that "Mr. Eliezer Ben-Yehuda is a great sympathizer of our Sephardic brothers."[126] Over two thousand individuals participated, including "a large quantity of our Sephardim and especially all of those emigrated from Palestine."[127] Their attendance suggests a notable population of former residents of the Land of Israel who might have been active in the dissemination of Sephardic-accented Hebrew in New York. *La America* reported that Judah Magnes, leader of the New York Kehilla, delivered his opening address "in the Hebrew language in the Sephardic pronunciation."[128] Ben-Yehuda's refusal on principle to attend Zionist conventions that were not conducted in Hebrew[129] may indicate that Hebrew was the language in which the entire event was conducted. The last speaker was Ben-Yehuda's son Ittamar Ben-Avi, a Hebrew journalist. "His sweet, resounding and clear speech, in a clean Sephardic dialect, intoned with the gestures of a sincere Jewish patriotism," Gadol reported, "made a deep impression on the entire audience."[130]

Ittamar Ben-Avi's varied activities in New York put him into close contact with the Sephardic community. In 1915, he was hired to head the Oriental Department of the Central Bank of the United States on Delancey Street, "in the interest of Sephardic clients."[131] Ben-Avi also taught Sephardic-inflected Hebrew to a "very large number" of students during his first few years in New York.[132] His guest lectures at a variety of Jewish gatherings may have had an even broader impact due to the size of the audiences and his penchant for speaking before large gatherings. Ben-Avi was a mesmerizing, arousing speaker fluent in English, French, German, and Hebrew.[133] His lectures to Hebrew and other language clubs in New York's public schools sometimes attracted student audiences as large as a thousand.[134] It was perhaps during this period that Ben-Avi addressed the Histadruth Ivrith Olamith and advocated that the U.S. Jewish community should officially adopt the Sephardic accent.[135]

One wonders what contact, if any, Ben-Avi had with Sephardic pedagogues and students.[136] On this detail, memoirs and biographers are silent.[137] This silence may speak to the rarity of Eastern Sephardim in Hebrew-language learning environments. Though some did enroll in Hebrew classes offered in public schools, the majority chose classes in Spanish, the closest language to the "Ladino they hear at home."[138] On the other hand, the Ladino press does attest to Ben-Avi's active participation in Sephardic political organizations. In July 1915 he attended a meeting of the Zionist Sepharadim of America. In a brief address he generously "proposed to speak at our meetings on any subject that we may demand." This endorsement by the first native speaker of Hebrew in modern times, who employed the Sephardic pronunciation, must have been a heady experience for New York Sephardim, who had been so often excluded from Yiddish- or *ashkenazis*-dominant organizations.[139]

But Ben-Avi did not always address his audience in Hebrew, which may speak to the weakness of that language among most Eastern Sephardim. In May 1917, he spoke at a meeting of the (Sephardic) Zionist Maccabee Society,[140] attended by three hundred individuals, mostly Sephardim. He addressed his audience in French, perhaps assuming that the majority of his audience members were both Alliance-educated and ignorant of spoken Hebrew. French would have also been a natural alternative for him, as it was then the international language in Palestine. Perhaps his theme—the situation of Jews in the Diaspora—also justified his use of a foreign tongue.[141] Later that year, the society's Women's Division (*Seksión de Damas*) organized a ball at Laurel Garden. Ben-Avi, the featured speaker, addressed his audience in both French and English. This event, organized by Women's Division president Mazal Emanuel (soon to be the wife of Rabbi Dr. Nissim Ovadia), attracted a large audience of both sexes.[142]

Another Ashkenazic leader who addressed his audience in Sephardic-inflected Hebrew was Bernard Drachman (1861–1945). Drachman, president of the Union of Orthodox Synagogues of America and a cultural mediator between the Sephardic and Ashkenazic communities, was one of the main speakers at a major meeting of the Zionist Sepharadim Society of New York. Responding to President Wilson's call for a day of national prayer for peace, the Zionist Sepharadim convened over six hundred men and women in July 1914. Presiding was president and chairman Moise Gadol, and talks were given in English, Hebrew, and Ladino. Drachman delivered a talk in both English and Hebrew, congratulating Sephardim "for our Sephardic Zionist movement and for the good initiative of the Society with the meeting of that day."[143] Drachman, who had learned Spanish in order to communicate with Eastern Sephardim,[144] may have mastered Sephardic Hebrew for similar reasons. As a student at the University of Breslau in the early 1880s, he had been exposed to this accent in classes offered by Jewish historian Heinrich Graetz.[145] By the time of his visit to Palestine in 1926, if not earlier, he could converse in fluent Sephardic Hebrew.[146]

Another possible influence on American Hebrew was the presence of Palestinian Jews, both Ashkenazim and Sephardim, who, unlike the aforementioned sojourners active in America during the 1910s, may have permanently settled in the United States. The reception organized in honor of Eliezer Ben-Yehuda in 1915, as we have seen, attracted a large number of Sephardim who had emigrated from Palestine.[147] Other sources confirm the numerical significance of these transplants. The records of the Industrial Removal Office note the transfer of eighty-seven mostly Ashkenazic Palestinian-born Jews between 1904 and 1922 from New York to the country's interior, including five "Hebrew teachers."[148] These numbers may point to a much larger presence of Palestinian Jews in New York, especially considering that most Jewish immigrants arrived and remained in that city. Mary Frank, a librarian who worked on the Lower East Side in the 1910s, also identified some recent arrivals in her neighborhood as Ashkenazim from Palestine.[149] David de Sola Pool noted in 1929 the presence in New York of "a large number of Palestinians, some of whom are here to study, others of whom are Palestinian teachers . . . many of whom as Palestinians are accustomed to the Sephardic pronunciation."[150] Indeed, by the 1920s there was a surplus of these instructors in the United States.[151] Most, if not all, of these instructors would have employed the Sephardic accent. Their presence, together with the American Jewish community's increasing orientation toward Palestine, may have encouraged Sephardic Jews in the United States to launch their own battle for Sephardic Hebrew.

The earliest evidence of such an attempt can be traced to the mid-1930s. In 1937, Pool made an official appeal to all Orthodox Jewish organizations to adopt the Sephardic accent. Later, this appeal was broadened to include a variety of U.S. Jewish religious and secular organizations. Not surprisingly, credit for this initiative goes not to London-born Pool but rather to his Palestinian wife, Tamar de Sola Pool (1890–1981). Tamar (née Hirschensohn) was born to a rabbinical family that had emigrated from Russia. Her parents had worked closely with Eliezer Ben-Yehuda in the revival of modern Hebrew and communicated with their five children in that language even after settling in the United States in 1903.[152] Tamar resolved to launch a campaign for Sephardic Hebrew in 1937 upon her return from a trip to the West Coast, apparently as a representative of both the Union of Sephardic Congregations (USC) and Hadassah. At a USC meeting, she recommended that the Union spearhead a campaign to endorse the Sephardic accent as the official one "for the purpose of creating unity." Following this recommendation, Reverend Pool distributed a resolution for discussion among various Jewish organizations, both religious and secular.[153] Ittamar Ben-Avi, who was in the United States around this time, may have influenced this initiative. Modern Hebrew's first native speaker had addressed Hadassah members at their annual opening tea in October 1936.[154] Around 1938, Ben-Avi gave public addresses at the Histadruth Ivrith Olamith meetings, as he had in years past, urging U.S. Jews to embrace Sephardic Hebrew.[155]

The resolution, sponsored by the Union of Sephardic Congregations, pointedly avoided the linguistic controversy over the historical accuracy of the Sephardic accent. Instead, the resolution focused on pragmatic reasons why both synagogues and other organizations employing Hebrew should embrace the "Sephardic or Palestinian pronunciation of Hebrew as the standard pronunciation":

WHEREAS the Palestinian pronunciation of Hebrew is recognized all over the world as the standard;

WHEREAS in universities and seminaries where Hebrew is taught to Jews and non-Jews the Palestinian pronunciation is always used;

WHEREAS an increasing number of teachers in religious schools are either Palestinians or have adopted the Palestinian pronunciation; and

WHEREAS in a rapidly increasing number of Ashkenazic synagogues and communities all over the world the Sephardic pronunciation of Hebrew is being adopted in order to conform to one classical standard pronunciation and to get away from the confusion of widely differing accents of Hebrew.[156]

The reactions of most organizations were at best tentative and at worse negative. Pool reported that the resolution had been discussed at the Convention of the Conservative Rabbis but that no action was taken. The Reform rabbis promised to appoint a committee to study the resolution. By May 1938, word arrived that the Central Council of American Rabbis had, at their most recent convention, appointed a committee to consider and report on the advisability of adopting the Sephardic pronunciation.[157] A few supporters of the resolution found certain statements unpalatable. One Western Sephardic respondent from Philadelphia thought that some people might object to Pool's characterization of Palestine, where so many secular Jews lived, as the "spiritual center of Jewish life." Reform Jews, who tended to reject the Land of Israel as the homeland of world Jewry, this respondent anticipated, might also object.[158] Strangely, Cyrus Adler was one of those who rejected the resolution. Adler, who as noted was raised in a Western Sephardic congregation and in 1923 had advocated the adoption of Sephardic Hebrew for the sake of religious unity,[159] feared that if U.S. Ashkenazic congregations adopted this intonation in their services, they would be separated from other diasporic Jewish synagogues.[160] It is difficult to determine what changed Adler's mind. Only Hadassah declared itself in favor of the resolution and adopted the Sephardic pronunciation, after its delegates voted unanimously.[161]

The preceding examples again suggest that Sephardic-inflected Hebrew gained ground in the United States thanks to Palestinian Jews, most of whom were Ashkenazic. As we have seen, David de Sola Pool's advocacy of Sephardic Hebrew was initiated by his Palestinian-born Ashkenazic wife, and its immediate success is unclear. The role of local Sephardim seems to have been secondary.

One final possibility of Sephardic influence is Nessim Behar, the Sephardic native of Jerusalem who taught the Hebrew-in-Hebrew method to Eliezer Ben-Yehuda. In 1901, the Alliance Israélite Universelle of Paris dispatched Nessim Behar to New York, where he was to reorganize the organization's work in the United States.[162] By the end of the year, when it became clear that his efforts were not financially successful, he turned his energies to other causes. These included publicizing the plight of Eastern European Jews and campaigning against the restriction of immigration to the United States.[163] Behar spent the last thirty years of his life in New York, participating actively in the local Sephardic community, where he was known as the "father of the colony" (*el padre de la kolonia*).[164]

Behar arrived on the cusp of the largest Sephardic wave of immigration from the Levant. One wonders what role, if any, he played in disseminating the Sephardic accent in the United States. Having served as a cultural broker among both Sephardim and Ashkenazim in various Ottoman cities, he would have been an ideal proponent of Sephardic-accented Hebrew. Moreover, his rabbinical lineage and staunch adherence to Jewish law would have facilitated the accent's introduction to religious Jewish schools, whose resistance in Palestine the secularist Ben-Yehuda had largely failed to break down.[165] In the decade of his arrival to the United States, Behar was often preoccupied with immigration and Americanization issues,[166] and his Zionist convictions seemed to have waned. During a trip to Boston in 1904 to reorganize the local branch of the Alliance Israélite Universelle, Behar declared, "Boston is our Zion and New York our Jerusalem, and we need not depart for Palestine, for we believe our salvation is possible in every country."[167]

Behar evidently experienced a change of heart in the 1910s, when he publicly spoke as an advocate of Zionism among New York's Eastern Sephardim.[168] His involvement in the Eastern Sephardic community also deepened at this time. In the early years of that decade, he became involved with efforts to establish a Sephardic Talmud Torah.[169] This religious school would have employed the Sephardic accent of Hebrew and possibly instructed its students in the "natural method." But alas, no evidence connecting Behar with the proliferation of Sephardic Hebrew has surfaced.

The story of Sephardic Hebrew's propagation in America would not be complete without a consideration of Syrian Jews. The role of Syrian Jews in modern Hebrew pedagogy in the United States is of special interest given Ben-Yehuda's aforementioned preference for Arabic-inflected Hebrew, which he described as "oriental" (*mizrahi*).[170] In fact, the institutional leaders of modern Hebrew, residing in Palestine, viewed the Aleppan dialect as especially desirable. As Benjamin Harshav notes, the dialect that was initially chosen for revived Hebrew "was essentially the dialect of the Jews of Syria; Aleppo, or Haleb, in Northern Syria had an influential Jewish community."[171] The Hebrew Language Committee of Jerusalem decided in 1915 "to compel all schools in Eretz-Israel to appoint a special teacher for pronunciation and to select for this position in particular one of the sages of Aleppo."[172] Among the features of this dialect are the useful distinctions made between letters that are pronounced identically in *ashkenazis* (e.g., *aleph* and *ayin*). One naturalized American Jew recalled that his native accent had been much esteemed among Ashkenazic pedagogues in Israel. Raymond Dayan, who spent part of his childhood in the newly founded State of Israel, recalled that his Torah teacher often called on him to read from the Bible. Dayan, whose father was born in Aleppo, reminisced in 2002, "It seemed that I had a very pronounced Sephardic accent, close to the original Hebrew, while most of my schoolmates were of Ashkenazi origin."[173]

The religious and communal intensity of American Syrian Jews ensured the preservation of their distinct Hebrew pronunciation, even as Sephardic Hebrew made inroads into the mainstream Jewish community. As early as 1945, Brooklyn's Syrian Jewish community offered language classes in both written and spoken Hebrew at its Magen David Hebrew Institute.[174] Separate classes for boys of the Community Junior League were offered by Sol Kassin and David Kassin.[175] Given the subethnic homogeneity of students and the necessity of a standardized pronunciation in language instruction, it is highly likely that the community's distinctive Judeo-Arabic accent was used.[176]

Activists in the State of Israel played an important role in instilling pride among Syrian Jews for Arabic-inflected Hebrew. In the 1960s and '70s, Avraham Matalon launched a campaign to standardize the Arabic dialect of Hebrew in the State of Israel. The Israeli linguist exposed the ways in which modern Israeli Hebrew was laden with inflectional distortions that taxed clarity and grammar and drained the language of its richness.[177] Moreover, he argued, Ashkenazic influence on the Israeli Hebrew accent was a form of colonialism and "distorted 'Western' geopolitical perspectives," from which all Jews must wrest themselves free. Adopting an Arabic-influenced accent would be true to Israel's history and geographic position globally and would help construct a "linguistic, spiritual, and political bridge" between Israel and Arab lands. Matalon's linguistic program, which he referred to as the "rehabilitation of the Hebrew language," also promised to "raise the self-esteem and spirit" of Jews hailing from the Middle East.[178] This last motivation was especially appealing to New York's Syrian Jewish community. While soliciting diasporic support for his project, Matalon succeeded in enlisting the support of a Syrian Jewish leader of Flatbush, who promised to collect funds from his Brooklyn constituents.[179]

The Hebrew traditions of Arabic-speaking Jews, however, have not affected the modern language as it is spoken elsewhere in the United States. As Baghdadi-born David Rabeeya has remarked sardonically, "the effect of Arab-Jews on . . . [modern Hebrew] is like snow in summer months."[180] Rabeeya, a self-described "progressive rabbi" who taught Hebrew and Judaic studies at Bryn Mawr College for thirty years, evidently speaks from personal experience.[181] As in Palestine, the Western disparagement of Arabic culture, which continued to inform majority culture, and the difficulty of most Westerners with this inflection help to explain why America's Arab Jews have not exerted a linguistic impact. The minority status of these Jews has also eroded the accent's vitality outside New York, as oral interviews suggest. In the late 1950s, Syrian Jewish children who left with their families for elsewhere in the country and enrolled in Hebrew school were forced to learn the language with an Ashkenazic intonation and prayers with Ashkenazic melodies.[182]

The sole known example of an Eastern Sephardic role in the dissemination of Sephardic Hebrew comes from Seattle. In the early 1970s, Rabbi Solomon Maimon worked with directors of the local Talmud Torah to introduce Sephardic Hebrew into the curriculum. His influence was bolstered by the city's significant Sephardic presence: of the school's 170 co-ed pupils, 50 (nearly a third) were Sephardic.[183] This anecdote is a reminder that the paradigm of impact may indeed be relevant for cities where Eastern Sephardim constituted a relatively large part of the local Jewish population.

Resistance to Change

Despite the central role that the State of Israel increasingly played in shaping American Ashkenazic identity, the dissemination of Sephardic Hebrew after 1948 was measured and has never completely displaced Ashkenazic dialects. Author Hayyim Schauss noted in 1950 that because "the Jews in America use mainly the Ashk'nazic pronunciation, many of the Hebrew terms when transliterated in accordance with S'fardic practice strike them as strange."[184] In the 1950s and early '60s, travel writer Ruth Gerber cautioned Americans that "the Israeli accent will be strange" to them, as they had probably "been speaking Hebrew with an Ashkenazic accent, the accent of Eastern and Central Europe."[185] As late as 1962, the author of a travel guide to Israel found it necessary to explain that Hebrew in that country "is spoken in the Sephardic way and not with the Ashkenazic accent which the Jews from Eastern Europe carried with them to the United States and other Western countries."[186] One observer of the U.S. Jewish community dates the widespread adoption of Sephardic Hebrew to the 1970s, when American Jewry basked in the sunshine of the Six-Day War and increasingly drew its ethnic identity from a militarily triumphant State of Israel.[187] As a possible confirmation of the impact of this event, a linguist observed in 1971 that Hebrew in the United States had been "*Lately . . . contaminated* with the simplified 'Sephardic' pronunciation of the new state of Israel, which has higher prestige and such a limited phonology that almost anyone can readily pick it up" (italics added).[188] Change has been especially slow as it relates to Ashkenazic religious and family traditions. Alfred J. Kolatch's first book on Jewish names, published in 1948, listed the Ashkenazic pronunciation of Hebrew names. Only in the 1989 edition of that book did he adopt a system of transliteration "in accordance with the Sephardic (rather than the Ashkenazic) pronunciation, which is now employed in Israel and in much of the Diaspora."[189]

The circles most resistant to change have been religious. Even those Jewish congregations that accepted Sephardic Hebrew for instruction in their religious schools debated its advisability for the synagogue service. Many communities, in fact, initiated a "diglossia" of intonations, with "Sephardi" implemented in classes and "*ashkenazis*" reserved for ritual use. As we have seen, this had also been a solution years before in the Land of Israel, where Palestine's Teachers' Association (founded 1892) decided that while the accent of instruction for all courses would be Sephardic, the Ashkenazic variant would be used for prayers.[190] In the 1940s, a number of congregations in the United Kingdom that had embraced Sephardic Hebrew for pedagogy also decided to preserve the Ashkenazic dialect for ritual use.[191] As in the United Kingdom, the movement in America to adopt a single Sephardic pronunciation in both classrooms and synagogues gained momentum in the late 1940s. The Reform and Conservative movements in the United States were the first to do so.[192] Some diasporic Ashkenazic congregations adopted Sephardic Hebrew for prayer specifically in reaction to the founding of the State of Israel.[193] One scholar noted in 1950 "the influences in liturgical expression of the Israeli Sephardic pronunciation now that it is on the way to being introduced into synagogue worship in this country."[194]

But decades later Sephardic Hebrew had failed to conquer all Ashkenazic congregations. In 1962, the rabbi of a Conservative congregation in Rockville Centre, New York, urged his members to accept Sephardic Hebrew because "that will bind us more closely to *k'lal yisrael*."[195] His successor, who assumed leadership in 1973, observed in 2007 that although the congregation has long used Sephardic Hebrew in its synagogue services, the current cantor (*hazan*), a Russian Jew, presides in the Ashkenazic intonation, and no one has pressured him to relinquish it.[196] In the late 1970s, an American rabbi testified that some Orthodox schools taught both ritual and conversational Hebrew in *ashkenazis*.[197] He also noted that "most synagogues continue to use that [Ashkenazic] dialect for prayer services."[198] Only in 2003 was the use of the Sephardic intonation in American Ashkenazic synagogues described as a "Zionist innovation" that was "almost universal."[199]

One of the reasons for resistance in religious circles to Sephardic pronunciation was that parents feared that the Sephardic accent as taught in modern Hebrew would confuse children when they attended synagogue, where the Ashkenazic pronunciation was often retained. This reason was voiced for example in Calgary when Aron Horowitz tried to introduce Sephardic Hebrew to the Canadian Ashkenazic Hebrew schools in the 1940s.[200] Another reason was halakhic. According to some rabbinical traditions, it is forbidden to abandon one's ancestral prayer rite for another.[201] This latter factor partly explains the perseverance of *ashkenazis* in ultra-Orthodox Jewish communities, which are the most defiant of linguistic change. In these communities, even among those outspokenly Zionist, and even in Israel, the Ashkenazic accent for liturgy prevails.[202]

The Impact of Sephardim on Hebrew in the United States

The various pieces of the puzzle point to an uneven dissemination of Sephardic Hebrew whose gradual acceptance in the diaspora often hinged on cultural developments in Palestine and the State of Israel. This, incidentally, helps to disprove the axiom among some scholars of American Judaism that Israel played an insignificant role in American Jewish religious life before 1967.[203]

It is true that Western Sephardim in colonial America and the United States exerted a disproportionate influence on Hebrew as it was pronounced and transliterated in the local Jewish community, in some cases until the early 1900s. This, parenthetically, is in consonance with the historical phenomenon of a vanquished civilization culturally influencing the dominant society because the conquerors deem the vanquished people as elite or superior. Western Sephardim long continued to exert a linguistic and ritual influence, even after they were outnumbered by Ashkenazim, because the latter viewed Western Sephardim as an elite to be emulated. Nevertheless, the Western Sephardic accent did not ultimately prevail. The Hebrew accent partly modeled on Eastern Sephardic intonation did.[204] Although the proliferation of this accent in the United States was concomitant with the mass immigration of Eastern Sephardim and Mizrahim, these populations had little if any impact on the broad acceptance of Sephardic Hebrew among American Jews.

Confirmation of these findings emerged from responses to the query of Sarah Bunin Benor, which was posted on the electronic discussion list H-Judaic in 2004. To reiterate her question, When and why did Hebrew schools in the United States shift from the Ashkenazic to the Israeli-Sephardic pronunciation? The responses—all of them either impressionistic or drawn from personal experience—affirm that the accent's dissemination was uneven, gradual, and much dependent on both political events in the Middle East and on secular versus religious environments. Another important factor was the importation of Israeli teachers, who sometimes imposed their accent on an otherwise Ashkenazic-accented curriculum.[205] Unlike in Palestine, where Sephardim occupied a central and direct role in Ben-Yehuda's work to revive Hebrew as a modern, spoken language and assisted him and other family members at critical moments of their personal lives and careers,[206] there is little evidence that Eastern Sephardim in the United States either directly or significantly influenced the propagation of Sephardic Hebrew.

This test case (together with other examples offered in the ensuing chapters of this book) makes it clear that the paradigm of impact current in American Jewish historiography does not generally work for Eastern Sephardi and Mizrahi Jews. Non-Ashkenazim after 1900 were largely excluded from the mainstream American Jewish community, and their distinctive traditions were not honored by the vast majority of their coethnics. The Eastern Sephardic impact on Hebrew intonation in America can be traced to Palestine (and later, the State of Israel), from where it was imported largely by Ashkenazic Jews. The failure of local Sephardim to have an impact on broader American Jewry endures even as U.S. Jews, in the past decade or so, have increasingly turned away from Israel as a cultural and religious model.[207]

The paradigm of impact persists as a leading theme in American Jewish history. Recently, the Goldstein-Goren Center for American Jewish History at New York University advertised a research position devoted "to the study of the mutual impact of the Jews and America."[208] Similarly, the opening line describing the *Encyclopedia of American Jewish History*, published by ABC-CLIO in 2007, reads, "Virtually every aspect of American culture has been profoundly influenced by Jewish immigrants and their descendants."[209] The apologetic nature of this approach should be immediately recognizable if one considers what is precisely meant by impact or influence. At least in Jewish studies circles, acceptable themes may include the role of American Jews in the garment and entertainment industries, but definitely not their possible impact on white-collar crime or racial oppression. Furthermore, impact or influence does not really tell us very much about American Jews. Their "contributions" or "accomplishments" may be disproportionate, but they are usually not incomparable. To quote an adage popularized by Eliot Cohen, "the Jews are like everyone else, only more so."[210] But what does the distinction of disproportion really tell us about American Jews?

If the paradigm of impact is problematic for American Jewish history, it is more so for Eastern Sephardi and Mizrahi Jews, whose marginalization has precluded influence on their immediate reference group, Ashkenazic Jews. Paradoxically, it is precisely this dynamic of exclusion that may serve as a more appropriate historiographical model. The dynamics that led to exclusion and encouraged liaisons outside the American Jewish community tell us much about Eastern Sephardim and Mizrahim and about the other groups—Jewish and non-Jewish—with whom they interacted.

3

East Meets West
Sephardic Strangers and Kin

Western Sephardim: The "Old" Sephardim

In 1933, Henry Pereira Mendes, Minister Emeritus of Congregation Shearith Israel, recalled his recent visit to a religious day school for Eastern Sephardim organized by the congregation's Sisterhood on the Lower East Side: "How well those children read and sang our ritual—some even acted as Hazan!" he enthused. "What magnificent material we have there from which to recruit upholders of Sephardic ritual, Sephardic melodies, Sephardic minhag, Sephardic traditions, Sephardic everything!" Nonetheless, British-born Mendes (1852–1937) considered automatic membership in the congregation ill-advised. Rather, Eastern Sephardim ought to be inducted through "gradual associate-membership and then gradual full membership, as the worldly conditions of the ones concerned improve."[1] This attitude of mixed respect and paternalism—evident since at least 1913—epitomizes relations between the two subgroups and explains both the successes and pitfalls of their joint endeavors.[2]

The distinctions between Western and Eastern Sephardim were most obvious to the groups themselves. The very term "Sephardic" became a national byword only in the early 1970s with the appearance of Stephen Birmingham's best-selling and recently reprinted *The Grandees*.[3] This popular history, though laden with distortions and factual errors and criticized for its gossipy nature, brought national attention to an obscure American subethnic group.[4] Birmingham devoted most of his exposé to the Western Sephardim whom Mendes represented: descendants of Portuguese- and Spanish-speaking Iberian refugees who had immigrated to North America via Western Europe, the Caribbean, and South America. The first Jews to settle in what is today the United States were drawn from this population and arrived in Nieuw Amsterdam

81

(present-day New York) via Recife, Brazil, in 1654. Among the illustrious descendants of the seventeenth-century arrivals are Isaac Touro (b. 1739), for whom the Touro synagogue in Newport, Rhode Island, is named; his son, merchant and philanthropist Judah Touro (1775–1854); politician, journalist, and playwright Mordecai Manuel Noah (1785–1851); Emma Lazarus (1849–1887), whose poetic verses are inscribed on the Statue of Liberty; Annie Nathan Meyer (1867–1951), a founder of Barnard College;[5] and U.S. Supreme Court justice Benjamin Nathan Cardozo (1870–1938).[6]

The community distinguished itself through such publicly renowned members and through a religious tradition, sometimes referred to as a Sephardic "enlightened orthodoxy," revered by Sephardim and Ashkenazim alike. This Jewish rite stressed dignity and decorum, in contrast to the unrestrained emotionalism of Eastern European Ashkenazim.[7] Long after Germanic Jews founded their own congregations at the turn of the nineteenth century, Ashkenazim of various European origins continued to join Western Sephardic synagogues and schools and openly imitated their coreligionists' rituals and customs. The first Jewish school in New York (Yeshibat Minhat Areb), founded by Western Sephardim in 1731, was reorganized after the American Revolution. Renamed after its Ashkenazic donor as the Polonies Talmud Torah, the school nonetheless retained its Western Sephardic rite until at least 1821.[8] The German Hebrew Society (Rodeph Shalom), which seceded from Philadelphia's congregation Mikveh Israel in 1795, carried over many Western Sephardic traditions, including the Spanish and Portuguese term *junto* to designate its board of directors.[9] It was a Western Sephardic Jew, Jacob da Silva Solis, who founded the mostly Ashkenazic congregation Shangaray Chasset (Gates of Mercy) in New Orleans in 1827. Solis, then residing in Westchester, New York, was convinced of the need for a synagogue during a business visit to that city. The congregants readily adopted the Western Sephardic rite, though most were not accustomed to it. One of the founding members confessed in 1828, "I do not know much about the portugaise minhag, still we came on pretty well."[10] Pioneering Jewish institutions associated with Germanic Jews, such as Philadelphia's Sunday school, founded by Rebecca Gratz in 1838, were established with the cooperation of the locally entrenched Sephardic elite.[11]

The Western Sephardic population in what is today the United States never rose above three thousand and probably numbered well below that by 1840, when it conceded communal hegemony to Central European

Ashkenazim. Already by 1720, Ashkenazim in America outnumbered their Western Sephardic coreligionists.[12] Western Sephardic descendants perhaps best understood how a tiny subgroup within the Jewish community could attract wide, public attention. As Annie Nathan Meyer commented, the "intense pride" and "strong sense of *noblesse oblige* among the Sephardim was the nearest approach to royalty in the United States."[13]

What exactly Western Sephardim had in mind when they referred to royal ancestry is worthy of remark. As we have seen, medieval Spanish Jews maintained that they descended from the Davidic dynasty of Judah, the southern kingdom of the ancient Land of Israel. Some, including George D. M. Peixotto of New York, traced their ancestry further back to the Resh galutha, or Exilarch of ancient Babylon. There was "no family living today more ancient than ours," Peixotto claimed in 1902.[14] Many twentieth-century Sephardim, however, stressed not *Jewish* but rather *Christian* noble ancestry. The Solis family, for example, claimed kinship not only with Catholic noblemen and women of crypto-Jewish heritage but also with Catholic monarchs entirely bereft of Jewish ancestry. This meant that they descended not only from the seventeenth-century Marquis of Turin in northern Italy and the (Spanish?) Count of Villa Real and Marquis of Monterrey, both of New Christian origin, but also from the first King of Portugal.[15] Although documenting their ancient Middle Eastern nobility was impossible, genealogical research could indeed verify early modern, and in some cases medieval, aristocratic descent. This is precisely what the initially skeptical historian Cecil Roth discovered to be the case in the 1920s, when he delved into various European archives in search of Western Sephardic progenitors. At the end of his archival investigation, Roth admitted to Jacob da Silva Solis-Cohen, Jr., that he "found much more solid basis in your family legend than (to be perfectly frank) I originally imagined."[16] One direct descendant of the Silva Solis family, Claire Carvalho Weiller (born sometime after 1882), gleefully remarked, "I feel quite gay that I can claim kindred with royalty with none of the dis-advantages."[17]

Another characteristic of many Western Sephardic families in the United States was their solid identification with the upper class. Memoirs of Western Sephardim who came of age in the second half of the nineteenth century are replete with tales of extravagance and opulence that rival any Edith Wharton novel, including year-long wedding journeys through Europe's "enchanted lands."[18]

The leading institution in the United States preserving Western Sephardic identity and communal cohesiveness was Congregation Shearith Israel, also known as the Spanish and Portuguese Synagogue. Tracing its founding to 1654, Shearith Israel was (and is) among New York City's most illustrious congregations. Through the centuries, Shearith Israel's leaders developed a reputation as representatives and spokesmen of Sephardim living both in New York and throughout the country. The synagogue proudly retained its ritual and traditions—largely modeled on the mother congregation in Amsterdam—and took great pride in its professional choir, regal service, and elegant building, hallmarks of Western Sephardic refinement.[19] It was thus natural that interactions between Western and Eastern Sephardim came to revolve around this synagogue and its leaders.

As the two groups quickly learned, class, cultural, and historical differences made ethnic kinfolk seem more like strangers. Perhaps the deepest division was class. Congregation Shearith Israel was acutely conscious of the exalted pedigree of its affiliates. A number of congregants, including social activist Alice Davis Menken (1870–1936), traced their ancestry back to colonial and revolutionary America and took great pride in their ancestors' role in the struggle for American independence. In 1932, Menken filed applications on behalf of her seven-year-old granddaughter, Marilyn Marise Menken, for membership in the National Society of the Children of the American Revolution. The granddaughter was accepted to the society by virtue of her direct descent from no less than three ancestors, including Lisbon-born Isaac Mendez Seixas (1709–1780), a signatory of the nonimportation agreement of 1770, and Benjamin Mendez Seixas (1747–1817), a Lieutenant in Battalions in New York City.[20]

The ethos of Western Sephardim was in part self-fashioned, but it also derived from a literary and scholarly myth cultivated by Ashkenazim since at least the sixteenth century.[21] Beginning with the Golden Age of medieval Spain and ending with the Inquisition and Expulsion, the myth emphasizes ancestral nobility, both secular and religious accomplishments, as we have seen, and heroic responses to oppression. Sephardim evoked this myth when presenting themselves to both the wider Jewish community and the public at large. The obituary of Mortimer Morange Menken (1867–1930), a New York City lawyer and husband of Alice Davis Menken, characterized him as a descendant "of those Spanish and Portuguese Hebrews, who in the so called Golden Era of Spain and Portugal, contributed so extensively to science and literature and were of the entourage of the Royal Houses."[22] This storied ancestry shielded family members from the anti-Semitism generally reserved for Jews newly arrived from Eastern Europe. Annie Nathan Meyer declared that anti-Jewish prejudice was uncommon in her experience, particularly in the city of New York—perhaps, she mused, because of her family's "long and distinguished history both here and in Europe."[23] Perhaps, too, the anglicized names of many Western Sephardim provided a convenient camouflage.

Western Sephardim took great pride in their integration into Anglo-American society. Annie Nathan Meyer's parents and relatives enjoyed close camaraderie with many (white) Christian families; a bridesmaid of her mother was a "Quakeress."[24] Her older sister Maud Nathan recalled, "all our companions, outside of the large family circle of cousins, were Christians." Her mother instilled in her children a deep reverence for Christianity, teaching them "to respect the customs and conventions" of Christianity and forbidding them from practicing piano or playing croquet on Sundays.[25] The funeral of cousin Benjamin Cardozo was held in a church at a ceremony organized by the Interfaith Movement.[26] The complete acceptance of Western Sephardim into white elite society is perhaps what permitted them publicly and unflinchingly to highlight their ethnic differences when appropriate.

Such a high degree of acceptance had its costs. On the eve of mass immigration from Eastern Europe, the Balkans, and the Middle East, Western Sephardim were struggling to maintain their boundaries as a distinct ethnoreligious group. Some of the literature documenting this period refers to them as "old Sephardim," a term that unwittingly communicates more than just chronology.[27] Native-born Jews who identified as Sephardim were nearly superannuated. Throughout the centuries, acculturation as well as marriage with Ashkenazim and gentiles weakened the distinctive traits of Western Sephardim.[28] Congregation Shearith Israel's members were emblematic of this dilution. The congregation's ethnic makeup had become increasingly Ashkenazic through intramarriage and acceptance of non-Sephardic Jews as members. In the first three decades of the twentieth century, the synagogue's pews attested to the diminishing number of Western Sephardim and the consequent threat to their distinct heritage.[29]

Acculturation into gentile white society had already begun in colonial times. Travelers' descriptions, memoirs, letters, and genealogies suggest a community in an advanced stage of integration with white Protestant society. Life in an environment that stressed "consent" over "descent" (i.e., an individual's choice over the constraints of tradition), and whose ruling class accepted Sephardim on some levels as equals, facilitated this integration, as did the legacy of a former Christian existence.[30] Male members of the short-lived original Jewish community of Savannah, Georgia, first established in 1733, engaged in military service and were permitted to bear arms. A Lutheran pastor noted disdainfully in 1738 that the "Englishmen, nobility and common folks alike treat the Jews as their equal. They drink, gamble and walk together with them; in fact, let them take part in all their fun. Yes, they desecrate Sunday with them, a thing no Jew would do on their Sabbath to please a Christian!"[31] The sons of Dr. Samuel Nunes, the community's heroic founding father, occasionally attended church. The only Iberian traits preserved by American-born Gershom Mendes Seixas (1745–1816), son of the aforementioned Isaac and cantor of Congregation Shearith Israel, "were his name and his Sabbath dish of *albóndigas* [meatballs]."[32] Supreme Court justice Benjamin Cardozo confessed in 1937 that his family preserved neither the Spanish language nor Iberian cultural traditions. Malcolm Stern's thorough genealogical research of the 1950s revealed so many Christian branches grafted onto the trunks of colonial Jewish family trees (some forty thousand individuals) that it made sense to title the first edition of his book *Americans of Jewish Descent*.[33] The acculturation of colonial Sephardim throughout the colonies paralleled similar patterns among contemporaneous Ashkenazim. Both groups, aspiring to middle-class status, quickly learned to emulate Christian ideals. To "act respectably" was to adopt the mores of Protestant white, middle-class society.

The last vestiges of a distinct Judeo-Iberian ethos were often retained through religious devotion, however nominal.[34] Though he stopped attending synagogue after his *bar-mitzvah* and declared himself an agnostic, Cardozo maintained a family pew in Shearith Israel his entire life.[35] The synagogue itself waged a successful battle against "the rising tide of innovation"—an allusion to the Reform movement—maintaining both its orthodox ritual and elements of Spanish and Portuguese heritage until today.[36] By the turn of the nineteenth century, most Western Sephardim no longer preserved the languages of their ancestors,[37] but traces of Spanish and Portuguese remained in a few synagogue terms (such as "Parnas Presidente" and "Adjunta") and prayers (such as "Bendigamos" and part of the prayer for the government). Well into the 1960s, congregants still referred to their house of worship as "Esnoga"

(Portuguese for "synagogue"), designated the lifter of the Torah scroll as the "Levantador" (Spanish for "he who lifts"), and called their supplementary prayers "Rogativas" (Spanish for "rogations," or solemn supplications).[38]

During their roughly 250-year residence in North America, the "Grandees" had defined what it meant to be a Sephardic Jew in the United States. The influx of fifty to sixty thousand Eastern Sephardic Jews reshaped this definition, for these newcomers—economically disadvantaged, with their distinct languages and mores—were "an altogether different sort."[39] As newcomers, Eastern Sephardim had no American colonial or revolutionary history of which to boast. Nor did their Sephardic rite easily unite them with the "Grandees," for the prayer books and religious melodies of the new immigrants were distinctly "Oriental." A number of their prayers were recited in Ladino, and the liturgical melodies reflected Levantine, not Western, musical traditions.[40]

Historical legacies, too, were dividing factors. The ancestors of Western Sephardim had dwelled in Christian lands in cities such as Amsterdam, Antwerp, and London, often as former crypto-Jews. Many families treasured heroic tales of escape from the Iberian Peninsula. One of the most celebrated is the story of Zipporah Nunez (1714–1799), great-grandmother of Mordecai Manuel Noah, who transmitted a harrowing account of her family's flight from the clutches of the Portuguese Inquisition in the early 1700s.[41] Some Western Sephardic families in America fetishized relics preserved from Inquisitorial times, a custom also noted for many centuries in Europe. The Lyons family of Columbus, South Carolina, cherished a cap supposedly "worn at prayers by one Lyons who was burned at the stake."[42] By contrast, Eastern Sephardic Jews had generally lived under Muslim dominion in the Ottoman Empire, and most had no direct ancestral connection to the crypto-Jewish legacy. Generally, they traced the origins of their Ottoman communities not to the forced conversions of 1391 and 1497 but rather to the Spanish Expulsion of 1492. This historical difference developed into a polemic in which the ancestors of Western Sephardim were criticized for having chosen conversion over expulsion.[43]

Despite these distinctions, the separate traditions of Western and Eastern Sephardim were similar enough to make bridge-building possible. After all, both groups traced their roots to the Iberian Peninsula, and the Inquisition and Expulsion from Spain were part of the collective Sephardic legacy. Both groups prayed according to Sephardic rites, and the similarity of Ladino to modern Spanish encouraged a shared identity. Moreover, mutual need acted as a powerful magnet. The diminished ranks of the Western Sephardic population could be replenished by tens of thousands of immigrants. The newcomers, in turn, looked to the established Sephardic community for philanthropy and guidance on the long road to adaptation. The quest for common ground, even when it sometimes failed, inevitably transformed both communities.

An Estranged Kinship

From the inception of the "Levantine" Jewish influx, Western Sephardim publicly acknowledged a shared historical, cultural, and religious continuum. In a 1912 sermon, David de Sola Pool (1885–1970), then Acting Minister of Congregation Shearith Israel, noted enthusiastically the influx of "ten thousand of our nearest kin."[44] For Pool (unlike his predecessor Mendes), shared rituals, Hebrew accent, ancestry, and history transcended class differences, and induction of Eastern Sephardim into the congregation was not only welcome but both a "paramount duty" and a "moral obligation."[45]

Women affiliated with Congregation Shearith Israel undertook much of the outreach work, largely through the Spanish and Portuguese Sisterhood. The Sisterhood had been founded in 1896 during a period when middle-class America began to reject the Calvinist ideology that poverty resulted from moral depravity as opposed to societal ills. Now, at the turn of the century, philanthropy and public responsibility became new catchwords. Women, assumed to be naturally religious and benevolent, dominated as social workers, and their benevolent societies proliferated under both Jewish and gentile auspices.[46]

Since its founding, the Spanish and Portuguese Sisterhood had fought to improve the education and welfare of Eastern European Jewish immigrants, focusing on the delinquency of girls and young women. During the second decade of the twentieth century, it redirected its efforts toward the newest Jewish immigrant group.[47] The Sisterhood's endeavors on behalf of Levantine Jewish immigrants were a natural continuum of its work with *Ostjuden* (Eastern European Jews), with all the accompanying intraethnic tensions and paternalism.

The Sisterhood flourished under the direction of Alice Davis Menken, a founder of the organization, who served as president from 1901 to

1928.[48] By 1916, Menken, unusual for her virtually "undiluted" Sephardic descent on both sides of the family,[49] achieved recognition as one of New York City's most influential women.[50] By 1912, the Sisterhood had founded the Oriental Employment Bureau, through which Levantine Jews could seek "honest employment," and also established a Talmud Torah, a traditional religious school for elementary-school-aged children,[51] which enrolled three hundred students by the mid-1920s.[52] Moreover, the Sisterhood organized a Special Committee on Oriental Jews to provide aid for the indigent and ill, offer instruction in the English language, reinforce synagogue activities, and help found religious schools.[53]

Perhaps the most famed accomplishment of the Sisterhood was the Settlement House.[54] This center had been organized as the Neighborhood House in 1896, on 128 Stanton Street, to serve Eastern European Ashkenazic immigrants of the Lower East Side.[55] Appropriately, it was located in a converted saloon and dance hall, places of leisure that Menken and other social reformers had identified as stimulants of vice among immigrant youth.[56] As the Sisterhood continued to expand its programs, it was obliged to relocate to larger buildings, to 86 Orchard Street in 1913 and to 133 Eldridge Street in 1918.[57] In its first location, the Sisterhood offered daily religious services, a kindergarten and Jewish religious afterschool program (Talmud Torah) for "Oriental Jewish Children," a reading room, and lectures. It also provided social services, such as relief and neighborhood visiting. The leisure time of beneficiaries was carefully directed to respectable activities, such as clubs and classes under the auspices of the Junior League of the Sisterhood, social entertainment, dancing, and a sewing circle, which met in Congregation Shearith Israel at West 70th Street, to provide clothing for the poor.[58]

When the Settlement House was rented and remodeled in 1918, it served as a religious, educational, and social center, primarily serving Sephardim and Mizrahim of Turkey, Greece, Syria, and the Arabian Peninsula.[59] By 1923, the center had redirected its services exclusively to Levantine Jews, and by 1925, it had further limited its focus to the needs of women and children.[60] The house operated largely independently, but it also received financial backing from New York's Ashkenazic community.[61]

These endeavors represented something of a revolution in elite Sephardic circles. Maud Nathan noted that in the 1880s there were no women's clubs to divert the attention of Jewish women of her class. "We had no civic duties, no public meetings to distract us from our homes and social duties," she recalled in the 1930s. Days were spent singing, playing piano, embroidering, paying social visits, entertaining, and running households staffed with maids and cooks.[62] The philanthropic endeavors stimulated by mass immigration transformed the lives of elite Sephardic women. Nathan noted with a tinge of regret that her friends and acquaintances in urban centers no longer enjoyed the social visits of yore. The club functions and civic and committee meetings that crowded the days eclipsed the "old-time form of friendly intercourse."[63] Social bonds among women now coalesced around common goals, rather than cliques or provincial class interests. Nathan's wistfulness notwithstanding, this new activism enriched the lives of female activists and broadened their social and political awareness.

Sisterhood activists were capable of showing great empathy and respect for their immigrant charges. Sisterhood president Menken took pride in the fact that her organization "sympathized" with the lives of Eastern Sephardim and Mizrahim in the Old Country and the "beauty of their traditions." According to her, the Sisterhood endeavored to impart Americanization while assisting the newcomers in retaining their Judaism. In a 1921 interview, she described Levantine immigrants as "cultured," "well educated," and "characterized by a deep sense of dignity, shyness, pride and self-respect."[64] In *On the Side of Mercy* (1933), her retrospective on over a quarter century of volunteer social work, Menken claimed she "helped to develop neighborhood resources for these foreign-born tenement settlers which would harmonize new obligations with old traditions."[65]

Yet philanthropic idealism had its limits. A report by the United Hebrew Charities concluded that Sisterhood volunteers generally "looked down upon" Levantine Jews.[66] Sisterhood volunteers were conditioned not only by Western Sephardic pride, which easily transformed into haughtiness, but also by paternalism—or, in this case, "maternalism"—a perhaps inevitable pitfall of charity. For many Sephardic elites, adaptation to a new land meant acquiring the gentility of the upper class. Proposing to introduce Western culture to Levantine Jews, Rachel Nahon Toledano (1867–1937) suggested in 1912 that girls learn to play the piano, a popular diversion among New York's white elites.[67] Her husband, Pinhas Habib (c. 1856–1936), volunteered to instruct the new immigrants in modern Spanish so that they might replace their Ladino with "the true Spanish-Castilian."[68] If Sephardic immigrants did not find the offers offensive, they did feel misunderstood. Moise Gadol, who reported on the meeting, called Pinhas's offer "mistaken." As a staunch advocate of Hebrew as the national Jewish language, he was uninterested in retaining any dialect of Spanish, a language that he associated with the auto-da-fe of Spain.[69] Moreover, acquiring piano and Castilian-language skills were not among the new community's pressing needs.[70]

A Question of Language: Ladino versus Spanish

Widespread regard for Ladino as a language in its own right did not come until many decades later. In the meantime, the Western Sephardic slight to the language was less consequential than its ill-informed equation with modern Spanish. The confusion was augmented by the tendency of some Ladino speakers to refer to their language as "espaniol" or "spaniol" (and, in English, as "Spanish"), whereby they unwittingly elided the distinctions between Judeo-Spanish and modern Castilian.[71] In some public venues, Sephardic elites blithely melted down these linguistic categories, perhaps in part to underscore intercommunal unity. Congregation Shearith Israel's Sisterhood included in its 1914 Purim celebration for Oriental Jews the presentation of songs in "both English and Spanish" and the performance of "an original Ladino comedy." Communal leaders from Congregation Shearith Israel, Rachel Toledano and Joseph de A. Benyunes, both fluent in modern Spanish, organized the event. The synagogue newsletter commented that this "Spanish entertainment for Spanish-speaking Jews from the Orient bears curious and instructive testimony to the unchanged tradition of the congregation and the unchanging nature of Jewish history."[72]

In reality, many Ladino-speaking Jews, particularly those of the first immigrating generation, encountered great difficulty understanding the Castilian spoken by some of their Western coethnics.[73] In the goal to homogenize the two groups, it was clear who bore the burden of linguistic conformity. Ladino, not modern Castilian, was in need of rehabilitation, partly for pragmatic reasons. Sisterhood activists recognized the economic potential of linguistic reform in 1924, when they hired Spanish professor Leo Pasternak to conduct free classes in Castilian at the Settlement House. These complimentary lessons were aimed at the economic betterment of the newcomers, particularly those hoping to enter businesses that conducted commerce with Spanish-speaking countries and those seeking positions as correspondents and secretaries in exportation houses.[74]

Some Eastern Sephardim, particularly those whose professions immersed them in the broader Hispanic world, readily embraced the goal to "update" the Ladino imported from the Orient. In the 1930s, native Ladino speaker and renowned Hispanist Maír José Benardete published a series of articles in *La Vara*. Though printed in Hebrew letters, the articles read like modern Spanish. Readers, including one Moise Angel, complained that they did not understand Benardete's "pure Castilian":

> Professor Benardete, in my humble opinion, is abusing the columns of *La Vara* and readers as well. His articles are always long, very long, [so long that] you would need intestines to read them. With regard to his language style, it is closer to Castilian than our Spanish. If Professor Benardete wishes to write in Castilian, he should write for *La Prensa,* a Spanish newspaper which appears in New York.[75]

In that same issue, subscriber Moshe Azuz added, with similar histrionics,

> not only can I not understand them, despite the many efforts I make to understand them, but I also become affright when I see them, being that they are very long, each one measuring a kilometer and a half, and [written] in a lofty language style, [so lofty it] reaches into the clouds.[76]

Chek Abrevaya publicly relieved himself of his shared disdain in the tabloid's next issue. Comforted that he was not alone, he heartily condemned Benardete's lengthy articles, written in a stilted Castilian, and yearned for writers who were less "Europeanized, and who employ a vocabulary more intelligible to the readers of 'La Vara.'"[77] By dint of these scathing critiques, the editor or linotypist was persuaded to translate Benardete's articles into Ladino, thus ensuring reader comprehension.[78]

The pressure that some Eastern Sephardim felt to "Hispanify" their Ladino finds its parallel in the country's Ashkenazic community, where Eastern European Jews sometimes Germanicized their Yiddish in deference to their Central European coreligionists. Germanicized Yiddish was sometimes employed in the meetings of *landsmanschaft* associations, as well as in the Yiddish press and on the stage, where its use was widespread by the late nineteenth century. For Yiddish speakers, German represented "culture, refinement, and modernity." The use of "daytshmerish," as it came to be known, was also a response to the need to express new political, cultural, social, and technical concepts and phenomena that did not exist in Old Country Yiddish. That the German of American Jews (as opposed to that of gentiles) served as the "normative model" affirms that newcomers looked to Central European Jews for cultural emulation. Eastern Sephardim, by contrast, had few Jewish Spanish-speaking models and were thus more influenced by the many dialects spoken by the city's gentile Hispanics. While Ladino progressively lost its distinctive qualities as a result of continual exposure to modern Spanish and unraveling ties to the Judeo-Spanish heritage, by the 1920s daytshmerish conceded victory to Yiddish, which had achieved maturity "as a language suitable for communal affairs."[79]

The Boundaries of Communal Belonging

Members of Congregation Shearith Israel who were fluent in modern Spanish commonly traced their recent ancestry to North Africa. Their presence in the Western Sephardic community is interesting for what it tells us about the borderlines of Western and Eastern Sephardic identity. It appears that the first Eastern Sephardi and Mizrahi immigrants to the United States were Maghrebi Jews who settled in New York in the 1880s. In 1885, they founded the Moses Montefiore Congregation (sometimes known as the Montefiore Sephardic Synagogue) to accommodate worshipers who lived too far from Congregation Shearith Israel. This, in fact, was "the first Sephardic offshoot" of Congregation Shearith Israel and was morally and financially supported by the mother congregation until its demise twenty years later. Most worshipers hailed from Gibraltar (much of whose population came originally from North Africa), and they were joined by Moroccan and other Sephardic Jews.[80]

Likewise, Rachel Toledano and her husband, Pinhas Habib, also natives of Morocco, clearly identified as Western Sephardim and were regarded as such by the Eastern Sephardic coreligionists whom they attempted to assist in the 1910s.[81] In their case, both high social and economic status as well as fluency in modern Spanish seem to have qualified them as "Western."[82] Another factor seems to have been arrival in the country before the mass influx of Eastern Sephardim and Mizrahim. The aforementioned Union and Peace Society (*La Sosieté Unión i Pas*), an English-speaking organization founded in 1899 by some of these wealthier North African, Balkan, and Middle Eastern Sephardim, is another example of "honorary" Western Sephardic identity. Many of the society's members worshiped at Congregation Shearith Israel and were perhaps more strongly identified as Western than as Eastern Sephardim. In 1912 the society counted almost two hundred members from Morocco, "Turkey," and Spain (no doubt recent émigrés from North Africa and the Ottoman Empire). Among them were the multimillionaire Schinasi brothers, of tobacco-factory fame. The society did not have a synagogue and during High Holy Days worshiped at Congregation Shearith Israel.[83]

One of these Maghrebi Jews seems to have shifted his communal belonging from West to East. David Z. Benoliel (b. 1845), a native of Oran, Algeria, arrived in the United States in 1866. He soon amassed a large fortune in the real-estate business and contributed generously to non-Jewish and Jewish charitable organizations. Benoliel was a member of Congregation Shearith Israel, but he ended his affiliation a few years before his death for cryptic reasons.[84] Toward the end of his life he founded and participated in a number of Eastern Sephardic organizations, including the Hevra Ozer Dalim Sefaradita Orientala. Eastern Sephardim, five hundred of whom attended his funeral procession, carried out the ritual washing of the body (rehisá).[85]

A final example demonstrates this elasticity of identity as it extended specifically to Jews from the Anatolian Peninsula. The "Descriptive Catalogue of the Shearith Israel Sisterhood Fair," which includes an account of the relics and book collection of art dealer Hadji Ephraim Benguiat, makes no reference to this man's Near Eastern precedents. The catalogue's introduction neglects to name Benguiat's place of birth, only describing him as "the descendant of an illustrious Spanish Jewish family which traces its origin as far back as the beginning of the eleventh century."[86] In fact, Benguiat was a native of Izmir who had also lived in Damascus and on Gibraltar before immigrating to the United States.[87] It seems that economically elite Eastern Sephardim, whose arrival in the country usually preceded the great influx of non-Ashkenazic Jews, were regarded on some level as Western Sephardim.

These attempts to elide differences were not effective vis-à-vis the majority of Eastern Sephardim. David de Sola Pool's idealistic proclamation in 1912 that the ritual of Eastern Sephardim "is our own" ignored distinctions that made common prayer difficult, if not impossible.[88] Pool was of course aware of these distinctions. In an article that appeared in an Anglo-Jewish periodical in 1914 he recognized Levantine Sephardim's "indefeasible right" to establish their own synagogue for the practice of their distinct religious traditions.[89] The importance of preserving Eastern Sephardic rites was also affirmed in the bulletins of Congregation Shearith Israel.[90] In 1913, the congregation's spiritual leader, Henry Pereira Mendes, sent an open letter to the editor of *La America*, acknowledging the preference of Oriental Sephardim to pray according to their own ritual and avowing to respect their desire to do so.[91]

The question was, whose rite would prevail if prayer services organized for Eastern Sephardim were held under Western Sephardic auspices? While Western Sephardic leaders claimed to cherish the distinctive traditions of their Eastern coreligionists, they also hoped to prevent the atomization of an emerging Sephardic community. Even as Pool encouraged the formation of new Sephardic synagogues, he decried the impulse of Levantine subgroups to form multiple congregations based on what he considered slight differences of Hebrew pronunciation.[92] Behind this quest for unity lurked some degree of cultural bias. The Middle Eastern tenor of the Eastern Sephardic rite could not but discomfit New York's elite Jews. Cyrus Adler, an American-born Germanic Jew who had been raised with the Western Sephardic rite, perhaps reflected the attitude of his audience members when he addressed the Sisterhood in 1916. It would be a pity, he declared, should their "particular form of worship" and "customs, *so far as they are good*, . . . be blotted out" (italics added).[93]

Parallel religious services and separate houses of worship for Eastern Sephardim were one solution to this conflict. Beginning in 1907, Congregation Shearith Israel offered free High Holy Day services for "our Oriental Sephardim" in the synagogue's assembly hall, a large room below the main sanctuary.[94] Congregation leaders graciously arranged for linguistic accommodations. The hundreds of Levantine Jews who attended these overflow services were greeted by a special usher conversant in Ladino, Arabic, and Greek.[95] This arrangement was short-lived, partly because of space constraints as the population of Levantine Jews steadily increased. Another difficulty was that until the 1920s, the majority of Levantine Jews resided downtown, on New York's Lower East Side, a good distance from Congregation Shearith Israel's West 70th Street locale. Traditional Jewish law forbids worshipers to drive or take transportation on the Sabbath and holy days. To remedy this situation, separate religious services for Sephardic newcomers were organized as early as 1911 at the aforementioned Neighborhood House.[96]

By 1913, these services gradually gelled into the Synagogue House, also known as Berith Shalom [covenant of peace] and operated under the direction of Congregation Shearith Israel's Sisterhood in its Orchard Street headquarters.[97] Founded by Gibraltar-born Joseph de A. Benyunes, in conjunction with the Sisterhood, the house of worship served the ten thousand Eastern Sephardim living on the Lower East Side and was meant to replace the halls that were periodically rented for Jewish worship, a practice initiated by Lower East Side Ashkenazim. A number of *kolonia* members objected to these makeshift synagogues, rendered unfit for worship by their usual use as dance halls, and hence the site of "the greatest immorality."[98] Benyunes, a businessman and ordained rabbi,[99] conducted Sabbath and holiday services in the new synagogue for over a year.[100]

Though organized for Levantine Jews, worship was apparently conducted according to the Western Sephardic rite and thus would not have included the Ladino prayers that characterize Eastern Sephardic religious traditions.[101] Synagogue bylaws, printed in Ladino and English for the years 1914–1915, were ambiguous on this matter. They promised that the "Prayers and Ceremonies that shall be performed at the Synagogue House, at 86 Orchard Street, shall be always according to the Sephardic Minhag, and read in the Hebrew Language, and in no case shall this be altered or changed."[102] Occasionally, Western Sephardic leaders did make superficial attempts to accommodate their Eastern Sephardic membership. In 1917, the Ladino tabloid *La Bos del Pueblo* announced that the downtown synagogue had hired Aharon Benezra, a rabbi who would deliver sermons in both Ladino and English.[103]

Benyunes, again with the cooperation of the Sisterhood, also founded and conducted a daily Talmud Torah. At its Eldridge Street location by 1918, the Talmud Torah offered Hebrew and religion studies and enrolled 175 Sephardic pupils, aged six to fourteen. In those years, the student body did not show signs of remarkable growth. Three years later it enrolled 180 children taught by five teachers.[104] This, with one unspecified exception, was the only such downtown institution offering Sephardic religious instruction to the thousands of Eastern Sephardic children. The rent of both the synagogue and Talmud Torah, as well as the teachers' salaries, were all paid by the Sisterhood, supplemented by revenues raked in by membership dues and offerings collected in synagogue.[105] In this case, too, it is reasonable to assume that this institute adhered to Western Sephardic traditions. The Sephardic Talmud Torah of "Uptown," also administered under the auspices of Shearith Israel, showed strong influences of the Western Sephardic tradition, particularly in its 1915 High Holy Day advertisement of "the best cantors accompanied by a magnificent choir."[106] In 1914, the Sephardic Jewish Community organized High Holy Day services intended to ritually unite Sephardim from all different parts of the (former) Ottoman Empire. These services, complete with a children's choir and "the strictest order and respect," likewise appear to have been influenced by the rites of Congregation Shearith Israel.[107]

The reaction of Eastern Sephardim to imposed ritual was mixed. Even those who resented what they perceived as Congregation Shearith Israel's condescension, or who preferred praying according to the "Oriental" rite, were mesmerized by the synagogue's "perfect services," choir, and the elegant dress of the worshipers.[108] Reactions were particularly enthusiastic during discussions about the potential affiliation of Eastern Sephardic religious organizations with Congregation Shearith Israel. The prospect of praying in the elegant, permanent building provided great incentive for religious unification.[109] Eastern Sephardic leaders also realized that membership would enhance the "honor" and "dignity" of their community in the eyes of the majority Ashkenazic community.[110]

But the path to membership was not always clear-cut. Henry Pereira Mendes had extended an ambiguous invitation to membership in Congregation Shearith Israel as early as 1913. In an open letter to *La America*, he had indicated that he considered all New York's Eastern Sephardim as members of Congregation Shearith Israel, but he declined to inform prospective congregants how they might join as bona fide members with all rights and privileges.[111] The following year, Berith Shalom worshipers were allowed to become associate members of the Spanish and Portuguese Synagogue upon the payment of monthly dues. Eastern Sephardim responded enthusiastically. The Lower East Side congregation embraced the plan unanimously, and sixty of its members immediately enrolled. Six months later that number doubled.[112] Over the next few years, the "form of application" was changed,[113] suggesting new obstacles to associative membership. This might explain why at a "Sephardic meeting" hosted by Pinhas Habib and Rachel Nahon Toledano in 1917, congregation members felt obliged to reaffirm their desire to affiliate Eastern Sephardim as Shearith Israel members.[114] By 1923, the official affiliation of Berith Shalom with Congregation Shearith Israel was complete,[115] but only two years later, the Eastern Sephardic congregation broke away due to irreconcilable differences.[116] By as late as 1933, as we have seen, Henry Pereira Mendes had returned to his ambiguous position of recommending "gradual associate-membership," contingent on the economic upward mobility of Eastern Sephardim.[117]

Class disparities were not the only cause for ambivalence among Western Sephardim, as semantic debates reveal. These heated discussions arose during the process of the formal naming of organizations founded to assist or represent Levantine Jews. The earliest controversy seems to have occurred during the establishment of a "Sephardic Bureau" in the Hebrew and Immigrant Aid Society in 1911. In January of the following year, HIAS formally inaugurated the new section as "Bureau for Sephardic Jewish Immigrants."[118] But Congregation Shearith Israel—probably with David de Sola Pool at its helm—"categorically opposed" this name and immediately began to pressure HIAS to change it. HIAS acquiesced, and the name became "Oriental Bureau" as of January 1912.[119] Again in 1912, a group of Eastern Sephardim formed a "Federation of Sephardic Societies" and approached Congregation Shearith Israel for assistance. According to Joseph M. Papo, Pool was willing to offer his support but exhorted the group to replace the term "Sephardic" with "Oriental." Pool's suggestion was accepted, and the organization was renamed "Federation of Oriental Jews."[120]

Pool continued his proprietary battle for the term "Sephardic" in 1914 when HIAS announced the establishment of its "Committee on Sephardic Jewish Immigrants." Pool urged HIAS to change the name to the "Committee on Oriental Jewish Immigrants."[121] HIAS official Isidore Hershfield informed Pool that the board of directors disapproved of the term "Oriental":

> on account of its liability to misconstruction into Chinese, Japanese, etc. "Eastern" would not fully or clearly express what we had in mind. "Levantine," while probably most correct, is an unusual word and not known to a very great majority of our members and the public. "Sephardic" was therefore agreed upon as being the nearest term which will popularly convey our meaning.[122]

But a month later, HIAS acquiesced to Pool's pressure.[123] HIAS president Leon Sanders wrote Pool that "the members at our Annual Meeting voted to change the name of the Committee on Sephardic Jewish Immigrants, so that it shall be known hereafter as the Committee on Oriental Jews."[124]

Kolonia members continued to protest long after these name changes became official. The name of the Federation of Oriental Jews, founded in 1912, bore the brunt of the attack. In a 1915 letter to *El Progreso*, "Ben Avi" demanded, "why should we give our future Sephardic community the name Federation of Oriental Jews? Does there exist in New York some federation of occidental Jews that we should call ourselves by an opposite name? Ashkenazim formed their Ashkenazic community, and we should form our Sephardic community."[125] At a federation meeting in March 1916, Moise Gadol threatened that "he would never speak in favor, but always against the federation" and would stir up popular opposition to that organization if it did not change its name from Oriental Federation to Sephardic Federation.[126] Interestingly, Joseph Gedalecia remembered in an interview that same year that Moise Gadol had been among the opponents who had originally "insisted [in 1912] that the name 'Oriental' was more appropriate." Gedalecia, who served as president of the Federation of Oriental Jews, commented that he himself had been one of those to initially suggest the term "Sefaradím." Now, in 1916, however, Gedalecia's approach to the semantic battle was allegedly one of indifference: "In effect, I don't think anything about this [matter] because I well know that names are created artificially."[127] Nonetheless, Gedalecia, who had left Istanbul at the age of eleven and traveled through Europe and parts of Asia and Africa before arriving in the United States, could not resist pointing out that Levantine Jews, wherever they went, were referred to as "Oriental." Moreover, when establishing themselves in the United States, they identified their businesses as such to the U.S. government. In the end, "Oriental" was for Gedalecia the preferred term.[128]

Gedalecia's claim that Gadol had changed his views on taxonomy was probably true. In 1915, Gadol had transformed the masthead of his newspaper from "Organ of the Judeo-Oriental Colony of America" to "Organ of the Judeo-Sephardic Colony of America." One reader, Ben-Sion Behar, noted that the substituted word ("Sephardic" for "Oriental") "is very small in content, though very large in its importance for the history of our Sephardic colony of America." Behar continued with a lengthy polemical enumeration of the historical, linguistic, and sociological reasons why Eastern Sephardim should be called Sephardim rather than Oriental. Historically, Eastern Sephardic communities had always referred to themselves as Sephardic, not Oriental. Linguistically, Ladino was a Western, not an Oriental language. Moreover, the word "Sephardic" was associated with "the glorious history of our ancestors of Spain" and brought Eastern Sephardim a reputation of "glory and aristocracy."[129] Gadol himself insisted on the term "Sephardic" over "Oriental" for the sake of communal unity. Gadol, a longtime campaigner for the merging of Western and Eastern Sephardim on an organizational and religious basis, also believed that Eastern Sephardic religious customs should be discarded as vestiges of the past. Following the dedication of the Shearith Israel–sponsored synagogue Berith Shalom in 1918, Gadol exhorted, "the word 'Sephardic' should shine everywhere and the name 'Oriental' should disappear completely from the midst of our people."[130]

David de Sola Pool's motivations for preserving separate identities are less clear and, like the views of Gadol and Gedalecia, seem to have evolved over time. According to Joseph M. Papo, Pool had urged HIAS to rename its Committee on Sephardic Jewish Immigrants in 1914 to Committee on Oriental Jewish Immigrants in order "to preserve for his Congregation the status of being the quintessential Sephardi group in America." Similarly, Marc D. Angel has suggested that "[s]ome of the old line Sephardim ... were afraid the term ['Sephardic'] would fall into disrepute."[131] But in an article published that same year, Pool emphatically objected to the term "Oriental." While he still found the term "Sephardim" as applied to the newcomers "the most objectionable of all," he felt the term "Oriental" was "too broad to be exact." Moreover, he explained, "Oriental" "leaves an impression in the mind of many that this immigration is one with the immigration of Hindoos, Japanese and other Eastern Asiatics." Pool also rejected "Turkish," since it would not encompass the "Greeks, Bulgarians, Servians, etc., . . . included among them" and because the public generally thought of Turkey "as comprising only Turkey in Europe without including Turkey in Asia." Similarly, Pool discarded the terms "Ladinos, Espanols or Spagnualis [Spaniolís]" since many of the Arabic- and Greek-speaking immigrants among them were entirely ignorant of Ladino. "Levantine," he concluded, was "more correct and more closely appropriate."[132]

It is highly plausible, as Papo and Angel argue, that Pool's concern for terminology demonstrated his anxiousness to preserve the social status of Western Sephardim.[133] But his quest for a term that would be culturally, geographically, and linguistically accurate should not be disregarded. He correctly noted that a "certain percentage of the immigrants in question are not Sephardim, *i.e.*, descendants of the Jews expelled from the Spanish Peninsula in the Middle Ages." Some of the immigrants were

Ashkenazim who had settled in the Near East, and many of the Greek Jews had no Spanish ancestry. For Pool, the term "Sephardic" referred to religious rite, not group identity. His "greatest objection" to the term, therefore, was "the fact that it classifies Jewish immigrants according to religious ritual." By this reasoning, Pool illustrated, "one would classify other immigrant Jews as Ashkenazic, Chassidic, Orthodox, Reform, etc." The only term that was "free from all of these objections," he insisted, was "Levantine." Pool preferred this term because of its geographical accuracy. As support for his view, he cited the definition for "Levantine" provided in the *Century Dictionary*: "the eastern Mediterranean and the coasts of Syria, Asia Minor and Egypt" and the "regions between Italy and the Euphrates." Pool concluded, "It would be as well if we could agree to use the term Levantine as the technical and standard description of this immigration." It is at once comprehensive and exactly descriptive of the locality whence come these immigrants, regardless of language and religious ritual."[134] Unfortunately, Pool did not explain why he had in 1911 and earlier in 1914 advocated the term "Oriental" for various organizations representing Eastern Sephardim and Mizrahim. Such inconsistencies are a sure sign of the increasing complexities of nomenclature and identity in both the Sephardic community and broader society.

Toward Unity

David de Sola Pool's efforts to ritually unite Western and Eastern Sephardim is consistent with his argument that "Sephardic" should refer to religious rite rather than subethnicity. This became clear in 1929 with the founding of the Union of Sephardic Congregations in New York City.[135] The union represented congregations in both the United States and Canada. Among its goals were to standardize the Sephardic prayer rite, train Sephardic religious leaders and teachers, and establish Sephardic religious schools.[136] The union's major achievement was the publication of the *Book of Prayers*, a standardized Sephardic Hebrew and English prayer book assembled under the editorial direction of Pool. The impetus for a new prayer book was not only the quest for communal unity but also the poor condition or unavailability of previously used editions.[137] An additional motivation may have been to discourage young Eastern Sephardim from rejecting the "old style of religious services" for Ashkenazic Reform services, a prospect so serious that Pool convened a conference of all New York Sephardic congregations in 1935 to discuss the matter.[138]

First published in 1936, the new prayer book was adopted by numerous Sephardic congregations in the United States and abroad and was distributed throughout the world, including Buenos Aires, Bucharest, Elisabethville (Belgian Congo), India, Rio de Janeiro, Salisbury (Rhodesia), and Suriname.[139] The process that brought the *Book of Prayers* into being stands as a liturgical testimony to the midcentury amalgamation of Western and Eastern Sephardic identities in the United States. Pool maintained that a standardized American Sephardic prayer book would

> overcome the division within the synagogue among those who would insist on preserving in this country every fine point of local minhag [custom] which they have brought with them from Salonica or Rhodes or Monastir or Janina or Aleppo or Jerusalem or Cairo or Mogador [now Essaouira, a city in Morocco west of Marrakesh] or Gibraltar or London or Amsterdam or Jamaica or Curacao, or any of the other places from which our American Sephardic communities are recruited.[140]

In addition to these *minhagim,* Pool noted, "there is a Sephardic tradition of nearly three centuries that has existed in New York, and with very slight differences also Philadelphia and Montreal." Unlike earlier debates over language, in which Western and some Eastern Sephardim insisted that modern Spanish prevail over Ladino, Pool adopted a more eclectic approach to liturgy. Pool emphasized that American Sephardic unity could only be achieved when all these rites were "merged and fused into one." This fusion was pragmatic, he noted, for division based on variant liturgical traditions was a luxury that the tiny Sephardic population could ill afford.[141] To ratify this amalgamation, Pool secured the approbation of the chief rabbi of New York's Syrian community, leading cantors (*hazanim*) of the city's "Oriental Jewish congregations," and the spiritual leaders of "the old American Sephardic communities."[142]

In Pool's preface to the second edition of the prayer book of daily and Sabbath prayers (1941), he acknowledged textual additions from the "Oriental Sephardic rite,"[143] though these concessions appear minimal. As in the early days of immigration, when Western Sephardim designed special services for their Eastern coreligionists, the tendency was to preserve the Western Sephardic tradition as the mainstay and add in Levantine traditions as superficial accommodations. This tendency is readily apparent in the English and Hebrew subtitles of the union's prayer books. The dominance of the Western Sephardic rite is suggested in the English subtitle: "According to the Custom of the Spanish and Portuguese Jews." A more ambiguous term is offered in the Hebrew subtitle, which would be translated as "according to the custom of the Sephardim in America."

The process of the prayer books' assembly was perhaps more important than the finished product. Joe Elias, son of Monastir-born cantor David Eliyahu Cassorla, recalls that Pool made sincere and wholehearted efforts to include the Eastern Sephardic rite in the new American Sephardic liturgy. Pool was, in fact, regarded as more receptive to Eastern Sephardim than his predecessors. Elias relates,

> I remember conversations in which they [Eastern Sephardic religious leaders] contrasted Rabbi de Sola Pool's open attitude with the previous attitudes they encountered.... De Sola Pool ... brought the [Eastern Sephardic] rabbis to meet with him in order to try to capture in one book the ... kind of service that the [Eastern] Sephardim offered.... They ... read to him, they showed to him the sections that they would use. That *siddur* [prayer book] was put together on the basis of his having these ongoing roundtable kinds of meetings with ... the Sephardic rabbis, ... Turkinos of my father's generation."[144]

Elias recalls that Pool "valued and treasured the Sephardic traditions that were brought from the Levant." The Eastern Sephardic rabbis whom Pool consulted, Elias adds, were deeply grateful for the honor given their liturgical traditions. These leaders "very much valued his reaching out to them."[145] The *Book of Prayers,* published by the Union of Sephardic Congregations, is today in its twelfth impression (1997) and remains one of the most enduring legacies of the merging of the two communities.

World War II heightened the urgency of Sephardic ritual unity. As was the case for Ashkenazim of Eastern European origin, this period witnessed the steady acculturation of Sephardic Jews to Anglo-American society. Congregation Mikveh Israel in Philadelphia was on the brink of the "abandoning of its Sephardic minhag," and Congregation Shearith Israel in Montreal faced an identical fate in the absence of a Sephardic rabbi. In fact, the only available Sephardic rabbi in the entire United States at that time was Solomon Maimon, a Seattle native and Yeshiva University graduate.[146] Overseas, Sephardic Jews were being slaughtered as part of Hitler's Final Solution. These factors made the question of

Sephardic ritual survival more acute than ever before. Nissim S. Saul, an Eastern Sephardic Jew who had worshiped in Congregation Shearith Israel from 1910 until his move to Los Angeles in 1935, wondered whether the Sephardim were "in their last episode." In 1944 he sent a plaintive letter to Pool asking, "Are we to be another lost tribe? Are we to be dispersed little by little until practically nothing is left? What is the future holding for us?"[147]

Pool deeply lamented the dearth of Sephardic rabbis in the United States and strove to remedy the situation. One solution, which reflected a new openness to subethnically diverse leadership, was to train Ashkenazic rabbis in the Western Sephardic rite. Among them was Dr. Louis C. Gerstein, who served Congregation Shearith Israel. Another strategy was to dispatch Western Sephardim to synagogues facing an imminent eclipse. In 1944, Congregation Shearith Israel released Rev. Cardozo from his duties so that he could take charge of Congregation Mikveh Israel in Philadelphia and rescue its Sephardic rite from abandonment.[148] Pool pointed out that the Union of Sephardic Jewish Organizations had been attempting to import from Europe Sephardic religious leaders or non-Sephardim who had served Sephardic congregations. Among them were Rabbi Kahan of Rhodes and Rome, who settled in Seattle, and Dr. Nissim J. Ovadia, chief rabbi of the Sephardic Community of Paris, who founded the Central Sephardic Jewish Community of America in 1941. But war conditions destroyed further possibilities. Pool noted despondently in 1944, "we have so little hope that any of them from the Balkans or such countries as Holland, France or Italy will survive."[149]

The influx of thousands of Sephardi and Mizrahi Jews from Arab lands, Persia (Iran), and Central Asia after 1948 augmented the non-Ashkenazic population of the United States to an unanticipated degree. While some of these refugees and immigrants helped fill the pews of Western and Eastern Sephardic congregations, the majority formed new congregations with their own distinctive rituals and prayer books.[150] Some historic Eastern Sephardic congregations reasserted their separate identities and brought back or updated their own distinctive liturgies.[151] Thus, the ritual unification that Pool spearheaded in the late 1920s proved both circumscribed and time bound. A more enduring coalition was accomplished by conceiving of American Sephardim not as a conglomerate drawn together by religious rite but rather as a secular entity united by group identity.

The same leaders devoted to religious unification undertook this effort to bring Sephardic societies under an inclusive, secular umbrella organization. These successive attempts, all of which ultimately failed, have been ably documented by Joseph Papo and need not be recounted in detail here. A brief overview of these organizations demonstrates how transient they were. The "Federation of Sephardic Societies," quickly renamed the "Federation of Oriental Jews" in 1912, was the first umbrella organization representing Eastern Sephardim, Mizrahim, and Ottoman-born Ashkenazim.[152] The organizations that superseded the federation all employed the term "Sephardic" and thus, at least nominally, encompassed both Western and Eastern Sephardim. These included the Sephardic Community of New York (1920–1922);[153] the Sephardic Jewish Community of New York (1923–1932);[154] and the Central Sephardic Jewish Community of America (1941), which ceased to be a major factor in the community by at least the early 1970s.[155]

The most enduring of these unification attempts came in 1972, when constituent societies founded the American Sephardi Federation. What Judith Mizrahi calls the "extended definition" of "Sephardic" was officially adopted in 1978 "at a symposium on Sephardim sponsored by the American Jewish Committee."[156] Today, the American Sephardi Federation defines "Sephardic" in its broadest, ahistorical sense and represents virtually all Jews who are not Ashkenazic.[157] In a study eventually published as *703 Sephardim in America*, Mizrahi sent questionnaires to "Bukharian," "Egyptian," "Greek," "Iraqi," "Moroccan," "Syrian," "Turkish," and "Early American" Jews, all of whom she identified as "Sephardim."[158] The irony of this conglomeration into one group is that non-Ashkenazim are collectively much more ethnically, linguistically, and culturally diverse than Ashkenazim. Most Eastern European Ashkenazim spoke Yiddish, whose various dialects were generally mutually comprehensible. Central European Jews traditionally spoke Western Yiddish or German, which though not always comprehensible to Yiddish speakers, was still a Germanic language. By contrast, the Jews represented by the American Sephardi Federation speak entirely unrelated languages such as Arabic, Ladino, Amharic, and Georgian.

Some Iberian-origin Sephardim have stridently objected to being drowned "in a sea of uniformity." In the words of Albert de Vidas, a New York–based Eastern Sephardic Jew of Egyptian origin, "What do the Arabic-speaking Jews of Syria or the Berber-speaking Jews of the Atlas mountains, or the Farsi-speaking Jews of Iran, or the Amharic-speaking Jews of Ethiopia have in common with our Hispanic culture and civilization? How can they relate to our history, before and after the expulsion?" Readers today should not mistake such exhortations for the cultural snobbery exhibited by some Western Sephardim in the early twentieth century. On the contrary, advocates of the circumscribed definition of "Sephardic," including de Vidas, feel strongly that Mizrahim and other non-Ashkenazim deserve to be publicly recognized for their own discrete heritage.[159]

It would be tempting to attribute, as do Vidas and others, the conglomerate term "Sephardic" to Ashkenazim in the State of Israel and the United States who could not comprehend the ethnic, cultural, geographical, and linguistic complexities of non-Ashkenazic Jews.[160] However, as demonstrated previously, the earliest drive for an overarching term actually originated among American Sephardim and Mizrahim themselves, as non-Ashkenazic leaders (and some Ottoman-born Ashkenazim) felt compelled to communally organize and publicly present themselves to outsiders. This occurred in the earliest days of their mass migration from the Ottoman Empire (as early as 1904) and represents a voluntary forging together despite disparate subethnic and linguistic backgrounds. Interestingly, a parallel force for a conglomerate identity emerged among world Sephardic leaders who began to organize at the beginning of World War I.[161] In 1915, non-Ashkenazic Jews formed the first Zionist Sephardic organization in Palestine, the *Histadrut Hatze'irim Ha-sefaradim*, later called the *Halutzei Hamizrah* (Oriental Pioneers). A series of conferences in the 1920s and 1930 led to the establishment of the World Federation of Sephardic Organizations, headquartered in Paris and then New York. Its main organ was *Le judaïsme sepharadi*, edited in Paris by Ovadia Camhy.[162] In both cases, political pragmatism impelled leaders to embrace a composite terminology. The shift from the terms "Sephardic" to "Oriental" and then back again to "Sephardic" directly parallels the taxonomical pendulum in America's non-Ashkenazic community.

Unaware of this history, observers in the second half of the twentieth century tended to justify the overarching term "Sephardic" by reading it backward into the past. Judith Mizrahi observed that the diverse groups of non-Ashkenazic Jews identified as a Sephardic unity already before the 1970s, a unity based on "common liturgy, shared . . . group feeling and . . . similar traditions and life perspective."[163] Yet a survey from the early 1980s, conducted by Mizrahi herself, suggested a wide divergence of opinion among U.S. non-Ashkenazic Jews as to what defines a Sephardic Jew. Some defined Sephardim as "The Syrians" or those "from Turkey, Iran, and Greece"; others, as "non-European"; and still others, as "Western European."[164] This inconsistency reinforces my argument that Sephardim and Mizrahim in the United States should be considered a social rather than an ethnic group.

Unlike the controversies that preoccupied David de Sola Pool and members of the Ladino-speaking colony, the last attempt at communal unification in 1972 apparently did not raise as many questions about nomenclature or communal inclusion. With the founding of the American Sephardi Federation (officially in 1973), it was clear that the tens of thousands of Eastern Sephardim and Mizrahim who arrived from Arab lands, Iran, and Central Asia after 1948 could be collectively represented as "Sephardim." The political exigency of organizational unity has triumphed over both precise terminology and historical self-ascription. Communal inclusion in the Ashkenazic community was a much thornier issue.

4

Ashkenazic-Sephardic Encounters

The Phenomenon of Coethnic Recognition Failure

Sometime between 1909 and 1913, a number of Ashkenazic Jews of the Lower East Side, protesting street disturbances and neighborhood disputes, petitioned Mayor William Jay Gaynor to remove the "Turks in our midst." The main problem with the complaint was that these "Turks" were actually fellow Jews. Upon learning of their mistake, the Ashkenazim—primarily Yiddish-speaking Jews of Eastern European origin—withdrew the petition, deciding to settle the matter "among themselves."[1] This phenomenon, which I have termed "coethnic recognition failure," is defined as a person's denial of a fellow group member's common ethnicity due to mistaken identity.[2] Coethnic recognition failure represents a central experience of a new group of immigrants that defied conventional categorization. The phenomenon raised new questions not only about Jewish ethnicity but also about the ethnic identity of the non-Jewish immigrants for whom Levantine Jewish immigrants were often mistaken. In the context of Jewish history, the phenomenon is a consequence of the dispersal of Jews throughout the world, which gave rise to cultural, religious, and (perceived) physiognomic gaps. One community could grow so distinct from another that one party (or, rarely, both parties) failed to recognize the other as belonging to the same people and religion.

Levantine Jews, with their unfamiliar physiognomy, Mediterranean tongues, and distinct religious and social customs baffled their Ashkenazic brethren. In the words of a contemporary satirist, "how could you be a Jew when you looked like an Italian, spoke Spanish, and never saw a matsah ball in your life?"[3] A female contributor to *La America* lamented in 1911, "our existence almost until the present day was not recognized even by our coreligionists, the Ashkenazim, some of them taking us for [gentile] Greeks, others considering us Italians or Turks, but none taking us for Jews."[4]

The denial of shared ethnicity and religion was the most painful and frustrating reaction that Eastern Sephardim encountered in their dealings with Ashkenazim, especially when it impeded them from attaining jobs. The problem of coethnic recognition failure was what initially impelled Moise Gadol to launch the country's first Ladino newspaper in 1910. The Eastern Sephardic men whom Gadol first met when he arrived in New York described this experience as their worst immigrant hardship.[5] In the same year, Gadol lamented that "many of our Turkinos, with tears in their eyes, tell us how, when they present themselves for employment, they are not believed by the Ashkenazim to be Jews, except with very great efforts and with all sorts of explanations." These experiences were not isolated incidents. Gadol related that "the columns of our small and precious journal would not suffice to recount one part of this sad situation."[6]

The multiple reports of this experience from a variety of sources—contemporaneous and reminiscent, Jewish and gentile—make it clear that coethnic recognition failure was neither folkloric nor a case of snobbery. Forged of genuine ignorance, it occurred in every place where Levantine Jews settled, including, aside from New York, in Atlanta, Baltimore, Seattle, Indianapolis, Chicago, and Los Angeles.[7]

Many Eastern Sephardi and Mizrahi immigrants encountered coethnic recognition failure for the first time upon their immigration to the United States, Latin America, and the Land of Israel, where the Ashkenazic population was numerically or culturally dominant. Yemeni Jews, studied by Dina Dahbany-Miraglia, are a classic example. Their "repertoire of ethnic identities" was based on language, religion, and regional origin and only acquired a fourth dimension, physiognomy, in the United States and in Palestine during the British Mandate. Dahbany-Miraglia argues that in the Middle East religion was the dominant criterion of ethnic categorization, whereas in the United States skin color and other physical markers often prevailed as ascertainers of Jewishness.[8]

In the United States, and perhaps also in Latin America, coethnic recognition failure betrays the parochial self-awareness of Jews who assumed that only "Yiddish and its associated cultural symbols defined Jewish identity."[9] The denial by Ashkenazim of shared ethnicity with Eastern Sephardim reflects the racialist idea, which intensified in the nineteenth century, that one defining marker of Jewishness is phenotype.[10]

Here it is important to stress that intraethnic tensions between Central and Eastern European Ashkenazim in Europe and the United States do not qualify as coethnic recognition failure. The latter group never genu-

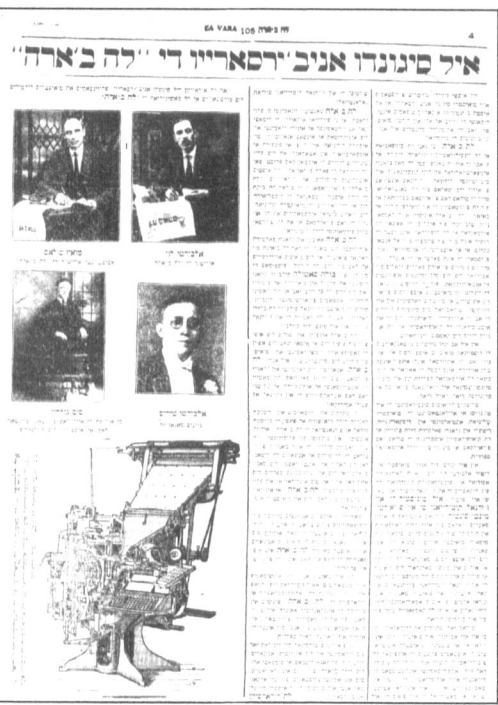

Photographs of the four staff members of La Vara in 1924. "El Segundo aniversaryo de 'La Vara'" [The Second Anniversary of La Vara], La Vara (August 29, 1924): 4. Counter-clockwise from upper right are Alberto D. Levy, Editor; Moise B. Soulam, Assistant Editor; Sam Golden, Printer and Distributor; and Alberto J. Torres, Business Manager. The drawing below represents the printing press.

inely doubted the Jewishness of their Reform coreligionists, even when they criticized their form or lack of Jewish observance.[11] This fact is reflected in the very nicknames that each group used for the other: *Yahudim* (Hebrew for "Jews") and *Ostjuden* (German for "Eastern Jews").[12] Similarly, when Orthodox Jews in the United States denigrated secular or Reform Jews as "goyim," as some still do, they were not imputing their coreligionists' Jewish belonging but rather criticizing their (lax) religious lifestyle.[13] Finally, coethnic recognition failure's most important dimension is subethnicity; thus, interdenominational relations do not fall under the concept's rubric.

In the early years of immigration, Eastern Sephardim who were rejected as Jews by the established Jewish community could sometimes rely on an enlightened Ashkenazic leader, typically a rabbi, who would undertake to enlighten his flock. Shortly after the first arrival of Ottoman immigrants in Indianapolis, a local Reform spiritual leader began to visit various Ashkenazic communities and synagogues in the area, affirming that the new arrivals were "real Jews."[14] In Seattle, the spiritual leader of

Front page of La America *(May 12, 1911), featuring an article in Yiddish directed at Ashkenazic readers. It is entitled, "To the Ashkenazic people."*

the city's Orthodox Jews often took "great pains to explain to his members that the Sephardim were just as Jewish as those of the Ashkenazim . . . and that they too were sons of Israel."[15]

The Ladino press was an important medium through which Sephardim struggled to secure recognition as Jews by their coreligionists. Between 1910 and 1948 as many as nineteen Judeo-Spanish periodicals appeared in the United States, all but two printed in New York. Moise Gadol's *La America*, dedicated to the adaptation of Eastern Sephardim to the United States, was the first enduring American Ladino tabloid and appeared from 1910 to 1925.[16] In one of the earliest issues, Gadol observed that Eastern Sephardim seeking positions in Ashkenazic establishments were often able to convince incredulous employers of their Jewish identity "by showing our tabloid with [its] Hebrew letters," peppered with announcements from the Ashkenazic Jewish press.[17] Addressing a rally of Eastern Sephardic female strikers in 1913, Gadol proclaimed that since the appearance of his journal and the establishment of the Oriental Bureau, responsible for receiving Levantine Jewish immigrants at Ellis Island, "all Ashkenazim are now clear that you are Jews of the same blood and faith."[18]

Other reports, however, contradict these triumphant affirmations. Ashkenazim of a generation later did not refrain from referring to their coreligionists as gentiles (e.g., "Turks"), an image that Eastern Sephardim sometimes internalized. "We used to speak about the Jewish guys, and the Sephardics were different," confessed American-born Ben Cohen, whose family had immigrated from Monastir in 1910. "Really strange."[19] When referring to the "Jewish guys," Cohen may have also had in mind the Ladino term for Eastern European Ashkenazim: "Yiddishim," composed of the word "Yiddish" (a reference to both the language and Jewishness) appended to the Hebrew plural suffix.[20]

The use of these peculiar ethnic labels suggests that both Eastern Sephardim and Mizrahim were complicit in reinforcing a model of "authentic" Jewishness. Syrian Jewish immigrants referred to Eastern European Ashkenazim as "Jewish" or "Iddish." A male Ashkenazic Jew was an "Iddshy," and a female was an "Iddshiyeh." Syrian Jews referred (and still refer) to themselves as "SYs," the first two letters of "Syrian," and nicknamed Ashkenazic Jews (of any background) as "JWs" or "J-Dubs," from the first and last letters of the word "Jew."[21] New York's Syrian Jews used these terms without self-consciousness, constructing a world trifurcated into "Syrians" (meaning Syrian Jews), "Jews" (Ashkenazim), and "Gentiles."[22] These ethnic terms, like the use of Ladino and Arabic words and phrases in English speech, undoubtedly cultivated an "'in-group' spirit," as Joseph A. D. Sutton suggests,[23] but reveal much more. If the established group was Jewish, what was the immigrant, minority group? The origin of these monikers within immigrant Jewish communities suggests that Sephardi and Mizrahi Jews in a part of their psyches assigned "true" Jewish identity to Ashkenazim, with the implicit negation of their own authentic Jewish belonging. Perhaps the most extreme example is the case of Yemeni Jewish immigrants who arrived after World War II and sometimes called one another *shvartze* and *shvartze khaye*, the derogatory Yiddish expressions for "nigger" (literally, "black") and "nigger beast" (literally, "black beast"), respectively, terms they heard from the mouths of their Ashkenazic contemporaries.[24] Here again a Jewish subgroup internalized the majority group's parochial (and in this case racist) perception. As we shall see, this phenomenon may partly explain the high incidence of out-marriage.

Many battles against coethnic recognition failure were fought in the pages of the Ladino press, where a few Ashkenazim chose to venture. In 1916, Russian-born Clara wrote to the editor of *La Bos del Pueblo* of her introduction to Jack, a young Sephardic Jew whom she met at a ball organized by that Judeo-Spanish newspaper. Clara was quite taken with Jack but was not certain of his ethnoreligious identity. "At first glance," she wrote, "I thought him Italian. The way he spoke, his countenance and his gestures were like those of the Italians. But later, when we began seeing each other, he swore to me that he is a Spanish-speaking Jew." Though the couple was in love, Clara's parents objected to the union because they did not believe that Jack was indeed Jewish. Addressing the editor, Clara wrote, "Now, I beg you to tell me through your esteemed newspaper if it is possible, that a Jew who doesn't speak Jewish, and doesn't look Jewish, can nevertheless have a Jewish soul." The young woman's question encapsulated what the country's Yiddish-speaking immigrants understood to be the defining elements of Jewishness: language, physiognomy, and metaphysical attributes. The editor's unenviable task was to assure his reader of something so basic, yet so difficult to prove: "Yes, 'Clara,'" he replied pedantically, "the boy speaking Spanish, having Italian gestures, who can read our newspaper, is Jewish. . . . No, we don't see any inconvenience in the intra-marriage of Sephardim with Ashkenazim. There are many examples of Sephardim living with Ashkenazim in the greatest harmony."[25]

The editor's attitude toward intramarriage was generous and may reflect the liberal mind frame of the Sephardic colony's leadership, which was often committed to the ideals of socialism. In reality, marital liaisons between Ashkenazim and Eastern Sephardim were exceedingly rare during the first immigrant generation.[26] For Ashkenazim of Seattle, a marital union between a Sephardic and Ashkenazic Jew "was tantamount to non-Jewish wedlock or even 'assimilation.'" Ashkenazic rejection of Sephardim as potential marriage partners may have played a role in the high rates of intermarriage among first- and second-generation Eastern Sephardim. According to estimates, unions between Sephardim and non-Jews in Seattle during the 1930s and early 1970s were four and three times as common, respectively, as marriages between Sephardim and Ashkenazim.[27]

Eastern Sephardim, however, were partly to blame, according to some observers. Their separatism and sense of superiority often hindered them from wedding Ashkenazim. Maurice B. Hexter, staff member of the Bureau of Jewish Social Research, observed in 1913 the "insolence of condescension" that Eastern Sephardim reserved for their Ashkenazic coreligionists. He noted that marrying a Yiddish-speaking Jew was "frowned upon as intermarriage."[28] Similarly, Louis M. Hacker intimated that the separation between Eastern Sephardim and Ashkenazim in the country was not only circumstantial but also self-imposed. According to him, "the Sephardim consider themselves a people apart; they are 'Spanish Jews,' with a distinct historical consciousness and often, an inordinate pride."[29] Eastern Sephardi and Mizrahi leaders confirmed this problem of social snobbery. Albert Matarasso, a leading religious leader of the *kolonia*, complained that "Sephardim, who glorify ourselves so much in our Spanish ancestors for their contributions to their people and to the world, think of ourselves as superior in character to our Ashkenazic brothers and try not to associate with them."[30] Similarly, Joseph A. D. Sutton points to the cultural ideal of *adamiyeh*, or ancestral gentility, that discouraged Syrian Jews from marrying out of the community. Marital alliances between Syrian Jews and Ashkenazim, even after the former moved into the largely middle-class Ashkenazic neighborhoods of Williamsburg, Brooklyn, in the late 1910s, was considered as "'intermarriage,' almost like marriage to a gentile."[31]

Yet it is important not to misinterpret these observations. Although some Eastern Sephardim and Mizrahim may have shared the Ashkenazic reluctance to intramarry, never did the former two groups deny the Jewishness of Central and Eastern European Jews. As one Sephardic immigrant noted in the 1970s, "The Sephardim in Turkey knew that there were Ashkenazim all over the world. But the Jews of America apparently did not know that there were Sephardim in existence."[32]

The Ashkenazic denial of the Jewishness of Sephardim was among the longest-lived of immigrant memories, perhaps because it affected the most crucial aspects of life: love and livelihood. Hank Halio, in his anecdotal recollections of the Sephardic Lower East Side, recalls the coethnic recognition failure that tormented him and his Sephardic friends as they began to date Ashkenazic girls and were introduced to Yiddish-speaking parents. "To try to prove we were indeed Jewish," he recalls, "we recited some Hebrew prayers, but we pronounced the words differently than they did, and they didn't believe us." Some contemplated a more extreme measure. "A certain unmentionable thought crossed the minds of some of the wise guys as a source of proof that they were Jewish," Halio notes euphemistically, "but I don't think any of them tried it."[33] The tell-tale sign of circumcision might have been convincing evidence of Jewishness, particularly given the small local population of Muslim Arab immigrants.[34]

But Halio was wrong about one thing: some Eastern Sephardic immigrants did dare to bare. One of them was David Eliyahu Cassorla, who immigrated to New York from Monastir in 1910 and eventually became an important religious leader in the Sephardic colony.[35] During Cassorla's first few years in the country, he befriended an Ashkenazic woman, the forelady in the garment factory where he worked. The woman's brothers, after meeting Cassorla, expressed their displeasure through physical aggression and cautioned him to stay away from their sister, "because what kind of Jew doesn't speak Yiddish?" Cassorla's son, Joe Elias, who shared the anecdote in the 1990s, recounted, "they took him into the bathroom to look at his [pause] machinery. They still weren't satisfied!"[36]

Albert J. Amateau, the aforementioned Sephardic colony leader who passed away in 1996 at the age of 106, was also subjected to such examinations while seeking boarding upon his arrival to New York in 1910. In 1986, he recalled the following:

> I had gone to two or three Ashkenazic [houses], and one asked me, "What's your name?"
> "Amateau."
> "What?"
> "Amateau."
> "Your Jewish name."
> "That's my Jewish name.
> "That's no Jewish name, that's a goy."
> "Well, I'm not a goy, I'm a Jew."
> "Come here!" Took me to the lavatory, he says, "Take your pants off, let me see." And even though he saw, he still says to his wife, "No, no, naah. . . . This fellow is a gringo of some kind, I don't know, he may be a Mohamedan or something, he's not a Jew." They wouldn't have me![37]

These occurrences, though recounted decades later in humorous tones, make up some of the bitterest chapters of the Sephardic-Ashkenazic encounter in the United States. Such anecdotes help explain why Joseph Gedalecia, president of the Federation of Oriental Jews in America, declared that Levantine and Eastern Sephardic Jews "feel more discrimination from the other wings of the Jews than they do from the non-Jew."[38]

These "tests" for Jewish belonging find their parallels in the experiences of Yemenite Jewish immigrants in Jerusalem, who after immigration to Palestine in the last two decades of the nineteenth century were often mistaken by Ashkenazim for Muslim Arabs and subjected to examinations to validate their Judaism, including the recitation of Hebrew prayers and the reading of the Talmud.[39] In the United States, too, Yemenite Jews were often not recognized as coreligionists by Ashkenazim.[40] This denial of shared ethnoreligious identity, however, carried with it a sharper racial sting. With their "dark skin" and "curly hair," Yemenite Jews were frequently mistaken for African Americans and resorted to strategies long familiar to the country's black community. When seeking apartments in Jewish neighborhoods, Yemenite Jews would dispatch a light-skinned family member or friend in their stead. When soliciting employment, particularly before the 1960s, they sought "the mediation of a friend or a relative."[41] Yemenite Jews, with no Judeo-Arabic newspaper that they might present to incredulous Ashkenazim as proof of their Jewishness, were forced to employ tactics traditionally used by many African Americans and Hispanics in a racially discriminatory America.

Coethnic recognition failure is not a phenomenon particular to Jews. It has developed among various diasporic peoples when time and geographical distance have created cultural, linguistic, and physiognomic diversity. While I was serving as a visiting fellow at the National University of Ireland, Galway, in 2002, one of my students was a Guyanese-born American of Hindu descent, whose ancestors had arrived in South America as indentured servants in the late nineteenth century. She recounted that while seeking employment in a Galway Indian restaurant, the owners did not believe that she was Indian and asked her to recite Hindi prayers to prove it. Undoubtedly, members of other diasporic groups have found themselves in similar situations.

The phenomenon of coethnic recognition failure should not be confused with the rejection of a coethnic group as a response to racism in mainstream society. An example in American immigration history is Cape Verdeans and peninsular Portuguese, whose shared Catholicism and Portuguese identity did not prevent the latter group from rejecting the former. Cape Verdeans, whose mass immigration began in the late nineteenth century, were perplexed to discover that they were not considered Portuguese by the "white" Portuguese, who excluded them from their organizations and ethnic neighborhoods. But this rejection was not forged of genuine ignorance that there were Portuguese nationals who happened to have African ancestry. Rather, the rejection of Cape Verdeans by peninsular Portuguese in the United States reflects the well-documented desire to dissociate from a people considered "black" by mainstream American society.⁴²

Similarly, northern Italians, who were the first of the peninsula to immigrate in large numbers, regarded southerners, especially Sicilians, as inferior and peasant-like.⁴³ Italians of the Mezzogiorno, meanwhile, associated northern Italians with the northern officials of the new Italian regime, the exploitative tax collectors of southern Italy. Although hostilities between these groups flared, they were never fueled by a mistaken denial of common ethnicity but rather by oppression and perceptions of inferiority. Comparable tensions, based on class, cultural, and religious differences, were also evident among Western Sephardim and Germanic Jews, and Germanic Jews and Eastern European immigrants. But never did these conflicts involve a denial of shared ethnoreligious identity.

The Phenomenon of Corporate Exclusion

For many Eastern Sephardim and Mizrahim, as we have seen, the experience of coethnic recognition failure began with their reception at Ellis Island. Ashkenazic officials stationed at that immigrant port were qualified to deal with Eastern European Ashkenazim but were not familiar with the languages or names of Ottoman Jews. Thus, most Ottoman Jews passed by Ashkenazic immigration officials unnoticed and did not receive the assistance to which they were entitled.⁴⁴ The most efficient way to solve this problem was to endow Eastern Sephardim with corporate representation within the Hebrew Immigrant Aid Society (HIAS), the organization responsible for receiving Jewish immigrants at Ellis Island since the late nineteenth century.⁴⁵ The new section created within HIAS in December 1911 was ultimately named the "Oriental Bureau."⁴⁶ Once this representation was set into place, Moise Gadol was certain that Ashkenazim would recognize Eastern Sephardim as fellow Jews "of the same blood and faith."⁴⁷ As he and other Eastern Sephardic leaders soon learned, corporate representation would assure their *recognition* as Jews but not their *equality* as Jews.

Interestingly, the impetus of HIAS to intervene on behalf of the "unfortunate Oriental Jewish immigrants of this city" came from outside the Ashkenazic community. One decisive force was Moise Gadol, who pointed out that HIAS was overlooking the Levantine Jewish immigrant population.⁴⁸ Another impetus was the Federation of Oriental

Jews, which influenced HIAS to form the Oriental Bureau.[49] An arguably stronger factor was that the plight of these immigrants had come to the attention of non-Jews in the city, including the North American Civic League for Immigrants. Embarrassingly, no "established" (read: Ashkenazic) Jewish organization, save for the Educational Alliance, which had recently organized English classes for Levantine Jews, had yet attempted to alleviate the economic hardships of the newcomers.[50] When financial support for the Oriental Bureau ran out in December 1915, despite fundraising efforts among the city's Sephardic organizations, HIAS decided to close down the section. Vigorous protests from the Federation of Oriental Jews convinced HIAS to appoint to its general staff a Sephardic Jew whose task would be to dispense advice and information.[51]

But HIAS expected the local Sephardic community to raise funds for the operation of the bureau, and this was not always possible. Consequently, HIAS sporadically closed and reopened the Oriental Bureau during the crucial year of 1915, when World War I made Jewish emigration from the Balkans and Middle East imperative.[52] During the bureau's intermittent collapses due to lack of funding, editors of the U.S. Ladino press or leaders of local Eastern Sephardic organizations stepped forward to bridge the gap.[53] Individuals, typically successful businessmen, also vouched for immigrants, even if they did not personally know them. Joseph Isaac Cohen, who arrived in the United States in 1906 and owned a barbershop, offered his Lower East Side business address as a reference to over two hundred families and met them at Ellis Island.[54] Various *kolonia* members, including Albert Amateau (1910–1911) and Monastir native Leon Alcosser (1915–1917), volunteered as interpreters at Ellis Island.[55]

Tellingly, the same year of the Oriental Bureau's establishment, HIAS decided to commission one of its representatives to survey economic opportunities in Cuba for Eastern Sephardim. A board member offered to publish the resulting report in his weekly newspaper, *Der Amerikaner*, and to provide HIAS with the type composition should the organization decide to publish the report in book form.[56] HIAS president Louis Sanders, a municipal judge born in Odessa in 1867, decided on Cuba because Levantine Jews were already immigrating to that island in significant numbers and HIAS had received numerous inquiries from other Levantine Jews about the conditions there.[57]

Sanders's reasoning for encouraging removal of Eastern Sephardim from the country, rather than investing in their adjustment, is worthy of note. After "due investigation," he became convinced that the miserable poverty of Levantine Jews was partly attributable to climate: the Northern Hemisphere brought on them a "lack of energy" that they would not confront in Cuba, whose climate was identical (!) to that of their native lands. Somewhat more justifiable was an argument about the language barrier that Eastern Sephardim encountered in businesses that employed immigrants. Their Spanish dialect was unknown in the Jewish neighborhoods in which they worked, rendering them vulnerable to the exploitation of their bosses.[58] Though it is true that Eastern Sephardim encountered fewer language barriers in the Spanish-speaking world, Sanders did not explain why Yiddish-speaking immigrants in New York would not also be vulnerable to the same exploitation at the hands of German- or English-speaking foremen. His logic is all the more ironic in light of his address at the third annual meeting of HIAS in January 1912:

> I rejoice that the history of our people in this country is a living demonstration of the fact that the primal ambition of the Jew is to become assimilated in the mass of the population, to familiarize himself with the glorious traditions of liberty, which are the corner stone of the republic, and to become, in company with his fellow citizens of other faiths, a cog in the wheel of progress. I further rejoice that the history of our people is a living refutation of the malicious calumny that all immigrants remain alien to our customs, language, and institutions, but that, on the contrary, from the day he lands at Ellis Island, the Jewish immigrant is consumed with the desire to hasten the approach of the day when he shall be qualified to enter upon the full enjoyment of the American franchise.[59]

In this address, Sanders was reacting against the conviction, popular in immigration restrictionist circles of the time, that Jews were the least assimilable of contemporaneous immigrant groups.

In the matter of Cuba, Sanders's remarks implying that Eastern Sephardim were inassimilable brings to mind the regard of German-Jewish Americans for Eastern European Ashkenazim as "uncouth Asiatics"[60] whose inability to Americanize was attributable to the "unscrupulous oppression" endured over the centuries.[61] Isaac Mayer Wise, editor of the *American Israelite*, had proposed in 1884 that New York State's restrictive immigration laws be reinstated in order to refuse the entry of some two hundred impoverished Russian Jewish refugees sailing aboard the SS *California*.[62] Sanders did not go so far as to advocate immigration restrictions against Levantine Jews. Still, his reasoning for removing Eastern Sephardim from the country seems extreme and inconsistent, particularly since climate and language were not generally seen as barriers to the adaptation of Eastern European Jews in the United States. In fact, many Ashkenazic leaders made efforts to retain the immigrants in the county while maneuvering them away from congested cities. Among them was philanthropist Jacob Schiff (1847–1920), who sought to establish a special territory for Jewish immigrants in Galveston, Texas.[63]

The organization principally responsible for transporting Jewish immigrants to less congested areas of the United States was the Industrial Removal Office (IRO), founded in 1901 with native-born Germanic Jews at the helm.[64] The largest group of beneficiaries was Eastern European Jews, but a tiny minority of Ottoman Sephardic Jews, mostly from Turkey, was also served.[65] Unlike HIAS, the IRO never established a subsection devoted to Levantine Jews.

However, the question of the corporate inclusion of Levantine Jews did preoccupy IRO leaders in 1913, just a year after HIAS inaugurated its Oriental Bureau. As was the case with HIAS, concern for the plight of Levantine Sephardim within the IRO was initiated by outside forces. Federation of Oriental Jews president Joseph Gedalecia, who had earlier fought for an Oriental Bureau, once again pressed for communal representation. Seeking a way to facilitate the adjustment of Levantine Jews to the United States, Gedalecia set his eyes on John Foster Carr's *Guide to the United States for the Immigrant Alien*. Nicknamed "The Little Green Book," the *Guide* was a vade mecum for immigrants of various nationalities. Selling in 1912 for a mere fifteen cents,[66] this guide was chock-full of advice and directives on procuring employment, learning English "practically and quickly," traveling, launching a profitable farm, and becoming naturalized. The necessity for translations was not merely linguistic, for each version of the guide included distinctive sections that catered to the specific needs of the particular ethnonational group.

By 1912, the guide had already appeared in Italian, Polish, Yiddish, and even in an English translation of the Yiddish, no doubt catering to German Jews involved in guiding new Jewish immigrants to Americanization. What was sorely lacking were versions in Ladino, Arabic, and Greek.[67] Levantine Jewish leaders energetically spearheaded efforts to raise funds for the three translations. On their behalf in November of that same year, John Foster Carr addressed the American Jewish Committee, notifying members that the federation was "exceedingly anxious to publish it in Spaniol, Arabic and Neo-Greek, and is now issuing a call for funds for that purpose." Carr pointed out that prospective immigrants could read and discuss the *Guide* during their oceanic journey and would thus arrive at Ellis Island savvy enough to avoid the common "legal difficulties" and behavior that was constantly "arousing the prejudice of Americans against them."[68]

The committee's response is not extant, but it was probably negative: we next find the Federation of Oriental Jews approaching the IRO itself. This time, the federation had reduced its goal to securing only a subvention for translation of the *Guide* into Ladino, "for the use of the Spaniol Jews in New York City." Undoubtedly, the spokesperson was the selfsame Joseph Gedalecia. The IRO board unanimously rejected the appeal. In the view of the board members, the proposal did not fall "within the fundamental purposes of our Society's activities."[69] This reasoning was strange for an immigrant-oriented organization, particularly given its statement of purpose, published just two years earlier. As declared in 1911, the IRO's mission was "to popularize the idea of distribution and to disseminate among the Jewish immigrant classes of New York City reliable and authentic information as to opportunities for a livelihood in the cities of the interior."[70] Certainly, a *Guide* in Ladino would have done just that.

Language translation also fell under the rubric of the IRO's activities. Since at least 1910 the IRO had dispensed its "reliable and authentic information" through public lectures given in the heart of New York's Jewish communities, and through pamphlets and leaflets. This information, of course, would have been transmitted in Yiddish. The IRO also published articles in the Yiddish press to disseminate information.[71] Its Emigrant Information Bureau distributed Yiddish-language "literature and printed matter ... as may form a valuable guide to the intended settler."[72]

Why would this organization not have seen fit to print similar material in Ladino? On this question the minutes from 1913 are cryptic. The anticipated benefit of a Ladino translation of the *Guide*, officials concluded, "from the point of view of it influencing eventually the Spaniol Jews to penetrate into the interior, was too problematic."[73] Ironically, less than three years later, the IRO board allocated funds to John Foster Carr for a revised Yiddish manual to provide immigrants with information regarding employment opportunities in the interior. Its rationale was that the Immigrant Publication Society, which Carr represented, was "supplementing the work of the IRO."[74] This evidence suggests that the IRO was willing to finance translation projects and the dissemination of information as long as the targeted population was Ashkenazic and the language was Yiddish.

By 1914, Sephardic communal leaders identified another administrative shortcoming. The previous year, the IRO transferred only seventy-eight "Levantine Jews" to the interior, a small fraction of those who applied for "removal." Jewish communities in the interior were apparently disinclined "to cope with the problem presented by Levantine Jews because of their inability to speak either English or Yiddish."[75] On the occasion of the National Conference of Jewish Charities in 1914, both David de Sola Pool and Cincinnati businessman and philanthropist Max Senior—also a Western Sephardic Jew—urged the IRO to "distribute Levantine Jews in the interior."[76]

Other examples of corporate exclusion likewise demonstrate that Eastern Sephardim and Mizrahim were generally not on the radar screen of the established Jewish community. In 1908, Germanic and Eastern European Jews formed the Kehilla, an umbrella organization that joined together 784 societies representing all types of Jews in America. Levantine Jews were the only ones missing.[77] In 1912, Asher Levy, a Jew from an unspecified Arab land, complained that he had found the American Jewish Committee unresponsive to the economic plight of Levantine Jews. Allegedly, he had turned to Joseph Gedalecia for intervention. Gedalecia had responded that "he can do nothing for the Arabian Jews, the Society is entirely for the (Hashkenasims)." Asher was perplexed. His sloppy typewritten response surely attests to his broken English and manual skills but may also indicate his distress: "We are all jews descendendant from the sam fathers, and I cant understandwhy there should be a different between the Hashkenasims and the Sephardims."[78] Louis M. Hacker admitted in 1926 that no thought (until that year) "has been given . . . to the 40,000 Sephardic Jews hailing from Levantine countries." To fill this gap, the "New York Federation" hired Hacker, under the auspices of the Bureau of Jewish Social Research, to compose a report on this population group.[79] Among Hacker's recommendations was that the New York Federation create an organization representative of the entire Sephardic community.[80]

A final example of communal exclusion relates to the Zionist movement in the United States. The Federation of American Zionists (FAZ), which was founded in 1897[81] and represented more than one hundred

Zionist organizations by 1915, did not initially include a single Sephardic organization.[82] Finally in April 1915, Louis Lipsky, an official in the FAZ since 1914, began to attend the meetings of the Zionist Sepharadim Society of New York and to address its members.[83] The following month, he extended the Zionist Sepharadim an invitation for membership in the FAZ.[84] But this inclusion did not meet the expectations of Sephardic Jews. Reporting on the near complete absence of Sephardim at the annual Zionist Congress of 1916, Gadol placed the blame squarely on Lipsky, then president of the FAZ, who "out of negligence did not make any propaganda among us one hundred thousand Sephardim of America."[85] In his report of the annual Zionist Congress of that year, Gadol fulminated over lack of references to Sephardim and accused the FAZ of neglecting "the best pioneers for Zionism."[86] Echoing complaints voiced by Sephardic Zionists worldwide, Moise Gadol concluded in 1921 that the "moral and material efforts of our Sephardim [on behalf of the Zionist movement] are considered insignificant, if they are not [entirely] denied by the Ashkenazim."[87] A few years earlier, Gadol had sarcastically dubbed that organization the Federation of *Ashkenazic* Zionists (italics added).[88]

The languages employed in the FAZ and in Ashkenazic-dominant Hebrew revivalist societies justify the legitimacy of these allegations of exclusion. Aharon Ben-Eliahu, president of the Sephardic organization Ivriya, noted in 1915 that Sephardic activists had been unable to find a place within already extant Hebrew revivalist organizations "being that all [these societies] employ the Ashkenazic pronunciation."[89] In 1920, Gadol complained that the district system of the FAZ—which classified members according to district of residence rather than by organization affiliation—meant that Sephardim would always constitute a minority at Federation meetings, unable to comprehend the Yiddish spoken there.[90] The use of Yiddish in the presence of Eastern Sephardim at public Jewish meetings—including those to which Sephardim were specifically invited—met with outrage on at least one occassion. At a meeting convened in 1912 at the Educational Alliance, where representatives lapsed into Yiddish, both Nissim Behar and Joseph Gedalecia left, reportedly, because they could not understand what was being said.[91]

The question of language emerged as a central concern of American Labor Zionist youths in the 1920s. The choice of Yiddish allowed them to evade the conflicting pressures of Americanization and adoption of Palestine's emerging Jewish language. The Poalei Zion Yugt (Young

Workers of Zion), a Labor Zionist youth group and official youth wing of the American Poalei Zion Party founded in 1920, was one such organization. The platform the group adopted that year declared Yiddish as the movement's language.[92] Other American Zionists advocated Yiddish as a pragmatic tool of communication, eventually to be superseded by English or Hebrew. Still others promoted Yiddish as a type of "secular spirituality, a quasi-religious alternative that linked them to Jews everywhere."[93] Whether deliberate or not, the unconscious equation of *Ashkenaziut* with Jewish nationalism and Hebrew revivalism resulted in the isolation of Sephardim from both these causes. This evidence suggests that Ashkenazic Zionist leaders ultimately viewed the involvement of Sephardim as unimportant, given their minority status, or simply overlooked Sephardim who, as non-Ashkenazim, were the "Jews who weren't there." As reinforcement of this interpretation, consider that corporate exclusion of Sephardim was often noted in the 1910s and '20s as a global problem in Zionist organizations, as the recent research of Ricardo Djaen has shown.[94]

The responses of HIAS, the IRO, the New York Federation, the FAZ, and Hebrew-language groups are paradigmatic of Ashkenazic-run societies in the first immigrant years. In both their infrastructure and self-conception, mainstream Jewish organizations in the United States were tacitly established to accommodate not Jewish immigrants but rather Eastern European Ashkenazic immigrants.[95] The first sign of this state of affairs is that the plight of Eastern Sephardi and Mizrahi Jews usually came to the attention of mainstream Jewish organizations through the charitable initiatives of non-Jewish societies. In this way, Ashkenazic-dominant organizations were "shamed" into stretching their corporate boundaries. This allowed Eastern Sephardim to volunteer their services within the existing societies. *Kolonia* leader Albert J. Amateau, a pro-bono interpreter for HIAS at Ellis Island, recalled, "we did all that work voluntarily, to prove to the leaders of the societies that their members needed these services. We thought that would convince them. But it did no[t], or they did not want to be convinced."[96] The ultimate symptom of this communal problem was the effective exclusion of Eastern Sephardim from Zionist and Hebrew revivalist circles, whose ideal was to unite all Jews under one political or cultural ideal.

In cases of corporate exclusion, the Jewishness of Eastern Sephardi and Mizrahi Jews was never questioned. However, time and again the assistance provided them was either circumscribed or time bound, and sometimes it eventually ceased entirely (as in the case of HIAS's Oriental Bureau). In many cases, the committees of these Ashkenazic organizations explained their limited assistance (or refusal to assist) in either cryptic or contradictory ways. To again scrutinize the decision process of HIAS, how can the benefits of translating an immigrant guide to Ladino be "too problematic"? One suspects that these odd responses reflect subconscious prejudices that were never forced into logical articulation. Yes, Eastern Sephardi and Mizrahi Jews were indeed fellow Jews. But they did not possess the cultural and linguistic characteristics associated with Ashkenazic Jewry. Moreover, the cultural and linguistic attributes that made them distinctive ("Spanish," "Arabic," and "Greek" heritage) marked them in the minds of decisive Ashkenazic leaders more as gentiles than as Jews. Therefore, there was no legitimate place for them in the Jewish community.

This dynamic, particularly pronounced in the early years of Levantine Jewish immigration, is suggestive of "incomplete allowance," a concept coined by historian Adina Cimet in her study of Ashkenazic Jews in Mexico.[97] Cimet defines this term as "a specific type of political violence which limits the rights of a minority to live its cultural difference fully—politically and philosophically."[98] This unequal treatment of minority groups developed during Mexico's nationalist movement in the 1910s through 1930. It established that the *mestizo* (an individual of Spanish and indigenous ancestry or of Spanish and a mixture of other ancestries) should rule the country, to the exclusion of the rights of other groups to their own culture. This resulted in the government's ambiguous approach to nonmestizo groups, including Jews, Chinese, and the indigenous, that implicitly cast doubt on their qualifications to be included as part and parcel of Mexican society.[99] The concept of incomplete allowance, which Cimet indicates is applicable to minority groups worldwide, is relevant to Ashkenazic-dominant organizations in the United States, which, as arbiters of Jewish belonging, manipulated and determined the boundaries of communal inclusion.

Interestingly, some of these same dynamics continue today, at least residually. When the Center for Jewish History was incorporated in 1994, no thought had been given to the inclusion of a Sephardic organization. The four founding institutions were YIVO (focusing on Yiddish language and culture), the Leo Baeck Institute (devoted to German Jewish history), the American Jewish Historical Society, and the Yeshiva University Museum. Only in 1998 was the American Sephardi Federation integrated as one of the five organizations constituting the Center for Jewish History. The late president of the ASF commented that "no Center for Jewish History can be complete without the inclusion of Sephardic history."[100] But the ideal of Jewish diversity may not have been the swaying argument, as Caryn Aviv and David Shneer have recently suggested. The explicit commitment of the ASF to Zionism may have been a subtle way for the center to represent Israel, as none of the other constituent organizations do.[101]

Images of Sephardim and Mizrahim

Another way to gauge Ashkenazic-Sephardic relations is through the images of Eastern Sephardim and Mizrahim in popular culture and printed media. In general, ethnic stereotypes of one group by another are often contradictory and sometimes even diametrically opposed. It is thus not surprising that coethnic recognition failure has a flip side: the exaltation of Eastern Sephardim and Mizrahim as superior Jews. Ashkenazic Jews were often familiar with legends describing the noble ancestry and medieval accomplishments of Sephardic Jews. These legends, cultivated by generations of Sephardim over the course of the centuries, were widely disseminated among both Ashkenazim and gentiles by the turn of the twentieth century.[102]

One peculiar image associated Eastern Sephardim and Mizrahim with Jerusalem. In an article from 1910, Moise Gadol noted in his newspaper, *La America,* that Eastern Sephardim were able to obtain credit from Ashkenazim quite easily since "the Ashkenazic-Jewish world of America believes that [Sephardim] of Turkey must be very honest Jews from Jerusalem, as they [Ashkenazim] call them."[103] Two years later, he remarked that Ashkenazic Jews in the United States favorably referred to Eastern Sephardim as "the Jews of Jerusalem."[104] Similarly, a Sephardic synagogue's lively parade in the spring of 1915 stimulated Ashkenazic admiration for the Jerusalemite origins of the marchers. The Love of Peace Society of Monastir organized an elaborate procession with thousands of Ladino-, Greek-, and Arabic-speaking marchers, in honor of a newly acquired Torah scroll. Winding their way through the streets of the Lower East Side, the marchers so impressed the "hundreds and thousands of our brothers, the Ashkenazim," that the latter declared the paraders the "true Jews of Jerusalem."[105] Eastern Sephardim played an important role in circulating this legend. In 1913, a reporter for the New York tabloid *The Sun* attended a triple wedding on the Sephardic Lower East Side and discovered that some of those present "traced their lineage back to the aristocracy of Jerusalem."[106]

These references to Jerusalem aristocracy perhaps harked back to the founding myth of Jews in Iberia, who pointed to the Book of Obadiah as evidence that they descended from the southern kingdom of Judah, whose capital was Jerusalem and whose monarch was King David. The city's location within the Ottoman Empire until World War I may have reinforced the association of Sephardim with such nobility.[107]

Syrian Jewish immigrants also presented themselves as ancestrally connected to the Land of Israel. Joseph A. D. Sutton recounts that Aleppo-born peddlers, when lunching on the traditional meal of bread and oil sprinkled with *za'atar* (a mixture of dried herbs), would explain to Ashkenazim sitting nearby that they were eating "the soil of the Holy Land," an allusion to the rabbinical regard for Aleppo as part of the Land of Israel.[108]

Reflecting the opposite extremes that stereotypes often embody, "Jerusalem Jew" was in other contexts employed as opprobrium. Moise B. Soulam notified his readership of this insult in a 1915 installment of his column "Words of a Woman." Soulam reconstructed a dialogue purportedly overheard on the Lower East Side between an Ashkenazic merchant and a Sephardic immigrant woman, who had engaged in aggressive bargaining. The merchant, apparently annoyed with his prospective customer, labeled her a "Jerusalem Jew." Soulam assumed his readers to be unfamiliar with the term. "Just so you know," he explained, "the Ashkenazim take all of us Turkinos for Jews who came from Jerusalem, and I swear to you that now, when they see a woman or man bargaining a lot, they call them Jerusalem Jew, and they think they're insulting us." The irony of the insult was not lost on Soulam, who recognized that Jerusalem was a revered city for Jews of all origins. "The truth is," he commented, "Ashkenazim are crazy for Jerusalem, and it is not fair that they call us Jerusalem Jews with such disgust. But, in seeing that cursed bargaining, and not knowing how to insult us, they insult us with that word."[109]

Joseph Saltiel, a reader of Soulam's column, defended the behavior of the immigrant woman in question and stressed the necessity of comparing prices in order to avoid being cheated by exploitative merchants. He wrote angrily to the newspaper's editor, "I would like to uproot from among that ignorant mass of Ashkenazim that grave insult that is hurled at us each and every day by many of their merchants." Saltiel advised his readers to "protest the insulting behavior of the Ashkenazim until the latter come to their senses."[110]

The city of Jerusalem was susceptible to this inversion because of its association until 1917 with the Ottoman Empire, perceived in much of the Western world as a place of desolation and lack of refinement. As Soulam correctly noted, Ashkenazim also had ties to that city. That they would insult Eastern Sephardim by identifying them derogatorily with Jerusalem suggests that Ashkenazim were ambivalent about their own ancestral and religious ties to the Middle East.[111]

That this insult was hurled in the context of bargaining reveals another dynamic of ethnic stereotypes. Middle Easterners in the Western world were often negatively associated with what Walter P. Zenner has called "economic 'Levantinism,'" defined as "a pride in shrewd haggling," shared by buyers and sellers alike.[112] The irony of derisively associating Eastern Sephardim with marketplace bargaining is that Ashkenazic immigrants engaged in the same practice.[113] Stereotypes are often projections bereft of self-awareness. In other words, Ashkenazim who derided Eastern Sephardim as aggressive hagglers could not at the same moment perceive the same fault in themselves.

This projection of unflattering public behavior is also observed among Ashkenazic subethnic groups. A Galician Jewish woman described her Russian Jewish neighbors in 1906 as a "strange sort of people" who "always shout and talk with their hands,"[114] cultural markers that gentiles often attributed to Jews as a whole. The anecdote is remarkably similar to Austrian-born Bertha Pappenheim's disparagement of the Jews she encountered in Galicia in 1902, whom she observed "shouting and gesticulating" in the marketplaces.[115]

Another legend through which Ashkenazim perceived Eastern Sephardim was "Golden Age" Spain. As we have seen, the term refers to a period of cultural efflorescence among Jews in Muslim Iberia.[116] During the Enlightenment era, Central European Jews, striving for integration into Christian society while maintaining their Jewishness, harked back to medieval Iberian Jewry as a community to be emulated.

The myth of Golden Age Spain formed part of the self-image of Eastern Sephardim in the United States. In a call for communal advancement, one *kolonia* member in 1911 urged his landsmen to demonstrate that "the blood of Maimonides, [Judah Ha]Levi, [and] the Abravanels still courses through our veins."[117] Mary Frank, a librarian in the Rivington

Street branch of the New York Public Library, made special efforts in the late 1910s to familiarize herself with Lower East Side immigrant Jews. In a 1919 report on her encounters with these Jews, she remarked on the pride displayed by the Eastern Sephardim: "We are the aristocrats of the Jews," one lad had told her.[118] Benjamin Varon (1918–1994), whose family had emigrated from Salonika and settled on New York's Lower East Side the year of his birth, taught his American-born children in the 1950s that Golden Age Spain was "the most important, distinguishing characteristic of his past."[119] Marguerite Saltiel, who was born in Salonika in 1900 and also arrived in New York the year of Varon's birth, informed her American-born children that "our roots indicated royal blood, as heirs *de reyes y reinas* in medieval Spain."[120]

Eastern Sephardim soon discovered that their Ashkenazic coreligionists were well acquainted with the myth of Golden Age Spain. Unfortunately, the myth did not always reflect well on Eastern Sephardim because it contrasted so starkly with their transplanted community, struggling with the usual challenges that new immigrants face. Meyer Berlin, a Polish-born rabbi,[121] succinctly demonstrated the deficiency of Golden Age Spain as a usable past. In an article published in 1917 in a New York Hebrew-language weekly, Berlin observed,

> In every place in which we, the Ashkenazim, chance upon Sephardim . . . they make a special impression upon us. This impression is a feeling of respect, of immediate admiration, a feeling of astonishment and, in the end, at times, also humiliation. Right away, they awaken in us a feeling of awe . . . , of admiration for the past. We see in them the descendants of the sages of the Golden Age, the Spanish period, which added a splendorous chapter to the history of our spiritual lives. In the end, when we draw nearer to them, when we contemplate their characteristics and their spiritual countenance, they awaken in us a feeling of distress, the same feeling evoked in us by a man who has lost all of his possessions.[122]

Exactly twenty years later, Philip A. Langh, rabbi of a Conservative congregation in Seattle, Washington, offered a similar analogy. During a synagogue event memorializing the Iberian Jewish exegete Isaac Abravanel, Langh delivered a sermon about a guest invited to dinner in a magnificent palace where only bread and water was served. The host explained that the palace was his inheritance but that bread and water were his only earnings. Langh specified that the parable was meant to represent contemporary Sephardic civilization, which possessed "a glorious inheritance but . . . little to offer of its own creation."[123] Marc D. Angel, spiritual leader of New York's Congregation Shearith Israel, recalls similar rhetoric from his childhood years in Seattle. Angel's Ashkenazic acquaintances would demand, "What have the Sephardim done since 1492? Whom have you produced? In all honesty, can your culture compare in any way with Vilna or Lodz or some other place?"[124]

Those who bore the brunt of this criticism could not have realized that this rhetoric reflected historiographical constructs—modern interpretations of the Jewish past that would be reassessed in later generations. These Ashkenazic critics were drawing on a long tradition of the Ottoman Empire as the "sick man of Europe," which considered the Jewish community as an infected body part. This tradition was created in part by Western travelers. A North American visitor to Istanbul described Sephardic Jews in 1835 as follows:

> I think it will hardly be denied that the Jewish nation in Turkey is in a complete state of indigence, as is sufficiently proved by the mean and vile employments to which individuals devote themselves. . . . There is no appearance of comfort, no appearance of competency among them; everything, where sight and smell are concerned, among them is extremely disgusting, and passing through their quarters, the sounds that assail the ears prove that they are a querulous race, destitute of domestic peace and comfort.[125]

This tradition of disparagement is evocative of the Christian idea of "fallen" Jews. Though once the chosen people of God, Jews became downtrodden as a result of their rejection of Christ and the Christian Bible. James Finn, in his 1841 history on Iberian Jews, applied this view to historiography when he declared Jews a "miraculous people" who "still command the attention of the world even in their fallen state."[126] Ashkenazim, in their simultaneous disdain and awe for Eastern Sephardim, perhaps subconsciously adopted this traditional anti-Semitic ideology.

How did Eastern Sephardim respond to this public denigration? Many internalized it. A contributor to *La America* identified as "Emiliana" noted in 1911,

> If we consider the intellectual and material situation of our brothers today and compare it with that of our forefathers established in the Orient upon their exodus from Spain, we shall see how much we have ret-

rograded, ... despite the liberty, tolerance, and protection offered by the Sultans. Although we bear their names, we are unfortunately no longer of those Spanish Jews who were the glory of their contemporaries, who marked our history with a page of gold. We are no longer of those Jews who possessed the courage to brave death for the sake of preserving their [religious] ideal."[127]

Like "Emiliana," Sephardic intellectual Maír José Benardete dismissed the Ottoman Sephardic legacy. Eastern Sephardim, he commented in the early 1950s, "retain an exemplary quality not so much derived from their own merit but from remote sources, ... their uninterrupted ascension from Peninsular glories." Only their preservation of *romances*—romantic ballads of medieval Spain—saved them from being "totally devoid of interest and significance for Hispanic letters and Jewish folkways."[128]

Eerily echoing the observations of rabbis Langh and Berlin before him, *kolonia* leader Albert Matarasso noted sometime before 1948, "despite the fact that our fathers were rich, we are dying of hunger. The accomplishments of the past cannot fill our stomach. The renown of yesterday cannot conserve the purity and nobility of our name today."[129]

Another response was the creation of a counter-myth emphasizing the glories of Ottoman Jewish history. Harry S. Mazal, secretary of the La Luz club, suggested that ancestral nobility and anti-Jewish oppression in Iberia had seasoned Ottoman Jews for survival and commercial accomplishments. In a letter to the editor of the *American Weekly Jewish News*, he pointed out that it was "a Sephardi who first introduced the Turkish tobacco industry in America, which gives work to thousands of laborers, and today the mostly [most] consumed brand of Turkish cigarette bears the name of that Sephardi."[130] Ben-Sion Behar, in a lengthy Ladino article in 1915, noted that in Egypt "the stock exchange as well as all commerce are largely in the power of Sephardim." He also remarked that despite the inferior state of the schools in Turkey, the important government officials there were Sephardic rabbis, lawyers, and judges, proof of "our ancient ability and intelligence."[131]

Like the myth of Golden Age Spain, this counter-myth found its precedents in historiography. One example is Maurice H. Harris's history on medieval Jews, published in 1916.[132] The British-born author's brief reference to Eastern Sephardim exalted those who, despite exile and impoverishment, "lost naught of their dignity of bearing or their cultured manners, which centuries of distinction had given them." Harris also dubbed

Ladino as a "half sacred" language and praised Sephardic Jews for their leadership capacity in Ottoman lands.[133] In the Ottoman "Golden Age" myth, Muslims played an important symbolic role, serving as a contrast to the achievements of Eastern Sephardim. Lady Mary Wortley Montague, who traveled to Adrianople in the 1810s, commented on the city's prosperous Jewish community and its important role in economic life and contrasted Jewish industry with the indolence of Muslim Turks:

> I observed most of the rich tradesmen were Jews. That people are in incredible power in this country. They have many privileges above all the natural Turks themselves, and have formed a very considerable commonwealth here, being judged by their own laws. They have drawn the whole trade of the empire in their hands, partly by the idle temper and want of industry in the Turks. Every pasha has his Jew who is his homme d'affaires; he is let into all his secrets and does all his business.... They are the physician, the stewards, and the interpreters of all the great men.[134]

Try as they might, Eastern Sephardim could not have rehabilitated their popular image through an Ottoman Golden Age. A Sephardic accomplishment myth for the Ottoman Empire did not strike a chord of familiarity among most Ashkenazim, nor among most Sephardim in America, for that matter. Nor were these achievements claimed as part of the legacy of the entire Jewish people, unlike the Spanish Golden Age. Instead, stereotypes highlighted the "fatalism and inertia" of Ottoman Sephardim and their "defective" Jewish nationalism, underscored by a tendency to assimilate "anywhere they go."[135] In the U.S. media, images of the Ottoman Empire as the "sick man of Europe" overpowered historical memories of Judeo-Ottoman civilization in all its splendor. In addition, the United States, a predominantly Christian country, looked askance at Islamic societies.

The self-representation of Levantine Jews in the Anglo-American and Anglo-Jewish press did not always produce the desired results. Interestingly, two of the most controversial portrayals of Levantine Jews were penned by immigrants whose full belonging in the Levantine Jewish community was ambiguous. Both created a sensation in the Eastern Sephardic community because they violated the unspoken rule regarding the airing of "dirty laundry" before a broader public.[136] In 1915, Moise Gadol took Joseph Gedalecia to task for his comments published in the Yiddish paper *Der Feder* in June of that year. According to Gadol,

Gedalecia "discredits to the nth degree the honor of our entire colony in front of all of our brothers, the Ashkenazim."[137] The article, which Gadol reproduced in Ladino in the next issue of his paper, depicted Levantine Jewish immigrants as lacking any viable trade or profession and being unable to unite on account of their diverse native languages. Gadol was primarily concerned that Ashkenazic readers would conclude "that we are elements of public charge being that, according to [Gedalecia], there is not one who can honestly support himself, they don't practice any trade, and not one is in a situation of independent self-support."[138]

Gadol also worried that the community's reputation would lead to restrictions on the immigration of "our people" to the country.[139] In another article in the same issue of his paper, he fretted that the use of the term "Oriental" to describe Eastern Sephardim would cause immigrant officials to confuse them with Asians, "against whom America manifests its most intense hatred."[140] He was no doubt aware of the Chinese Exclusion Act (1882) and subsequent bills that were vetoed but eventually led to the restrictive immigration laws of 1917 through 1924.[141]

The vitriol that Gadol reserved for Gedalecia (as a form of retaliation, he recommended excommunication) may have had something to do with Gedalecia's ambiguous ethnic background. Gadol advised his readers that "we should absolutely distance this gentleman from among our Sephardim and tell him that his place should be among his best brothers, the Ashkenazim, given that he does not know our languages, customs, or character."[142] Gadol insisted that Gedalecia should not "be at the head of our 20,000 Sephardim without being elected by our people." Alluding to Gedalecia's position as head of the Federation of Oriental Jews, Gadol added that "it would be an embarrassment for the 20,000 Sephardim to allow ourselves to be carried around by the nose by a Tudesko [Ashkenazic Jew] like Gedalecia. We have already told him that we don't want him anymore! He should go with the Tudeskos!"[143]

In reality, Gedalecia's ethnic makeup was not as clear as Gadol would have liked to believe. Joseph M. Papo, who personally solicited biographies of *kolonia* leaders, identifies Gedalecia, a native of Istanbul, as of Sephardic ancestry on his father's side and of Sephardic-Ashkenazic extraction on his mother's. Gedalecia's own direct descendants remain uncertain of his precise subethnic background.[144] Gedalecia had attended a German-Jewish school, was married to a Russian Ashkenazic immigrant, and was hence very involved in the Ashkenazic community. He was a member of the aforementioned Yiddish- and English-speaking Ori-

Joseph Gedalecia and family. Undated photograph of Joseph Gedalecia, Sarah Levy Gedalecia, and Edmond Gedalecia. Courtesy of David Gedalecia.

ental Progressive Society, a Levantine Jewish organization whose nearly sixty members in 1912 were almost all Ashkenazim from the Ottoman Empire. Gedalecia's fluency in German and Yiddish, extensive affiliation with and full acceptance by the Ashkenazic community, as well as his ignorance of Ladino,[145] cast suspicion on him as both a Sephardic leader and colony member.

The conflict between Gedalecia and Gadol may have also had much to do with age at immigration and length of sojourn in the United States. Having arrived in America in 1889 at the tender age of thirteen,[146] Gedalecia spent some of his formative years in his adoptive land. By the time he locked horns with Gadol, he had lived in the county for over twenty-five years and had integrated himself into the Ashkenazic community. Before assuming the presidency of the Federation of Oriental Jews, in fact, Gedalecia had served on the staff of the Kehilla.[147] By contrast, Gadol, who was forty-one in 1915, had resided in America for only five years.

Another dividing line was type of leadership: newspaper man versus communal leader. Gadol's profile matches that of most Ladino press editors in that he came of age in his native land and learned his trade abroad. Gedalecia's profile more closely approximated that of many leaders of Ashkenazic federations, who arrived in the country at a young age and received some formative education here. Jacob Carlinger, who headed the Russian-Polish Federation, arrived at age twelve; Samuel Goldstein of the Romanian Federation, at age fourteen; Pierre Siegelstein of the American Union of Roumanian Jews, at fifteen or sixteen; Bernard Semel, president of the Federation of Galician and Bucovinean Jews, at fourteen; and Samuel Margoshes of the Galician Federation, at age eighteen.[148]

It would be incorrect to assume that the conflict between Gedalecia and the pugnacious Gadol was driven solely by personality differences, for in 1916 Gedalecia was taken to task by the socialist tabloid *La Bos del Pueblo*. Again, the issue consisted of a number of articles published in the Yiddish press. The editors of *La Bos del Pueblo* accused Gedalecia of "denigrating" "our element in America."[149] Unfortunately, the Passover holidays curtailed the next issue of the newspaper from eight to four pages, and the storyline was lost. Although details of this second disagreement are unavailable, it is significant that two widely differing tabloids, the religiously conservative *La America* and the socialist *La Bos del Pueblo*, shared the same concern about Gedalecia's contributions. This suggests that the editors of Ladino tabloids, whatever their ideological leanings and personalities, envisioned their role as public advocates of the Levantine Jewish colony. Although all felt free to censure their community privately, within the pages of their respective publications, their larger public duty was to defend the honor of the *kolonia*.

Another ethnically ambiguous leader who provoked much internal controversy was Samuel M. Auerbach. Also born in Istanbul, Auerbach had immigrated to the United States in 1907 and served as a social worker and investigator at a number of institutions, including the Bureau of Industries and Immigration and the New York State Department of Labor.[150] Auerbach's last name suggests an Ashkenazic ethnicity, and his membership in the Oriental Progressive Club indicates his identification with the Levantine Jewish community.[151]

Auerbach's article "The Levantine Jews," published in the *Immigrants in America Review*, is striking in that, were readers unaware of the author's background, they would assume that the article was written by a non-Levantine Jew. Auerbach was perhaps cognizant of this probability when he decided to adopt the voice of an outsider unfamiliar with Levantine Jewish cultures.[152] In this voice, he wondered about the identity of the "strangers" he glimpsed sitting at coffeehouses, smoking "strange-looking waterpipes," and imbibing "dark liquid from tiny cups." Auerbach depicts Lower East Side Sephardim in caricature-like form, describing their "strange languages, customs, manners and traditions."[153]

Auerbach's dramatization of Levantine Jewish customs and mores reflects a journalistic tendency to sensationalize, as noted by Maurice Nessim. In an August 1916 issue of *La Bos del Pueblo*, Nessim published a strident refutation of Auerbach's article, stating that "many passages of the article do not correspond with reality." "Mr. Auerbach tried to make our element stand out so much and attract the attention of our neighbors to us that as a result," Nessim observed, "he made us appear strange, bizarre, and ridiculous."[154] *La Bos del Pueblo* serialized Auerbach's article, both in Ladino translation and in the original, under the English heading "A Wrong Interpretation of the Life of the Sephardim Jews."[155] For the benefit of his English-speaking readers, Nessim also published an editorial in English in that same newspaper in which he questioned Auerbach's qualifications as a commentator on Eastern Sephardim. Noticeably avoiding any reference to Auerbach's non-Sephardic background, Nessim commented, "Since he has been in this country, he has not kept in touch with our people."[156]

Perhaps it was Nessim's socialist background that inhibited him from explicitly challenging Auerbach's authority on ethnic grounds. In keeping with Marxist ideology, Nessim may have equated ethnic affiliation with bourgeois values. Whatever Nessim's allegations, Auerbach had an entirely different self-perception. "I feel that I am, by birth and experience," he insisted a few months later, "competent to speak authoritatively about any subject affecting Oriental Jews." "During the past nine years," he stated, with an implicit nod toward Nessim, "I have been in close touch with our Oriental Jewish community in this city, and interested myself in a great measure toward studying and solving some of their problems."[157]

Aside from the obviously irksome adjectives "strange, bizarre, and ridiculous," what precisely was "wrong" with Auerbach's descriptions of Eastern Sephardim? Its opening paragraph depicted Sephardim in their leisure activities (playing backgammon, imbibing Turkish coffee, and smoking waterpipes). Although "picturesque," to borrow a term often used to describe immigrants in the 1910s, these descriptions evoked the stereotype of the indolent "Oriental," reinforcing, as Nessim noted, images of lethargy and idleness (rather than resourcefulness and industry). Moreover, many Eastern Sephardic leaders who had graduated from the Alliance Israélite Universelle may have balked at the mores of non-Western-educated Jews.

The cultural symbols that Auerbach highlighted were visually the most easily identifiable characteristics of the new arrivals. These symbols of ethnicity, however, did not reflect their Jewishness and had not defined Levantine Jews in their homelands. In the Old Country, Eastern Sephardic immigrants identified themselves according to their religion and cities or villages of birth, and they possessed their own conceptions of their regional distinctions.[158] Outsiders in the United States, in contrast, viewed these immigrants as a Near Eastern conglomerate and sought to attach to them distinguishing characteristics not specific to Jewish culture.[159] Auerbach's depiction could only exacerbate the coethnic recognition failure that so plagued colony members.

The Auerbach controversy raged for months. In October 1916, upon the republication of Auerbach's "harmful article" in the *Jewish Immigration Bulletin*, the official organ of the Hebrew Immigrant Aid Society, *La Bos del Pueblo* expressed surprise that the society would "allow to pass [an] article injurious to our element." The journalist further chastised the editor for failing to approach the editorial offices for a candid and informed interview.[160]

Interestingly, Gedalecia's and Auerbach's journalism rhetorically approximates that of Ashkenazic journalists born in Eastern Europe. One of these, Joseph Kotovski, a.k.a. Marion Golde, was a reporter for the *American Weekly Jewish News*. In 1918, Kotovski covered a story on Eastern Sephardic immigrants in New York. He had personally visited the editorial offices of *La Bos del Pueblo* beforehand to interview editor Maurice Nessim. The resulting article, in Nessim's opinion, was "injurious." Under the sensational title of "Children of the Inquisition," Kotovski described the Ladino language as an "outlandish speech" and depicted Eastern Sephardim as "sluggish in temperament, slow in thought, and non-progressive."[161] Kotovski based his article not on his interview with Nessim but rather on an extensive meeting he had with an anonymous young man whom he met in "a corner of a cafe on Eldridge street," in whose voice the bulk of the article is written.[162] The essential point of the article was that Sephardim "left Spain branded with the scars of their martyrdom" and "acquired the characteristics of the people among whom we lived," specifically, the "indolence" of the Turks.[163]

Maurice Nessim expressed his sense of betrayal in a front-page editorial of his newspaper:

> Mr. Kotovski begged us to be impartial and to tell him the good and the bad of our colony. Being certain that our good qualities would outdo our defects, we told him all that was happening. What was our surprise when last week we read in the [*American Weekly*] *Jewish News* an article filled with insults against us! To be frank, we should admit that a part of the assertions were fair, but they were also exaggerated and told very partially. The reporter had the fantasy of exposing only the bad points of our colony, and ignored totally the good that we had told him.[164]

What is most interesting here is that Nessim agreed with some of Kotovski's depictions. This would suggest that editors of the Ladino press were arguing with Ashkenazic journalists not necessarily over facts but rather over emphasis and tone. In short, they objected to the extreme representations inherent in stereotypes.

Maurice Nessim was especially horrified that both the masthead of his paper and his photograph appeared on the first page of "Children of the Inquisition." His letter of protest in English appeared in the next issue of the *American Weekly Jewish News* and also on the front page of his tabloid.

> I wonder if you can realize the shock that the article "The [sic] Children of the Inquisition," by Marion Golde, published in your valuable magazine last week, produced upon the Sephardic community in America. It was one of those blows that the Jewish press aims at us every now and then. It threw our people into a turmoil, and, had I not interfered, you would have been overwhelmed with a storm of protests.... I want to protest, not only against Marion Golde, but also against that clique of Jewish writers whose trick it is to sneer at our people, for their selfish purposes.[165]

Several letters, representing the "storm of protests" that Kotovski provoked, were published in both the *American Weekly Jewish News* and in *La Bos del Pueblo*. The letters published in the former newspaper stressed ancestral heroism and the achievements of the Sephardim during their relatively short sojourn in the United States.[166] But the most insightful (and biting) responses to Kotovski were reserved for the Ladino press. A letter of protest submitted under the pseudonym "Sefaradí" accused the Ashkenazic journalist of denigrating Eastern Sephardim in order to achieve his goal, "which is that of leaving a great name of a literary writer."[167] León Yafo claimed that the defects the journalist perceived in Sephardic newcomers were the same that plagued Ashkenazic immigrants. To highlight Kotovki's hypocrisy, Yafo applied the Ladino proverb "the camel doesn't look at his own hump, but rather ... at the hump of the camel in front of him."[168] Yafo unwittingly pinpointed a key attribute of the stereotype and its agent: lack of self-awareness. One recurring critique reflected in Kotovski's article and elsewhere was that Eastern Sephardim clung too tenaciously to their regional origins and were thus unable to achieve communal unity.[169] This criticism conveniently ignored the fact that Ashkenazic immigrants suffered from the same problem. Ashkenazic authors who dispensed directives for proper organizational administration claimed from the turn of the century that Eastern European Jews lacked managerial know-how.[170]

These letters, published in the Ladino press, triggered an internal debate about verbal strategies of self-defense.[171] One of them, submitted by Maurice Nessim, helps to explain the sensitivity of Eastern Sephardim to public misrepresentation. "There isn't an Ashkenazic periodical that hasn't profited from our communal weakness by insulting us shamelessly and to our greatest detriment," Nessim wrote. "The merchants also do not fail to contribute to this stain. There doesn't pass a day when our women are not insulted on Orchard Street and in Harlem because of the fact that we are Sephardim."[172]

All these letters published in *La Bos del Pueblo* demonstrate that the Ladino press was a much safer forum for open discussion among Eastern Sephardic immigrants than was the English-language press. In the columns of Ladino newspapers, *kolonia* members felt freer to express their ire against Ashkenazim and disagree about methods of self-defense. This candid aspect of the Ladino press is generally characteristic of other foreign-language American Jewish tabloids that were, as Jonathan D. Sarna notes, "often bolder and more critical of America and American Jewish life than English-language ones."[173] This analysis provides yet another reason to focus on the Ladino press and other public fora where conversational privacy was assumed.

Toward a Rapprochement

The dynamics of coethnic recognition failure, corporate exclusion, and Sephardic stereotypes should not overshadow the cooperation that developed between Ashkenazim and Eastern Sephardim since the early years of immigration.[174] Indeed, in many cases there is no evidence of any of these divisive phenomena. These examples demonstrate that Eastern Sephardim and Ashkenazim were capable of fruitful interaction in a wide variety of mutual endeavors.

Some of the earliest signs of cooperation occurred during the founding of immigrant societies. The Rhodes League of Brothers Aid Society, a mutual-aid organization founded in 1910, received its charter thanks to four established Ashkenazim, friends of Eastern Sephardim, who were already American citizens. Their names were listed as founding members for the charter but served only as "dummies." According to state legislation, two-thirds of the society's directors had to be American citizens, and the two founders from Rhodes were not.[175] So, too, in the case of the Filo Center, founded in 1918 by a group of Eastern Sephardim in Harlem who sought to establish a meeting place to "develop and exchange ideas, promote cultural and philanthropic causes, and foster friendly and social relations among themselves." They obtained their charter in 1920 when an Ashkenazic attorney named Louis Rosett applied for one.[176] These relationships suggest not only sincere friendship but also an appreciation for Eastern Sephardic communal life.

For all its polemics, the Ladino press is replete with examples of mutual respect and joint endeavors motivated by both pragmatism and idealism. In 1911, J. Farhi suggested that *La America* undertake the rapprochement of the two groups so that Sephardim would be able to make "good business" and secure "better paying and more honest positions."[177] The achievement of such a rapprochement was Moise Gadol's main mission. In numerous articles printed in his paper, he encouraged Eastern Sephardim to learn both English and Yiddish in order to secure employment more easily. He also urged Ashkenazim in commerce and industry to employ Levantine Jews and New York Yiddish journalists to take interest in Sephardic issues.[178] With the hope of attracting an Ashkenazic readership, Gadol published in *La America* a series of articles in Yiddish entitled "Tsu dem Yiddishen," a survey of the history of the Ottoman Empire and its Sephardim, and English-Yiddish-Ladino conversational lexicons.[179]

The Ashkenazic press took notice of *La America* shortly after it debuted in late 1910. The following year a number of "important articles" appeared in the New York Ashkenazic newspapers, especially in *Der Yidishe Tagblatt*. Moise Gadol noted with pleasure that thanks to this coverage, "the entire Ashkenazic Jewish world knows about this [element of] our Jews, who were until now unknown ... and will in the future be looked upon with a good eye."[180] Gadol, who partly due to his fluency in German could also speak and read Yiddish, was a lively respondent to articles on Sephardim appearing in the Yiddish press.

Gadol also sought to unite Jews under the common banner of Jewish nationalism. During the Hebrew year 5673 (coinciding with the years 1912–1913), he printed bilingual Rosh Hashanah (Jewish New Year) greeting cards, encouraging Sephardim and Ashkenazim to "exchange greetings in the spirit of cementing the bond of brotherhood."[181] The card, with the Ladino caption "the union of Israel" (and in Yiddish, "the unity of all Jews"), declared in Ladino, "We, all the Sephardic Jews of the countries of the Orient, convene with the Ashkenazic Jews of the entire world and clasp hands of brotherhood for our holy promise to labor in common agreement for our national Jewish ideal and to help each other in every respect."[182]

Thanks to his fluency in Yiddish and English, Gadol served as an effective Sephardic spokesman to both the Ashkenazic and non-Jewish world. He urged the Union of Orthodox Jewish Congregations of America to involve itself more with Sephardim and negotiated with the New York Kehillah, HIAS, and numerous other organizations.[183] Among the earliest successes toward Sephardic integration was the decision of Congregation Peace and Brotherhood of Monastir and the Union and Peace Society to join New York's Kehillah in 1911. By 1913, all but two Eastern Sephardic societies had officialized their affiliation with that Ashkenazic communal organization.[184] They perhaps responded to the Kehillah's aggressive efforts in 1909 and 1910 to recruit all unaffiliated Jewish societies.[185]

Eastern Sephardim, in turn, encouraged Ashkenazic leaders to participate in their events. Zionist gatherings were among the most successful in achieving an integrated audience. The Sephardic Zionist Union, led by Moise Gadol, organized an evening celebration for Hanukah in 1914. Over one thousand attended, including some one hundred Ashkenazim.[186] During World War I, Louis Lipsky, Eliezer Ben-Yehuda, and his son, Ittamar Ben-Avi, were frequent guest speakers at the Sephardic

Zionist Union. Ashkenazic endorsement of Sephardic Zionist activities represented a definitive and public recognition of both the Jewishness of Sephardim and their commitment to Jewish nationalist causes.

The Ashkenazic community cultivated its own leaders who advocated reconciliation between the two groups. Rabbi Dr. Bernard Drachman, president of the Union of Orthodox Jewish Congregations, was an ideal intermediary given his knowledge of Spanish. One of Drachman's main motivations in studying that language had been his desire to communicate with Eastern Sephardim.[187] In his 1948 memoir, Drachman reminisced, "I was greatly interested in these new brethren. I admired their Jewish loyalty—their great majority was strictly observant of their religious traditions—I respected the devout and decorous manner of their worship, I loved their sonorous and melodious pronunciation of the Hebrew and their dignified and courtly demeanor suggestive of the Orient and, remotely, of medieval Castile."[188] Drachman advocated the Sephardic cause in the Ashkenazic community, served as an intermediary between Congregation Shearith Israel and Eastern Sephardim, and on occasion was asked to help settle disputes between various Sephardic leaders.[189]

Knowledge of Ladino helped Ashkenazim build commercial bridges as well. In 1916, Hayim Hausdorff advertised his new Harlem pharmacy as a "Spanish Pharmacy." Hausdorff's advertisement described him as "a native of Jerusalem who can speak Judeo-Spanish well."[190] Meir London's matsah factory on Grand Street also catered to a Sephardic clientele.[191] Some Ashkenazim, stimulated by their knowledge of modern Spanish, corresponded with the editors of the Ladino press and even subscribed. In 1915 a Bureau of Jewish Education researcher named Max Schurman sent a letter to *El Progreso* indicating that with his modest knowledge of Spanish he was able to read that Ladino newspaper with some effort and that he appreciated the editors' "toilsome mission."[192]

The progressive breakdown of social provincialism among Eastern Sephardim, especially through intramarriage, opened the doors to Ashkenazic membership in Eastern Sephardic communal organizations. At some point, every such society began to admit Jews regardless of subethnic background. In 1932 the Rhodes mutual-aid society, with headquarters on Forsythe and Rivington streets, decided to admit all Jewish men married to Sephardic women "so that our Ashkenazim [sic] brothers could become part of us."[193] Abravanel, the Sephardic Masonic lodge founded in the 1930s, allowed non-Sephardim (including non-Jews) to join.¹⁹⁴ The Chios Brotherhood Society, organized in 1917, appointed an Ashkenazic Jew, Louis Weinman, as a member of the Constitution Revision Committee and as second vice president in the late 1960s.¹⁹⁵ Statistics concretize the extent of communal integration. Nearly all Sephardim who immigrated in the early twentieth century married fellow Sephardim; by the third generation, intramarriage "had become the rule, rather than the exception." Hayyim Cohen found in the early 1970s that 72 percent of second-generation Sephardim had married non-Sephardic women; that figure jumped to 90 percent in the third and fourth generations.¹⁹⁶

One notable exception to this high rate of intramarriage among non-Ashkenazic Jews is the Syrian community of Brooklyn. Since their immigration in the early twentieth century, Syrian Jews have by and large successfully resisted extracommunal marriage, whether with Ashkenazim, gentiles, or converts to Judaism. Unlike their Balkan and Turkish brethren, Syrians consistently established their own Jewish day schools and, when public education became mandatory, afterschool programs that maintained their children within the traditional cultural orbit.¹⁹⁷ In the 1960s, 90 percent of New York Syrian Jews enrolled their children in *yeshivot* and *Talmudei Torah,* and by the next decade Syrian Jews were considered "the best organized Sephardi-Eastern Jewish community in the U.S.A." both materially and spiritually.¹⁹⁸

The central reason for this success was the presence of a strong rabbinical leadership representing insular Old Country values and, more importantly, the official acceptance of such values by all Syrian Jewish organizations. The relative rarity of intramarriage and almost nonexistent out-marriage can be traced to a 1935 decree in Hebrew signed by five Syrian rabbis in Bensonhurst, ratified in 1942 and 1946 and reaffirmed in 1972 and 1984. Joseph A. D. Sutton writes, "Such marriages would not be accepted under any circumstance, even when the non-Jewish partner had converted to Judaism; even if the conversion was not for the purpose of facilitating marriage." A man accepting a gentile or converted spouse would be effectively excommunicated, deprived of religious honors in the synagogue, forbidden burial in the communal cemetery, and his children barred from Syrian schools and rejected as legitimate marriage partners.¹⁹⁹ The edict was most recently ratified in 2006 (this time by 225 rabbinical and lay leaders), and the community's rabbis are expected to discuss it from the pulpit at least once yearly.²⁰⁰

Cooperation between Ashkenazim and both Eastern Sephardim and Syrian Jews gradually intensified, particularly after World War II, which broke down many of the old barriers between various ethnic communities. Emblematic is the leadership positions that Ashkenazic rabbis accepted in non-Ashkenazic congregations. Rabbi Arnold B. Marans served eight years as rabbi of the United Sephardim of Brooklyn before accepting a position as spiritual leader in the Conservative and newly founded Sephardic Temple of Cedarhurst, Long Island, in 1963. Marans's congregation was formed by young men from New York's Monastir-origin community who had come into contact with the conservative rabbinate during their military service. In order to preserve the traditions of his congregants, Marans learned about their heritage and actively tried to foster Sephardic traditions among younger members.[201] Similarly, in 1942 the Syrian Jewish community of Brooklyn hired Abraham Hecht, an Ashkenazic rabbi with connections to the Lubavitcher movement, to serve as assistant rabbi to the community's chief rabbi, Jerusalem-born Joseph Kassin. Hecht, who served for twenty-five years, learned Syrian Jewish customs and adopted the community's pronunciation of Hebrew.[202] The move to hire Hecht was organized by a group of first-generation American-born men who regarded the traditional Syrian synagogue and its religious leadership as inflexible and outmoded, particularly the Shabbat sermons delivered in Arabic.[203] The Balkan Sephardic congregation of Los Angeles was served by the Ashkenazic rabbi Jacob Ott, and in Seattle, William Greenberg presided over the Rhodes congregation.[204] These congregations are perhaps the only corporate examples of Ashkenazic adoption of Eastern Sephardi and Mizrahi culture in the United States.

The Legacy of Ashkenazic-Sephardic Relations

Given the development of such cooperation, it would be reasonable to assume that coethnic recognition failure is no longer a dynamic in Ashkenazic-Sephardic relations. The breakdown of Jewish communal insularity during World War II and the immense cultural influence of the State of Israel, whose Jewish population was until recently mostly non-Ashkenazic, would also support this assumption. But, in fact, the end of this phenomenon is difficult to pinpoint in time.

Albert Daniel Saporta, a native of Salonika living in New York, had met "many Ashkenazic Jews who never had heard of a Jew of Spanish descent." Sometime during the 1940s, one of his business associates was certain that Saporta was "trying to assume the Jewish religion for mysterious reasons" and subjected him to the proverbial Hebrew reading test. Saporta recalls,

> He got up from his seat at the bench and walked to a shelf and getting hold of a tiny bible he proceeded to make me read the first page. I am not a bible expert but I knew by heart the first paragraph of it and I recited to him "Bereshit bara elohim et ashamayim ve et haarets," and from that moment on his whole mien changed. He offered me a chair next to him and he continued with his work asking me all kinds of questions. It was evident that he had met for the first time a Jew of my kind and he was pleased with what I told him.[205]

Similarly, Leonard Gold, a college student from Cleveland, Ohio, admitted in 1949 that he had for many years "thought that . . . as long as I knew Yiddish . . . I could hold a coherent conversation with any Jew whom I would meet."[206] Feminist scholar Melanie Kaye/Kantrowitz, who came of age in New York in the 1950s and early '60s, never heard the term "Ashkenazic" growing up and equated the Yiddish culture of her grandparents with Jewishness.[207] When Indian-born Rachel Wahba, a Jew of Iraqi and Egyptian origin, arrived in Los Angeles in 1964, she found Ashkenazic Jews questioning whether she was "really Jewish."[208] As late as the mid-1970s a young Sephardic Jew in Los Angeles testified that Ashkenazim often asked him "how I can be Jewish if I don't speak Jewish."[209]

The increasing ancestral diversity of the American Jewish community in recent years has ensured the continuation of coethnic recognition failure as a significant force. "Jews of Color," who trace their non-Ashkenazic ancestry to conversion, inter- and intramarriage, or adoption, suggest that many Ashkenazic Jews are "generally unaware of Jewish multiculturalism."[210] Like the Eastern Sephardi and Mizrahi Jews considered in this study, "Jews of Color" are often asked to explain or "prove" their Jewishness.[211]

Images of Eastern Sephardi and Mizrahi Jews are also reminiscent of times past. A popular history of American Jewry, published in 1992 and spanning nearly one thousand pages, devotes a scant three pages to non-Ashkenazim in the early twentieth century. In these pages, Eastern Sephardic immigrants are noted for their "cultural deprivation," "communal disunity," and the effects of the "atrophy of economic and cultural resources" that reigned in their native lands. The same author tells us that alcoholism, prostitution, and wife abandonment were "far more extensive among them than among Ashkenazic immigrants." Ladino newspaper editor Moise Gadol, we read, was "in no sense comparable to Abraham Cahan of the *Forverts*." And "efforts to formulate a single Sephardic prayer book" came to naught.[212] This approach is eerily reminiscent of the sensationalist journalism that mortified Eastern Sephardic immigrants nearly one hundred years ago. With a little tweaking, these observations might have appeared in an Anglo-American or Anglo-Jewish newspaper from the 1910s or '20s.

It may be useful to ask again, what is "wrong" with these depictions? First of all, these remarks are not placed in relational context. If they had been, readers would also note that Ashkenazic Jews of the same period failed to achieve communal and ritual unity. The New York Kehilla, a cooperative endeavor of Germanic and Eastern European Jews, collapsed in 1922 after it failed to confederate.[213] Another tendency is to impressionistically appraise the vices of Eastern Sephardim as more extreme than those of Ashkenazic immigrants, while their accomplishments never attain the same level. Finally, the third problem is simply historical inaccuracy. Regarding Sephardic prostitution, we do not learn from which comparative study the author draws, but it certainly was not the report of Alice Davis Menken, who in 1922 declared that out of some eight thousand Jewish women during the previous ten years, "no Sephardic Jewish women have been arraigned in the Women's court."[214] According to this report, prostitution was a decidedly Ashkenazic problem: in the mid-1910s some 18 percent of the women charged with prostitution were Jewish (read: Ashkenazic).[215] Nor, apparently, is the author aware of the inclusive Sephardic prayer rite (*nusach*) that David de Sola Pool developed in the 1930s, now in its twelfth impression (1997).

Another tendency, also evocative of early-twentieth-century reportage, is to portray Eastern Sephardim and Mizrahim as bizarre or ridiculous in their differences. One example, surprisingly, comes from the field of anthropology. The author, who "discloses" his New York Ashkenazic roots in the introduction to his study of world Jewry, describes Yemeni rites of passage—complete with slaughtered animals and animal-skin diapers—as "exotic" but assures his readers that these Jews otherwise maintained all "standard Jewish practices."[216] Similarly, a recent historical survey of Jewish communities in Africa and Asia liberally employs the adjective "exotic," prominently displayed in its title.[217] Such studies unconsciously present Ashkenazic culture as a touchstone against which other Jewish communities are qualified and understood. In describing these communities as "isolated from the major centers of Jewish civilization,"[218] they ignore the fact that centers of Jewish civilization have periodically migrated over the centuries. Moreover, these studies assume the existence of an objective "normative Judaism" to which all these communities in theory should conform in order to assert Jewish belonging.[219] As divergent from the "norm," Levantine Jews appear so "strange" that their Jewish belonging or authenticity is tacitly, if not consciously, questioned.

Non-Jewish authors have perpetuated similar images. A renowned Polish American professor of Middle East politics once described Yemeni Jewish immigrants in the new State of Israel as "a backward, oriental, and almost alien mass of refugees" who were "lice-infested, Arabic-speaking, brown-skinned, and superstitious."[220] Similarly, a best-selling book on American Sephardim portrays Eastern Sephardim as poor, uneducated, "frozen in time," and hermetically sealed off from developments in the rest of the Jewish world. This survey spends an inordinate amount of space describing the odd superstitions and "hyper-ritualistic" and "incomprehensible" customs of Eastern Sephardim, omitting all references to similar folklore common to the largest branch of world Jewry.[221]

Here, it is important to recall that many Ashkenazim exalted Sephardic immigrants as an aristocracy descended from Jerusalem or as heirs to the "sages of the Golden Age."[222] From this perspective, too, Eastern Sephardi and Mizrahi Jews are the "Jews who weren't there." Life in the kingdom of ancient Judah or medieval Spain can teach us very little about "real live" Sephardim who immigrated to the United States from the Ottoman Empire. The persistence of these historical paradigms, in fact, does little to rehabilitate the historiography of the Eastern Sephardic past or to assure its inclusion in the canon of Jewish studies. As a fellow graduate student once remarked to me sardonically, "the only good Sephardim are dead Sephardim."[223]

In the foregoing examples, Eastern Sephardim and Mizrahim are portrayed in the extreme: they are either lofty or despicable. To reiterate an earlier observation, stereotypes often situate ethnic groups at opposite extremes of positive and negative representations.[224] As such, they tell us little about the experiences, struggles, and perspectives of Eastern Sephardim and Mizrahim.[225] How can scholars of American Jewish studies overcome these omissions and avoid such misrepresentations? One approach is to shift the camera from center to margin. What would the American Jewish community look like if the spotlight were repositioned to the missing 4 percent of its constituents and if history were told from its perspectives?

Another approach to less commonly studied Jewish communities is relational. In the context of medieval Spain, Ivan Marcus has argued that "all Jewish communities and their cultural achievements should be treated as a part of the complex fabric of the Jewish historical 'culture,' in the anthropological sense of the word. Above all, we should not place special value on some Jewish cultures and their elites at the expense of others."[226] Similarly, David Biale emphasizes the need for "the examination of a culture in all its registers with the use of a wide range of disciplinary techniques" and reminds us that "Jewish culture has no single geographical center."[227] To successfully implement this relational approach, the study of Jewish civilization must be "decentered"; both Sephardim and Ashkenazim must be studied in a global Jewish context. As Rachel Wahba writes, "Our experience [as non-Ashkenazic Jews] is so consistently considered strange, inferior, or irrelevant, when in fact it is such an integral part of the Jewish story."[228]

But in the context of American Jewish history, such implorations for a paradigm shift have largely fallen on deaf ears. Eastern Sephardi and Mizrahi Jews have yet to emerge from a twentieth-century paradigm that has erased or demeaned them as the "exotic exception." Ironically, one must look outside the field of American Jewish studies to locate leading specialists of minority groups who unwaveringly embrace Sephardic civilization. The Recovering the U.S. Hispanic Literary Heritage program, founded in 1990 by Nicolás Kanellos at the University of Texas at Houston, includes Ladino periodicals as well as the literature of southwestern Sephardim in its campaign to redeem the pre-1960s Hispanic contribution from oblivion. Whether they wrote in Hebrew-scripted Judeo-Spanish, Spanish, Portuguese, or English, the writings of these Jews are acknowledged as integral to the tapestry and are never relegated to marginalia or an interesting footnote. This disproportionate interest from a Hispanic cause is reminiscent of the scholarly community's reaction to the decimation of Europe's Judeo-Spanish populations during World War II. As Denah Lida notes, "probably the greatest outside concern was expressed by the Hispanists, the scholars of Spanish letters and culture. To everyone else the Sephardim were so many more Jews, and there was no reason to single them out."[229] As we shall see, these examples are part of a much older tradition that has linked non-Jewish Hispanics and Eastern Sephardim in the United States through the ties of language and cultural affinity.

5

The Hispanic Embrace

In the 1980s, historian Germán Rueda was immersed in a study of Spanish immigration to the United States. In the course of his research, he stumbled on a group of early-twentieth-century newcomers who, though born and raised in the Ottoman Empire, identified their country of origin as "Spain." Rueda realized emotionally that these individuals were Sephardim, Jews whose ancestors had resided in *Sefarad* for over a millennium before Ferdinand and Isabel expelled them in 1492. He concluded that these handful of examples gave testimony to the thousands of Sephardim who "for more than four centuries had preserved the language, customs, and something more than just a memory of their ancestors' country."[1]

Elsewhere, we read that Ottoman Jews of Iberian ancestry "had no sense of identification with Spain.... Moreover, Sephardim in no way seem to have communicated with other Spanish-speaking groups in this country."[2] This astonishing statement, published in a 1986 historical survey of U.S. Hispanics, would have dismayed a small but influential group of university educators and communal leaders who facilitated some of the most intense and public cooperative efforts between gentile Hispanics and Ladino-speaking Jews. These personalities, active in the city of New York during the first half of the twentieth century, proved the elasticity of the relatively new concept "Hispanic" and its power to reconfigure ethnic identity.[3]

Rueda's discovery, suggesting a nostalgic tie with Spain, was but a small facet of a broad phenomenon that linked Eastern Sephardim and gentile Hispanics mainly through the common bond of language. Arguably, language was a stronger connective force among Eastern Sephardim and gentile Hispanics than any awareness of common geographical origins. Ladino, in its many linguistic variations, often extended a bridge of communication to speakers of Spain's many peninsular and diasporic dialects. Though written in Hebrew characters, in its spoken form Ladino was often intelligible to speakers of Spanish vernaculars. A librarian who worked on the Lower East Side in the 1910s maintained that if "you know modern Spanish, you will have a very satisfactory, if occasionally halting, means of communication" with Eastern Sephardim.[4] Such was also the experience of Bernard Drachman, an American rabbi who learned modern Spanish partly in order to communicate with Eastern Sephardim. On one occasion in the 1910s, he delivered an address to an Eastern Sephardic organization in Spanish and was understood.[5] Another example is "Madame Esther Tuvi," who remarked in 1935 that her Catholic friend, fluent in Spanish, could understand the Hebrew-scripted articles in New York's Ladino weekly *La Vara* when Tuvi read them aloud to her. Alas, Tuvi does not mention her friend's ethnicity, perhaps demonstrating that for some Sephardim religion and language were more important identifiers than national origin.[6]

Linguists have long recognized the centrality of language to the demarcation of communal boundaries. As one noted in 1977, "After the blood tie, nothing unites like the language."[7] Language often functions as a "common code" and fosters group solidarity and group identification.[8] In a multilingual or multidialectical environment, language has the power to open and close membership to an ethnic group.[9] Recent sociological and anthropological studies have affirmed the primacy of language in interactions that test the boundaries of ethnic belonging. Sociolinguist Ben Rampton examines the use of Panjabi among adolescents of African-Caribbean and Anglo descent, of Creole among adolescents of Panjabi and Anglo origins, and the use of stylized Indian English among British youths to challenge racial and economic stratification.[10] Linguistic anthropologist Dina Dahbany-Miraglia recorded cases from the 1970s of Yemenite-descended Jews who, by responding in African American Vernacular English during momentary encounters with American blacks, tacitly avowed an African American identity.[11] Body language and personal appearance can also operate as self-conscious identity markers. Katya Gibel Azoulay, an American-born cultural anthropologist of self-described "Jewish and West Indian descent," noted that while attending high school in the early 1990s, one of her children "consciously adopted the gestures, dress codes, and hairstyle that would mark him as "Black."[12]

No such studies exist for the U.S. Sephardic community, but archival evidence, oral interviews, and contributions to the Ladino press all suggest similar dynamics among Ladino and Spanish speakers during the first half of the twentieth century. The camaraderie and tensions evoked by shared language stimulated encounters most notably with Puerto Rican and Spanish-origin peoples, particularly in New York and Los Angeles.

Hispanic Encounters in the "Big Mango"

When Puerto Rican activist Bernardo Vega arrived in New York in 1916, one of his first visits was to the immigrant neighborhood of Harlem, where the largely Catholic Caribbean population was just beginning to swell. In 1916, New York's *Boricua* community numbered some six thousand souls; by 1927, one hundred thousand of his brethren reportedly dwelled in the "Big Mango."[13] The thirty-one-year-old Vega (1885–1965) dined in a restaurant called La Luz, and, as its name seemed to promise, he soon experienced an enlightened epiphany: the proprietor was not a fellow islander but rather a Sephardic Jew. Seating himself at a table with his companions, Vega found his senses both confounded and delighted. Conversations in "ancient Spanish or Portuguese" swirled around them, and the cuisine he sampled was at once familiar and foreign. The seasoning tasted decidedly alien, but the sauces seemed of Spanish origin. "The restaurant impressed me because it was so hard to believe that it was located in the United States," he reminisced in the late '40s. "The atmosphere was exotic. The furnishings and décor gave it the appearance of a café in Spain or Portugal. Even the people who gathered there, their gestures and speech mannerisms, identified them as from Galicia, Andalusia, Aragon, or some other Iberian region. I began to understand what New York really was: a modern Babylon, the meeting point for peoples from all over the world."[14]

La Luz was one of dozens of Lower and Upper East Side establishments launched by Sephardic immigrants from the disintegrating Ottoman Empire.[15] Though they traced their remote ancestry to the Expulsion of Jews from Spain in 1492, their immediate predecessors had dwelled in what are today Turkey and the Balkans for over four hundred years.[16] Their primary means of communication was not "ancient Spanish or Portuguese," as Vega imagined, but rather the oft-romanticized Ladino, a fusion language based on early modern Castilian, with admixtures of Hebrew, Aramaic, Portuguese, Italian, Greek, French, and Arabic, and traditionally written in Hebraic letters. Even when unaware of the Iberian origins of their mother tongue, they referred to their language as

"Spaniól" ("Spanish"), often bore Hispanic surnames, such as Calvo, de Castro, Torres, and Toledo, and sang *romansas*, romantic ballads evocative of medieval Iberia.[17] By 1916, the year of Vega's arrival, some twenty thousand Eastern Sephardic Jews had already immigrated to the United States, the overwhelming majority settling in the city of New York.[18] Their neighborhood in Harlem, sometimes referred to as a "little Jerusalem" (*chiko Yerushalayim*),[19] represented for some upward mobility, for others a much anticipated escape from Lower East Side congestion, and for most the promise of improved housing at affordable cost.[20] By 1911, *La America* reported that there were six Ottoman Sephardic cafés and restaurants in the center of downtown on Chrystie, Rivington, and Allen streets.[21] In ensuing years, the number of food establishments catering to the Eastern Judeo-Spanish palate mushroomed, both downtown and uptown, responding to an ever-increasing wave of immigration, halted only intermittently by World War I.

The ethnic landscape of Harlem remained both Spanish Caribbean and Eastern Sephardic until the 1930s, by which time probably most Ottoman-origin Jews had migrated to new neighborhoods in the Bronx and Brooklyn.[22] Max Aaron Luria, during the course of his research on Ladino dialects in the late 1920s, was delighted to discover the two linguistic traditions unsuspectingly juxtaposed on the storefronts of the Upper East Side:

> By a curious coincidence one stumbles across a considerable Porto-Rican [sic] colony in this very district. Even the most exigent Romanic [sic] scholar cannot demand a greater linguistic thrill than the sight of a shop displaying a sign in Spanish, but Spanish transcribed in Hebrew characters while on the show-window of the store adjoining he reads that he can obtain "Espesialidades [sic] de las Antillas."[23]

Many Sephardic eating establishments probably displayed their signs in Latin letters as well as Hebrew letters, as suggested by business cards and advertisements in the Ladino press. Restaurants and cafés such as La Luz of Harlem, and El Paladar, La Estrella, and El Amaneser, all of the Lower East Side, nominally capitalized on the Hispanic aspects of Ottoman Sephardic heritage.[24] Others, like La Vida Orientala, owned by Hayim D. Levy (b. 1882), and Constantinople, stressed through their names the Middle Eastern strain of this legacy.[25] Regardless of the name, and contrary to the exclusively "Spanish" flavors that Vega may have "read into" his food, these eating houses offered an array of Eastern Sephardic dishes and beverages. A customer could awake to a breakfast of *bumuelos* (sweet doughnuts or fritters) or *sutlaches* (flan-like puddings), spend his lunch break munching on *boyos* (pastries filled with either meat or cheese), or enjoy an afternoon snack of *asoplados* (meringue puffs), also known as "Oriental candy Kisses." In the evening, he might return for a dinner of *kababes* (shish kababs), washed down with a cup of Turkish coffee or *raki* (an alcoholic anise drink).[26]

For Sephardic Jews of the former Ottoman Empire, cafés and restaurants were much more than places to satisfy hunger pangs, quench thirst, or provide a spirituous buzz. They were also social centers for meeting friends, playing cards, dominoes, billiards, and backgammon (*sheshbesh*), and exchanging advice on immigrant adaptation and employment opportunities. Sephardic leaders found the central location of these eating establishments ideal for hanging political announcements or invitations to public events, and intellectuals and reporters met there to discuss cultural and social matters.[27] Clients often read Ladino newspapers as they sipped their drinks, and some even received their mail there. A number of cafés entertained their customers with the Sephardic and Near Eastern melodies of Turkish-style bands. These immigrant sanctuaries provided a warm, familiar atmosphere and an escape from overcrowded, frigid, and often filthy tenements.[28] Given that most early immigrants were single men, these establishments could serve as a heartening substitute for home cooking.[29] The comfort of sharing conversations over familiar nourishment and refreshments provided a means of maintaining cultural connections to the Old Country, while creating bonds between Sephardic immigrants of diverse Ottoman origins. Arguably, cafés and restaurants surpassed Sephardic clubs and organizations, which often held their events in the evening, as centers of Sephardic social and cultural life. Since many Sephardim labored after hours in movie theaters, hotels, and nightclubs, and since unemployment was common in the early immigrant years, these establishments were frequented by day as well as by night.[30]

The food industry is a savory example of ethnic self-representation, demonstrating how Ottoman-born Sephardim chose to emphasize a particular facet of their composite heritage to passersby and customers alike, while rendering it comprehensible and appealing to a clientele largely Sephardic and probably only incidentally gentile Hispanic.[31] If a culture combining the Spanish language with Middle Eastern culture was immediately recognizable to an "Oriental" Sephardic Jew, it likely mystified most everyone else. Vega himself seemed unaware of the four-hundred-year Ottoman "sojourn," during which his fellow diners had developed a new language and a singular heritage that combined Judeo-Spanish with Near Eastern cultural elements.

Vega's appreciation for Eastern Sephardic cuisine, albeit based on historical distortions, may indicate an aspect of gentile Hispanic receptivity that could potentially develop into cultural camaraderie. Still, most confirmed examples of such openness—whether in business, platonic, or romantic relationships—point to language as a unifying factor. David Altchek, a native of Salonika and father of eight who immigrated to the United States in 1914, relocated from the Lower East Side to Spanish Harlem partly because he "felt more comfortable with Spanish-speaking people."[32] His son Emanuel opened a Spanish-speaking medical practice in the mid-1920s in Harlem, where he served a primarily Puerto Rican and Cuban clientele.[33] He and his youngest brother, Victor, a surgeon, became so integrated into the Spanish-speaking community of New York that they appeared in the *Who's Who,* published in 1964 for that population group.[34] Another physician brother, Salvator, who practiced in Brooklyn, was known affectionately in the Puerto Rican community as "Alcheca." This Altchek routinely offered his service pro-bono to indigent patients and treated them "as though they were Park Avenue residents."[35] As late as the 1960s, Ladino-speaking garment workers in the International Ladies' Garment Workers' Union (ILGWU) were placed in positions of leadership because they were able to communicate with the Shirtmakers' Union's largely Puerto Rican labor force. An interpreter was an ongoing necessity since the 1950s because Puerto Ricans, Cubans, and other Latin American workers, as "birds of passage," were reluctant to learn the English language.[36] Language also functioned as a bridge of communication outside New York. A 1976 study found that several Sephardic immigrants who arrived in New York during the first decades of the twentieth century ultimately decided to settle in Los Angeles mainly because of the preponderance of the Spanish language. Many of these migrants chose to live not among fellow Jews (Ashkenazim) but rather among non-Jewish Spanish speakers. This linguistic commonality greatly contributed to the adjustment of Sephardim to their new city of residence.[37]

Romantic liaisons between Eastern Sephardim and gentile Puerto Ricans occurred with sufficient frequency to merit notation, but they were not always welcome in the Jewish community. One Dr. H. Goldstein of the Jewish Center noted in a 1926 interview that "Porto Ricans (non-Jews) in large numbers had moved to the district of his center [Harlem] and had driven out the Sephardim because of the fear of intermarriage, many moving to the Bronx—one group forming a Synagogue in the Grand Concourse."[38] In the late 1920s and early '30s Moise Soulam, a columnist for *La Vara*, reported a rising incidence of Sephardic girls running away from their parental homes to clandestinely elope with non-Jewish Puerto Ricans. Anecdotes of married Sephardic women leaving their husbands for gentile Puerto Rican men were also described.[39] In 1933, Henry Pereira Mendes, Minister Emeritus of Congregation Shearith Israel, also fretted over the conjugal choices of New York's Eastern Sephardic women: "I know a case where the girls (pure Sephardic Orientals) have thrown off all Jewish loyalty. I know of cases of intermarriage with Porto-Ricans or other Spanish-speaking people."[40]

It would be too simple to assume that these negative attitudes toward interethnic romances were merely religiously motivated. The Puerto Ricans with whom Sephardic girls eloped troubled journalist Moise Soulam less because of religious differences than because of skin color. "Why do [Sephardic] girls prefer Puerto Rican men with their brown or mulatto skins to white-skinned Sephardim and Ashkenazim?" he wondered in 1929.[41] To fall in love with Puerto Ricans with dark skin, he maintained, was beneath their dignity.[42] Not coincidentally, Sephardic denigration of Puerto Ricans was pronouncedly directed toward males, suggesting that some members of Harlem's Sephardic community viewed Puerto Rican men as sexual predators. This hypothesis finds support in Soulam's anecdote about a Puerto Rican man who attempted to bribe a Sephardic girl with candy but was thwarted from doing so just in time by the appearance of her father.[43] Likewise, Pereira Mendes's use of the word "pure" (in his reference to girls whom he described as "pure Sephardic Orientals") suggests a concern about sexuality as much as ethnoreligious loyalty. It cannot be happenstance that he juxtaposed his remark of 1933 with a reference to Jewish women arraigned for sex crimes in the Women's Night Court and Sephardic white slavery in Argentina.[44] By implicitly linking intermarriage with gentile Puerto Ricans and prostitution, Pereira Mendes unwittingly betrayed a fear that intermarriage would lead to—or indeed constituted—sexual immorality. Soulam commented that falling in love with "dark-skinned" Puerto

Ricans was worse than falling for gentile Poles or Italians.[45] In the mind of these Sephardic leaders, perceived "dark skin" was apparently linked with sexual depravity.[46]

On the other hand, Sephardic fears about the sex industry in Harlem were not entirely unfounded. Prostitution was also a concern in the Puerto Rican migrant community, as the memoirs of Bernardo Vega reveal.[47] Moise Soulam's reports in the 1920s and '30s about Sephardic women serving as madames and sex workers in Puerto Rican prostitution dens of both Harlem and the Bronx were probably not fanciful, especially since these accounts proliferated during the Depression.[48] Apparently, the local Puerto Rican community was also aware of the participation of Eastern Sephardim in the sex industry. In a column from 1928, Soulam recounted an embarrassing interaction between a Puerto Rican "good-for-nothing" (*penzil de Portorikenyo*) who mistook two Harlem Sephardic women for "ladies of the night." These women had been innocently conversing in Ladino about sexual relations with their husbands, unaware that a non-Jew might understand them.[49]

Soulam consistently portrayed Sephardic involvement in prostitution either as a misunderstanding or as scandalous and, therefore, anomalous. His disparagement of Puerto Ricans may reflect broader anxieties about Sephardic social status in U.S. society. Sephardic Jews and (predominantly Catholic) Puerto Ricans were both, to varying degrees, "inbetween peoples."[50] Soulam's physical depictions of Puerto Ricans served to distinguish Sephardim from "brown-skinned," "mulatto," or "black" peoples, thus affirming the white identity of Ladino-speaking immigrants. This distinction was particularly crucial in the *kolonia*, for Sephardim were often imagined by Ashkenazim and other outsiders as Mediterranean gentiles, Arabs, and other inbetween peoples and were often linked in the Anglo-American press, pseudoscientific literature, and immigration classifications with "Orientals" and, therefore, marked as not (completely) white.

Preoccupation with skin color was also rife in the Puerto Rican community. Journalist Jesús Colón (1901–1974) decried in 1927 the ambition of Puerto Rican women to marry Euro-American men for the sake of whitening or "advancing" the race (*adelantar la raza*).[51] His older brother, Joaquín Colón López (1896–1964), who arrived in New York in 1917, testified to the prejudice against African-origin Puerto Ricans both on the island and in "the Big Mango."[52] Religious and racial anti-Semitism were also deeply rooted in the *Barrio*. As Jesús Colón admitted in 1943, "The Jew, for most Hispanics, is the landlord, . . . the exploitative owner of the factory in which we work, . . . the man who betrayed Christ."[53] Lest one assume that these negative stereotypes were solely stimulated during the Nazi regime, already in 1928 we find Colón urging his Hispanic readers in Harlem not to "augment hateful legends . . . despising the Hebrew race."[54]

These racialist opinions may be understood in the broader social context of Anglo-American society. Puerto Ricans, whose homeland had been annexed in 1898 as a U.S. territory, were, like Eastern Sephardic Jews, an "inbetween people." They were shuttled back and forth between a relegated status, in Bernardo Vega's words, as "an expendable species—an ignorant, juvenile, and uncultured people,"[55] and U.S. citizens (beginning in 1917) whose ethnicity—not race—was Hispanic.[56] The aspiration for lighter skin as well as disparaging remarks about Jews was perhaps impelled by a desire to escape this ambiguous status. It was against this backdrop of ascribed identity that Puerto Ricans and Sephardim interacted, clashed, and sometimes united. The common linguistic and geographical heritage that connected them raised tantalizing questions about Spanish and Hispanic identity, eagerly explored by a small but influential group of activists and intellectuals for whom Spain was paramount.

Bridges to Spain

The Repatriation Campaign

In the late 1920s, the aforementioned scholar Max Aaron Luria undertook seven months of philological research among Eastern Sephardic Jews of New York to prepare himself for his linguistic study on the Ladino of Monastir. Luria found his local informants eager to learn of Spain and the differences between their native language and modern Spanish. Although Luria found no customs that he perceived as "essentially Spanish," he did detect "a deep-seated, tender memory and a pronounced nostalgia reverting to the Spain of their ancestors, the home of their fathers for so many centuries." Luria concluded that this living memory proved that the love of Sephardim for Spain's soil was almost tantamount to their devotion to Jerusalem.[57] Luria was perhaps partly conditioned by his own romantic expectations, but many Eastern Sephardim shared his sentiments.

Although Eastern Sephardim and Spaniards did not dwell in the same neighborhoods, they would not have had to venture far to hear one another's language. New York City's Spaniards tended to cluster in four zones. Most settled in Southeast Manhattan.[58] Perhaps ten thousand immigrants lived there in the 1920s, a number that climbs to twenty-five to thirty thousand if their American-born children and grandchildren are included. Others settled in East Manhattan, especially in an area known as "little Spain,"[59] as well as in Brooklyn and in Astoria.[60] The principal settlements of Sephardim (until they fanned out to Brooklyn and the Bronx in the 1920s) were the Lower East Side, just south of the area harboring the highest concentration of Spaniards, and Harlem.[61]

This proximity fostered casual encounters between the two groups. Sephardic émigré and Brooklyn College professor Maír José Benardete observed in the 1940s that non-Jewish Hispanic Americans, especially Spaniards in New York, would sooner or later inevitably hear the "archaic Spanish" spoken by Ottoman-born Sephardim.[62] Another testament to these linguistic interactions is the New York Ladino press, which over the years made increasing accommodations to modern Castilian. This adjustment delighted Benardete, who, with patent hostility to his own mother tongue, observed in 1953 that the "outlandish excrescences [of Ladino] are filed away or dropped off" during encounters between Sephardim and modern Spanish speakers.[63] The imprint of Ladino, however, was never entirely effaced, as the writings of Eastern Sephardic intellectuals demonstrate. Salonika-born Henry V. Besso, active in both Eastern Sephardic and Spanish scholarly circles, frequently injected Ladino grammatical forms into his writings, and Benardete's own wife, Paula Ovadia de Benardete, an instructor of Spanish at Brooklyn College, peppered her Spanish-language correspondence with Judeo-Spanish vocabulary.[64]

Another opportunity for contact with Spaniards in the first half of the twentieth century was the realm of politics. The immediate roots of these interactions can be traced to 1904, when Spanish senator Ángel Pulido Fernández, during a voyage on the Danube, overheard some fellow passengers speaking what sounded to him like archaic Spanish. These passengers were Eastern Sephardic Jews, and their language was Ladino. His "discovery" led to renewed efforts to "repatriate" Ottoman Sephardim, whom he dubbed "Spaniards without a fatherland."[65] Pulido also had plans for Ladino, during that era sometimes called "Oriental Spanish" (*castellano oriental*). He advocated both preserving that language and making efforts to close the linguistic gap between the two tongues so that they would not progressively differ over time. This, he hoped, would facilitate the forging of both commercial and cultural relations with Eastern Sephardim.[66]

Following Pulido's lead, the Spanish embassy launched a campaign in New York in about 1912 to repatriate Eastern Sephardic Jews to Spain.[67] The promoters' underlying economic motives did not escape public attention. In a 1913 article on Ladino-speaking immigrants, journalist Mary Brown Sumner noted that Spain had recently sent representatives to Turkey to invite Sephardim back, "evidence that that country believes them to have qualities that would be an asset to the country of their choice."[68] Two years later, Joseph Gedalecia, president of the Federation of Oriental Jews, noted that this seemingly high-minded scheme was aimed to "place Spain in the front rank of the South American trade."[69] Gedalecia's skeptical critique did not stifle the enthusiasm of one Levy Friedman, a private American citizen residing in New York, who began diplomatic negotiations with the Spanish ambassador to "return" Eastern Sephardim to their ancestral land.[70] To some *kolonia* leaders, Friedman's Ashkenazic identity was not inconsequential. Gedalecia, for one, resented the fact that the Eastern Sephardic community was not notified of Friedman's efforts.[71] The leading Jews in the United States involved in the campaign seem to have been all Ashkenazim. The Anglo-American Jewish press reported in 1915 that Oscar Straus, a German-born Jew who had served as the U.S. minister to the Ottoman Empire during the late 1880s and '90s and again in 1909–1910, was working assiduously with Friedman and the Spanish ambassador to the United States in order to realize this plan.[72]

Non-Ashkenazic leaders also objected to the plan for ideological reasons. Gedalecia maintained that "Jews of the orient, though they have no feelings of resentment or animosity against Spain, have not forgotten the sufferings of their ancestors," and he hoped that his Eastern Sephardic brethren would "receive the magnanimous condescension of the Spanish Government with an eloquent shrug."[73] Moise Gadol was likewise distressed when in 1915 the Spanish American press and Spanish ambassador in Washington solicited his participation in the movement. More trenchantly than Gedalecia, he remarked that the Sephardim had still not forgotten the bitterness of the "cruel and barbaric" Inquisition in which thousands were tortured and thrown into the pyre of the auto-da-fe. Eastern Sephardim, he maintained, "would not be so ignorant as to return to a country that left us with such sad memories." Moreover, the anti-Semitism of the Spanish people was not a phenomenon of the past. Gadol pointed to recent letters that he had received from Eastern Sephardic readers of *La*

America residing in Madrid and Barcelona, begging him to mail their subscriptions with the Hebrew letters carefully concealed in wrapping.[74]

The issue of common language that surfaced during this campaign testifies to the limits of linguistic commonality in interethnic bridge building. One of the arguments Spanish delegates used to advocate repatriation, as Gadol noted in 1915, was that Eastern Sephardim spoke the language of Spain. Gadol responded that "we speak and write this language against our will, being that our ancestors did not take pains to resurrect our own ancient Hebrew language." Rejecting all national ties with Spain, Gadol asserted that the only remedy for Sephardim was to "work for the honor and dignity of our nation under the new national Jewish ideal, Zionism," namely, the resettlement of Jews in Palestine.[75] This linguistic hostility is also represented in the family history of scholar Denah Lida, whose Greek-speaking grandfather, Behor Semopolos (b. 1846), refused to allow "Spanish," that "accursed language of the country that expelled us," to be spoken in the house.[76] For a variety of reasons, the repatriation campaign of the 1910s was not generally successful, either in the United States or in the (former) Ottoman Empire.[77] Nonetheless, an expanding circle of Eastern Sephardim residing in the United States soon embraced their "Spanish" identity in the intellectual environment of Columbia University.

In the Ivory Tower

"The Philo-Sephardic movement in Spain,"[78] which developed at the turn of the century, included campaigns to repatriate Sephardim and to spread awareness of the Ladino language. Among its followers were Ángl Pulido, Benito Pérez Galdós, Marcelino Menéndez y Pelayo, Ramón Menéndez Pidal, and Rafael Cansinos-Asséns, all of whom encouraged Eastern Sephardim "to maintain their traditions and reverentially love and study them."[79] For some of these Spaniards, interest in Sephardic civilization led to an empathic ethnoreligious identity. Pulido, the so-called apostle of the Sephardim, came to suspect that he himself had Sephardic roots.[80] Spanish novelist and critic Rafael Cansinos-Asséns (1883–1964), through kabbalistic calculations, arrived at the conclusion that his ancestors were crypto-Jews. His conviction led him to join the small group of Moroccan and European Sephardim who dwelled in Madrid, and he saturated his pamphlets, essays, short stories, poems, and novels with Sephardic themes.[81]

This philo-Sephardic movement found its spiritual offspring in Spanish intellectual circles in the United States. The catalyst was Federico de

Faculty members from the Hispanic Institute and its Sephardic Section. Courtesy Hispanic Institute. Caption on back reads, "Sentados [seated]: Carneiro (Brasil); Concha Romero James, Ciro Alegría (Perú); Gilbert (ecuatoriano), Luis Valcárcel (Peruano), F. de Onís. De pie [standing]: A. Iduarte, M. J. Benardete, A. del Río, T. Navarro, Francisco García Lorca. Año 1941."

Onís (1885–1966), professor of Spanish languages and literatures at the University of Salamanca and the Center for Historical Studies in Madrid and renowned as one of the world's leading scholars of Spanish and Latin American literature. In 1916, Columbia University president Nicholas Murray Butler appointed Onís to organize Hispanic studies on a new foundation. Butler was responding to an exponential increase in the popularity of Spanish academic studies, witnessed nationwide, particularly in the fields of language and literature. One scholar describes the boon in Spanish studies during the years on either side of World War I as "arguably the biggest and most dramatic surge ever in the history of U.S. Spanish studies."[82]

Matriculation in the century's first decade had already stretched Columbia University's Spanish professors beyond capacity. Then, from 248 students enrolled during the academic year 1911–1912, enrollment rose to 1,626 in 1915–1916, peaking at 2,923 undergraduates during the

Cast members from the Sephardic Studies Section, performing Lope De Vega's The Rape of Dina. *The cast members are local Eastern Sephardim, underscoring the regard for Ladino as a petrified medieval Spanish. Caption on back reads, "Instituto, Fiesta de la Lengua, May 2, 1941, Representación de Lope de Vega, El Robo de Dina, representado por la sección sefardí."*

Cast members from the Sephardic Studies Section, performance of Jean Racine's Athalie. *The play was performed several times in March and April 1936, on both the Lower East Side and uptown. The performance in the MacMillin Theatre, Columbia University, was attended by about a thousand Eastern Sephardim and persons of various nationalities, including Spaniards and Latin Americans. This play, performed in Ladino, is set in Jerusalem, c 700* B.C.E. *Cast members, flanked on either side by Frederico de Onís (right) and Alberto Matarasso (left), include Mollie (Dina) Hakim as the Queen, Joseph Kattan, and Robert Nassi. Reprinted from Revista Hispânica Moderna 3:1 (October 1936): 95.*

1920–1921 academic year. A new maximum was achieved in 1948–1949, with 4,169 students (among them 1,050 graduate students and 3,042 undergrads). With regard to Hispanic studies, Columbia University was distinctive nationally, for since 1916 graduate matriculation in Spanish exceeded parallel enrollment in all other universities nationwide.[83]

Onís, who arrived in the United States in September 1916, had initially intended to remain in the United States for just a year, but he eventually resolved to settle permanently. His sojourn on the mainland was only interrupted thirty-years years later, upon his retirement to Puerto Rico. In a 1955 retrospective of his mainland career, Onís reflected that in North America he felt "more in the center of Spain than when . . . in Spain itself," where he had spent the first thirty years of his life.[84] In this sense, Onís may have been exceptional among U.S.-based intellectuals of Spanish birth, who tended to separate themselves from the local Spanish colony.[85]

At Columbia University, Federico de Onís founded the Instituto de las Españas en los Estados Unidos (Institute of the Spains in the United States), later known as the Instituto Hispánico or Hispanic Institute.[86] It was the beginning of a long-lived academic alliance between Spanish and Eastern Sephardic thinkers and led to a veritable efflorescence in Sephardic studies. Onís explained the plural usage of the word "Spain" as

> [a]ll of the various forms that Spain has taken across time and through the peoples in its fertile and magnificent historical career. For the complete success of this work, the collaboration of everyone is necessary: Spaniards of every region, Hispano-Americans of all countries, Jews of Spanish origin and North Americans dedicated to the study of our culture should join in the House of the Spains and convert it into what it aspires to be and what it in fact is already to a large extent: a common home where everything that unites us among ourselves and entwines us with the rest of the world is maintained alive, that which is highest, most universal and most eternal in Spanish culture.[87]

Initially, the Instituto had no building of its own, and activities took place in various edifices of the university. But in 1930 President Butler decided to fund a center that would house the institute's programs. The building, just one block north of Columbia's main campus, became known as the "Casa Hispánica," to match the institution's new name, "Instituto Hispánico."[88] A perhaps unintended consequence of the new name was the allowance of potential inclusion—at least taxonomically—of Eastern Sephardim as fellow Hispanics. This consequence became significant in later decades, as the term "Hispanic" gained currency as a designator of all Spanish-speaking peoples in the United States. The selection of the name may have also been a nod at New York's Hispanic Society of America, founded in 1904 by American Hispanist Archer Milton Huntington and located further uptown. It was Huntington who in 1916 was appointed by Nicholas Murray Butler to select an academic from Spain to organize Hispanic studies at Columbia, and Huntington had handpicked Federico de Onís.[89]

The time was auspicious for both programmatic expansion and conceptual revolution. Infrastructural reorganization at Columbia University in 1929 had divided the Department of Languages and Romance Literatures into three sections. This allowed Spanish scholars to adopt the term "Hispánico" to designate their newly independent section.[90] This independence seems to have opened the doors to a multicultural approach to Spain. Brazilian-born Spanish historian Américo Castro (1885–1972) spearheaded such a scholarly approach in the following decade. Castro served as visiting professor at Columbia University's Hispanic Department in 1923 and may have influenced Onís's conceptualization of Spanish historiography.[91] A more direct impact on Onís was novelist Miguel de Unamuno, who had been his principal teacher in Spain, and who spoke of "the blood of the spirit" that united all Spanish speakers "through the tie of the language."[92]

The expansive approach that Onís introduced to the Hispanic Institute may be related to "Pan-Americanism," a trend that developed around 1915 and challenged Spain's central position in American Hispanic studies. Previously, as Edith Helman has noted, there existed "no division between the Spanish and the Spanish-American language and culture. In order to learn Spanish, you read the works of the great Spanish writers. And in reading Spanish literature, you learned about the Hispanic mind and character in America as well as in the Peninsula."[93] The new trend, coinciding with World War I, allowed academics to give primacy to Hispanic culture as it developed outside Spain. Nevertheless, even among the proponents of this new focus, manifestations of Hispanic culture were often circuitously linked back to Spain.[94]

These historical and political trends prepared the ground for an expanding view of Hispanicity, but they do not entirely explain how the borders of the "Spains" were stretched to include Jews in and from the (former) Ottoman Empire. To elucidate this stretching of the borders, one must consider the philo-Sephardic Spaniards of the late nineteenth and early twentieth centuries who sought to embrace Eastern Sephardim as part of Spain's heritage and who, like Ángel Pulido and Rafael Cansinos-Asséns, often exhibited an empathic Sephardic identity. Federico de Onís, soon to become a cultural mediator between gentile Hispanics and Eastern Sephardim at Columbia University, also briefly flirted with his possible Sephardic origins.[95] This empathic identity suggests that the interest of gentile Spaniards in Sephardim was not only intellectual but also existential.

This philo-Sephardism spurred the founding of the Hispanic Institute's "Sección Sefardí" (hereafter referred to as the "Sephardic Section") sometime in the late 1920s or early '30s.[96] Its mission to advance the study of "Spanish-Jewish culture" included research projects and publications in the fields of history, literature, and folklore. The intention to study Sephardic civilization both historically and "as it is preserved today in the traditions of the Sephardic people" suggests the study of Sephardim in the former Ottoman Empire and the anticipated participation of New York's local Eastern Sephardic community. In casting its eyes eastward, the Sephardic Section blazed a trail, for until then the Ottoman Jewish legacy had been sorely neglected by gentile and Jewish historians alike.[97]

Onís invited Maír José Benardete to direct the Sephardic Section.[98] Their relationship, and indeed, Onís's interest in Sephardim, long preceded the establishment of the section. In 1923, Onís had encouraged Benardete to begin a thesis at Columbia University on Spanish ballads preserved among Eastern Sephardim of the "slums of the East Side and Harlem."[99] Onís, Benardete reported two decades later, imbued in Eastern Sephardic students a love for their heritage, which they had been taught by their own community to despise.[100] In the late 1920s, Onís had also assisted Ashkenazic graduate student Max Aaron Luria with his project on the Monastir dialect of Ladino, which appeared as a lengthy article in the 1930 issue of *Revue Hispanique*.[101] That same year, Onís invited Simy (Suzanne) Nahón de Toledano, sister of a Columbia University graduate student, to record Moroccan Judeo-Spanish ballads at the Casa de las Españas. He built up an impressive archive of Eastern Sephardic Ladino songs thereafter, culled from informants born in Salonika and Rhodes.[102] When Henry V. Besso sought to enroll in the Spanish Department as a prospective graduate student around 1931, Onís warmly welcomed him and initiated a long-enduring personal and professional friendship.[103]

Though Onís apparently did not teach Sephardic-related courses, a multicultural orientation to Spanish civilization developed under his directorship. The Hispanic Institute offered such courses as "La Cultura Española," an interdisciplinary course bearing three credits and cross-listed with an astounding number of departments (Anthropology, Architecture, Art, French, Geology, History, Latin and Greek, Philosophy, Law, and Semitic Languages). The course consisted of a series of English-language lectures on various aspects of Spanish civilization, including a two-day lecture by Salo Wittmayer Baron on "The Hebraic Civilization in Spain" and a one-day presentation by German-Jewish anthropologist Franz Boas on "The Diffusion of Spanish Folklore in Africa, Asia and America." Considering that Boas had directed a study on North African Judeo-Spanish around 1912, his course may have included Sephardic material as well. Benardete offered history lectures on Sephardic Spain, including "El judío en la España cristiana del Medioevo" (summer 1935).[104] The array of courses is all the more impressive when one recalls that during this time academic scholarship and instruction on Jewish civilization in Christian Spain (and indeed Jewish history in general) were in their infancy.[105]

It was mainly Benardete, however, who developed Sephardic studies programming at the Hispanic Institute. Benardete was an obvious choice for the position of director. Born and raised in Dardanelles in the Ottoman Empire, he arrived in the United States in 1910 at the age of fifteen, old enough to be fully immersed in his native language and culture but young enough to be fundamentally shaped by America's institutions of higher education. He graduated from the University of Cincinnati and received his M.A. and Ph.D. degrees from Columbia University, mastering Spanish literature and completing both theses on the topic of Sephardic civilization.[106] His M.A. thesis project in the early 1920s represented the first endeavor to gather and record Judeo-Spanish ballads in New York.[107] Benardete was a regular contributor to the New York Ladino press from the 1910s through the 1940s, and readers energetically responded to his articles.[108] In 1953, he published his Columbia University Ph.D. dissertation *Hispanic Culture and Character of the Sephardic Jews* under the imprint of the institute.[109] Though he was affiliated with Columbia University through its Hispanic Institute, Benardete's academic career as a professor of Spanish literature mostly developed at Hunter College and Brooklyn College, where he taught from 1930 until his retirement in 1965.[110]

Benardete encouraged Eastern Sephardic scholars to pursue their own studies on the Judeo-Spanish legacy. In the 1930s, as a result, Michael Molho completed a study on the *MeAm Lo'ez*, an eighteenth-century classic of Ladino literature.[111] In 1924, Benardete met a young Henry V.

Besso.[112] He invited Besso to speak at the Hispanic Institute in 1931 on the relationship between Sephardim and Spain. It was Besso's first public lecture in Spanish. Benardete encouraged Besso to publish his "first serious contribution" on Sephardic folklore in the *Bulletin Hispanique* (1935) and to speak at the "Octocentennial Celebration of Moses Maimonides" in 1935.[113] He appointed Besso assistant director of the section in 1936[114] and arranged for his election as a Sephardic delegate to the First Congress of Hispanic Culture, which met in Madrid in June 1963.[115]

The position of director of the Sephardic Section afforded Benardete a great deal of creative freedom both to develop Sephardic research and programming and to involve the local Ladino-speaking population. Under Benardete's direction, the Sephardic Section sponsored lectures on Sephardic civilization, generated articles for the institute's *Revista Hispánica Moderna* (*RHM*), and published a Ladino/Spanish commemorative volume on the medieval Iberian-Jewish poet Yehudah Halevi. Artistic endeavors included staged performances in Judeo-Spanish, among them a 1934 dramatic and musical presentation set in the time of Cervantes. The cast included native speakers of Ladino: student Jennie Abolafia, Benardete himself, and Henry V. Besso.[116] These theatrical presentations took place during the annual "Fiesta de la Lengua" ("Language Festival"), inaugurated in 1920 to "celebrate all who are united through the tie of the language, the blood of the spirit, as [Miguel de] Unamuno has called it."[117] The 1941 showing presented Lope de Vega's *El Robo de Dina*, animated once again by native Ladino-speakers of New York, mostly students. The festival's idealistic goal was to instruct individuals in "how to be nationalistic and universalistic at the same time" and to realize that "a language and a spirit," in belonging to the Spanish people, "belong to everyone."[118]

The organization's "inclusive exclusiveness" had its limits. The dramatic events sponsored by the Hispanic Institute and its Sephardic Section seemed to operate under the narrow conviction that Ladino was a petrified medieval Spanish, the Spanish of the Golden Age.[119] Sephardim, in turn, were portrayed as a long-lost component of Spanish civilization, frozen in time and ready for reclamation. This approach was in keeping with the aforementioned "Pan-Americanism," which tended to circuitously link diasporic Hispanic cultures back to Spain.[120] In its scholarly output, however, the institute treated Ladino as distinct from medieval Spanish. Max Aaron Luria's *A Study of the Monastir Dialect of Judeo-Spanish Based on Oral Material Collected in Monastir, Yugo-*

Slavia appeared under the Hispanic Institute's imprint, and the institute also demonstrated its awareness of Ladino as a singular, living language through its subscription to a Hebrew-scripted Ladino periodical.[121]

Still, Christian Spain was clearly the nucleus around which everything else revolved. There is no evidence, for example, that students were encouraged to study Arab expansionism or the Hebrew or Arabic alphabets, which would have deepened and possibly transformed understanding of the other "Spains." The Hispanic Institute's manifesto noticeably omitted Hispano-Muslims and their descendants, though the institute's publications acknowledged them through, for example, a volume on Hispanized Muslims and references to a newly founded Arabic institute in Granada, Spain.[122] In a 1936 lecture, Federico de Onís clarified that it was due to lack of interest that no Arabic studies section would be formed alongside the parallel Spanish, Portuguese, Hispano-American, and Sephardic studies sections.[123] This apparent apathy probably had much to do with both U.S. demographics and historical memory. Eastern Sephardic Jews, by virtue of their numbers and links to the established Jewish community, had a much stronger presence than the handful of Arab Muslims in the United States who may have claimed ancestral ties to the Iberian Peninsula.[124] Moreover, Eastern Sephardim were associated not with Catholic Spain's politically charged military defeat of Muslim Granada in 1492 but rather with the romantic ideal of cultural and linguistic retention despite the Expulsion and the legacy of the Inquisition.

Stepping its way gingerly into politics, the Sephardic Studies Section also addressed the repatriation campaign that had so irked Joseph Gedalecia and Moise Gadol in the 1910s. In April 1931, Maír José Benardete mediated and presided over a discussion on "the new attitude of Spain towards the Sephardim." A synopsis of the event stated that the subject matter was "of special interest to a number of students of the department, who are of Judeo-Spanish origin." Numerous Eastern Sephardim living in New York and some students, professors, and members of the institute participated.[125]

These attempts of Spanish and Eastern Sephardic intellectuals to achieve a rapprochement with New York's Eastern Sephardic community set a receptive stage for native Ladino speakers, who in years to come would enroll in the university in intellectual search of their own storied heritage.[126] In the summer of 1943, just after receiving her degree in Spanish from Hunter College, twenty-year-old, Harlem-born Denah Levy Lida (daughter of the aforementioned restaurateur Hayim D. Levy) decided to pursue her academic interest in Ladino. She learned of a Spanish professor at Columbia University who was interested in language and would perhaps be responsive to "her Spanish." Lida found Tomás Navarro Tomás, an adviser to the Hispanic Institute, in his office and introduced herself, proposing to write a master's thesis using her own family members as linguistic and folkloric repositories.[127] Navarro Tomás exhibited "enormous interest, personal curiosity, and warm encouragement," Lida recalls. Under his direction, Lida studied Spanish literature and also enrolled in a seminar designed to further her M.A. thesis. It was in this latter course that Lida came to fully appreciate her heritage and ceased to disdain Ladino as "kitchen Spanish." Navarro Tomás asked her pointed questions, instructed her to gather specific vocabulary ("what do they call the jamb of a door?"), and handed her his own standard linguistic questionnaires.

Navarro Tomás's intense curiosity was not just lexical but also cultural. Suddenly, Judeo-Spanish and its heritage seemed very important to Lida. "I realized through him that we could learn much about medieval Spanish and poetry that had been preserved in Ladino," she reflected in 1999. Navarro Tomás transformed her entire perspective toward her native language. This "distinguished, elderly man" even asked about Sephardic cuisine. She brought in lists of gastronomical vocabulary, and when no equivalent existed in modern Spanish, her task was to write detailed descriptions that stimulated Navarro's academic interest no less than his tastebuds. He then requested samples of these delicacies. Lida's mother obliged by preparing mouth-watering morsels that her daughter brought in as part of the course syllabus. Navarro Tomás relished these moments, "especially when his wife was away." He sampled Turkish and Greek Sephardic pastries, such as *baklava* and *kuraviedes* (baked dough stuffed with chopped almonds and topped with powdered sugar), and exclaimed, "Ah, éste está muy bueno."[128] Tomás also encouraged Lida to retain her native pronunciation of the letter "s," which differs markedly from the lisp pronunciation of modern peninsular Spanish. This validation of her own linguistic heritage left a deep pedagogical imprint. When Lida found "ghetto children" among her students, she urged them not to suppress their dialects, informing them that they had something crucial to communicate to the larger world.[129]

For intellectual patrons of Judeo-Spanish scholarship such as Navarro Tomás, Sephardic civilization was not frozen in a mythical Golden Age, nor was it a legacy of Near Eastern decline (what I have termed "The Fallen Sephardi"), but rather it was a living tradition, encompassing sounds and tastes, no less than words and ideas. In contrast to the alternatively hyperbolic and denigrating paradigms with which many Ashkenazim approached their Eastern Sephardic coreligionists, the Hispanic Ivory Tower embraced its distant cousins as part and parcel of the Spanish-speaking world, past and present. In the words of Federico de Onís, "Séneca, Lucano, San Isidoro, Averroes, and Maimonides are as Spanish as Góngora and Cervantes."[130] This approach helps to explain why these encounters could be so fruitful. Moreover, as Maír José Benardete noted, "better educated" Sephardim in the former Ottoman Empire and Spain tended to respond more warmly to cooperative ventures with gentile Spaniards than did Sephardim from other walks of life.[131] The same observation may be applied to the United States. Eastern Sephardim who initiated contact with Columbia University's Hispanic circles were probably intellectually predisposed toward such bridge-building endeavors.

Sephardic programming at the Hispanic Institute continued sporadically through the 1960s, but the heyday of the Sephardic Section was the 1930s. The halt of the mass immigration of Eastern Sephardim in the 1920s no doubt contributed to the gradual waning of Sephardic involvement in the Hispanic Institute. This cessation of immigration weakened the status of Ladino as the community's primary spoken language. The incidence of intramarriage with Ashkenazim, which accelerated beginning with World War II, also weakened the prospects of transmitting a strong Sephardic identity. In 1948, the country's only Ladino newspaper folded due to the illness of its sole redactor. By the 1960s, most of the city's Eastern Sephardic population no longer conversed in Ladino and had largely intramarried with Ashkenazim or (more rarely) outmarried.[132] On the other hand, sea-changing events in Spain augmented the population of Spanish ex-patriot intellectuals. The Spanish Civil War (1936–1939) and the fall of the Second Spanish Republic in 1939 stimulated the exile of "a small but highly significant group of refugees and exiles," among them leading Spanish intellectuals, many of them transplanted to the United States.[133]

The collaboration between gentile Spaniards and Eastern Sephardim in U.S. academic circles was very much a New York story. Sections, chapters, and affiliates of the Hispanic Institute were opened after 1920 all over the country in such cities as Atlantic City (1937), Austin (1941), Chicago (1935), Los Angeles (1939), New Orleans (1933–1935), Newark (1936), Omaha (1936), San Francisco (1935), Washington, D.C. (1933–1935), Winter Park, Florida, at Rollins College (1933), and in

New Mexico (1935).¹³⁴ But there is no known evidence that any of these chapters developed a coexisting Sephardic Section.¹³⁵ Columbia University's Hispanic Institute was in this respect singular. Of all the cities where offshoots of the Hispanic Institute were established, none (except perhaps Chicago) harbored a significant Ladino-speaking population by the 1930s. New York was the only city that was home to vibrant gentile Spanish and Sephardic populations of roughly the same size. Moreover, the city's *kolonia* was home to the nation's most prominent Eastern Sephardic leaders and intellectuals.

The Hispanic Institute's evening lectures held on Mondays (*veladas de los lunes*) continued to feature Sephardic-related topics through the 1960s. Some of the presenters, including Beraha Safira, who performed Eastern Sephardic songs in 1950,¹³⁶ were obviously native Ladino speakers. Sephardic-related *veladas* seem to have largely ceased after Maír José Benardete's retirement from Brooklyn College in 1965, a possible indication of the fragility of the Sephardic endeavor in an institute of higher learning.¹³⁷

During its roughly forty years of active existence, the Hispanic Institute attempted to narrow the cultural and political gap between the Spanish diaspora and Eastern Sephardim residing in the New York City area. This rapprochement was accomplished largely through the efforts of its two most visible leaders: Federico de Onís, remembered as a "great friend of the Sephardim,"¹³⁸ and Maír José Benardete, who styled himself as a bridge between cultures and scholarship and who, upon retirement, was credited for his success in "placing the Sephardim of this country in closer relationship with the Hispanic world."¹³⁹

In 1971, William J. McGill, Columbia University's president, decided to suspend the Casa Hispánica's bibliographical service, which he apparently regarded as superannuated. Responding to an open letter of protest submitted by Henry V. Besso, McGill stressed that both the Hispanic Institute and the Casa Hispánica, administered under the direction of the Department of Spanish and Portuguese, represented the university's "recognition of the large Spanish community which surrounds Columbia." He promised that the activities of the institute and its building would be maintained and promoted, but his resolve to terminate bibliographical services effectively transformed the institute's archival collection into an abandoned warehouse.¹⁴⁰

The enduring influence of Spanish émigrés on the local Spanish-speaking population remains an open question. What is certain is that for perhaps two decades Spaniards played a pivotal role in intensifying

Hispanic identity in hundreds, if not thousands, of Sephardic Jews living in the city of New York.[141] The Sephardic Section endeavor, in turn, allowed idealistic Spanish intellectuals and their students to promote an ecumenical vision of Spain beyond itself. The activities of Columbia University's Hispanic Institute functioned as a bridge between the Ivory Tower and New York's Eastern Sephardic Jews, a bridge constructed by Spanish intellectuals who, despite their occasional view of Ladino speakers as petrified relics of a glorious medieval age, were appreciative of Eastern Sephardim as real-life people. Because the links between Spaniards and Sephardim beginning in the 1920s appear to be so time bound, perhaps their relationship is best described as a drawbridge, extended for a relatively brief moment in time and then forever lifted as the local Sephardic population acculturated to Anglo-American society and Spanish intellectuals made way for more pressing Hispanic concerns.

Masonic Connections: The La Fraternidad and Abravanel Lodges

The aforementioned records of Spanish immigration to the United States, analyzed by Germán Rueda in the 1980s, indicate that dozens of Sephardim emigrating from Ottoman lands designated Spain as their "country of origin." In assessing this self-identity, one should not discount their attempt to obscure their "Oriental" background, particularly in view of the Act of April 27, 1904, which reaffirmed and indefinitely extended the Chinese Exclusion Act of 1882.[142] Once settled in New York, however, many Eastern Sephardim electively affiliated with La Fraternidad No. 387, the country's first Spanish-speaking Masonic lodge. In the first three decades of the twentieth century, in fact, Eastern Sephardim were disproportionately represented as members.

La Fraternidad was founded in 1855 and chartered in 1856 as the first Spanish-speaking lodge in North America. Its earliest members were predominantly Cuban.[143] The first brother who is identifiably Sephardic (based on both name and birthplace) was Salomon Emmanuel, a merchant from Palestine born in 1875 and initiated in 1900. The proportion of Eastern Sephardic brothers steadily increased just at the moment when other Masonic lodges in the United States, fueled by anti-Semitism, were beginning to exclude Jews.[144] In 1900, 9 percent of La Fraternidad's new members were Sephardic, and this number rose exponentially during the following three decades. In 1901 and 1905, 20 and 50 percent of the newly initiated, respectively, were Sephardic. The peak year in terms of proportion was 1909, when 63 percent of new members were Sephardic. From then until 1931, new or restored members who were Eastern Sephardim represented between 20 and 40 percent in most years. After 1931, their presence drops off markedly, until it finally disappears after 1956.[145]

Memories of Eastern Sephardim in La Fraternidad continued long after their numbers began to dwindle. One non-Jewish brother noted in 1955 that after the great influx of immigrants to the United States in the 1880s, the lodge included "a notable number" of Sephardim.[146] That year (1955), when La Fraternidad celebrated its centennial anniversary, roughly 12 percent of its 302 active members were verifiably Sephardic.[147] The impact of Sephardim on La Fraternidad's institutional memory was also related to the longevity of some its members and their leadership positions. The first identifiably Eastern Sephardic Master was Elie I. Contente, who served in 1910.[148] Following him were Raphael S. Amado (1913), Salomón Emanuel (1918), perhaps the aforementioned Salomon Emmanuel initiated in 1900, Solomón Contente (1920), Jacques M. Habib (1924), and Louis J. Opal (1929, 1943, and 1944).[149] Albert J. Torres, longtime editor of the Ladino weekly *La Vara*, served a few times as treasurer in the 1930s.[150] In 1977, Ottoman-born Victor Nahum (1892–1981) was the member of longest standing in the lodge. He had been initiated in 1918 and served the lodge for sixty years. Among his contributions were his endeavors as a liaison between the La Fraternidad lodge of New York and that of Israel.[151]

The decision to initiate the lodge's first Sephardim may have been motivated in part by the desire to bolster membership, which was depleted after Cuba attained its independence in 1898 and many brothers returned to the island.[152] Masonic regulations usually oppose active solicitation for members, but the prospect of the lodge's diminution may have stimulated greater openness to the acceptance of Jews.[153] This receptivity also reflects ongoing discussions in Spain concerning its political and ideological reconstruction in the wake of territorial losses.[154]

What was the appeal of the lodge for Eastern Sephardic immigrants? Material benefits may have tempted some. The Masonic Life Association, in business since 1873, offered monthly and yearly plans at about one-half of "Old-Line" insurance companies.[155] But Jewish descendants and acquaintances of Fraternidad brothers reject this theory. Lenny Lubitz, a third-generation member of Abravanel No. 1116 lodge, an offshoot of La Fraternidad, explains that struggling immigrants think first and foremost about day-to-day survival. Once they are more stationed in life, then they have the luxury of seeking out higher ideals, such as fraternity and universalism.[156] Moreover, Masonic lodges would have been familiar to many Eastern Sephardic immigrants. The first lodge in Salonika was established in 1904 by Jewish leaders in that city under the sponsorship of the Grand Orient de France. By 1908 a handful of Greek, Armenian, and Muslim men had joined, but Jews continued to dominate numerically.[157]

The historical persecution of Masonic groups carried out by Catholic churches and governments, as well as Masonic opposition to many Church teachings, including the identification of Jews as Christ's crucifiers, may have facilitated warm relations between gentile Hispanic and Sephardic brothers. Masons who were alienated from their Catholicism or who were only nominally Catholic may have rejected the animosity toward Jews and Judaism prevalent in their Spanish-speaking lands of origin.[158] Political factors may have also played a role in building commonalities. Most of the lodge's founders and early members were refugees from Cuba who had fought against what they viewed as despotic Spanish rule.[159] Perhaps some Eastern Sephardic brothers, aware of the Expulsion of Jews in 1492 and long-lived Inquisition, shared this antipathy for Spain.

But the most important bond was language. Without knowledge of Ladino, similar in many ways to Spanish, Eastern Sephardic members could not function in this Hispanophone Masonic lodge. Fluency in Spanish was not merely a pragmatic prerequisite for initiation into the lodge. That "beautiful language," as one lodge leader called it in 1955, was precious to the founding members because it conveyed La Fraternidad's lofty ideals. That the Eastern Sephardim also preserved this "sweet Castilian speech" must have endeared them to gentile brothers. Moreover, their preservation of a Hispanic language served both as proof of their affection for a more tolerant Spain and as a "terrible accusation" against postexpulsion "intolerance and fanaticism."[160]

At the same time, there existed within the lodge an ideology that Jewishness somehow mitigated Hispanicity. At its sixtieth-anniversary banquet in 1915, the lodge's Senior Warden, Manuel Crespo, proudly acknowledged the geographical diversity of his lodge brothers, including those born "on the frozen shores of the Baltic" and those "whose cradles were rocked under the green fig trees of Jericho." Referring to Eastern Sephardic Jews, Crespo observed that because their eleventh-century ancestors "founded extensive colonies in the interior of Spain" and "married native women," they were to be considered "our brothers in blood, proud to be called Spaniards, as we are proud to call them brothers."[161] Thus, the "Spanishness" of Sephardic Jews was not transmitted through them but rather through their intermarriage with Iberian gentiles. Evidently, Crespo did not consider that many Spaniards of the Catholic faith, including those of pagan Visigoth and North African Muslim origins, also had non-Iberian ancestry. Such a multicultural awareness of Spanish society was probably not popularized until the publication of Américo Castro's groundbreaking works on Iberian history in the 1940s.[162]

The presence of Eastern Sephardim in La Fraternidad was apparently a one-generation phenomenon, slacking off beginning in the 1930s. Not coincidentally, this diminution coincided with the founding of the Abravanel lodge, identified by its founders as the first Sephardic Masonic organization in the United States of America.[163] The Abravanel Lodge No. 1116, chartered on May 5, 1932,[164] was named after Isaac Abravanel and founded by Eastern Sephardim who were active masons,[165] including Louis J. Opal (Master elect), Jacques M. Habib (Senior Warden elect), and Salomon Emmanuel (Junior Warden elect).[166] These three men were longtime members of La Fraternidad, Opal having joined in 1924, Habib in 1919, and Emmanuel in 1900, with the latter two joining at age twenty-five.[167] In 1930, these masons had begun to speak of founding a Masonic lodge "whose membership would be predominantly Sephardic," though from the beginning, non-Sephardim (including non-Jews) were also allowed to join. Abravanel was to be the only Masonic lodge in the world whose membership was mostly Sephardic.[168] The lodge met from 1932 to 1934 at the recently constructed Pythian Temple on 70th Street in Manhattan, fortuitously located near Congregation Shearith Israel.[169]

One wonders why members of La Fraternidad would found an offshoot of their longtime lodge in the midst of the Depression. By the 1930s, the Eastern Sephardic community had largely abandoned the Lower East Side as a center of residence, and many in the younger generation possessed only a passing knowledge of Ladino. Linguistic exigencies, then, may have occasioned the founding of Abravanel, as one current member of the lodge affirms,[170] as well as the desire to pass on Masonic brotherhood to the next generation. The founding of Abravanel does not appear to have been a rash act of adolescent rebellion; in 1932 Habib and Emmanuel would have been in their late thirties and fifties, respectively.[171] Still, it is possible that internal dissension contributed to the founding of this offshoot. Consider, for example, that conflict within La Fraternidad between Spaniards and Cubans led to the formation of another Spanish-speaking lodge, La Universal of Brooklyn. All lodges in the district, including La Fraternidad, unanimously approved the petition for the new lodge, thereby demonstrating "the tenets of the Masons' profession, brotherly love and affection."[172] Similarly, Eastern European Jews had founded the Order of Sons of Benjamin in 1879 as a result of discrimination that they felt in the largely German-oriented Jewish lodges, including the Order B'rith Abraham, established in 1859.[173]

Nevertheless, descendants of pioneering members of the Abravanel lodge deny there was internal dissension. One, recalling a conversation with an Abravanel founding member, maintains that these Eastern Sephardic founders simply "wanted their own identity."[174] This testimony and published evidence point to warm relations between the two lodges from early on. In 1935, the La Fraternidad newsletter asked its members to be punctual at a social meeting so that brothers could attend the banquet and dance of "our sister lodge Abravanel."[175] In 1941, La Fraternidad presented the Abravanel lodge with a gift of the "Gabo," a ceremonial gavel used to maintain decorum in meetings.[176] In 1987, Abravanel was identified in its newsletter as "an offshoot of La Fraternidad," and relations between the two lodges still appeared to be close.[177] Abravanel's first Master, Louis J. Opal, continued to be very active in La Fraternidad through the 1960s.[178] Opal joined La Fraternidad on November 22, 1924,[179] and served as an officer in various capacities from the 1930s through the 1960s.[180] Although Abravanel's members were predominantly Eastern Sephardim, Hispanics of the Catholic faith also joined. The lodge's Abravanel Square Club, whose mission it was to organize social events, was founded in 1943 by Jacob Hassid, David N. Barocas, and Tomas Santana,[181] identified by current Abravanel brothers as a Catholic from the Canary Islands.[182]

The 1930s appear to have been pivotal years for the transformation of Sephardic identity in the United States. During that decade, as we have seen, Sephardic masons founded Abravanel, a specifically Sephardic offshoot of the Spanish-speaking La Fraternidad lodge. Ashkenazim could join the English-speaking Abravanel lodge, but, unless they happened to speak Spanish, they could not become brothers of La Fraternidad. Thus, Abravanel served as a meeting place for Eastern Sephardic and Ashkenazic brothers under (Sephardic) Jewish auspices. The process of Anglo-Americanization was apparently stimulating the Jewish (as opposed to Hispanic) side of Eastern Sephardic identity. Another sign of this shift is that the Hispanic Institute's Sephardic Section, which had fostered Hispanic identity in Eastern Sephardim, was beginning to atrophy. The virtual cessation of immigration from the former Ottoman Empire after 1924 and the ensuing weakening of the Ladino language and Eastern Sephardic identity help to explain the waning of Hispanic Sephardic identity. By the 1930s, Eastern Sephardim had achieved a much greater degree of integration into the Ashkenazic-dominant Jewish organizations than they had in the 1910s and '20s, and they often accomplished this integration while still maintaining their distinct communal identity as Eastern Sephardim.[183] The weakening of Hispanic identity among Eastern Sephardim, therefore, may have been as linked to acceptance in the mainstream Jewish community as it was to linguistic and population attrition.[184] But this cultural erosion did not decisively sever the Hispanic-Jewish connection, as future developments would demonstrate.

The Crypto-Jewish Movement of the American Southwest

If language was arguably the strongest unifier of Eastern Sephardim with gentile Hispanics, the connection was bound to unravel with acculturation to Anglo-American culture. The phenomenon of modern-day crypto-Judaism that emerged in the 1980s demonstrates that Jewish historical consciousness could also serve as catalyst for close relations between Jews and non-Jewish Hispanics.[185] In contrast to Hispanic-Jewish alliances of the first half of the twentieth century, Ashkenazic Jews have been in the forefront as mediators of this contemporary "hidden heritage."

The crypto-Jewish movement is based on the largely popular conviction that many forcibly converted Jews in Spain and Portugal, as well as their descendants in both the Iberian Peninsula and the Americas, never fully abandoned their Jewish identity or practices. The major forced conversions of Jews took place in Spain and Portugal in 1391 and 1497, respectively. When faced with expulsion, conversion, or death in 1492, many additional Spanish Jews chose conversion, while most fled over the border to Portugal, where Judaism remained a legal religion until 1497. Even after the establishment of the Spanish and Portuguese Inquisitions in 1478 and 1536, respectively, in Lima (Peru) in 1570, in New Spain (present-day Mexico) the following year, and in Cartagena (present-day Colombia) in 1620, many scholars and laymen have argued, Catholic descendants of forced Jewish converts in the Iberian Peninsula and Spanish America continued to cultivate Jewish identity or practices.

It is historically indisputable that a portion of these early modern Sephardic descendants did indeed preserve a Jewish identity or embraced Mosaic laws and customs. Among the best-known examples is Luis de Carvajal the Younger, a peninsular immigrant who settled in New Spain in the latter half of the sixteenth century and detailed his occult convictions and practices in an autobiography and series of letters, writings recorded not under compulsion—a fundamental methodological problem of Inquisitorial testimony—but rather of his own free will.[186] Historical links between early modern crypto-Jews and their twentieth-century descendants—notably those of Belmonte, Portugal, who retained Jewish self-awareness and praxis—have also been clearly established.[187] Thus, modern-day Hispanos (descendants of Spanish colonists) who claim crypto-Jewish roots could *theoretically* be heirs to an unbroken chain of transmission. The question concerns the *evidence* that self-identified crypto-Jews and scholars have offered in support of a diachronic secret Judaism in the American Southwest.[188]

The "dean" of the crypto-Jewish movement, Stanley Hordes, recorded some of the earliest modern-day claims to Hispano-Jewish descent while serving as New Mexico's state historian in the early 1980s.[189] In 1990, he and Joshua Stampfer, a rabbi of Portland, Oregon, founded the National Society for Crypto-Judaic Studies, self-described as "the major academic organization conducting and encouraging research on the Crypto-Jews." Striving to delineate the boundary between the academic and the personal, the society recently resolved to make a clearer distinction between scholarly papers and reflections or life stories and to professionalize its organ, a quarterly newsletter/journal, *Ha-Lapid: The Journal of the Society for Crypto-Judaic Studies.*[190] In a recent book on the phenomenon (*To the End of the Earth*), Hordes uses Inquisitorial archival records, genealogical and genetic research, oral tradition, and folklore to argue that there is an unbroken thread of identity or practices linking twenty-first-century Hispanos with their alleged sixteenth-century crypto-Jewish ancestors in what is today New Mexico.

The methodology employed by proponents of the crypto-Jewish continuity theory has come under the skeptical scrutiny of historians, folklorists, and journalists. Judith Neulander has discovered that many of the purportedly Jewish customs, such as a game with a spinning top akin to a dreidl, are at best of Ashkenazic (not Sephardic) origin. Neulander has called crypto-Jews an "imagined community."[191] She and others suggest that the will to be Jewish stems from racism turned inward. In the view of these scholars, Chicanos and Hispanos strive to dissociate themselves from their Native American ancestry by grasping on to Jewish identity "as a postmodern marker for ethnic purity."[192] David Gitlitz, a scholar of crypto-Jewish studies, points to the general extinction of hidden Judaism by the late eighteenth century. The assumption that Jewish ancestry renders one Jewish, he argues, is a "major misconception."[193] Thus, in Gitlitz's view, Hordes's most recent project—to verify the Jewish ancestry of the claimants—would not prove crypto-Jewish authenticity. Scholar Seymour Drescher has noted that the Inquisition was largely successful in its goals. Even after the wars of independence, secret Jews of Iberian origin (if any survived) did not openly revert to Judaism. Roman Catholicism remained the dominant religion in Spanish- and Portuguese-speaking Latin America, and only in some isolated villages in Portugal and the Americas was crypto-Judaism "rediscovered or *reinvented* in the late twentieth century" (italics added).[194]

At the other end of the spectrum are academics who accept the self-proclaimed identity at face value and do not seriously address the historicity of oral tradition or the raging controversy about invented heritage.[195] The fact that most of these academics are social scientists is crucial. Scholars in this discipline are generally not trained to assess the past and are generally more preoccupied with self-understanding than with historicity and historical links.[196] Despite this lack of historical focus, their work has not been seriously challenged historiographically, and some historians continue to base their arguments on these findings.[197] The emotion that has fueled much of the controversy has regrettably obscured just this point: the real problem is not historical plausibility but rather methodology.

Ambivalence about historical authenticity is not as strident in the organized Jewish community, but doubts have sprung up there as well. Rabbi Marc Angel, spiritual leader of Congregation Shearith Israel, while inspired by the romanticism of the phenomenon and embracing the ancestors of self-proclaimed crypto-Jews as his own, has nonetheless issued a halakhic recommendation that such claimants formally convert to Judaism in order to eliminate all ambiguity.[198] Conversely, Daniel Bouskila of Sephardic Temple Tifereth Israel in Los Angeles believes that those who seem sincere and have authentic family traditions should be "welcomed back to the community" without conversion.[199]

The modern-day crypto-Jewish phenomenon has also raised considerable controversy in the country's non-Jewish Hispanic communities, a fact often downplayed in Jewish lay and academic circles alike. Historian Elmer Martínez, director of Albuquerque's Spanish History Museum, is dubious about the historicity of Southwest crypto-Judaism. He notes the absence of "solid documentation" and concluded in the early 1990s, "All we have is rumors and people reading between the lines to try and find it."[200] Numerous families in the region have been torn apart by members claiming Jewish descent. Some, echoing Judith Neulander's contention, see this as a fantasy heritage that betrays a shame for *mestizo* ancestry.[201] On the other hand, Hispanos whose families have embraced civil-rights activism as well as their own "nonwhite" phenotypes and ancestry reject this prestige claim as deeply offensive. With the rise of anti-Semitism, some ask rhetorically, what could they possibly gain by being Jews?[202]

The secret Jewish revival has raised many legitimate questions that are often stifled beneath accusations that Jews are reluctant to admit descendants of Native Americans and Hispanics into their ranks or are orthodox "bigots" lacking compassionate tolerance.[203] For the historian, however, these legitimate questions cannot be dismissed by imputations of racism. Nagging inconsistencies include the intense identification with Spain, even as the overwhelming majority of New Christians who immigrated to the Americas, whether Judaizing or not, were of Portuguese origin. The word "judío" (Jew), which modern-day crypto-Jews claim was used as a self-descriptive in their families, could refer in the seventeenth- and eighteenth-century Iberian Peninsula to liberals, Freemasons, or others considered politically threatening. The disdain for Catholicism, which some crypto-Jews point to as proof of their origins, could also theoretically originate from Native American hostility toward an imposed European religion. Self-proclaimed crypto-Jews who have been exposed as imposters motivated by eagerness for fame and financial gain have also encouraged scholarly caution. Finally, the contemporary media's role in creating and shaping crypto-Jewish ethnic identity, not yet extensively explored by any scholar, is crucial to understanding this modern phenomenon.

Of particular interest is the creation of self-identified crypto-Jews who embrace a specifically Sephardic identity. In Albuquerque, New Mexico, about a dozen congregants of the messianic Jewish congregation Adat Yeshua identify as "Sephardim for Yeshua," the Hebrew name for Jesus. They were raised as Catholics, believe Jesus is the Messiah, and have been accepted in the congregation as fellow messianic Jews.[204] Whatever their ensuing struggle for recognition in the mainstream Jewish community, these individuals and congregations are building potential bridges between Jews and Hispanics, even as they test the sensitive boundaries between Christianity and Judaism.

The identification of many Hispanos as descendants of Sephardic Jews can be compared to Catholic Spaniards who in the early twentieth century were involved in the campaign to repatriate Eastern Sephardim to Spain and spread knowledge of the Ladino language. As noted earlier, many of these Spaniards came to suspect their own Sephardic roots, and some asserted a Jewish identity. Skeptical family members sometimes punctured these Sephardic daydreams. Cansinos-Asséns's sister, with whom he lived all his life, rejected his assertions that their family descended from crypto-Jews.[205] Empathic ethnic identity also inspired Ashkenazic Jews. José Máximo Kahn donned a Sephardic identity by moving to Spain and joining philo-Sephardic intellectual circles. Adopting the pseudonym Medina Azara, Kahn briefly served as Spanish consul in Salonika, moved to Madrid, and later relocated to Buenos Aires, where he continued "his youthful love for everything Sephardic."[206] Thus, the contemporary crypto-Jewish movement should not be reduced to a modern phenomenon fueled by internalized racism. From a broad perspective, it is part and parcel of a long-enduring mutual attraction between the Jewish and Hispanic worlds.

The Arabic Embrace

Eastern Sephardic relations with non-Jewish Hispanics share many parallels with relations between gentile Arabs and Mizrahi Jews. This theme, limited here to a brief overview focusing on Syrian Jews, merits in-depth investigation.[207] Many Syrian Jews, in the first decades of their immigration to the United States, sustained close commercial relations with non-Jewish Syrian-Lebanese merchants.[208] Aleppo-born Shayah Shalom, who arrived in 1907 at the age of sixteen, established a booming supply house at 70 Orchard Street, where many of his goods were acquired from local Christian Arab merchants.[209] Even after Syrian Jews moved in the late 1910s to Williamsburg, Brooklyn, neither sufficiently numerous nor well entrenched in their new neighborhood to open their own establishments, they continued to obtain their "Oriental" merchandise from the Christian-Syrian community on Washington Street in lower Manhattan.[210]

There is evidence that some Syrian Jews were ascriptively identified as Arabs upon immigration. Abraham and Rachel Esses, along with (presumably) their children Mazzal, René, and Aslan, were all listed as "Arab" when they arrived at Ellis Island in 1921.[211] In the case of many Syrian Jewish passengers, the "Race or People" rubric on the ship manifest form was initially typewritten as "Syrian" and, later, apparently as a corrective or supplementary afterthought, handwritten as "Hebrew."[212]

In later years, there are indications of overt self-identity as "Arab" or "Arabian" in Brooklyn's Syrian Jewish community. One of the local clubs, founded in 1939, was named the Arabian Knights.[213] During World War II, Syrian Jews identified strongly with aspects of Arabic culture that were not specifically "Jewish." As in the case of relations between gentile Hispanics and Sephardic Jews, common language was key to close relations between Jews and gentiles of Arab lands. Leisure programming in the community over the decades underscores this interethnic camaraderie. Brooklyn's Syrian Jewish community organized Arabic concerts and film screenings to raise funds for the war effort. One of these events, sponsored by the Girls Junior League in 1943, featured the Syrian film *Happy Day,* starring Egyptian singer and movie celebrity Mohammed Abdul Wahab (1907–1991).[214] The hundreds of spectators who attended this and other events, collectively described as "Syrians" or "Syrian people," probably included non-Jews.[215]

The North African front during World War II stimulated the expression of Arabic ethnic identity. Syrian Jewish soldiers serving in the U.S. Army forged close ties with the gentile Arabs whom they encountered in the Maghreb. These connections were reinforced by common language. Pvt. David A. Beyda reported that he met a royal sheik who was "so glad to meet an American soldier speaking Arabic, that he invited him to his home for dinner" and "presented him with a ring to cement friendship between them."[216] These close contacts are explained in part by Joseph Sutton, who notes that in contrast to Eastern European Ashkenazim, Syrian Jews in Aleppo and Damascus for centuries shared a common language and cultural life with their Muslim and Christian Arab neighbors. Whereas Ashkenazim cultivated few ties to their homelands, which they often associated with oppression, Syrian Jewish immigrants "felt that they were *in exile*" (italics in original).[217]

Linguistic and cultural affinity, sustained in part by new immigration waves during the second half of the twentieth century, has continued long after Eastern Sephardim largely abandoned their own ancestral language and loosened their ties with local Spanish-speaking populations. In the late 1970s, Joseph Sutton noted that Syrian families often purchased records at an Arabic record shop on Brooklyn's Atlantic Avenue. Arabic music, performed live by Christian and Muslim Arabic musicians, was the featured entertainment at a variety of family celebrations.[218]

These examples of confluence and self-ascription continue even as Jewish Arab identity has become increasingly untenable for political reasons. William F. Haddad, the Reform Democratic candidate in the 1964 New York elections, whose father was born in Aleppo, claimed that he always identified as an "Arab Jew."[219] Herbert Hadad, a freelance writer of Syrian Jewish descent, joined an Arab American organization during college and was elected its president, albeit while masquerading as a non-Jew. Later, he began to openly espouse an identity as both Jewish and Arab, which elicited both ridicule and disbelief. Largely due to political tensions in the Middle East, Ashkenazic Jews and gentile Arabs alike generally assumed, "You can't be both. It is impossible."[220] Hadad's own father maintained his dual loyalties in tact while keeping his "Arabic upbringing . . . separate from current politics of the Middle East."[221]

Persistent coethnic recognition failure has also challenged the development of a public Arab Jewish identity. In 1964, the primary campaign in the Nineteenth Congressional District focused on the background of Reform Democratic candidate William F. Haddad. Haddad's father, Charles Haddad, grew up in Cairo's Jewish community. The younger Haddad, in his campaign brochures, openly spoke of his father's Arab Jewish origins and in an interview claimed that "he had always described himself as 'an Arab Jew.'"[222] Nevertheless, rumors circulated in New York's (largely Ashkenazic) Jewish community that Haddad "is an Arab and therefore could not possibly be a Jew."[223] In the words of Ella Shohat, the conflation of "Jew" with European origin, along with political conflicts in the Middle East, has made Arab Jewish identity tantamount to "an ontological subversion."[224] Today, a burgeoning group of activists and writers in the United States, both gentile Arab and Jewish, are legitimizing through their various activities and publications the identity of Mizrahim as Arab Jews.[225] As with Eastern Sephardim, the identity of Jews who trace their descent to Arab lands is complicated, varied, and often controversial. Although developed largely on the periphery of American Jewish society, the identity of these Jews should not be marginal to discussions of communal history and identity.[226]

The interactions between Spanish-heritage gentiles and Ladino-speaking Jews took place as Eastern Sephardim were being forced to rethink their identity as both Jews and Sephardim in an environment that often denied their Jewishness and alternately denigrated and celebrated their medieval and postexpulsion Iberian heritage. Through intellectual enterprise, platonic relationships, and intermarriage, Hispanic non-Jews sometimes expanded the boundaries of their own communities to include Eastern Sephardim. Even as common Iberian roots were an important link between gentile Hispanics and Eastern Sephardim, the most powerful magnet was language. The intense connection was thus bound to attenuate, since the influx of Ladino speakers, which tapered off in the early 1920s, did not keep pace with the immigration of Spanish speakers from Spain and Latin America. Nor was the Old Country pool of Ladino speakers, estimated at 350,000 for the years 1900 and 1925, nearly as large as the pool of Spanish speakers.[227]

These cross-ethnic interactions in the first half of the twentieth century are largely overlooked in both lay and scholarly accounts of American Jewish history, and they are almost completely ignored in the media. Recent articles in both the U.S. Anglo-Jewish and Anglo-American press that do consider the Hispanic-Jewish nexus focus on the late twentieth century and deal exclusively with Ashkenazic Jews and their alliances with non-Jewish Latinos. These publications explore the development of the conservative political alliance between Jews and gentile Hispanics that emerged in the United States during the 1980s and '90s, and American Jewish philanthropic endeavors among U.S. Hispanics and in Latin America, including domestic neighborhood revitalization and international disaster relief. The key word in these articles is "Jew," which authors tacitly (and no doubt unconsciously) employ as a synonym for "Ashkenazic." Such contributions reinforce popular understanding of Jewishness as Ashkenazic. Moreover, they obscure the longer-lived, varied, and more intense relationships forged between U.S. Hispanics and Ladino-speaking Sephardim since the turn of the twentieth century.[228]

The recent alliance between largely Ashkenazic Jews and the self-identified descendants of crypto-Jews of the American Southwest demonstrates the influence of Sephardic survival myths on the country's majority Jewish population. The simplistic image of forced converts to Christianity heroically maintaining their Jewish practices and identity has been a memorable component of the U.S. Jewish school curriculum and continues to inform popular imagination.[229] Generally uncritical acceptance of the claim to Sephardic ancestry and to uninterrupted religious traditions have persisted despite internal inconsistencies of family testimony, historical discrepancies, and fundamental misunderstanding of Jewish traditions (e.g., references to Ladino and dreidls as indigenous to crypto-Jewish culture).[230]

Arguably, southwestern Hispanics who claim Sephardic ancestry serve to foster U.S. Ashkenazic identity and perpetuate the image of diasporic Jews as heroic survivors of religious and racial persecution. In the process, however, justice is not being served to the internal cultural and ideological variations within the southwestern population itself, although interviewees often highlight their own ethnic and religious diversity. As one expressed it, "I do believe many northern New Mexicans have some Jewish ancestry, just like we have from many other races, including ... the Native Americans."[231] Another bluntly admits, "I don't feel any connection to Judaism. However, I'm proud of my heritage and tell my children that they have an Apache, Basque, and Jewish heritage."[232] Gloria Golden, author of a recently published collection of oral testimonies, acknowledges that "most of the individuals I interviewed consider themselves Catholic and Spanish."[233] Yet endorsers of her book flatten out all these complexities by referring solely to Jewish identity. One blurb proclaims that the book will show "what it means to discover and embrace one's Judaism." Another, penned by an academic, describes the group of interviewees as "the returning converso Jews in the American West."[234]

Most astonishing is that perhaps the majority of U.S. Jews involved in this movement continue to embrace these "returnees" even when so many of them strongly identify as Christian or Messianic Jews.[235] This attitude contradicts a strong impulse in the organized Jewish community to draw a distinct line between Christianity and Judaism over the nature of Jesus Christ.[236] Also noteworthy is that Ashkenazic mediators of the modern crypto-Jewish movement seem untroubled by certain stereotypical physical and behavioral traits identified by interviewees as Jewish. Many of these identified traits have no factual basis as markers of Jewish identity, and others have blatantly anti-Semitic overtones.[237] This unusual tolerance for religious ambiguity and racist conceptions of Jewishness suggest the intense need for a myth that would foster Jewish identity in what is, according to some demographic reports, a rapidly assimilating community.[238]

Peter Novick, in his study on the role of the Holocaust in the contemporary U.S. Jewish community, offers a similar argument to explain the post-1960s emphasis of American Jews on that genocide.[239] Observers have remarked that the twentieth-century U.S. Jewish community has lacked a unified leadership.[240] In a community bereft of consensus, Novick argues, the idea of "shared victimhood" serves to create a solidarity to address the "survival anxiety" that has fretted communal policymakers and leaders since the post–World War II period.[241] Interestingly, some self-identified crypto-Jews indicate that their first suspicion of their Jewish ancestry came from the suggestions or prodding of often Ashkenazic Jewish acquaintances, suggesting that modern crypto-Judaism may be partly an ascriptive identity serving the identity needs of both groups.[242] The appeal of the crypto-Jewish movement comes partly from the fact that the Holocaust and Inquisition have become the "twin towers" of Jewish persecution, so much so that they are erroneously conflated in the popular mind as driven by the same motivation: to obliterate the Jewish population.[243]

The crypto-Jewish movement of the American Southwest may also be a barometer of a new expansiveness of the U.S. Jewish community's borders. Embracing a population, many of whose members are considered (and consider themselves) nonwhite or minorities, suggests a sea change in Jewish identity politics. If the organized American Jewish community has, since the third wave of immigration, militated against ethnic labels in favor of religious designation, Jewish interest in embracing nominally Catholic and Protestant Hispanics—who according to today's U.S. census constitute an ethnic group that may identify as either white or nonwhite—shows an openness to multiheritage Jewishness.[244] Perhaps this receptivity may eventually transform the way American Jewish history is taught and remembered.

6

Conclusion
A View from the Margins

A recent demographic study sponsored by the American Jewish Committee found that Jews are "the most distinctive" among ethnic and religious groups in the United States. The study was based on surveys carried out by the National Opinion Research Center from 1972 to 2002, and it compared "Jews" to "German, Brits, Blacks, Irish, Hispanics, Italians, Native Americans, Scandinavians, French, Eastern European, Asian, Polish, Other Whites," and "others."[1] What is striking about this research is that American Jews are implicitly imagined as an Ashkenazic ethnic conglomerate discrete from other ethnic and "racial" groups. The author explains Jewish "distinctiveness" by pointing to Ashkenazic historical experiences, such as a "tradition of radicalism and support for socialism in Europe" and a "democratic, reformist tradition against authoritarian government in Europe."[2] In the entire narrative portion of the book, there is no indication that American Jews are anything other than European and Ashkenazic in origin. Only at the back of the book, in the statistical section, do we read, "If Jews are eliminated as an ethnic category and Jews are assigned to other ethnic/racial groups: 95.7% are non-Hispanic white and 4.3% other races and ethnicities (2.2% Black, 1.2% Hispanic, 0.9% Asian)."[3] This tendency can also be observed in the decennial National Jewish Population Survey. The directors of the 1990 survey apparently gave no thought to including questions meaningful to Sephardi and Mizrahi Jews until they were prompted to do so by ASF leaders in 1988.[4]

These demographic studies mirror the two major features of contemporary American Jewish scholarship and communal consciousness: non-Ashkenazic Jews are either entirely ignored or relegated to a tangential remark. These studies are but two examples of a widespread phenomenon that is experienced on both individual and institutional levels. The present book is replete with relevant historical examples, but it is important to emphasize that exclusion and exoticization is an ongoing academic and communal problem. One recent college graduate remarked that over the course of ten years of Jewish education, "everything I learned about the Jews of North Africa, the Middle East, and Latin America came from home."[5] Similarly, Julie Iny, who traces her paternal ancestry to Iraq and India, claims that she learned "next to nothing" about Jews of Arab lands during fourteen years in the socialist-Zionist youth movement.[6] Lital Levy relates that her Hebrew school taught Judaism "as if it were a monolithic tradition," with the only diversity expressed through denominations (Reform, Conservative, and Orthodox).[7] New York's Sephardic House, now a cultural division of the ASF, was established in 1978 partly because "the Sephardic community felt very much ignored by the mainstream American-Jewish community." As founding member Marc D. Angel explained in the late 1990s, "Our contributions to history and civilization were almost totally neglected. The Sephardic component in Jewish life was simply not part of the over-all agenda of the American-Jewish intellectual and cultural establishment."[8] Rachel Amado Bortnick, founder of the online chat room Ladinokomunita, remarked recently, "I always notice that when there is a concert of songs in Yiddish and Hebrew they call it "Jewish Music," but when it is in Ladino it is "Sephardic music."[9]

It is tempting to seek causal connections between this ongoing exclusion and coethnic recognition failure, the historical phenomenon by which Ashkenazic Jews, out of genuine ignorance, denied a shared sense of peoplehood with Sephardim or Mizrahim. However, there are probably very few Jews in America today who are unaware of the existence of Sephardim and Mizrahim. On the other hand, many American Jews are unaware of so-called Jews of color, who have proliferated in recent years as a result of conversion, inter- and intramarriage, or adoption. These "diverse Jews," as they are sometimes called, now bear the brunt of coethnic recognition failure.[10]

Generally speaking, the problem today concerns not genuine ignorance about the existence of non-Ashkenazic Jews but rather what I term corporate exclusion: the failure to consider them a legitimate part of American Jewish history and community. The present book contains numerous examples, including some of the most recent manifestations. When Sephardi and Mizrahi Jews are included in scholarship or cultural programming that focuses on American Jews, they are often inserted as mere tokens and are not integrated into the overarching narrative. Another aspect of this tokenism is extreme representation. Eastern Sephardim and Mizrahim are often described, in the words of author and activist Loolwa Khazzoom, as either "barbaric, primitive, uneducated, dirty, and violent" or as "different, unusual, mysterious, fascinating, and exotic."[11] These stereotypes—whether depicting Sephardim as exalted or denigrating them as backward—are not informative of "real live" Eastern Sephardi and Mizrahi Jews. They tell us nothing of their experiences, struggles, and aspirations as non-Ashkenazi Jews. Whether entirely ignored in American Jewish scholarship or depreciated as the exotic exception, non-Ashkenazi Jews are in either case "the Jews who weren't there."

After decades of academic and communal efforts to spread awareness of non-Ashkenazic Jews in America and weave them into the warp and woof of scholarship, some scholars and activists have concluded that the failure to integrate is not a function of benign ignorance but rather of laziness, parochialism, or intention. The equation of Jewishness with *ashkenaziut* avoids raising uncomfortable questions regarding the place of Jews in the world and their relations with some of their gentile neighbors. A consideration of Eastern Sephardic ties with gentile Hispanics, or Mizrahi connections with non-Jewish Arabs, for example, might dislodge many American Jews from their comfortable niche as white ethnics whose Jewishness is generally confined to religion.[12] It might also force examination of the "Germanness" or "Eastern Europeanness" of an identity widely presumed to be simply "Jewish."

Another possible reason for this exclusion or marginalization is the tendency of many American Jews to self-identify as a religious, as opposed to an ethnic or racial, group. American Jewish demographic studies continue to frame Jewishness in primarily religious terms. This tendency becomes clear when one considers the four screening questions applied to the American Jewish Identity Survey of 2001, which asked participants, "What is your religion, if any?" "Do you or does anyone else in your household have a Jewish mother or a Jewish father?" "Were you or anyone else in your household raised Jewish?" "Do you or anyone else in your household consider himself or herself to be Jewish?" None of these questions explicitly directs the informant to consider identity in ancestral or subethnic terms.[13] Recent attention to secularism as a major force among American Jews has done little to broaden this approach.[14] Moreover, studies on internal divisions within the American Jewish community over the past several years have focused not on ethnic or racial variation but rather on religious practice and communal policy.[15]

In order to properly evaluate coethnic recognition failure and the corporate exclusion of Eastern Sephardim and Mizrahim from the broader Jewish community, a global perspective is imperative. One noteworthy comparison group is non-Ashkenazim of Sydney, Australia, composed mainly of immigrants from Egypt, Iraq, and India. They began to arrive in the late 1940s and first organized in the early 1950s.[16] Its members have testified to the Ashkenazic denial of their shared ethnoreligious identity in ways remarkably similar to the cases documented in the United States.[17] Moreover, non-Ashkenazim found that the Executive Council of Australian Jewry, established in 1945 to welcome and assist all Jewish immigrants admitted into the country, failed to include Jews from Arab lands and in many instances refused to represent prospective Eastern Sephardi and Mizrahi immigrants.[18] Anthropologist Naomi Gale concludes that Ashkenazic Jews sought to disassociate themselves from Middle Eastern and Asian Jews because they feared losing their status as white Australians. She also suggests that the government's anti-immigration policy, which often viewed Eastern Sephardim and Mizrahim as "half or at most three-quarter caste," would implicate Ashkenazim as nonwhite.[19] This comparative example stimulates new questions about Ashkenazic-Sephardic relations in the United States. One wonders, for example, if the provincial definition of Jewishness that led to coethnic recognition failure had been universal among all Eastern European Ashkenazic communities from which Ashkenazic immigrants hailed. One might also speculate if the phenomenon of corporate exclusion was an impulse among Ashkenazim wherever they settled or whether it was conditioned by their status as a numerical majority among Jews and by national racial and immigration policies. There is evidence, for example, that corporate exclusion was a serious issue for Sephardim in the global Zionist movement in the 1920s and '30s. An interesting test case for these questions would be France, whose largely Mizrahi population in many structural ways dominates the broader Jewish community.

Students of Jewish history are often trained to seek the impact of Jews on broader society. Indeed, this impact is sometimes seen as a justification for studying the topic. The evidence considered for this book suggests that Eastern Sephardi and Mizrahi Jews had no perceptible impact on their immediate reference group, American Ashkenazim, during the first half of the twentieth century. One main reason for this lack of impact can be explained through the "tipping point," a term popularized in the 1970s that refers to a moment when a population achieves a certain proportion (often around 20 percent) significant enough to make a crucial impact on larger society.[20] Before 1948, non-Ashkenazic Jews in the United States numbered well below 1 percent of the general American Jewish population, far short of a "critical mass" that might have had a direct influence on broader Jewish society. Today, non-Ashkenazim form about 4 percent of the U.S. Jewish population, still well below the proportion theoretically necessary to have a visible impact on the broader community.[21]

This lack of influence, however, does not mean that non-Ashkenazic communities are unworthy of study. The records that Eastern Sephardi and Mizrahi Jews left behind, particularly as they relate to intra- and interethnic dynamics, are eloquent indicators of Jewish self-identity and of the self-conception of gentile Hispanics and Arabs. These records, unearthed and examined up to one hundred years after their creation, may hold the key to a paradigm shift in American Jewish history and communal identity.

How do we integrate the "Jews who weren't there" into the field of American Jewish history? One answer lies in viewing the past from their perspective. This "history from the margins" can paint a more complete portrait of American Jewry. But more importantly, it will tell us much about Jewish self-identity that a focus on mainstream Jewry cannot. In this book I have attempted to distinguish scholarship from social activism (group advocacy is not the task of the historian). Thus, my findings and analyses should by no means be taken as a guide to effect change in Jewish communal policy. Rather, the hope here is to stimulate new research and approaches to the study of American Jewish history. If my arguments for the worthiness of including Eastern Sephardim and Mizrahim in the narrative of American Jewish history do not suffice, perhaps sheer scholarly boredom with a very old historiographical paradigm will.

Appendix
Population Statistics of Non-Ashkenazic Jews in the United States of America

Estimates of the non-Ashkenazic Jewish population of the United States since 1880 vary widely. Statistical ambiguity is a characteristic of the U.S. Jewish population in general. Salo Wittmayer Baron observes, "our information about the number of Jews residing in the United States in any period, but especially since the enormous increase at the turn of the twentieth century, is conjectural." This uncertainty exists because national decennial censuses since 1790 were not permitted to record religious affiliation. The tallies of religious bodies, carried out under governmental supervision, are likewise unreliable, as they rely heavily on "varying denominational interpretations." Since the 1870s, Baron observes, estimates of the Jewish population were left to the Jewish community itself (Baron, *Steeled by Adversity*, 269–70). As the chart below suggests, the uncertainty is all the more pronounced for the nation's population of non-Ashkenazic Jews.

Year	Population	Description	Source
"before 1900"	"a few hundred"	"Sephardic Turkish immigrants from the Ottoman Empire" in "New York"	Albert J. Amateau, "Turkish-Jewish Pioneers in the US," *Turkish Times* (March 1, 1991)
1900 to 1905	"hardly a few dozen"	Sephardic immigrants from the Oriental Mediterranean in the United States	M. J. Benardete, "Saver i ser: Nessim Behar en los Estados Unidos," *La Vara* (April 5, 1940)
1912	1,000	Arabian Jews in New York	Asher Levy to H. Pereira Mendes, December 15, 1912, CSISA
1912	20,000	Eastern Sephardic Jews	[Moise Gadol], "El emportante raporto del Bureau Oriental," *La America* (January 12, 1912): 2
1914	10,000–15,000	"Oriental Jews" in New York, including Ladino-, Arabic-, and Greek-speaking	"Oriental Jews Gather," *New York Times* (June 8, 1914): 7

Year	Population	Description	Source
1915	20,000	"Sefaradím" of New York; Ladino-speaking	[Moise Gadol], "Basta Piedrer Tiempo en Vazío," *La America* (October 22, 1915): 4; and [Moise Gadol], "La Vieja Istoria Se Repita" (December 24, 1915): 6
1916	100,000	"Sephardim of America"	[Moise Gadol], "Nada por Nuestros Sefaradím," *La America* (July 7, 1916): 3
1918 to 1919	4,000–5,000	Syrian Jews in Williamsburg	Joseph A. D. Sutton, *Magic Carpet: Aleppo-in-Flatbush: The Story of a Unique Ethnic Jewish Community* (New York: Thayer-Jacoby, 1979), 35
1923	50,000	Ladino-speaking Sephardim in the United States	Maír José Benardete, "Los Romances Judeo-Españoles en Nueva York," M.A. thesis, Columbia University, 1923, viii
1923	20,000–25,000	Ladino-speaking Sephardim in New York City	Benardete, "Los Romances Judeo-Españoles en Nueva York," viii
1924	50,000–100,000; 40 percent in New York City	"Levantine Jews in the United States"	"Levantine Jews in America," *The Interpreter* (New York: Foreign Language Information Services) 4:10 (December 6, 1925): 5
1926	50,000–60,000 (of whom 40,000 lived in New York)	"Sephardim," referring to all non-Ashkenazic immigrants from the Levant	Louis M. Hacker, "The Communal Life of the Sephardic Jews in New York City," *Jewish Social Service Quarterly* 3:2 (December 1926): 32, 34
1900 to 1930	100,000	"Sephardic Turks"	Amateau, "Turkish-Jewish Pioneers in the US," citing HIAS statistics without specific attribution
1935	50,000	"Spanish" Jewish population in North America	Susan Bassan [Warner], "Judeo-Spanish Folk Poetry," M.A. thesis, Columbia University, 1947, 19, citing E. M. Torner, *Temas folklóricos-música y poesía* (Madrid: Faustino Fuentes, 1935), 52
1939	75,000	"Sephardi Jews"	David Sitton, *Sephardi Communities Today* (Jerusalem: Council of Sephardi and Oriental Communities, Jerusalem, 1985 [1962]), 328
1941	250	Yemeni Jews in the United States	Dina Dahbany-Miraglia, "Acculturation and Assimilation: American Yemenite Jews," *Perspectives: Research, Instruction and Curriculum Development, a Journal of the Faculty, New York City Technical College*, CUNY 10 (1987–1988): 125

Year	Population	Description	Source
1946	55,000 (of whom 40,000 lived in New York)	"Sephardim"; no distinction made	Joseph M. Papo, "The Sephardic Community in America," *Reconstructionist* 12 (October 20, 1946): 12–18
1953	60,000	"Hispano-Levantines" in the United States; over half in New York	Maír José Benardete, *Hispanic Culture and Character of the Sephardic Jews*, 1st ed. (New York: Hispanic Institute, 1952), 141
1954	65,000 in the United States of America	"Sephardim"	Isaac I. Schwarzbart, "Toward Unity between Sephardim and Ashkenazim: A Survey of World Jewish Congress Organization Activities to Attain This Goal and Comparative Chart of the Sephardim in the World Jewish Population, 1950–1954," April 1954, unpublished typescript, box 11, folder "Speeches," Joseph M. Papo Papers, AJA, p. 2
1962	60,000 in Greater New York	Divided as follows: half from Balkan lands and Turkey, half from Arab lands (known as the Syrians)	Sitton, *Sephardi Communities Today*, 333
1966	55,000–60,000 (40,000 in New York City)	"Sephardim"; broadly defined	Helen Shirazi, "The Communal Pluralism of Sephardi Jewry in the United States," *Le Judaïsme Sephardi* (new series) 31 (January 1966): 23–25
1972	Over 150,000 in the United States, according to author's investigation; nearly 200,000, according to Ashkenazic communal workers and historians with whom author consulted. Of the author's estimate, 20,000 are Syrian Jews in New York.	"Sephardi and Eastern Jews"	Sitton, *Sephardi Communities Today*, 327, 330

Year	Population	Description	Source
1973	100,000	"Sephardic and Oriental Jews" in the United States	Daniel Elazar, as cited in "Organization Set Up by Sephardic Jews to Promote Culture," *New York Times* (February 26, 1973): 22
1976	180,000	Jews from Spain, "Portugal, Turkey, Greece, Syria and Islamic countries"	"The Minority within a Minority," *Human Behavior* (June 1976): 62
1977	25,000	Syrian Jews of Brooklyn	Bernard Gwertzman, "Syrian Proxy-Marriage Plan Lets Jewish Women Emigrate to U.S.," *New York Times* (July 31, 1977): 1
1979	20,000–25,000	Syrian Jews in Flatbush, Brooklyn; "Sepharadi Jews"	Sutton, *Magic Carpet*, ix, 3.
1983	200,000	"Sephardi and Eastern Jews"	Matti Ronen, "Sephardi Jews in the United States," *Sephardi Heritage* (winter 1983): 23
1987	5,000	Yemeni Jews in the United States	Dahbany-Miraglia, "Acculturation and Assimilation," 125
1992	100,000	Sephardim of Iberian origin	Albert de Vidas to Editor of *Jewish Week*, August 16, 1992. box 9, Joseph M. Papo Papers, AJA
1996	400,000	"Sephardic and Oriental Jews across the United States"	Edwin Shuker to Yuri Shcherbak, September 4, 1996, box 9, folder "ASF Concerns about the state of the Jewish cemetery in Lviv (Ukraine), 1996," ASF
2004	250,000	Non-Ashkenazic Jews	Randy Belinfante, personal communication, August 26, 2004

Abbreviations

AJA	American Jewish Archives (Cincinnati, Ohio)
AJHS	American Jewish Historical Society (New York, New York)
ASF	American Sephardi Federation (New York, New York)
CSISA	Congregation Shearith Israel Sisterhood Archives (New York, New York)
FAZ	Federation of American Zionists
HIAS	Hebrew Immigrant Aid Society
IRO	Industrial Removal Office
PAJHS	*Publications of the American Jewish Historical Society*

Notes

NOTES TO THE ACKNOWLEDGMENTS

1. Giselle Hendel-Sebestyen, "The Sephardic Home: Ethnic Homogeneity and Cultural Traditions in a Total Institution," Ph.D. diss., Columbia University, 1969, 32, 35.

NOTES TO THE INTRODUCTION

1. Milas is in present-day southwestern Turkey. The use of the phrase "the Jews who weren't there" to describe the exclusion of Sephardim and Mizrahim from scholarship originates from Marianne Sanua, "'The Jews Who Weren't There': Integrating Sephardim and Mizrachim into the Jewish Studies World View," session 5.3, "When Diasporas Meet: Interactions between Sephardi/Mizrahi and Ashkenazi Jews in Modern Times," paper presented at the Association for Jewish Studies Conference, December 1998.
2. Albert J. Amateau, "The Immigrant from Turkey," unpublished typewritten manuscript, 13 pages, box 7, folder "Salo Baron," Joseph Papo Papers, AJA, p. 1. Amateau arrived on August 18.
3. Gloria Ascher, "'Smyrna to New York': Alfred Ascher's Judeo-Spanish Diary," available online at http://istanbulsephardiccenter.com/index.php?contentId=121&mid=114 (accessed January 29, 2008). Ascher is now working on a critical edition of this diary.
4. Albert J. Amateau, "One Century in the Life of Albert J. Amateau, 1889–: The Americanization of a Sephardic Turk," interview conducted by Rachel Amado Bortnick, March 26, 1986 (Berkeley, CA: privately reproduced, 1989), 55, 66.
5. Gloria Ascher, email correspondence to author, December 10, 2007.
6. Examples, still accumulating in various media, are too numerous to compile here. See, for example, Dina Dahbany-Miraglia, "An Analysis of Ethnic Identity among Yemenite Jews in the Greater New York Area," Ph.D. diss., Columbia University, 1983, 24–25; Brigitte Sion, "Where Have All Sephardim Gone?" *Los Muestros* 36 (September 1999): 11–12; Rachel Wahba, "Benign Ignorance or Persistent Resistance?" in Loolwa Khazzoom, ed., *The Flying Camel: Essays on Identity by Women of North African and Middle Eastern Jewish Heritage*, 47–65 (New York: Seal Press, 2003), 51–59; and Melanie Kaye/Kantrowitz, *The Colors of Jews: Racial Politics and Radical Diasporism* (Bloomington: Indiana University Press, 2007). For parallel examples in the State of Israel, see H.

Toledano, "Time to Stir the Melting Pot," in Michael Curtis and Mordecai S. Chertoff, eds., *Israel: Social Structure and Change*, 333–48 (New Brunswick, NJ: Transaction Books, 1973), 341–42.

7. Among the works that elide Sephardi and Mizrahi Jews are Jeffrey S. Gurock, *When Harlem Was Jewish, 1870–1930* (New York: Columbia University Press, 1979); Deborah Dash Moore, *At Home in America: Second-Generation New York Jews* (New York: Columbia University Press, 1981); Edward S. Shapiro, *A Time for Healing: American Jewry since World War II* (Baltimore: Johns Hopkins University Press, 1992); and Paula E. Hyman, *Gender and Assimilation in Modern Jewish History: The Roles and Representation of Women* (Seattle: University of Washington Press, 1995). Hyman explains her omission of Eastern Sephardim and Mizrahim on p. 7.

8. Works with passing references to Western Sephardim include Leon A. Jick, *The Americanization of the Synagogue, 1820–1870* (Hanover, NH: Brandeis University Press, 1976), 3–4, 55; Jonathan Sarna, ed., *The American Jewish Experience* (New York: Holmes & Meier, 1997 [1986]), in which "Sephardic" is not in the index; Gerald Sorin, *A Time for Building: The Third Migration, 1880–1920* (Baltimore: Johns Hopkins University Press, 1992), 2, 71, 90, 102, 153, 175, 181; Henry L. Feingold, *A Time for Searching: Entering the Mainstream, 1920–1945* (Baltimore: Johns Hopkins University Press, 1992), with a brief mention of Western Sephardim on pp. 32 and 137–38; Hasia R. Diner and Beryl Lieff Benderly, *Her Works Praise Her: A History of Jewish Women in America from Colonial Times to the Present* (New York: Basic Books, 2002), 9–10, 25–26, in which Ladino is incorrectly identified as the *lingua franca* of Spanish Jews and Iberian Jewish exiles in Amsterdam and Brazil; Marc Lee Raphael, *Judaism in America* (New York: Columbia University Press, 2003), 41–43; Dana Evan Kaplan, *The Cambridge Companion to American Judaism* (Cambridge: Cambridge University Press, 2005), 24, 25, 31, and a brief allusion to Ladino music on p. 376; Eric Goldstein, *The Price of Whiteness: Jews, Race and American Identity* (Princeton, NJ: Princeton University Press, 2006), 130–31; Norman H. Finkelstein, *American Jewish History* (Philadelphia: Jewish Publication Society of America, 2007), in which Sephardim disappear from the narrative by the mid-nineteenth century; and Beth S. Wenger, *The Jewish Americans: Three Centuries of Jewish Voices in America* (New York: Doubleday, 2007), 3.

9. Works reflecting, to varying degrees, awareness of Eastern Sephardim are Salo Wittmayer Baron, *Steeled by Adversity: Essays and Addresses on American Jewish Life* (Philadelphia: Jewish Publication Society of America, 1971), 280; Jack Wertheimer, ed., *The American Synagogue: A Sanctuary Transformed* (Cambridge: Cambridge University Press, 1987), with a chapter on the Eastern Sephardic synagogues of Seattle; Howard M. Sachar, *A History of the Jews in America* (New

York: Vintage Books, 1992), 337–40; Daniel Soyer, *Jewish Immigrant Associations and American Identity in New York, 1880–1939* (Cambridge, MA: Harvard University Press, 1997), 2, 46, 117, 123; Jack Glazier, *Dispersing the Ghetto: The Relocation of Jewish Immigrants across America* (Ithaca, NY: Cornell University Press, 1998), 15, 111, 129, 145; and Ilana Abramovitch and Seán Galvin, *Jews of Brooklyn* (Hanover, NH: Brandeis University Press, 2002). Historiography on Eastern Sephardim in Florida, home to the third-largest Sephardic community in the country, is now developing, as seen in Henry Alan Green, *Mosaic: Jewish Life in Florida: A Documentary Exhibit from 1763 to the Present* (Coral Gables, FL: Mosaic, 1991), 21–22.

10. Hasia R. Diner, *A New Promised Land: A History of Jews in America* (Oxford: Oxford University Press, 2003); and Jonathan D. Sarna, *American Judaism: A History* (New Haven, CT: Yale University Press, 2004). On Sarna's omission within the context of American Jewish multiculturalism, see Ilan Stavans, "Multiculturalism and American Jews: Oy, Are We a *Pluribus?*" in *The Jewish Identity Project: New American Photography*, 27–45 (New York: Jewish Museum/New Haven, CT: Yale University Press, 2005), 31.

11. Hasia R. Diner, *The Jews of the United States, 1654 to 2000* (Berkeley: University of California Press, 2004), 81.

12. See, for example, Rudolph J. Vecoli, "Immigration," in Paul S. Boyer, ed., *The Oxford Companion to United States History* (Oxford: Oxford University Press, 2001), 359–66; James Ciment, ed., *Encyclopedia of American Immigration*, 4 vols. (Armonk, NY: M. E. Sharpe, 2001), 1:95 and passim, where the Jewish immigrants who arrived in 1654 are not specified as Sephardim. Western and Eastern Sephardim as well as Mizrahim are better represented in John Powell, *Encyclopedia of North American Immigration* (New York: Facts on File, 2005).

13. Marc D. Angel, "Sephardic Culture," *Jewish Spectator* (December 1972): 23; Abraham D. Lavender, "The Sephardic Revival in the United States: A Case of Ethnic Revival in a Minority-within-a-Minority," *Journal of Ethnic Studies* 3:3 (1975): 21–31; "The Minority within a Minority," *Human Behavior* (June 1976): 62; Matti Ronen, "Sephardi Jews in the United States," *Sephardi Heritage* (winter 1983): 23; Glazier, "The Indianapolis Sephardim: An Essay," *Shofar* 3:3 (1985): 27; Judith Laikin Elkin, review of Joseph M. Papo's *Sephardim in Twentieth Century America*, *American Jewish History* 77:3 (March 1988): 502; Richard Kostelanetz, "Two Views of Jewish American Literature: A Norton Anthology," *Midstream* 47:6 (September-October 2001): 37; David Rabeeya, *Encyclopedia of Wisdom and Jewish Mythology* (Xlibris, 2003), 164–65, 173; David Rabeeya, *The Journey of an Arab-Jew: Through the American Maze* (Xlibris, 2007), 17, 23; David Shasha, review of Lucien Gubbay, *Sunlight and Shad-*

ow: *The Jewish Experience of Islam* (Other Books, 2001) and "Sephardic Literature: The Real Hidden Legacy," *Zeek* (September 2005).

14. See, for example, José Faur, "Introducing the Materials of Sephardic Culture to Contemporary Jewish Studies," *American Jewish Historical Quarterly* 43:4 (June 1974): 340–49; Alan D. Bennett, "The Rewakening of American Sephardim: Lesson Plan Summary," *Keeping Posted* (November 1974): 9–10; H. J. Campeas, "The Inclusion of a Sephardi Dimension in American Jewish Education," *New Directions: A Publication of the Annual Workshop on Innovative Jewish Education* (American Jewish Committee, March 13, 1978), 47–56; Lea-Nora Kordova, Annette Labovitz, and Eugene Labovitz, *Our Story: The Jews of Sepharad: Celebrations and Stories* (New York: Coalition for the Advancement of Jewish Education, 1991); Jane S. Gerber, ed., *Sephardic Studies in the University* (Madison, NJ: Fairleigh Dickinson University Press, 1995); and Tamar Frank, "The Sephardic Heritage in the Jewish Curriculum: Current Practices and Future Directions," in Yedida K. Stillman and Norman A. Stillman, eds., *From Iberia to Diaspora: Studies in Sephardic History and Culture*, 533–45 (Leiden: Brill, 1999).

15. "Roundtable on Integrating the Sephardi/Mizrahi Experience," session 6.5, AJS conference, December 2003; AJS Sephardi/Mizrahi Studies Caucus, panels and lunch sessions organized annually since 1997. For a broader discussion of Jewish historiography and paradigm shifts, see Michael A. Meyer, "The Emergence of Jewish Historiography: Motives and Motifs," *History and Theory* 27 (1988): 160–75; Jacob Katz, "Emancipation and Jewish Studies," *Jewish Emancipation and Self-Emancipation* (Philadelphia: Jewish Publication Society, 1986), 75–85; and David Biale, "Challenging the Boundaries," *AJS Perspectives* (fall/winter 2003): 12.

16. Denah Lida, "The Vanishing Sephardim," *Le Judaïsme Sephardi*, New Series 24 (July 1962): 1037; Isaac Jack Lévy, "Folklore and Reality: The Key to a People," *Sephardic Scholar*, Series 2 (1972–73): 29.

17. "Sephardic Studies Program," *American Sephardi* 4 (autumn 1972): 119; Ben G. Frank, "The Sephardic Revival," *Keeping Posted* 20 (November 1974): 6.

18. "The American Society of Sephardic Studies," *American Sephardi* 2 (1968): 13–14; Isaac Jack Lévy, "Foreword," *Sephardic Scholar*, Series 2 (1972–73): 5; "Organization Set Up by Sephardic Jews to Promote Culture," *New York Times* (February 26, 1973): 22. Yeshiva University also publishes the *Sephardic Bulletin*. As part of the "Sephardic revival," three Sephardic high schools were established in New York in the course of three years, and New York Sephardic leaders established the Foundation for the Advancement of Sephardi Studies and Culture (FASSC) in 1969. Raymond Harari, "The Awakening of Sephardic Youth," *Keeping Posted* 22 (November 1974): 22; Frank, "The Sephardic Revival," 6.

19. Western Sephardic Jews in America were outnumbered by Ashkenazim by the 1720s, but no reliable statistics are available. Estimates for the contemporary American Sephardi and Mizrahi population hover at around 3 or 4 percent of the U.S. Jewish population. See chapter 1 of this volume and Judith Mizrahi, *703 American Sephardim: Diversity within Cohesiveness* (New York: Gemini Books, 1993), 1.

20. Roth's remark, made in the context of broader Sephardic civilization, equally applies to American Jewish literature. Norman Roth, "What Constitutes Sephardic Literature?" in Yedida K. Stillman and Norman A. Stillman, eds., *From Iberia to Diaspora: Studies in Sephardic History and Culture*, 247–63 (Leiden: Brill, 1999), 262.

21. David Shasha, "A Jewish Voice Left Silent: Articulating 'The Levantine Option,'" *Secular Culture & Ideas* (2008), online journal sponsored by the Posen Foundation and available at http://www.jbooks.com/secularculture/index.htm.

22. Minutes Meeting of the Board of Directors of the American Sephardi Federation, November 26, 1997, box 1, Board of Directors Meeting, November 1997, ASF, p. 2.

23. Lavender, "Sephardic Revival in the United States," 306. Lavender observed in 1976 that Sephardim constituted 16 percent of world Jewry and 60 percent of Israel's Jews. See also "Minority within a Minority."

24. Lynn Davidman, *Tradition in a Rootless World: Women Turn to Orthodox Judaism* (Berkeley: University of California Press, 1991), 47; for statistics, see Daniel J. Elazar, "Communal Reflections: A Report on What Is Known," *Jewish Education* 59:2 (fall 1991): 13; Jim VandeHei, "Future of Orthodox Jewish Vote Has Implications for GOP," *Washington Post* (August 3, 2006): A6.

25. Quoted in Davidman, *Tradition in a Rootless World,* 47. See Jill Julius Matthews, *Good and Mad Women: The Historical Construction of Femininity in Twentieth-Century Australia* (Sydney: Allen & Unwin, 1984).

26. Charles Selengut, "American Jewish Converts to New Religious Movements," *Jewish Journal of Sociology* 30:2 (December 1988): 95–109; Rodger Kamenetz, *The Jew in the Lotus: A Poet's Rediscovery of Jewish Identity in Buddhist India* (San Francisco: Harper, 1994), esp. 132ff. Social scientists today generally prefer the term "New Religious Movement" over "cult."

27. M. Mitchell Serels, "Sephardic Printing as a Source of Historical Material," in Issachar Ben-Ami, ed., *The Sephardi and Oriental Jewish Heritage: Studies*, 123–31 (Jerusalem: Magnes, 1982), 123.

28. Rabeeya, *Encyclopedia of Wisdom*, 165; and for similar statements, see Rabeeya, *Journey of an Arab-Jew*, 13, 17.

29. Walter P. Zenner and Shlomo Deshen, "Introduction: The Historical Ethnology of Middle Eastern Jewry," in Shlomo Deshen and Walter P. Zenner, *Jewish Societies in the Middle East: Community, Culture and Authority* (Washington, DC: University Press of America, 1982), 1.

30. For an analysis of the image of Sephardim and Mizrahim in modern Hebrew literature, see Lev Hakak, *Inferiors and Superiors: The Image of Sephardim and Near Eastern Jews in Modern Hebrew Short Story* (Kiryat-Sefer, 1981); and Lev Hakak, "The Image of Sephardim in the Modern Hebrew Short Story," in Issachar Ben-Ami, ed., *The Sephardi and Oriental Jewish Heritage: Studies*, 297–310 (Jerusalem: Magnes, 1982).

31. Jacob R. Marcus, "The Periodization of American Jewish History," *PAJHS* 47:3 (March 1958): 126–27. For a critique of the "generation" model, which divides American Jewish history according to the heaviest waves of Jewish immigration, see Sarna, *American Judaism*, xviii–xix.

32. Reflections of Marina Rustow and Sarah Abrevaya Stein, as cited in Kaye/Kantrowitz, *Colors of Jews*, 93.

33. Edouard Roditi, "'Those Other Jews' in Fiction," *Midstream* 28:8 (October 1982): 55.

34. Wahba, "Benign Ignorance," 58.

35. This book is a revision and expansion of my "Where Diaspora Met: Sephardi and Ashkenazi Jews in the City of New York—A Study of Intra-Ethnic Relations, 1880–1950," Ph.D. diss., Brandeis University, 1998. The earliest use of the phrase "minority within a minority" applied to the U.S. Sephardi and Mizrahi communities seems to date to the 1970s. See Lavender, "Sephardic Revival in the United States"; "Minority within a Minority"; Eliezer Chammou, "Migration and Adjustment: The Case of Sephardic Jews in Los Angeles," Ph.D. diss., University of California Los Angeles, 1976, 181; and Joseph A. D. Sutton, *Magic Carpet: Aleppo-in-Flatbush: The Story of a Unique Ethnic Jewish Community* (New York: Thayer-Jacoby, 1979), 228, in which Sutton refers to a "minority *within another minority*" (italics in original).

36. On Greek-speaking Jews, see Steven B. Bowman, *The Jews of Byzantium, 1204–1453* (Tuscaloosa: University of Alabama Press, 1985); and Annette B. Fromm, *We Are Few: Folklore and Ethnic Identity of the Jewish Community of Ioannina, Greece* (Lanham, MD: Lexington Books, 2007).

37. For a recent example of this paradigm, see Stephen H. Norwood and Eunice G. Pollack, eds., *Encyclopedia of American Jewish* History, 2 vols. (Santa Barbara, CA: ABC CLIO, 2007), 1:xiii–xiv.

38. For a critique of this aspect of U.S. Jewish historiography (the neglect of interethnic dimensions of American Jewish history), see Robert Singerman, "Introduction," and Scott Cline, "Jewish-Ethnic Interactions: A Bibliographical Essay," *American Jewish History* 77:1 (September 1987): 4–5, 135–54.

39. The statistic is from Dash Moore, *At Home in America*, 21.

40. For a list of subscribers to *La Vara* in these and other American cities, see *La Vara* (July 25 and September 9, 1924). Only the first two communities ever reached the three thousand mark during the first half of the twentieth century.

41. For a consideration of Jewish communities of New York as compared to other Jewish settlements in the country, see Louis Wirth, *The Ghetto* (Chicago: University of Chicago Press, 1928), 204–5. These distinctions are sometimes a factor of relative size. In Seattle, for example, Eastern Sephardim at one time constituted up to one-third of the general Jewish population.

42. Two previous books on American Sephardim were written by a congregational rabbi and communal activist, respectively. Marc D. Angel's *La America: The Sephardic Experience in the United States* (Philadelphia: Jewish Publication Society of America, 1982) focuses on the first American Ladino newspaper, *La America,* and its somewhat idiosyncratic editor, Moise Gadol, a Bulgarian immigrant who arrived in New York in 1910. Joseph M. Papo's *Sephardim in Twentieth Century America: In Search of Unity* (San Jose and Berkeley: Pelé Yoetz Books and Judah L. Magness Museum, 1987) concentrates on organizational unity and ultimate communal fragmentation within the American Sephardic community. Joseph A. D. Sutton (*Magic Carpet: Aleppo-in-Flatbush*) explores the Arabic-speaking Syrian community of New York.

43. Deb Hammacher, "Latino Immigrants Are Changing the Face of America, Say Emory Experts," press release from Emory University, May 28, 2002, available online at http://www.news.emory.edu/Releases/latinoforum1022617768.html (accessed September 27, 2007); Sam Roberts,

"In Name Count, Garcias Are Catching Up to Joneses," *New York Times* (November 17, 2007): 1 and A13. On trends affecting the coverage of peoples from the Middle East, see Amaney Jamal and Nadine Naber, eds., *Race and Arab Americans before and after 9/11: From Invisible Citizens to Visible Subjects* (Syracuse, NY: Syracuse University Press, 2007).

44. Diane Kaufmann Tobin, Gary A. Tobin, and Scott Rubin, *In Every Tongue: The Racial and Ethnic Diversity of the Jewish People* (San Francisco: Institute for Jewish and Community Research, 2005), 20–21.

45. Ibid.; Kaye/Kantrowitz, *Colors of Jews*; Joel Sanchez, "Wrestling with the Angel of Identity: Jews of Color," M.S.W. thesis, Smith College, 2006.

46. *El Mesajero* ("The Messenger") appeared in Los Angeles from 1933 to 1934; *El Emigrante* ("The Émigré") appeared in New Brunswick, New Jersey, in 1917. See Aviva Ben-Ur, "In Search of the American Ladino Press: A Bibliographical Survey, 1910–1948," *Studies in Bibliography and Booklore* 21 (winter 2001): 10–52.

47. For a heavily genealogical account of Syrian Jewish immigrants, focused mainly on the author's family, see Robert Chira, *From Aleppo to America: The Story of Two Families* (New York: Rivercross, 1994). Two fine articles are Walter P. Zenner, "Syrian Jews in Three Social Settings," *Jewish Journal of Sociology* 10:1 (1968): 101–20; and Marianne Sanua, "From the Pages of the *Victory Bulletin*: The Syrian Jews of Brooklyn

during World War II," *YIVO Annual* 19 (1990): 283–30.

48. The manuscript is tentatively titled "Yemenites in America: The 'Invisible' Jews." Dina Dahbany-Miraglia, email correspondence to author, September 28, 2007.

49. On "Janinan" Jews, see Rae Dalven, *The Jews of Ioannina* (Philadelphia: Cadmus, 1990); and Fromm, *We Are Few*. The latter includes information on Ioanninan Jews in the United States.

50. In 1914, an article in *The Survey* mentioned that Levantine Jewish immigrants were "conducting newspapers of their own in Ladino, Arabic and Greek." See "Oriental Jews Will Finance Their Own Social Work," *The Survey* 31:18 (January 31, 1914): 518. A minutes review of a meeting on the unification of the Oriental Jewish community of New York specifically instructs officials to publicize organizational efforts in "each Hebrew, Greek and Arabic newspaper in New York." The first line reads, "In Order to quickly organize on a sound and permanent basis:—." Untitled circular, CSISA, p. 1.

51. Traditionally, both Judeo-Greek and Judeo-Arabic are printed in Hebrew letters. But circulars announcing upcoming events in the colony have survived, and these announcements are printed in Greek and Arabic—as opposed to Hebrew—letters, which suggests that if these groups did indeed produce their own newspapers, they were not printed in Judeo-Greek or Judeo-Arabic.

52. José M. Estrugo, *El retorno a Sefarad: Un siglo después de la inquisición* (Madrid: Europa, 1933), 37. The phrase "the other Jews" is borrowed from Daniel J. Elazar, *The Other Jews: The Sephardim Today* (New York: Basic Books, 1989). See also Roditi, "'Those Other Jews' in Fiction."

53. Estrugo, *El retorno a Sefarad*, 35–36 and, for other details, 35–38. The translations are mine. The communal minutes identifying Estrugo as a founder of the Los Angeles Sephardic community (now Sephardic Temple Tifereth Israel) are quoted at the Sephardic Temple Tifereth Israel website, http://home.earthlink.net/~benven/STTI.htm (accessed November 18, 2007).

54. Isaac da Costa, "The Jews of Spain and Portugal," in Isaac da Costa et al., *Noble Families among the Sephardic Jews* (London: De Navorscher, c. 1857; 2nd Dutch edition, 1876); Haim Beinart, "Cuando llegaron los judíos a España?" *Estudios* 3 (1962): 6–8; Ivan G. Marcus, "Beyond the Sephardic Mystique," *Orim* 1 (1985): 44.

55. Beinart, "Cuando llegaron los judíos a España?" 6.

56. As suggested in da Costa, "Jews of Spain and Portugal." Juan de Mariana (*Historia General de España*, 1733) linked Toledo to Toledot (the Hebrew word for "generations"), and Yepes, Escalona, Noves, and Maqueda with Jope (Jaffa), Ascalon, Nobe, and Magedon, respectively. See Beinart, "Cuando llegaron los judíos a España?" 8. See also James Finn, *Sephardim; or, The History of the Jews in Spain and Portugal* (London: J. G. F. & J. Rivington, 1842), 18–19.

57. Susan Bassan [Warner], "Judeo-Spanish Folk Poetry," M.A. thesis, Columbia University, 1947, 3.

58. Yosef Kaplan, "The Travels of Portuguese Jews in Amsterdam to the 'Lands of Idolatry' (1644–1724)," in Yosef Kaplan, ed., *Jews and Conversos: Studies in Society and the Inquisition* (Jerusalem: World Union of Jewish Studies and the Magnes Press, Hebrew University, 1955), 198. *Conversos* in this context refer to Iberian Jews forcibly converted to Catholicism in 1391 in Spain and in 1497 in Portugal. Their descendants are also called *conversos*. Ashkenazic Jews also used false Hebrew etymologies to express their sense of belonging in diasporic lands. One legend tells that Poland derives its name from the Hebrew *poh-lin* ("here you shall dwell"), the command of a heavenly voice to Jewish exiles who left Spain in 1492. Diane K. Roskies and David G. Roskies, eds., *The Shtetl Book* (New York: Ktav), xiii.

59. Patricia Seed, *Ceremonies of Possession in Europe's Conquest of the New World, 1492–1640* (Cambridge: Cambridge University Press, 1995), 163, 165, 174–76.

60. The most famous exception is Judah Halevi, who in 1141 forsook his respectable, upper-class life in Spain and embarked for Palestine, then under Crusader rule. On the age-old tendency of Jews to remain in the diaspora even when immigration to Palestine was possible and safe, see A. B. Yehoshua, "Exile as a Neurotic Solution," in Etan Levine, ed., *Diaspora: Exile and the Contemporary Jewish Condition* (New York: Steimatzky, 1986), 15–35.

61. See Harold Fisch, trans., *The Holy Scriptures* (Jerusalem: Koren, 1989).

62. *Sefarad*, like Roman *Hispania*, encompassed the entire Iberian peninsula; Portugal did not emerge as an independent kingdom until the twelfth century.

63. For rabbinical commentaries on Obadiah 1:20, including those of Yonatan ben Uziel, Rabbi Abraham Ibn Ezra, Rabbi David Kimchi, and Isaac Abravanel, see *Nevi'im Aharonim* [in Hebrew] (Berlin: Schocken, 1937/1938), 311a. They use the term "Aspamiah," a corruption of the Roman word for the peninsula. See also H. Freedman and Maurice Simon, eds., *Midrash Rabbah Leviticus* 29:2 (London: Soncino, 1983), 370–71 (esp. 371); I. Laredo and David Gonzalo Maeso, "El nombre de Sefarad" and "Sobre la etimología de la voz Sefarad," *Sepharad: Revista de la Escuela de Estudios Hebraicao* 4:2 (Madrid 1944): 349–63; and S. Krauss, "The Names Ashkenaz and Sepharad" [in Hebrew], *Tarbiz* 3 (5692 [1931/1932]): 423–35.

64. Beinart, "Cuando llegaron los judíos a España?" 30. Consider, too, the Talmudic reference to "Aspamia" in Baba Batra 38:1, as discussed in ibid.

65. Epitaph of Salomonula, Adra, Spain, third century, in Emil Hübner, *Inscriptiones Hispaniæ Latinæ* (Berlin: G. Reimerum, 1869), 268; and for an analysis of the tombstone and its epitaph, see José Amador de los Ríos, *Historia social, política y religiosa*

de los Judíos de España y Portugal, 2 vols. (Madrid: Turner, 1984), 1:68.

66. Haim Beinart dates a Jewish sarcophagus discovered in Tarragona to the first or second century C.E. Haim Beinart, "Cuándo llegaron los judíos a España?" 21. An amphora discovered in Ibiza (an island off the east coast of Spain) in 1907 and dated by one scholar to the first century C.E. suggests the presence of Jewish merchants but not necessarily a Jewish community. David Noy, *Jewish Inscriptions of Western Europe*, vol. 1, *Italy (Excluding the City of Rome), Spain and Gaul* (Cambridge: Cambridge University Press, 1993), 239.

67. Recommended overviews are Eliyahu Ashtor, *The Jews of Moslem Spain* (Philadelphia: Jewish Publication Society, 1973); and Yitzhak Baer's classic *A History of the Jews in Christian Spain*, 2 vols. (Philadelphia: Jewish Publication Society, 1992 [1971]).

68. The term "Spanish Golden Age" was first employed by Christian Hebraist Franz Delitzsch, in reference to periodization of Spanish-Jewish poetry. Ismar Schorsch, "The Myth of Sephardic Supremacy," *Leo Baeck Institute Year Book* 34 (1989): 60–61.

69. Estimates range from 150,000 to 400,000, though some figures reach much higher. Avigdor Levy, *The Jews of the Ottoman Empire* (Princeton, NJ: Darwin, 1994), 4, 126n. 17; Henry Kamen, "The Mediterranean and the Expulsion of Spanish Jews in 1492," *Past and Present* 119 (May 1988): 31; and Henry Kamen, "The Expulsion: Purpose and Consequence," in Elie Kedourie, ed., *Spain and the Jews: The Sephardic Experience, 1492 and After*, 74–91 (London: Thames and Hudson, 1992), 85; Baer, *History of the Jews in Christian Spain*, 1:27.

70. David M. Gitlitz, *Secrecy and Deceit: The Religion of the Crypto-Jews* (Philadelphia: Jewish Publication Society, 1996), 27. According to Baer (*History of the Jews in Christian Spain*, 2:438), a majority of between 100,000 to 120,000 Jews fled to Portugal.

71. Yosef Kaplan, "Bom Judesmo: The Western Sephardic Diaspora," in David Biale, ed., *Cultures of the Jews: A New History*, 639–69 (New York: Schocken, 2002), 642. Kaplan does not explain why the tie to Portugal would have been even stronger than to Spain.

72. In the kingdom of Navarre, this happened in 1498. Benjamin R. Gampel, *The Last Jews on Iberian Soil: Navarrese Jewry, 1479–1498* (Berkeley: University of California Press, 1989).

73. David L. Graizbord, *Souls in Dispute: Converso Identities in Iberia and the Jewish Diaspora, 1580–1700* (Philadelphia: University of Pennsylvania Press, 2004).

74. See Kaplan, "Bom Judesmo."

75. See, for example, Marc D. Angel, *Remnant of Israel: A Portrait of America's First Jewish Congregation* (New York: Riverside, 2004), 14.

76. For a refutation of the year 1654 as the congregation's founding, see Leo Hershkowitz, "By Chance or Choice: Jews in New Amsterdam 1654," *de Halve Maen: Journal of the Holland Society of New York* 77:2 (summer 2004): 23–30.

77. Henry Hart Milman claimed in the late nineteenth century that "of those who fled from Spain, ... 50,000 are estimated to have been admitted into that country [the Ottoman Empire]." Henry Hart Milman, *The History of the Jews* (London: Darf, 1986 [1892]), 574. According to Henry Kamen, there is no evidence of a dramatic Sephardic influx into the Ottoman Empire in 1492, but "many undoubtedly went there in the course of the sixteenth century." Kamen, "The Expulsion," 90. Early-sixteenth-century records indicate that "within two or three decades after their expulsion, tens of thousands of Iberian Jews had become established in many Ottoman cities and towns." Avigdor Levy, *The Sephardim in the Ottoman Empire* (Princeton, NJ: Darwin, 1992), xiii. See also Aron Rodrigue, "The Sephardim in the Ottoman Empire," in Elie Kedourie, ed., *Spain and the Jews: The Sephardi Experience, 1492 and After*, 162–88 (London: Thames and Hudson, 1992), 165.

78. Imanuel Aboab, *Nomologia o discursos legales* (Amsterdam: n.p., 5487 [1726–1727]), 317 (my translation from the Castilian).

79. Rodrigue, "Sephardim in the Ottoman Empire," 164.

80. Ibid., 165–66.

81. Levy, *Sephardim in the Ottoman Empire*, 3–4.

82. Ibid., 12; and Levy, *Jews of the Ottoman Empire*, 12.

83. Avigdor Levy, introduction to Levy, ed., *Jews, Turks, Ottomans: A Shared History, Fifteenth through the Twentieth Century* (Syracuse, NY: Syracuse University Press, 2002), xix.

84. Bernard Lewis, *The Jews of Islam* (Princeton, NJ: Princeton University Press), 120–48; Levy, *Sephardim in the Ottoman Empire*, xiii.

85. Levy, *Sephardim in the Ottoman Empire*, 72–73.

86. Ibid., 71.

87. Ibid., 74.

88. Moshe David Gaon, *A Bibliography of the Judeo-Spanish (Ladino) Press* [in Hebrew] (Tel Aviv: Monoline, 1965). Gaon's bibliography is not exhaustive. For example, he counted only twelve American Ladino periodicals, as compared to my count of nineteen. Aviva Ben-Ur, "The Ladino (Judeo-Spanish) Press in the United States, 1910–1948," in Werner Sollors, ed., *Multilingual America: Transnationalism, Ethnicity, and the Languages of American Literature*, 64–77 (New York: New York University Press, 1998).

89. Levy, *Sephardim in the Ottoman Empire*, 121; and Levy, introduction to *Jews, Turks, Ottomans*, xviii. In 1905, 60,000 of Salonika's 130,000 inhabitants were Sephardim.

90. Levy, *Sephardim in the Ottoman Empire*, 120.

91. Ibid., 121.

92. Haïm Vidal Sephiha, *L'Agonie des Judéo-Espagnols* (Paris: Éditions Entente, 1977), 65.

93. Maír José Benardete, *Hispanic Culture and Character of the Sephardic Jews*, 2nd ed. (New York: Sepher-Hermon Press for the Foundation for the Advancement of Sephardic Studies and Culture and Sephardic House at Congregation Shearith Israel, 1982) (unless otherwise indicated, subsequent references to this book are to this edition),

56, referring to "the two or three main languages of the Peninsula" that Sephardic exiles transported.

94. There is an ongoing debate about what to call this language among both laymen who are native speakers and scholars. Terms include Ladino, Judezmo, romance, espaniolit, sefardí, lingua franca, jargón, espanyol (Spanish), judeo-espanyol (Judeo-Spanish), gudió, and gidió. My own preference is for Ladino, a term often used by native speakers in the United States. See, for example, Denah Lida, "The Vanishing Sephardim," *Le Judaîsme Sephardi*, New Series 24 (July 1962): 1036 and Susan Bassan [Warner], "Judeo-Spanish Folk Poetry," M.A. thesis, Columbia University, 1947, 32. David M. Bunis observes that the term *Ladino* is the most widely used today among lay people. David M. Bunis, "Judezmo Language and Literature: An Experiment at Columbia University," in Issachar Ben-Ami, ed., *The Sephardi and Oriental Jewish Heritage: Studies*, 383–402 (Jerusalem: Magnes, 1982), 387].

95. David M. Bunis, *A Guide to Reading and Writing Judezmo* (Brooklyn, NY: Adelantre!, 1975), 1–2; Stanford J. Shaw and Ezel Kural Shaw, *History of the Ottoman Empire and Modern Turkey*, 2 vols. (Cambridge: Cambridge University Press, 1995 [1977]), 2:386. In printed form, Ladino appeared in either Rashi script or block Hebrew letters. Handwritten Ladino appeared in solitreo, the cursive of the Sephardic Jews. The verb *seletrear* denotes "to correspond," in the sense of "to communicate."

96. Calque, from the French *calquer,* "to trace," refers to translations of Hebrew religious texts into Judeo-Spanish that preserve the Hebrew syntax.

97. M. L. Wagner, *Caracteres generales del judeo-español de Oriente* (Madrid, Hernando, 1930), 20.

98. Aviva Ben-Ur, "Ladino in Print: Towards a Comprehensive Bibliography," *Jewish History* 16:3 (2002): 309–26.

99. Uriel Weinreich, *College Yiddish: An Introduction to the Yiddish Language and to Jewish Life and Culture* (New York: YIVO Institute for Jewish Research, 1992), 143–44. See also Max Weinreich, *History of the Yiddish Language*, trans. Shlomo Noble (Chicago: University of Chicago Press, 1980), 1–2.

100. These observations are based on Bernard Lewis, *Semites and Anti-Semites: An Inquiry into Conflict and Prejudice* (New York: Norton, 1987), 63. One notable exception is Aleppo, Syria. Although Iberian exiles arriving there in the sixteenth century formed only "a separate minuscule Sephardi community," Ladino initially dominated as the main Jewish language. Joseph A. D. Sutton, *Aleppo Chronicles: The Story of the Unique Sephardeem of the Ancient Near East—in Their Own Words* (New York: Thayer-Jacoby, 1988), xi–xii.

101. Arthur Ruppin, *Soziologie der Juden* (Berlin: Jüdischer Verlag, 1931): 2:131. Another source estimates the population of Ladino speakers in 1935 at 650,000. Bassan [Warner], "Judeo-Spanish Folk Poetry," 16. Hen-

ry V. Besso stated in 1968 that there were a million or a million and a half Judeo-Spanish (Ladino-speaking) Jews and their descendants in the world. Henry V. Besso, "Los Sefardíes y el Idioma Castellano," *Revista Hispánica Moderna* 34:1–2 (January–April 1968): 178.

102. Asher Birnbaum, "Jewish Languages," *Encyclopedia Judaica* (New York: Macmillan, 1971), 10:67. In 1948 there were reportedly 220,000 Ladino-speaking Sephardim in the State of Israel. Besso, "Los Sefardíes y el Idioma Castellano," 192.

103. The classic article on this theme is Schorsch, "Myth of Sephardic Supremacy."

104. Heinrich Graetz, *Divrei Yemei Israel* (Warsaw: Ahisefer, 1893), 7:11–12, 40; Max Grünbaum, *Jüdisch-Spanische Chrestomathie* (Frankfurt am Main: J. Kauffmann, 1896), 4; Moritz Kayserling, "Sephardim," *The Jewish Encyclopedia* (New York: Ktav, 1901–1905), 2:197; Marcus Ehrenpreis (trans. Alfhild Huebsch), *The Soul of the East: Experiences and Reflections* (New York: Viking, 1928), 40–41. The word in modern Spanish would be *grandeza*.

105. Kayserling, "Sephardim."

106. Maurice Henry Harris, *History of the Mediaeval Jews: From the Moslem Conquest of Spain to the Discovery of America* (New York: Bloch, 1907), 308; "Rev. Dr. Harris Dies; Dean of Rabbinate," *New York Times* (June 24, 1930): 21. Harris was of British birth.

107. Raphael Patai and Jennifer Patai, *The Myth of the Jewish Race*, rev. ed. (Detroit: Wayne State University Press, 1989), 25–30; John M. Efron, *Defenders of the Race: Jewish Doctors and Race Science in Fin-de-Siècle Europe* (New Haven, CT: Yale University Press, 1994), 24, 82, 88, 104, 114–19, 179. These scholars included both Jews and non-Jews in their racial categories. Other anthropologists divided Jews into three or more racial categories.

108. Laikin Elkin, review of Joseph M. Papo's *Sephardim in Twentieth Century America*.

109. Haim Vidal Sephiha, "Plan d'urgence de recherches dans le domaine des langues et literatures judéo-espagnoles," in Issachar Ben-Ami, ed., *The Sephardi and Oriental Jewish Heritage: Studies*, 353–82 (Jerusalem: Magnes, 1982), 354. Sephiha's observations relate to France but are equally applicable to the United States.

110. Mark R. Cohen, "The Origins of Sephardic Jewry in the Medieval Arab World," in Zion Zohar, ed., *Sephardic and Mizrahi Jewry: From the Golden Age of Spain to Modern Times* (New York: New York University Press, 2005), 36.

111. For early examples of this application, see David de Sola Pool, "The Levantine Jews in the United States," *American Jewish Year Book* 15 (1913–1914): 211; and Alice Davis Menken, response to David de Sola Pool's Report on the Brith Shalom Congregation, November 1922, CSISA. Heading reads, "To the Board of Trustees, Congregation Shearith Israel."

112. See, for example, Ernestine Rose, *Bridging the Gulf: Work with the*

Russian Jews and Other Newcomers (New York: Immigrant Publication Society, 1917), 5; Mary Frank, *Exploring a Neighborhood: Our Jewish People from Eastern Europe and the Orient* (New York: Immigrant Publication Society, 1919), 1; "Levantine Jews in America," *The Interpreter* (New York: Foreign Language Information Services) 4:10 (December 6, 1925): 4–8.

113. Papo, *Sephardim in Twentieth Century America*, 52.

114. Joseph A. D. Sutton, for example, argues that the Iberian Peninsula was a linguistic, religious, and economic continuum of the ancient and medieval Middle East and that Iberian Jews were therefore "none other than descendants of Middle East *ancestors*" who hailed from Egypt, Baghdad, North Africa, Palestine, and Syria. This argument overlooks the fact that all Jews, presumably, originally descend from the Middle East. Sutton, *Magic Carpet*, 251–52. For a similar view, see David de Sola Pool, "The World of the Sephardim: A Personal Survey," 5–21, and Abraham Lopes Cardozo, "The Music of the Sephardim," 37–70, both in David de Sola Pool, Raphael Patai, and Abraham Lopes Cardozo, eds., *The World of the Sephardim* (New York: Herzl, 1960), 5, 37–38; Elazar, *The Other Jews*; Ammiel Alcalay, *Keys to the Garden: New Israeli Writing* (San Francisco: City Lights Books, 1996).

115. These scholars argue that non-Ashkenazic Jews should be classified on the basis of ancestral language and region and that "Sephardic" as a blanket term is simply erroneous. Among them are Alan D. Corré, "Sephardim," *Encyclopaedia Judaica* (Jerusalem: Keter, 1972), 14:1164–71; Sephiha, "Plan d'urgence," 354; Besso, "Los Sefardíes y el Idioma Castellano," 178. On examples of cultural and religious differences between Eastern Sephardim and Mizrahim, see Stephen Stern, "Ethnic Identity among the Sephardic Jews of Los Angeles," in Issachar Ben-Ami, ed., *The Sephardi and Oriental Jewish Heritage: Studies*, 133–44 (Jerusalem: Magnes, 1982), 135; and Nitza Druyan, "Early Contacts between the Sephardic Community and the Yemenite New Immigrants in Jerusalem at the End of the 19th Century," in Issachar Ben-Ami, ed., *The Sephardi and Oriental Jewish Heritage: Studies*, 157–64 (Jerusalem: Magnes, 1982), 162–63.

116. For examples, see Yosef Hayim Yerushalmi, review essay of Simposio de Estudios Sefardíes, *American Jewish Historical Quarterly* 42:2 (December 1972): 184; Laikin Elkin, *The Jews of Latin America* (New York: Holmes & Meier, 1998), 180, and Richard Glaser, "The Greek Jews in Baltimore," *Jewish Social Studies* 38:3–4 (summer-fall 1976): 327.

117. Isaac Jack Lévy, "Sephardic Scholarship: A Personal Journey," in George K. Zucker, ed., *Sephardic Identity: Essays on a Vanishing Jewish Culture*, 11–25 (Jefferson, NC: McFarland, 2005), 17–25.

118. In this sense their behavior is similar to non-Ashkenazic Jewish immigrants in Latin America, who also organized according to native tongue. Laikin Elkin, *Jews of Latin America*, 180.

119. Bernard Lewis, *The Jews of Islam* (Princeton, NJ: Princeton University Press, 1987), 121, 127; Norman A. Stillman, *The Jews of Arab Lands: A History and Source Book* (Philadelphia: Jewish Publication Society, 1979), 90, 289.

120. Ella Shohat, "The Invention of the Mizrahim," *Journal of Palestine Studies* 29:1 (autumn 1999): 5–20. Farsi-speaking Jews from what is today Iran were numerically negligible in the United States until the second half of the twentieth century, as were Aramaic-speaking Jews from Central Asia. On Farsi-speaking Jews, see Daniel Tsadik, *Between Foreigners and Shi'is: Nineteenth-Century Iran and Its Jewish Minority* (Stanford, CA: Stanford University Press, 2007).

121. Greek-speaking Romaniote Jews in New York established Kehila Kedosha Janina, a still-functioning congregation on the Lower East Side. The synagogue maintains a museum on its premises at 280 Broome Street.

122. For early discussions on nomenclature, see David de Sola Pool, "The Immigration of Levantine Jews into the United States," *Jewish Charities* (Baltimore) 4:11 (June 1914): 12–13; Albert J. Amateau, "Sephardic Jews," *American Hebrew* (October 3, 1916): 792; and J. de A. Benyunes, "The Sephardic Jews of New York," *American Hebrew* (September 29, 1916): 718.

123. Annette B. Fromm, "Sephardic Remnants in Ioannina," in George K. Zucker, ed., *Sephardic Identity: Essays on a Vanishing Jewish Culture*, 75–80 (Jefferson, NC: McFarland, 2005).

124. For example, Jack Marshall observes that Jews (including, he states, possibly his father's ancestors) had lived in present-day Iraq for twelve hundred years but explains that the ancestors of "Arabic Jews" were expelled from Spain in 1492. Jack Marshall, *From Baghdad to Brooklyn: Growing Up in a Jewish-Arabic Family in Midcentury America* (Minneapolis: Coffee House Press, 2005), 16, 30.

125. Michael Pollak, preface to Ken Blady, *Jewish Communities in Exotic Places* (Northvale, NJ: Jason Aronson, 2000), xv.

126. Daniel Elazar (*The Other Jews*) notes that Moroccan Jews, for example, lived farther west than most European Jews. He also objects to the negative connotations of "East" when juxtaposed with "West."

127. My thanks to David Gedalecia for this point. Many leading scholars, however, prefer the term *edot ha-mizrah*. See, for example, Cohen, "Origins of Sephardic Jewry," 36.

128. Janet Liebman Jacobson, *Hidden Heritage: The Legacy of the Crypto-Jews* (Berkeley: University of California Press, 2002).

129. Stanley M. Hordes, *To the End of the Earth: A History of the Crypto-Jews of New Mexico* (New York: Columbia University Press, 2005).

NOTES TO CHAPTER 1

1. Isaac Azriel, "Letra de Elis Ailand," *La America* (June 11, 1915): 8; ship manifest (available via ellisiland.org). I have Anglicized his first name,

which, according to the Ladino accent, would be pronounced "Ishák." According to the ship manifest of May 28, Azriel was diagnosed with a deformity of the thorax (known today as rib hump).

2. Isaac Azriel, "Letra de Elis Ailand," and "Komo fui delivrado de Elis Ailand," *La America* (June 25, 1915): 6. For an account of similar scenes witnessed at Ellis Island from 1907 to 1910, see Fiorello La Guardia, *The Making of an Insurgent: An Autobiography: 1882–1919* (Westport, CT: Greenwood, 1984 [1948]), 64–65.

3. Legislation requiring a literacy test was passed in 1917. Baron, *Steeled by Adversity*, 289. The bill was successively vetoed by presidents Benjamin Harrison, Grover Cleveland, William H. Taft, and finally by Woodrow Wilson, but it was passed over Wilson's veto. Cyrus Adler to Lucien Wolf, 1922, in Cyrus Adler, *Selected Letters*, ed. Ira Robinson, 2 vols. (Philadelphia: Jewish Publication Society of American; New York: Jewish Theological Seminary of America, 1985), 2:51.

4. "Salvada de la deportasión kuando el vapor se aprejava a partir," *La Vara* (January 19, 1923): 3. I have Anglicized Kamhi's first name, which, according to the Ladino accent, would be pronounced "Sará."

5. David Barocas, audiotape address for the Sephardic Brotherhood of America, May 19, 1963, private audio collection of Albert Matarasso, courtesy Dora Matarasso Green.

6. Isaac Azriel, "Letra de Elis Ailand," *La America* (September 8, 1915): 8. Another term for Ellis Island was "island of tears." David M. Brownstone, Irene M. Franck, and Douglass L. Brownstone, *Island of Hope, Island of Tears* (New York: Rawson, Wade, 1979), 14, 166, 168, 170, 192, 195–96, 203, 227; Leo Hershkowitz, "Ellis Island," *The Oxford Companion to United States History* (Oxford: Oxford University Press, 2001), 222.

7. See, for example, *La America* (October 1 and November 19, 1915) and *El Progreso* (October 10 and November 5, 1915).

8. Linguistic barriers, of course, also affected non-Jewish immigrants. For an example, see Amateau, "Immigrant from Turkey," 5.

9. Peter Mesenhöller, *Augustus F. Sherman: Ellis Island Portraits, 1905–1920* (New York: Aperture, 2005), 6–7; Barbara Benton, *Ellis Island: A Pictorial History* (New York: Facts on File, 1985), 7; Brownstone, *Island of Hope*, 203. However, no more than 2 percent of immigrant detainees at Ellis Island were deported annually. Benton, *Ellis Island*, 7, 54, 92, 96.

10. Roger Daniels, "Immigration Law," *The Oxford Companion to United States History* (Oxford: Oxford University Press, 2001), 365. There were seventy ports of entry in the United States in the early 1900s, but 90 percent of all immigrants entered through Ellis Island. Benton, *Ellis Island*, 7.

11. Daniels, "Immigration Law," 365.

12. Mae M. Ngai, "The Architecture of Race in American Immigra-

tion Law: A Reexamination of the Immigration Act of 1924," *Journal of American History* (June 1999): 69.

13. Brownstone, *Island of Hope*, 95.

14. The Arabian peninsula, Egypt, Iraq (Mesopotamia), and Morocco (French and Spanish Zones and Tangier) were allotted 100 each; Syria and Lebanon (French Mandate) were allotted 123; and Turkey and Greece, 226 and 307, respectively.

15. Mesenhöller, *Augustus F. Sherman*, 6; Hershkowitz, "Ellis Island."

16. Mesenhöller, *Augustus F. Sherman*, 7.

17. Soyer, *Jewish Immigrant Associations*, 138–39.

18. Ibid., 139–40. In 1909, the Hebrew Sheltering Home Association (Hakhnoses Orkhim) merged with the Hebrew Immigrant Aid Society, and in its composite form was generally known as HIAS. Jocelyn Cohen and Daniel Soyer, ed., *My Future Is in America: Autobiographies of Eastern European Jewish Immigrants* (New York: New York University Press, 2006), 312.

19. *La America* (December 17, 1915). Despite these barriers, many Eastern Sephardi and Mizrahi Jews had received assistance from HIAS from early on. Dahbany-Miraglia's Yemeni Jewish informants reported that a few of the earliest immigrants (who began to arrive in 1905) took advantage of its services. Dahbany-Miraglia, "Analysis of Ethnic Identity among Yemenite Jews," 136.

20. Joshua Cohen, "Report on the Oriental Bureau for the Year 1917," typewritten manuscript, box "Masa-

da," folder "YIVO Institute," Joseph M. Papo Papers, AJA, p. 2. For more on HIAS and the Oriental Bureau, see chapter 5 of this volume.

21. Angel, *La America*, 139. For references to children working to help support their impoverished families, who arrived between 1900 and 1920, see David N. Barocas, *The History of the Broome & Allen Boys Association, Inc.* (New York: Foundation for the Advancement of Sephardic Studies and Culture, 1969 or 1970), 6–7; and Leon Alcosser, "My Life's Memoirs," unpublished manuscript, dated 1970–1981 (photocopy in author's possession, courtesy of Ed Alcosser).

22. *La Vara* (August 1, 1924).

23. *La Vara* (September 12, 1924).

24. *La America* (April 30 and May 7, 1915).

25. HIAS, Report of Committee on Oriental Hebrews, unpublished typescript, box 11, folder "Speeches," Joseph M. Papo Papers, AJA, p. 1.

26. Cohen, "Report on the Oriental Bureau for the Year 1917," 1.

27. The dangers of these bombings became acute early in 1917, when the imperial German government announced that it would use its submarines to bomb all ships coming into Great Britain's ports or into ports administered by Germany's enemies. La Guardia, *Making of an Insurgent*, 138.

28. HIAS, Report of Committee on Oriental Hebrews, 1–3.

29. Rachel Amado Bortnick, *One Century in the Life of Albert J. Amateau, 1889–: The Americanization of a Sephardic Turk: An Interview Con-*

ducted by Rachel Amado Bortnick on March 26, 1986 (Berkeley: privately reproduced, 1989), 52–53; [Moise Gadol], *La America* (February 17, 1911); and [Moise Gadol], "El importante raporto del Buro Oriental," *La America* (December 29, 1911): 2.

30. Anecdotes about the Schinasi family, transmitted by Izmir-born Mathilde Benforado, are recorded in Sally Bowen Benforado, *Bring Me a Story* (Oakland, CA: Floricanto, 1986), 29–32, 53. Mathilde lived for a time with the Schinasis, and her brothers worked in their Turkish cigarette factory. Sally, a gentile of English and Irish ancestry, was Mathilde's daughter-in-law. Larchmont is located on the shore of the Long Island Sound. The Victrola was invented in 1906 and was popular through the 1920s.

31. *La America* (February 17, 1911).

32. Sephardic Jewish Community of New York, mimeographed bulletin, 2:97 (year unspecified; either 1928 or 1929).

33. Papo, *Sephardim in Twentieth Century America*, 29–30; *Souvenir Programme First Annual Ball of the Sephardic Jewish Community of New York, Inc.*, Sunday Eve., February 13, 1927, folder "Sephardic Jewish Community of New York," Joseph M. Papo Papers, AJA, pp. 1, 50 (unpaginated).

34. "Obituary," *New York Times* (October 31, 1933): 24. This obituary specifies "Turkey" without including the city of birth.

35. *Scrap Book of the Sisterhood of the Spanish and Portuguese Synagogue*, from 1897, *Shearith Israel Sisterhood Fair Descriptive Catalogue of a Collection of Objects of Jewish Ceremonial*, n.d., probably c. 1915, CSISA; Grace Cohen Grossman with Richard Eighme Ahlborn, *Judaism at the Smithsonian: Cultural Politics as Cultural Model* (Washington, DC: Smithsonian Institution Press, 1997), 54. According to Cyrus Adler, the family was from Damascus, and Ephraim Benguiat, the elder of the family, was living in Boston by 1892. Cyrus Adler, *I Have Considered the Days* (Philadelphia: Jewish Publication Society of America, 1941), 174. I have not ascertained Ephraim Benguiat's year of immigration to the United States.

36. Amateau identifies this as the 1904 World's Fair, held in St. Louis, Missouri. Albert J. Amateau, "Turkish-Jewish Pioneers in the US," *Turkish Times* (March 1, 1991).

37. This obstacle was surmounted through the acquisition of "certificates of travel," issued by transport companies. Kemal H. Karpat, "The Ottoman Emigration to America, 1860–1914," *International Journal of Middle East Studies* 17 (1985): 187. The depression of the 1890s was another deterrent to immigration.

38. Testimony of Ida Mouradjian, an Armenian from the Ottoman Empire who survived the Armenian Holocaust during World War I, as transcribed in Brownstone, *Island of Hope*, 71.

39. Pool, "Immigration of Levantine Jews," 21.

40. [Moise Gadol], "El emportante raporto del Bureau Oriental," *La America* (January 5, 1912): 2.

41. Ibid.

42. Jewish immigration from the Near East first became noticeable in approximately 1903, but the greatest influx began after the Young Turk revolution of 1908. Pool, "Levantine Jews in the United States," 207.

43. "Levantine Jews in America," 5; David de Sola Pool, *H. Pereira Mendes* (New York: n.p., 1938), 22; Papo, *Sephardim in Twentieth Century America*, 30. Papo (p. 30) identifies the Levantine Jews who immigrated after 1908 as often lacking formal education and vocational skills.

44. [Moise Gadol], "El importante raporto del Buro Oriental," *La America* (December 29, 1911): 2; [Moise Gadol], "El emportante raporto del Bureau Oriental," *La America* (January 5, 1912): 2; [Moise Gadol], "El servisio military en Turkía," *La America* (January 19, 1912): 1; Ezra Sitt to David de Sola Pool, April 17, 1913, CSISA, pp. 1–2; Cohen, "Report on the Oriental Bureau for the Year 1917," 1; "Levantine Jews in America," 5; Albert Franco, "History of The Rhodes League of Brothers' Aid Society, Inc.," undated typescript, c. 1950s, photocopy in author's possession, p. 3; Benardete, *Hispanic Culture and Character of the Sephardic Jews*, 1st ed. (New York: Hispanic Institute, 1952), 139; Angel, *La America*, 11–12, without a citation; Sutton, *Magic Carpet*, 127. Leon Ligier, who was born in Vidin, Bulgaria, in 1879, also cited military conscription as a reason for leaving his native land. Chammou, "Migration and Adjustment," 60.

45. Before that time, non-Muslims had been permitted to secure an exemption from military service through the *bedel-i-askeri* tax. Mandatory conscription for all the republic's ethnoreligious groups was an effort to introduce equality among all citizens, but loopholes in the law existed as a means of producing much-needed revenue for the constitutional government. Feroz Ahmad, "The Special Relationship: The Committee of Union and Progress and the Ottoman Jewish Political Elite, 1908–1918," in Avigdor Levy, ed., *Jews, Turks, Ottomans: A Shared History, Fifteenth through the Twentieth Century*, 212–30 (Syracuse, NY: Syracuse University Press, 2002), 227.

46. Angel, *La America*, 11–12, without a citation; [Moise Gadol], "El importante raporto del Buro Oriental," *La America* (December 29, 1911): 2; [Moise Gadol], "El emportante raporto del Bureau Oriental," *La America* (January 5, 1912): 2; [Moise Gadol], "El servisio military en Turkía," *La America* (January 19, 1912): 1; Cohen, "Report on the Oriental Bureau for the Year 1917," 1; Amateau, "Immigrant from Turkey," 8.

47. Sutton, *Magic Carpet*, 7, 185. See also See Marc D. Angel, "The Sephardim of the United States: An Exploratory Study," *American Jewish Year Book* 74 (1973): 86.

48. Ezra Sitt to David de Sola Pool, April 17, 1913, CSISA, pp. 1–2.

49. Albert J. Amateau to Lee Iacocca, December 24, 1991, box 7, folder "Salo Baron," Joseph M. Papo Papers, AJA, p. 1.

50. For example, David Barocas cited "want and need" as the primary motivation for immigration. Barocas, audiotape address for the Sephardic Brotherhood of America. Albert Amateau brought his younger sister to the United States in 1920 because all available Jewish men in their city had been conscripted. Amado Bortnick, *One Century*, 59.

51. Adler, *Selected Letters*, 1:222. Some Jews fled to Izmir, Edirne, and Istanbul. Ahmad, "Special Relationship," 227.

52. "Moise Soulam in America," *La America* (September 12, 1913): 3.

53. *La America* (September 12, 1913): 4.

54. Cohen, "Report on the Oriental Bureau for the Year 1917," 1.

55. Hayyim J. Cohen, *The Jews of the Middle East, 1860–1972* (New Brunswick, NJ: Transaction Books, 1973), 64; *The Statistical Bases of Sir John Hope Simpson's Report on Immigration Land Settlement and Development in Palestine,* pamphlet (London: Jewish Agency for Palestine, 1931), box 3, folder 10, Solis Family Papers, AJHS, pp. 30–31; Dahbany-Miraglia, "Analysis of Ethnic Identity among Yemenite Jews," 51.

56. Dahbany-Miraglia, "Analysis of Ethnic Identity among Yemenite Jews," 131.

57. "Immigration and Emigration, and Net Gain or Loss, 1908 to 1923, by Race," *Eleventh Annual Report of Secretary of Labor for the Fiscal Year Ended June 30, 1923,* as quoted in Roy L. Garis, *Immigration Restriction* (New York: Macmillan, 1927), 210.

58. Derived from "Statistics of Jews," *American Jewish Year Book* (1914–1915): 352. These statistics are for the year ending June 30, 1914. The real numbers for European Turkey are the following: 1,408 Jews arrived from European Turkey, and 67 Jews from European Turkey left the United States, compared to 2,461 non-Jews who left. The real numbers for Asian Turkey are the following: 844 Jews arrived, and 11 departed, compared to 2,232 non-Jews who left.

59. Jews accounted for some 15 percent of the total immigrant population from European Turkey, but only 5 percent of those who departed the United States in those years were Jews. Similarly, Jews represented about 14 percent of the total number of immigrants admitted from Asian Turkey but only about 5 percent of all those departing. Derived from "Statistics of Jews," *American Jewish Year Book* (1923–1924): 348. The real numbers are the following: 147 Jews from Greece were admitted, and only 5 Jews departed, compared to 7,501 gentiles who did. The real numbers from European Turkey are the following: a total of 1,660 were admitted, among them 241 Jews; of these, 10 Jews departed, compared to 191 gentiles who did. The real numbers for Asian Turkey are the following: 287 Jews were admitted, out of a total of 1,998; 92 Jews departed, compared to 1,639 gentiles who did.

60. For anecdotal evidence on reverse migration, consider Albert Daniel Saporta (1898–1979), whose

immigration to America was followed by several years in Palestine. Albert Daniel Saporta, *My Life in Retrospect* (New York: n.p., 1980).

61. Simon S. Nessim, "Amerikanizasión," *La Luz* (October 16, 1921): 1.

62. Samuel Joseph, "Jewish Immigration to the United States," *Studies in History, Economics and Public Law* 59:4 (1914): 503.

63. Pool, "Immigration of Levantine Jews," 19.

64. "Statistics of Jews," *American Jewish Year Book* (1914–1915): 347; Susan Cotts Watkins, ed., *After Ellis Island: Newcomers and Natives in the 1910 Census* (New York: Russell Sage Foundation, 1994), 25–26.

65. Pool, "Immigration of Levantine Jews," 20.

66. Albert J. Amateau to Joseph M. Papo, March 18, 1976, 5 pages, Joseph M. Papo Papers, AJA, p. 3.

67. The statistic is from Joseph, "Jewish Immigration to the United States," 511.

68. Ibid., 578.

69. This information is based on ibid., 509–10. This possibility also exists for the statistics representing the United Kingdom and British North America, the majority of whose (Ashkenazi) Jewish emigrants were transmigrants or transient Eastern European Jews (ibid., 511). On this point see also Pool, "Levantine Jews in the United States," 209n. 1.

70. "Statistics of Jews," *American Jewish Year Book* (1914–1915): 348. The rubric on the census forms is "Yiddish and Hebrew." The unidentified author attributes the latter term to "the fact that Yiddish is printed in Hebrew" (347).

71. [Moise Gadol], "El emportante raporto del Bureau Oriental," *La America* (January 5, 1912): 2.

72. "Discussion," *Jewish Charities* 4:2 (1914): 29.

73. Pool, "Levantine Jews in the United States," 209.

74. Ibid., 214.

75. Sutton, *Aleppo Chronicles*, 14.

76. Albert Levi, "El menester de un jurnal kotidiano se aze fuertemente sentir," and "Por la prima vez en la istoria de los Sefaradím de Amérika: Grandioza kompanía de publisidad Sefaradít" (editorial announcement), *La Vara* (December 14, 1923), 2, 4.

77. "A los lektores de 'La Vara': Nuestra seksión en Ingléz" (editorial announcement), *La Vara* (August 10, 1934), 8.

78. Angel, "Sephardim of the United States," 126–30; and Hayyim Cohen, "Sephardi Jews in the United States, Marriage with Ashkenazim," *Dispersion and Unity* 13–14 (1971–1972): 151–60. Syrian Jews, in contrast, have until today largely eschewed both inter- and intramarriage. See Sutton, *Aleppo Chronicles* and *Magic Carpet*.

79. For more details on immigration figures, see the appendix.

80. Edwin Shuker, Executive Director of the ASF, to Yuri Shcherbak, Ambassador to the Republic of Ukraine, September 4, 1996, box 9, folder "ASF Concerns about the state of the Jewish cemetery in Lviv (Ukraine), 1996," ASF; Randy Belinfante, personal communi-

cation, August 26, 2004. Communal leaders consulted by Belinfante offer the following figures: 75,000 Eastern Sephardim of Ladino-speaking background; 50,000 Syrian Jews; 50,000 Bukharian Jews in the United States and Canada, of which 40,000 live in New York; 30,000–40,000 Iranian Jews, of which 4,000 are Mashadi; 30,000 Yemeni Jews; 15,000 Iraqi Jews.

81. Pool, "Levantine Jews in the United States," 211, 214; Maír José Benardete, "The Sephardic Jews in the United States," *Hispanic Culture and Character of the Sephardic Jews* (New York: Sepher-Hermon, 1982), 164; Papo, *Sephardim in Twentieth Century America*, viii; Angel, *La America*, 6.

82. "Mother-Tongues of New York," *The World* (New York) (February 21, 1914): 10; Lloyd P. Gartner, Hillel Halkin, Edward L. Greenstein, and Yehuda Ben-Dror, "New York City," *Encyclopedia Judaica* (Jerusalem: Keter, 1971), 12:1078.

83. Albert Adatto, "Sephardim and the Seattle Sephardic Community," masters thesis, University of Washington, 1939, 53. Pool ("Levantine Jews in the United States," 216) also notes that Constantinopolitan and Salonikan Jews tended to be more educated than other Levantine Sephardic groups.

84. Alice Davis Menken, "Our Neighbor-Friends," 1921, CSISA; Alcosser, "My Life's Memoirs," 75.

85. Giselle Hendel-Sebestyen, "Role Diversity: Toward the Development of Community in a Total Institutional Setting," *Anthropological Quarterly* 52:1 (January 1979): 25.

86. On Sephardic Seattle, see Joan Dash, "Sephardim in Seattle," *National Jewish Monthly* (May 1963): 12–13, 49–50; David Romey, "The Sephardim of Seattle," *Jewish Life* 31:5 (May-June 1964): 47–55; Allen H. Podet with Dan Chasen, "Heirs to a Noble Tradition: Seattle's Storied Sephardim," *Jewish Digest* 13:12 (September 1968): 30–40; Marc Dwight Angel, "'Progress'—Seattle's Sephardic Monthly, 1934-5," *American Sephardi* 5 (1971): 90–95; "The Sephardic Theater of Seattle," *American Jewish Archives* 25:2 (November 1973): 156–61; and "Notes on the Early History of Seattle's Sephardic Community," *Western States Jewish Historical Quarterly* 7:1 (October 1974): 22–30.

87. See, for example, Adatto, "Sephardim and the Seattle Sephardic Community"; Emily Adatto, "A Study of the Linguistic Characteristics of the Seattle Sefardi Folklore," master's thesis, University of Washington, 1935; and Emma Adatto and George Umphrey, "The Linguistic Archaisms of the Seattle Sephardim," *Hispania* (May 1936). Language attrition among immigrants generally occurs more slowly in rural than in urban centers. Barbara Kirshenblatt-Gimblett, "Traditional Storytelling in the Toronto Jewish Community: A Study in Performance and Creativity in an Immigrant Culture," Ph.D. diss., Indiana University, 1972, 37.

88. *El Mesajero* ran from September 21, 1933, to at least December 2, 1934, the latest issue that I have been able to locate. *El Mesajero* was the official organ of the Peace and Progress

Society. On Los Angeles Sephardim, see Aron Hasson, "The Sephardic Jews of Rhodes in Los Angeles," *Western States Jewish Historical Quarterly* 6:4 (1974): 241–54; Stephen Stern, *The Sephardic Jewish Community of Los Angeles* (New York: Arno, 1990); and Stern, "Ethnic Identity among the Sephardic Jews of Los Angeles." By 1933, Seattle's Eastern Sephardic population had climbed to three thousand but had fallen into third place, ranking behind the burgeoning Sephardic settlement of Los Angeles. Lionel Hill, "Seattle," *The Universal Jewish Encyclopedia* (New York: Ktav, 1969), 9:451; and Robert E. Levinson, "Seattle," *Encyclopedia Judaica* (Jerusalem: Keter, 1971), 14:1082–83.

89. Angel, "Sephardim of the United States," 128.

90. Cohen, "Sephardi Jews in the United States."

91. [Moise Gadol], "Insidentes dezagradavles," *La America* (April 23, 1915): 1. The article dates the incident to the previous year; the inference that this restaurant, located at 170 or 175 Forsyth Street (Gadol lists both addresses), was Eastern Sephardic is mine.

92. [Moise Gadol], "Un aklaramiento," *La America* (December 24, 1915): 4.

93. Eric Hobsbawm, *The Age of Empire, 1875–1914* (Gloucester, MA: Peter Smith, 1997), 53.

94. For an overview of this theme, see Jason McDonald, *American Ethnic History: Themes and Perspectives* (New Brunswick, NJ: Rutgers University Press, 2007).

95. Ibid., 16.

96. Ibid., 22.

97. Ibid., 3, 13.

98. Gerda Lerner, *Why History Matters: Life and Thought* (New York: Oxford University Press, 1997), viii, 184–97.

99. For another definition of "ethnicity," see Jack Glazier and Arthur W. Helweg, *Ethnicity in Michigan: Issues and People* (East Lansing: Michigan State University Press, 2001), 2–3. Ethnic distinctions became more complex with the emergence of modern nation-states. Greek-born Jews and their descendants are illustrative of this complexity. Their reconstituted community in Baltimore in the 1970s identified variably as Greeks or Greek Jews, with no differentiation between Sephardim and Romaniote Jews. Glaser, "Greek Jews in Baltimore," 327. This observation may have been exacerbated by the interviewer's apparent disinterest in subethnic identity. As mentioned earlier, he classified both groups under the "Sephardic" label.

100. This distinction is inspired by Naomi Gale, *The Sephardim of Sydney: Coping with Political Processes and Social Pressures* (Brighton, UK: Sussex, 2005). Gale identifies Eastern Sephardi and Mizrahi Jews in Australia as a social, rather than an ethnic, group (19–21).

101. Cecil Roth, "The Last Days of Jewish Salonica: What Happened to a 450-Year-Old Civilization," *Commentary* 10:1 (July 1950): 49–50; Adler, *Selected Letters*, 1:30. Adler, in this letter sent from Constantinople in 1890, does not specify that the geographical names are Iberian.

102. Joseph Néhama, *Histoire des Israélites de Salonique* (Paris and Salonika: Librairie Durlacher and Librairie Molho, 1936), 3:66.

103. "Philologist Finds 22 Dialects among the Sephardic Jews in New York," *Sephardic Bulletin* 1:4 (February 1929): 1.

104. "Una lingua ke non es lingua," *La Vara* (October 13, 1922): 4.

105. Benardete, *Hispanic Culture and Character of the Sephardic Jews*, 169, 173–75. On the exceptional subcultural tenacity of Monastir-origin Jews, see Mark Cohen, *Last Century of a Sephardic Community: The Jews of Monastir, 1839–1943* (New York: Foundation for the Advancement of Sephardic Studies and Culture, 2003), 193–94.

106. Hendel-Sebestyen, "Role Diversity," 23–25.

107. Néhama, *Histoire des Israélites*, 66.

108. Benardete, *Hispanic Culture and Character of the Sephardic Jews*, 172.

109. William Isaac Thomas, *Old World Traits Transplanted* (Montclair, NJ: Patterson Smith, 1971 [1921]), 202.

110. Baron, *Steeled by Adversity*, 351–52.

111. Arthur A. Goren, *New York Jews and the Quest for Community: The Kehilla Experiment, 1908–1922* (New York: Columbia University Press, 1970), 249; and for other factors, see Alexander Dushkin, *Living Bridges: Memoirs of an Educator* (Jerusalem: Keter, 1975), 22.

112. Max Raisin, "Splendid Results of Reform Due to Organization," *American Jewish Chronicle* 2:6 (December 15, 1916): 169.

113. Baron, *Steeled by Adversity*, 356; Cyrus Adler to Simon Wolf, 1905, in Adler, *Selected Letters*, 1:108–9. The Board of Delegates of American Israelites, an American Jewish defense group, was absorbed by the Union of American Hebrew Congregations in 1878 (Adler, *Selected Letters*, 109n. 2).

114. Adler, *Selected Letters*, 2:123.

115. Baron, *Steeled by Adversity*, 655n. 101.

116. Baron applies this argument to explaining the proliferation of religious groups; it may also be applied to Jewish organizations in general. Baron, *Steeled by Adversity*, 373.

117. Franco, "History of The Rhodes League of Brothers' Aid Society," 6. Franco refers to these exceptional members as "strangers" (including the quotation marks), which is no doubt a translation of *ajeno,* the term used to identify Sephardim from a city or region not one's own.

118. Ibid., 9.

119. Ibid., 11.

120. Jonathan D. Sarna, "From Immigrants to Ethnics: Toward a New Theory of 'Ethnicization,'" *Ethnicity* 5 (1978): 370–78. On this tendency among Jews in the Arab world, see, for example, Ella Shohat, "Reflections of an Arab Jew," in Loolwa Khazzoom, ed., *The Flying Camel: Essays on Identity by Women of North African and Middle Eastern Jewish Heritage*, 115–21 (New York: Seal, 2003), 115.

121. Saporta, *My Life in Retrospect*, 31 (where the "Sabbath goy" is referred to as the "Turkito").
122. Asher Levy to H. Pereira Mendes, December 9, 1912, CSISA.
123. E. Silvera to David de Sola Pool, April 21, 1913, CSISA (my translation from the French).
124. Sarna, "From Immigrants to Ethnics."
125. "Entrevista enteresante," *La Bos del Pueblo* (March 26, 1916): 2.
126. Benardete, *Hispanic Culture and Character of the Sephardic Jews*, 165.
127. Néhama, *Histoire des Israélites*, 3:66; Esther Benbassa and Aron Rodrigue, *Sephardi Jewry: A History of the Judeo-Spanish Community, 14th–20th Centuries* (Berkeley: University of California Press, 2000).
128. Certificate of name change, November 2, 1921, undated typescript, folder "Certificates of Incorporation," Joseph M. Papo Papers, AJA.
129. "Dos palavras por el trokamiento de nuestra kavesera," *La Vara* (April 19, 1935): 1.
130. Pool, "Immigration of Levantine Jews," 16; and untitled article in the *Sephardic Bulletin* (February 1938), as cited in Max J. Cohen, "Sephardic Jews in the Bronx," unpublished typescript, 1944?, box 11, folder "speeches," Joseph M. Papo Papers, AJA, p. 4.
131. "Entrevista enteresante," *La Bos del Pueblo* (April 14, 1916): 2; Papo, *Sephardim in Twentieth Century America*, 52. There were five Greek-speaking societies at the time.
132. Pool, "Levantine Jews in the United States," 218–19.

133. Albert E. Castro to editor, "Tribuna Libera," *La Bos del Pueblo* (January 7, 1916): 4.
134. The federation collapsed due to financial struggles, internal dissent, and efforts to replace this national organization with one that would exclusively cater to New York's Levantine Jewish population. Angel, *La America*, 81. It was dissolved by proclamation on December 15, 1952. Louis J. Lefkowitz to Joseph M. Papo, April 9, 1974, box "Sephardic organizations," Joseph M. Papo Papers, AJA.
135. Sarna, "From Immigrants to Ethnics."
136. Benardete, *Hispanic Culture and Character of the Sephardic Jews*, 169.
137. Mordecai Soltes, *The Yiddish Press: An Americanizing Agency* (Philadelphia: Jewish Publication Society, 1950 [1924]), 20.
138. Most of the members of this community hailed principally from the cities of Aleppo and Damascus; their identity as Syrian Jews is a manifestation of ethnicization on a regional scale.
139. *Victory Bulletin* 1:1 (July 1942): 1.
140. *Victory Bulletin* 1:2 (August 1942): 1.
141. Ibid., 5.
142. "In the Memory of Murdered Israel We Appeal to All Syrian Jews!" *Victory Bulletin* 3:3 (September 1945): 6.
143. *Victory Bulletin* 1:2 (August 1942): 5; personal observation.
144. See, for example, Morris J. Rothman, "The Magen David Syrian

Jewish Community," *Orthodox Union* 10:5 (June 1943): 6–7.

145. An example of Iberian heritage is Fred Laniado, a Brooklyn Syrian Jew who contributed a column to the *Victory Bulletin* in the 1940s and winked at his own Hispanic heritage by using the pseudonym "Don Frederico." *Victory Bulletin* 1:1 (July 1942): 8. His column was entitled "Syrio-Syncrasies."

146. David Sitton, *Sephardi Communities Today* (Jerusalem: Council of Sephardi and Oriental Communities, 1985), 338.

147. Ibid., 335.

148. Albert Passy, interview with author, Los Angeles, August 3, 2000.

149. Zosa Szajkowski, "The Yahudi and the Immigrant," *American Jewish Historical Quarterly* 63:1 (September 1973): 37.

150. Glazier, *Dispersing the Ghetto*, 84.

151. Szajkowski, "Yahudi and the Immigrant," 37.

152. Baron, *Steeled by Adversity*, 42.

153. Ngai, "Architecture of Race," 81.

154. Ibid., 84.

155. By the 1910s, the term "Oriental" was still largely associated with the Chinese and Japanese, while "Levantine" was "an unusual word and not known to a very great majority of our members and the public." Isidore Hershfield (HIAS official) to David de Sola Pool, concerning the committee to be established by HIAS for Eastern Sephardic immigrants, January 23, 1914, "Oriental Jews—Correspondence, 1912–1917," CSISA. Similarly, Maurice Nessim protested that readers of an article entitled "The Levantine Jews in the United States" would not understand from the title that it referred to members of the *kolonia*. Maurice S. Nessim, "The Oriental-Sephardim vs. 'The Levantine Jew,'" *La Bos del Pueblo* (August 25, 1916): 2.

156. [Moise Gadol], "Kualo devemos azer?" *La America* (June 18, 1915): 4. Other sources that communicate this fear are Hershfield to Pool, January 23, 1914; Nessim, "Oriental-Sephardim vs. 'The Levantine Jew.'"

157. This act was again ratified in 1894 and 1902 through a treaty and legislative enactment. Both Western and Eastern Sephardim were concerned about this legislation. See, for example, Hershfield to Pool, January 23, 1914; and Nessim, "Oriental-Sephardim vs. 'The Levantine Jew.'"

158. Ngai, "Architecture of Race," 69, 72–73, 80. Besides the Chinese, subject to the Chinese Exclusion Act of 1882, most Asians had already been barred from citizenship in 1917 due to the creation by Congress of the "barred Asiatic zone" (ibid., 80).

159. David M. Katzman and William M. Tuttle, Jr., eds., *Plain Folk: The Life of Undistinguished Americans* (Urbana: University of Illinois Press, 1982), 165.

160. Papo, *Sephardim in Twentieth Century America*, 54.

161. Benyunes, "Sephardic Jews of New York," 718. On his subethnic identity and its possible role in his approach, see chapter 4 of this volume.

162. Ben Avi, "Tribuna Libera," *El Progreso* (October 30, 1915): 3. Unless this "Ben Avi" is Eliezer Ben-Yehuda's son, it is probably a pseudonym.

163. Joseph Gedalecia, "Discussion," *Jewish Charities* 4:11 (June 1914): 29. It is hard to resist mentioning the incidental fact that David Gedalecia, one of Joseph's grandsons, is a Chinese historian married to a non-Jewish woman from China. I am grateful to David Gedalecia for this and other information he shared in several email correspondences in 2006 and 2007.

164. "Turkish Jews Latest Comers on East Side," *The World* (New York) (February 22, 1914): 1N (Second News section).

165. Samuel M. Auerbach, "The Levantine Jew," *Jewish Immigration Bulletin* (August and September 1916): 10. For a contemporary reflection on the multifaceted background of Judeo-Spanish Levantines, see Victor D. Sanua, "Growing Up as a Jew in Cairo," *Image* (April 1997): 20.

166. Aron Rodrigue, *French Jews, Turkish Jews: The Alliance Israélite Universelle and the Politics of Jewish Schooling in Turkey, 1860–1925* (Bloomington: Indiana University Press, 1990); and "Discussion," *Jewish Charities* 4:11 (1914): 28–31.

167. "Discussion," *Jewish Charities* 4:2 (1914): 29.

168. Albert J. Amateau to Joseph M. Papo, April 7, 1976, 2 pages, Joseph M. Papo Papers, AJA, p. 1.

169. Ibid., 2.

170. Marcos DeFunis, telephone interview with author, July 20, 2000.

171. For this eulogy, see David Balint, "In Memoriam: Marco DeFunis," available online at http://www.balintlaw.com/serendipity/index.php?/archives/56-In-Memoriam-Marco-Defunis.html (accessed November 20, 2007).

172. "Only Hispanic in America," *Globe and Mail Report on Business* (March 11, 1992). The case is listed as *Bennun v. Rutgers*, 941 F.2d 154, 56 F.E.P. Cases 747, 762 (3rd Cir. 1991).

NOTES TO CHAPTER 2

1. Benor's original query read, "Can anyone direct me toward research about when and why American Hebrew schools shifted from Ashkenazic to Israeli pronunciation norms?"; it appeared in the March 9, 2004, issue of H-Judaic.

2. There were three hundred thousand non-Ashkenazic Jews living in Israel in the early 1950s. This figure includes Mizrahi Jews with no Iberian origin. "Sefardíes," in Eduardo Weinfeld and Isaac Babani, eds., *Enciclopedia Judaica Castellana*, 10 vols., 9:496–519 (México: Editorial Enciclopedia Judaica Castellana, 1951), 9:517.

3. Judges 12:6. For scholarly discussions of these differences since antiquity, see Moshe Atar, *Hebrew: A Living Language* [Hebrew: *Ivrit safa haya*] (Tel Aviv: Sh. Friedman, 1989), 95; William Chomsky, *Hebrew: The Eternal Language* (Skokie, IL: Varda Books, 2001 [1957]), 50–51, 54, 91;

and G. R. Driver, "The Modern Study of the Hebrew Language," in Arthur S. Peake, ed., *The People and the Book*, 73–120 (Oxford, UK: Clarendon, 1925), 113.

4. Atar, *Hebrew*, 95.

5. Irene Garbell, "The Pronunciation [sic] of Hebrew in Medieval Spain," *Homenaje a Millás-Villacrosa*, 2 vols. (Barcelona: Consejo Superior de Investigaciones Científicas, 1954), 1:647–96. The author also considers Portuguese, but her conclusions are generally inconclusive due to lack of material.

6. Chomsky, *Hebrew*, 91.

7. A polemic about the superiority of the Sephardic rite, in some ways related to the question of accent, can be traced to the period immediately following the Expulsion of the Jews from Spain. Samuel de Medina (1506–1589), a Salonikan rabbi and *dayan* (judge), described this rite as "fresh and sweet" and gave Ottoman Ashkenazim halakhic sanction to adopt it. Samuel de Medina, *She'elot u-Teshuvot* (Salonika, 1797). See also Leah Bornstein, ed., *Index to the Responsa of Rabbi Shmuel de Medina* [in Hebrew] (Jerusalem: M. Safra, 1979).

8. Simha Assaf, ed., *Mekorot le-Toldot ha-Hinuh be-Israel* (Tel Aviv: Devir, 1925–1942), 1:234. Wessely's ideas appear in the fourth letter, chapter 17, of *Divrei Shalom Ve-Emet*. On Wessely, see Israel Zinberg, *A History of Jewish Literature* (Cincinnati: Hebrew Union College Press; New York: Ktav, 1976), 60ff; and Schorsch, "Myth of Sephardic Supremacy," 53. For additional sources on the Ashkenazic regard for Sephardic speech, see Schorsch, "Myth of Sephardic Supremacy," 54; Graetz, *Divrei Yemei Israel*, 12; Antoine Guénée, *Letters of Certain Jews to Monsieur Voltaire* (Covington, KY: G. G. Moore, 1845), 65–66; and Kayserling, "Sephardim," 198.

9. Schorsch, "Myth of Sephardic Supremacy," 54. On the prestige of Sephardic or Oriental pronunciation among early Jewish enlighteners, see also "Sichah bein Yachin Uvein Bo'az," *Hameasef* 8 (Iyar 5569 [1809]), 217–30; Chaim Rabin, "The Revival of the Hebrew Language," *Ariel* 25 (winter 1969): 26; and Moshe Pelli, "The Revival of Hebrew Began in Haskalah: 'Hame'asef', First Hebrew Periodical, as a Vehicle for the Rejuvenation of the Language" [in Hebrew], *Leshonenu La'am* 50:2 (January-March 1999): 59–75.

10. Jay R. Berkovitz, *The Shaping of Jewish Identity in Nineteenth-Century France* (Detroit: Wayne State University Press, 1989), 147, 217.

11. Bernard Drachman, *The Unfailing Light: Memoirs of an American Rabbi* (New York: Rabbinical Council of America, 1948), 105.

12. Yaakov Saphir, *Sefer Masa Teiman* (Jerusalem: Levin Epshtayn, 1944).

13. Ibid. David Ben-Avraham's English translation, quoted here, is available online at http://www.umass.edu/sephardimizrahi/past_issues/051218.html.

14. Kayserling, "Sephardim," 198. For allusions to this article, see, for example, Annie Nathan Meyer, *It's Been Fun: An Autobiography* (New York: Henry Schuman, 1951), 11.

15. Alexander M. Dushkin, *Jewish Education in New York City* (New York: Bureau of Jewish Education [Lipshitz Press], 1918), 30.

16. Dash, "Sephardim in Seattle," 13.

17. Jessie Ethel Sampter, *A Guide to Zionism* (New York: Zionist Organization of America, 1920), 114.

18. Thomas Sugrue, *Watch for the Morning: The Story of Palestine's Jewish Pioneers and Their Battle for the Birth of Israel* (New York: Harper, 1950), 23; Hayim Halevy Donin, *To Raise a Jewish Child: A Guide for Parents* (New York: Basic Books, 1977), 161.

19. An observation attributed to Jewish pioneers in Palestine in Donin, *To Raise a Jewish Child*, 161. Eliezer Ben-Yehuda deemed the "oriental" Hebrew accent objectively beautiful and the oldest among Jews. Eliezer Ben Yehuda, "Ha-Mivta be-Lashon ha-Ivrit," in *ha-Sifrut ha-Ivrit va-Atidotehah* (New York: HaHistadrut ha-Ivrit be-Amerikah, 1917), 14.

20. See, for example, Marie Syrkin, *Way of Valor: A Biography of Golda Myerson* (New York: Sharon Books, 1955), 21.

21. Among those who disparaged the Ashkenazic dialect for this reason was the Hebrew writer Shlomo Tsemakh (1886–1974), a Polish Jew who arrived during the Second Aliya (which began in 1903), as cited in Benjamin Harshav, *Language in Time of Revolution* (Berkeley: University of California Press, 1993), 156. On the other hand, other Ashkenazic Jews, apparently referring to the Arabic inflection, disparaged Israeli Hebrew as "hard, clipped, guttural, the pronunciation of a people afraid to catch sand in its throat" and described the Ashkenazic intonation as "soft" and "caressing." Abraham Moses Klein, *The Second Scroll*, ed. Elizabeth A. Popham and Zailig Pollock (Toronto: University of Toronto Press, 2000), 148.

22. Chomsky, *Hebrew*, 115. For linguistic sources that consider the Sephardic intonation older, and thus presumably more "authentic," see ibid., 112–13; and *American Journal of Semitic Languages and Literature* 19 (1941): 233.

23. Louis Hurwich (Aryeh Leib Hurvich), *Memoirs of a Jewish Educator [Zichronoth Mehanech Ivri]*, 3 vols. (Boston: Bureau of Jewish Education; Tel Aviv: Sefarim M. Neuman, 1960), 1:143. Nessim Behar, who pioneered the method, called it *ha-shitah ha-tivi'it*. Nessim Behar, "The History of the 'Natural Method'" [in Hebrew], *HaDoar* 11:12 (January 30, 1931): 193.

24. Hurwich, *Memoirs of a Jewish Educator*, 3:39.

25. Ibid., 1:178; T. Preschel, "Hebrew," in Raphael Patai, ed., *Encyclopedia of Zionism and Israel*, 471–73 (New York: Herzl Press/McGraw-Hill, 1971), 473. Neumann's was the first exclusively Hebrew-speaking school in the United States. Another pioneer was Hebraist Abraham Isaac Saklad, who came to Boston from Russia in the early 1880s and established a school in which the language of instruction was Hebrew. Jacob Rader Marcus, ed., *This I Believe:*

Documents of American Jewish Life (Northvale, NJ: Jason Aronson, 1990), 151.

26. Hurwich implies this when he mentions that he had to accustom himself to speaking Sephardic Hebrew during his trip to the Land of Israel in 1934. Hurwich, *Memoirs of a Jewish Educator*, 3:28. Another Jew with an apparent "diglossia" in terms of Hebrew intonation was Cyrus Adler, who grew up in the Western Sephardic tradition in Philadelphia's Congregation Mikveh Israel and mastered that Hebrew accent but from the early 1890s through at least the 1920s used the Ashkenazic accent in written correspondence (e.g., "Shabbas," "Cosel Magrabi," "rachmonus," "Kotel Maaravi," "Kotel Maarabi"), as published in Cyrus Adler, *Selected Letters*, 1:31, 42, 2:125 (Adler to Israel Davidson in Jerusalem, 1926), 182 (Adler to Louis B. Namier in London, 1930), 199 (Adler to Judah L. Magnes in Jerusalem, 1930), 212 (Adler to Chaim Weizmann in London, 1931).

27. Daniel J. Elazar, "The National-Cultural Movement in Hebrew Education in the Mississippi Valley," in Alan Mintz, ed., *Hebrew in America: Perspectives and Prospects*, 129–54 (Detroit: Wayne State University Press, 1993), 139.

28. Aron Horowitz, *Striking Roots: Reflections of Five Decades of Jewish Life* (Oakville, Ontario: Mosaic, 1979), 48–49.

29. For examples of this omission, see, for example, Salo Wittmayer Baron's address on Hebraic studies in the United States in his *Steeled by Adversity*, 106–26; and Shuly Rubin Schwartz, "Camp Ramah: The Early Years, 1947–1952," *Conservative Judaism* 40:1 (fall 1987): 12–41. There is also no mention in Menahem Sheinkin (1871–1924), *Sefatenu (Lish'elat ha-Safa ha-Ivrit ve-ha-Safot HaMedubarot be-Ameinu)* (New York: HaHistadrut HaIvrit BeAmerika, 1917).

30. Jack Fellman, *The Revival of a Classical Tongue: Eliezer Ben Yehuda and the Modern Hebrew Language* (The Hague: Mouton, 1973), 25–26, 30; and Jack Fellman, "Eliezer Ben-Yehuda: A Language Reborn," *Ariel* 104 (1997): 31.

31. Reuven Sivan, "Ben-Yehuda and the Revival of Hebrew Speech," *Ariel* 25 (winter 1969): 38; Hemda Ben-Yehuda, *Nose HaDegel: Hayyei Ittamar Ben-Avi* (Jerusalem: HaMa'arav, 1943?).

32. Eliezer Ben-Yehuda, *A Dream Come True* (Boulder, CO: Westview, 1993), 33–34.

33. Hemda Ben-Yehuda, *HaLohem HaMeushar: Hayei Eliezer Ben-Yehuda* (Jerusalem: Tsiyyon, 1931), 38. In this conviction he had the agreement of his close friend and confidant, the gentile Russian journalist Tshashnikov, who visited him in Algeria and thought that this accent was prettier than the Ashkenazic. Later, Ben-Yehuda encountered a Jew from Palestine, again an Ashkenazic Jew, who spoke Hebrew with the accent current in that land. During their conservations, he became accustomed to employing this accent (ibid., 42).

34. Ben-Yehuda, *A Dream Come True*, 53.

35. Ibid., 65–66.
36. Ibid., 63–64.
37. Ibid., 65–66.
38. Ibid., 78–79 (chap. 9). See also Eliezer Ben-Yehuda, "Arba ha-Rishonot," *Luah Ahi'ever* 1 (1918): 21–27; and E. R. Lipsett, "Nissim Behar: The Man, His Battles and His Burdens," *American Hebrew* (March 29, 1918): 565.
39. Jacques Bigart, *A la mémoire de Nissim Behar, 1848-1931* (Paris: Alliance Israélite Universelle, 1931), 7; Hana Magid, *Toldot LeShoneinu* (Israel: Karni, 1984), 151–52; Solomon Harmati, *Shelosha SheKadmu LeBen Yehuda* (Jerusalem: Yad Itshak Ben Zvi, 1978); Nessim Behar, "The History of the 'Natural Method'" [in Hebrew], *HaDoar* 11:12 (January 30, 1931): 193. Fellman (*Revival of a Classical Tongue*, 49) gives a slightly different version of events, also basing his account on Behar's article.
40. Nathan Elkan Adler, *Jews in Many Lands* (Philadelphia: Jewish Publication Society of America, 1905), 62. Adler (1861–1946) identifies the school as the "Institution Israélite pour l'Instruction et le Travail: Fondation, Lionel de Rothschild," with Nissim Behar as its director and the Alliance Israélite Universelle as among its financial supporters.
41. Fellman, *Revival of a Classical Tongue*, 49–50. Yellin was one of Ben-Yehuda's first teacher-observers and substituted for Ben-Yehuda after he took ill (ibid., 52–53).
42. Ibid., 51. The "b'nai bilu," who settled in Jaffa, were the pioneers of Hebrew-speaking agricultural settlements. Ben-Yehuda, *HaLohem HaMeushar*, 51.
43. Fellman, "Eliezer Ben-Yehuda," 31; Tudor V. Parfitt, "The Use of Hebrew in Palestine, 1800–1881," *Journal of Semitic Studies* 17:2 (1972): 237–52.
44. Ben-Yehuda, *HaLohem HaMeushar*, 42; Parfitt, "Use of Hebrew in Palestine." Another eyewitness claims that in the 1910s in Palestine, Sephardic Jews spoke Arabic with their Ashkenazic neighbors. Ben-Yehuda, *Nose HaDegel*, 108.
45. Parfitt, "Use of Hebrew in Palestine," 251–52.
46. Adler, *I Have Considered the Days*, 122. See also Cyrus Adler to Sarah Sulzberger Adler, April 24, 1891, in Adler, *Selected Letters*, 1:42–43, referring to Ephraim Cohn-Reiss (1863–1943), director of the German-Jewish Hilfsverein schools in Palestine.
47. The year 1901 is given by A. L. Hurviz, *Ha-Zevi* 2 (1901): 1–2, as cited in Fellman, *Revival of a Classical Tongue*, 89–90. Other sources offer the year 1900. Tudor V. Parfitt, "Ahad Ha-Am's Role in the Revival and Development of Hebrew," in Jacques Kornberg, ed., *At the Crossroads: Essays on Ahad Ha-am* (Albany: State University of New York Press, 1982), 23; Haim Blanc, "The Israeli Koine as an Emergent National Standard," in Joshua A. Fishman, C. A. Ferguson and J. Das Gupta, eds., *Language Problems of Developing Nations*, 237–51 (New York: Wiley, 1968), 239–40. Harshav states that the Sephardic intonation "was already a *fait*

accompli" by 1903, the official start of the Second Aliya. Harshav, *Language in Time of Revolution*, 153.

48. Chaim Rabin, "The Revival of the Hebrew Language," *Ariel* 25 (winter 1969): 26; Fellman, *Revival of a Classical Tongue*, 98, 100; Harshav, *Language in Time of Revolution*, 109.

49. Fellman, *Revival of a Classical Tongue*, 101. However, the Ashkenazic script would be maintained in these schools.

50. Fellman, *Revival of a Classical Tongue*, 103.

51. Ben Yehuda, "Ha-Mivta be-Lashon ha-Ivrit," 9.

52. *Ha-Maggid*, no. 14 (Lyck, 1857), 55 (*"in spanischer Weise"*), and *Jewish Intelligence* 5 (1839): 267 ("in the Spanish way"), both cited in Parfitt, "Use of Hebrew in Palestine," 246, 247. See also Adler, *I Have Considered the Days*, 122 ("Spanish pronunciation," in an anecdote relating to the 1890s).

53. Ben Yehuda, "Ha-Mivta be-Lashon ha-Ivrit," 9, 14.

54. Harshav, *Language in Time of Revolution*, 159; Fellman, *Revival of a Classical Tongue*, 82.

55. Ittamar Ben-Avi, "Of One Accent," circular printed c. 1938, box 4, folder "Sephardic Pronunciation, 1937–1940," Union of Sephardic Congregations, ASF, p. 1. See also the appendix to this volume. Ben-Avi (1882–1943) was born Ben-Zion Ben-Yehuda and after he changed his name to Ben-Avi was sometimes known Ben-Avi Ben-Yehuda.

56. David de Sola Pool contributed to the confusion when he urged his congregation in 1912 to embrace the Eastern Sephardic newcomers, "whose Hebrew accent is our own." David de Sola Pool, "The Numbering of the People," in Marc D. Angel, ed., *Rabbi David de Sola Pool: Selections from Six Decades of Sermons, Addresses and Writings*, 28–32 (New York: Leon Amiel/ Union of Sephardic Congregations, 1980), 31. Ladino-speaking Sephardim traditionally pronounce the *tsadi* not as a Germanic "z" but rather as an "s" (thus, the word Zion is pronounced SiON). Moreover, they do not distinguish between the *aleph* and the *ayin*. Israeli linguist Avraham Matalon noted that Jews from Turkey and Salonika pronounced the *aleph* and *ayin* as if they were a *heh* and in so doing desecrated Hebrew prayers. Avraham Matalon, *Ha-Ivrit ha- mitnavenet be-Yisrael* [The Deterioration of Hebrew in Israel] (Ashdod, Israel: h.mo.l. [Avraham Maladon?], 1965), 13. For examples of Western Sephardic Hebrew pronunciation, see Emily Solis-Cohen (1886–1966), *David the Giant Killer, and Other Tales of Grandma Lopez* (Philadelphia: Jewish Publication Society of America, 1938 [1908]), 96, 140, 173, 249–50.

57. Bureau of Curriculum Development, Division of Secondary Education, New York State Education Department, *Syllabus in Modern Hebrew* (Albany: State University of New York Press, 1949), 12.

58. Avraham Matalon, for example, noted that Israeli Jews of North African origin pronounced the letter *shin* as an "s" and in so doing repeated the self-betrayal of the children of Efraim,

who in the Book of Judges gave themselves away by pronouncing the word *siboleth* instead of *shivolet*. Matalon, *Ha-Ivrit ha- mitnavenet be-Yisrael*, 13.

59. Meir Medan, "The Academy of the Hebrew Language," *Ariel* 25 (winter 1969): 42.

60. For other descriptions of the differences, see Donin, *To Raise a Jewish Child*, 161; Raphael Patai, *Journeyman in Jerusalem: Memories and Letters, 1933–1947* (Lanham, MD: Lexington Books, 2000), 73–74; Chomsky, *Hebrew*, 91, 108.

61. For an analysis of modern Israeli Hebrew, see Preschel, "Hebrew," 471; Blanc, "Israeli Koine," 243; Fellman, *Revival of a Classical Tongue*, 83–86; and David Tene, "Israeli Hebrew," *Ariel* 25 (winter 1969): 49.

62. Ben-Yehuda, *Nose HaDegel*, 61. See also Ben-Avi, "Of One Accent," 1.

63. Fellman, *Revival of a Classical Tongue*, 24, 94.

64. The widespread acceptance of Ashkenazic handwriting for Hebrew cursive necessarily displaced the Sephardic tradition. Benjamin Harshav argues that adopting Sephardic Hebrew encountered less opposition than would have the imposition of the Sephardic script for handwritten Hebrew, because there was already a time-honored tradition of Hebrew script among Ashkenazim. Harshav, *Language in Time of Revolution*, 154–55.

65. Mordecai H. Lewittes, "Hebrew Enters New York High Schools," *Menorah Journal* 26 (spring 1938): 239.

66. The introduction of Hebrew-in-Hebrew around 1905 is attributed to Zvi Malacovsky, a Russian immigrant and educator. Gurock, *When Harlem Was Jewish*, 100.

67. Hurwich, *Memoirs of a Jewish Educator*, 1:244.

68. Gurock, *When Harlem Was Jewish*, 110, citing *Morgen Journal*, June 5, 1910, p. 5, and June 5, 1911, p. 5.

69. Israel Friedlaender, "The Problem of Jewish Education in America and the Bureau of Education of the Jewish Community of New York City," in *Report of the Commissioner of Education for the Year Ended June 30, 1913*, vol. 1, 365–93 (Washington, DC: Government Printing Office, 1914), 383, 389.

70. Lewittes, "Hebrew Enters New York High Schools," 237. On the Hebrew curriculum committee was one Avraham Aaroni, perhaps a Sephardic Jew. Bureau of Curriculum Development, *Syllabus in Modern Hebrew*, 5.

71. Lewittes, "Hebrew Enters New York High Schools," 238.

72. Ibid., 240.

73. See, for example, Horowitz, *Striking Roots*, 56.

74. These textbooks included David Yellin's *Lefi HaTaf*, available in New York in 1904. Hurwich, *Memoirs of a Jewish Educator*, 1:143. See also Harry Blumberg and Mordecai Henry Lewittes, *Ivrit hayah: le-limud ha-lashon ha'ivrit ve-dikdukah le-mathilim bogrim* [*Modern Hebrew: A First-Year Course in Reading, Grammar and Conversation, Part* One] (New York: Hebrew Publishing Company, 1956 [1946]). This textbook used the Sephardic intonation "since it is the

Sefardic pronunciation which is used in every-day speech in Israel" (ix). Nonetheless, exercises at the back of the book contain footnotes indicating Ashkenazic pronunciation for those who wish to learn *ashkenazis* (xv).

75. Mark Raider, *The Emergence of American Zionism* (New York: New York University Press, 1998).

76. Ibid., 59–60.

77. Hurwich, *Memoirs of a Jewish Educator*, 3:28.

78. A. P. Gannes and Levi Soshuk, "The Kvutzah and Camp Achvah," *Jewish Education* (1949): 63. On Habima, see Freddie Rokem, "Hebrew Theater from 1889 to 1948," in Linda Ben-Zvi, ed., *Theater in Israel* (Ann Arbor: University of Michigan Press, 1996), 57. Throughout his career in the United States, Benderly was controversial among traditional Jews for the innovations he introduced to Jewish education (e.g., female Hebrew teachers; the use of Hebrew as a secular language; the use of stereopticon slides to teach the Bible), but before Camp Arverne the so-called Benderly System apparently did not include the Sephardic accent. Alexander M. Dushkin, *Jewish Education: Selected Writings* (Jerusalem: School of Education of the Hebrew University and the Ministry of Education and Culture by the Magnes Press, 1980), 152; and Dushkin, *Living Bridges*, 10–12.

79. Irving White, "Response to Perry London and Allissa Hirschfeld," in David M. Gordis and Yoav Ben-Horin, eds., *Jewish Identity in America*, 51–59 (New York: Ktav/Susan and David Wilstein Institute of Jewish Policy Studies, 1991). The *Irgun Tsvai Leumi* was the military army of the *Herut*, an Israeli right-wing political group, and functioned from 1931 to 1948. It clashed with the *Hagganah*, the regular army in Palestine responsible for fighting Arab enemies and maintaining peace within the land's borders.

80. Dushkin, *Living Bridges*, 10–11.

81. Gannes and Soshuk, "Kvutzah and Camp Achvah," 63.

82. Dushkin, *Jewish Education*, 148–49.

83. Alexander M. Dushkin, who lived in Palestine from 1920 to 1921 and witnessed Benderly's ridicule by Palestinian Jewish youth (Dushkin, *Living Bridges*, 10–11), had apparently already adopted the Sephardic accent.

84. For examples, see Yehoash [Solomon Bloomgarden], *The Feet of the Messenger* (New York: Arno, 1977 [1917]), 35, 39, 59; and Harshav, *Language in Time of Revolution*, chap. 27.

85. Raphael Patai, *Apprentice in Budapest: Memories of a World That Is No More* (Lanham, MD: Lexington Books, 2000 [1988]), 177.

86. Aron Moskovits, *Jewish Education in Hungary (1848–1948)* (New York: Bloch, 1964), 255.

87. Jeffrey Shandler, *Awakening Lives: Autobiographies of Jewish Youth in Poland before the Holocaust* (New Haven, CT: Yale University Press, 2002), 78 (and for biographical details, 51).

88. Harriet Pass Freidenreich, *The Jews of Yugoslavia: A Quest for Community* (Philadelphia: Jewish

Publication Society of America, 1979), 93. Freidenreich does not specify a year; based on another date in the same paragraph, I have surmised that the language shift occurred during the 1920s.

89. Horowitz, *Striking Roots*, 106; Rabbi Aron Horowitz, ed., *The Yearbook of the Calgary Hebrew High School* (Calgary Hebrew School, 1945), 12.

90. Shandler, *Awakening Lives*, 78.

91. White, "Response to Perry London and Allissa Hirschfeld," 53–54 and, for the author's background, 296.

92. Raider, *Emergence of American Zionism*, 164; Arieh Bruce Saposnik, "'. . . Will Issue Forth from Zion'? The Emergence of a Jewish National Culture in Palestine and the Dynamics of Yishuv-Diaspora Relations," *Jewish Social Studies* 10:1 (2003): 163.

93. In this novel, protagonist Menakhem-Mendl, a journalist working in Warsaw, attends the Eleventh Zionist Congress and notes the opposition of many delegates to this policy. Sholem Aleichem, *The Further Adventures of Menachem-Mendl*, trans. Aliza Shevrin (Syracuse, NY: Syracuse University Press, 2001), 142. The author did indeed attend a Zionist congress (p. viii), and the anecdote may be partly based on actual experiences, as much of the novel is. I was unable to locate the minutes from the 1913 Congress. *Bericht des Actions-Comités der Zionistischen Organisation an den XI. Zionisten-Kongress* (Vienna, 1913) includes no information on Hebrew accent. See also the discussion of Sholem Aleichem's anecdote in Philologos [pseudonym], "Sephardic Hebrew, Part II," *Forward* [New York] (October 13, 2000): 5.

94. "Zionist Congress Opens Tomorrow," *New York Times* (August 20, 1933): N1 ("Hitherto the official language of Zionist congresses has always been German").

95. Before 1907, languages employed at the Zionist Congress also included Yiddish and Russian. "Zionists Enthusiastic," *New York Times* (August 25, 1907): C3. At the Eleventh Zionist Congress, convened in September 1913 in Vienna, at least one speaker (listed as "Dr. S. Levin") addressed the audience in Hebrew. "Zionist Congress Opens," *New York Times* (September 3, 1913): 4; "Nordau Criticises Zionist Executive," *New York Times* (September 4, 1913): 4.

96. Letter to the editor, *Jewish Chronicle* (March 4, 1949).

97. Horowitz, *Striking Roots*, 107.

98. Bureau of Curriculum Development, *Syllabus in Modern Hebrew*, 5.

99. Ibid., 5, 7. This text indicates that the same syllabus had been used since 1930 and suggests that prior to 1948 the language was taught as a dead language. It is difficult to reconcile these two views; perhaps historical amnesia is at play.

100. Bureau of Curriculum Development, *Syllabus in Modern Hebrew*, 12, 22, 24, 26, 35, 44. Hebrew language instruction in Semitic Languages departments had long employed the "oriental" accent. While a graduate student at Johns Hopkins University in the early 1880s, Cyrus Adler indicated that "Hebrew is

pronounced here in the eastern way; an extremely strong guttural, also found in Arabic and Assyrian." Adler, *Selected Letters*, 1:4. The next year, Sabato Morais informed him that the "early grammarians knew no distinction in the *'ayin*, which demonstrated that "even it if it had existed it must have died out in early times" (ibid., 6).

101. Zvulun Ravid, "When Was Hebrew Language Instruction Initiated?" [in Hebrew], *Shevilc-ha-hinukh* 40 (December 1980): 78.

102. Chomsky, *Hebrew*, 114.

103. L. Gertner, "Pronunciation of Hebrew, A Cultural Link" (letter to the editor), *Jewish Chronicle* (August 13, 1949). Gertner was secretary of the Education Department of the Zionist Federation of Great Britain and Ireland.

104. "Adopting Sefardi Pronunciation: Suggestion for Glasgow Classes," February 10, 1950, unnamed newspaper, probably the *Jewish Chronicle*, box 6, Union of Sephardic Congregations, ASF.

105. Rabbi Dr. L. Rabinowitz, "Pronunciation of Hebrew; Palestinian Accent in S. Africa" (letter to the editor), *Jewish Chronicle* (August, 1948).

106. Jacob Rader Marcus, *The Colonial American Jew, 1492–1776*, 3 vols. (Detroit: Wayne State University Press, 1970), 2:1004.

107. Judah Monis, *Dickdook Leshon Gnebreet: A Grammar of the Hebrew Tongue, Being an Essay to bring the Hebrew Grammar into English to Facilitate the Instruction of all those who are desirous of acquiring a clear Idea of this Primitive Tongue by their own Studies* (Boston: Jonas Green, 1735). Strangely, Monis claims that, with the exception of England, "all the Jewish Nation in all their Dispersions, do pronounce it as I do." For a discussion that briefly addresses but does not resolve the question of accent, see George Alexander Kohut, "Judah Monis, M.A., the First Instructor in Hebrew at Harvard University (1683–1764)," *American Journal of Semitic Languages and Literatures* 14:4 (July 1898): 217–26.

108. Chomsky, *Hebrew*, 254, 256. For an example of Leeser's Western Sephardic pronunciation, see, for example, *Services for the Fast Days According to the Sephardi Tradition* (Philadelphia: Haswell, Barrington and Haswell, 1837–1838).

109. Joseph Aaron, *Sefer Mafteah el Lashon Ibri we-Hokhmat ha-Dikduk Meforash im Nekudot. Sha'ar ha-Rishon* [A Key (or Beginners') Book of the Hebrew Language and the Knowledge of Grammar, with Vowels. First Part] The author is identified as a "Hebrew Professor and Teacher of Hebrew Grammar." As discussed in Chomsky, *Hebrew*, 252–53.

110. Israel Goldstein, *My World as a Jew: The Memoirs of Israel Goldstein*, 2 vols. (Cranbury, NJ: Associated University Presses, 1984), 1:31.

111. The anecdote is from Dash, "Sephardim in Seattle," 13. My assumption is based on the fact that mass immigration of Eastern Sephardim to the United States had only just begun.

112. W. Gunther Plaut, *The Jews in Minnesota: The First Seventy-five Years* (New York: American Jewish Historical Society, 1959), 78–80.

113. Adler, *I Have Considered the Days*, 122. See also Cyrus Adler to Sarah Sulzberger Adler, April 24, 1891, in Adler, *Selected Letters*, 1:42–43, referring to Ephraim Cohn-Reiss (1863–1943), director of the German-Jewish Hilfsverein schools in Palestine.

114. Cyrus Adler to Henry Pereira Mendes, 1923, in Adler, *Selected Letters*, 2:77.

115. [Moise Gadol], "Primera Sosietá Sionista de Sefaradím en NevYork," *La America* (July 31, 1914): 2. On the Language Council, see Fellman, *Revival of a Classical Tongue*, 89–93; and Medan, "Academy of the Hebrew Language," 42.

116. Ben-Sion Behar, "Sefaradím, Ma No Orientales," *La America* (October 29, 1915): 2.

117. In Ladino, "pronunsiasión Palestiniano." See A. Ben-Eliahu, "Por La Propaganda de el Ebreo," *La America* (February 12, 1915): 2.

118. In Ladino, "dialegto arsí-Israelít (Sefaradí)." [Moise Gadol], "El Miting de la Agudá Sionít Sefaradít," *La America* (June 25, 1915): 5.

119. [Gadol], "Primera Sosietá Sionista de Sefaradím en NevYork," 2. In Hebrew, this society was known as "Agudá Sefaradít BeNuYork," probably synonymous with the "Agudá Sionít Sefaradít."

120. [Gadol], "El Miting de la Agudá Sionít Sefaradít," 5.

121. *La America* (June 25, 1915).

122. [Moise Gadol], "El Progreso de la 'Ivriá,'" *La America* (February 19, 1915): 2. The society probably took its inspiration from the world organization Ivriya, founded in 1903 at the sixteenth Zionist Congress in Basel by Hebraists seeking to disseminate the Hebrew language. Preschel, "Hebrew," 473. An eponymous society was founded in Jerusalem and Jaffa in 1906 as a Hebrew cultural, educational, and social organization. The Palestinian *Ivriyya* is mentioned in Fellman, *Revival of a Classical Tongue*, 91.

123. Ravid, "When Was Hebrew Language Instruction Initiated?" 79; Baron, *Steeled by Adversity*, 403.

124. The period overlapping with World War I was a watershed for spoken Hebrew in New York. Hebrew educator Louis Hurwich, who returned to New York City in 1916 after a five-year lapse, was astonished to discover that the Hebrew-speaking population had grown enormously. He gave credit to the hundreds of thousands of Jewish immigrants from (Eastern) Europe who had brought with them a living Hebrew that had spread in their home regions before World War I. Among them were thousands who spoke Hebrew fluently. Hurwich, *Memoirs of a Jewish Educator*, 1:324. Yet, even during this period, Ashkenazic Hebraists largely ignored the question of pronunciation. See, for example, Sheinkin, *Sefatenu*.

125. M.G. [Moise Gadol], "El Sionizmo Sefaradí de NuYork," *La America* (May 7, 1915): 8.

126. [Moise Gadol], "Fiesta de Resivo en Onor de Eliezer Ben Ye'uda," *La America* (June 11, 1915): 3.
127. *La America* (June 18, 1915).
128. Ibid.
129. Hemda Ben-Yehuda, *Ben-Yehuda: Hayav UMifalo* (Jerusalem: Mosad Bialik, 1990 [1941]), 275.
130. [Moise Gadol], "La Grandioza Fiesta en Onor del S. Eliezer Ben Ye'uda i su Famiya," *La America* (June 18, 1915): 1.
131. [Gadol], "El Miting de la Agudá Sionít Sefaradít," 5; and [Moise Gadol], "Otro Grande Akto del S. Josef Markos," *La America* (July 2, 1915): 1.
132. Ittamar Ben-Avi, *Avi* (Jerusalem: Hassolel, 1927), x.
133. On his penchant for large audiences, see Ben-Yehuda, *Nose HaDegel*, 251–52.
134. Lewittes, "Hebrew Enters New York High Schools," 242. The author alludes to one gathering held at the auditorium of the Thomas Jefferson High School, without specifying the year.
135. Ben-Avi, "Of One Accent," 1. Ben-Avi states, "Some years ago at meetings of the Histadruth Ivrith Olamith I advocated that America should follow suit."
136. For evidence of such pedagogues, see the advertisement of an *ivrit-be-ivrit* teacher, *La America* (October 8, 1915): 1. This teacher, also a cantor (which confirms both his gender and Sephardic identity), had five years of experience teaching the language.
137. Ben-Avi makes a sole reference to the four years he spent in the United States, limiting his comments to his propaganda on behalf of English sovereignty in Palestine. Ittamar Ben-Avi, *L'Enclave* (Paris: Éditions Rieder, 1931), 237. Hemda Ben-Yehuda devotes a chapter to the New York sojourn but mentions no Sephardim. Ben-Yehuda, *Ben-Yehuda*, 271–78 (chap. 43). Eliezer Ben-Yehuda's autobiography, *Halom VeShivro*, penned in 1917–1918, focuses on Palestine and makes no reference to his New York stint.
138. Lewittes, "Hebrew Enters New York High Schools," 239. Similarly, a census conducted from 1916 to 1918 indicates that the number of Ashkenazim speaking revived Hebrew in Israel far surpassed the number of both Sephardim and Mizrahim (excluding Yemenis). Bernard Spolsky, "Multilingualism in Israel," *Annual Review of Applied Linguistics* 17 (1996): 138–50; Roberto Bachi, "A Statistical Analysis of the Revival of Hebrew in Israel," *Scripta Hierosolymitana* 3 (1956): 187.
139. [Gadol], "El Sionizmo Sefaradí de NuYork," 8.
140. In Hebrew, "Agudá Sionít Makabí."
141. Reporter, "Miting de los Sionistas Sefaradím," *La Bos del Pueblo* (May 11, 1917): 4. Most Sephardim did not understand spoken Hebrew, but many, especially those educated in the Alliance Israélite Universelle, were fluent in French. Ben-Avi published some of his works in French, including Ben-Avi, *L'Enclave*. On French as Palestine's international language and the local government's

official language in the 1910s, see Ben-Yehuda, *HaLohem HaMeushar*, 97, 139.

142. Reporter, "Nuestras Ijas Salen a Luz," *La Bos del Pueblo* (October 12, 1917): 4. On Emanuel, see Papo, *Sephardim in Twentieth Century America*, 39, 113. Nissim Ovadia had served as chief rabbi of Vienna's Sephardic community before fleeing to the United States during the Holocaust.

143. [Moise Gadol], "Las Orasiones por la Paz," *La America* (October 9, 1914): 2. Drachman was an English-speaking rabbi and among the earliest U.S.-born university-trained pulpit rabbis in Harlem who served the neighborhood's native-born, upwardly mobile Jewish community. The spiritual leader of Congregation Zichron Ephraim in 1902, he had cooperated that year with Congregation Shearith Israel's Rabbi H. P. Mendes and other Harlem Jews to establish Congregation Shomre Emunah (at 121st Street and Madison), an Orthodox synagogue that emphasized decorum during religious services. Drachman became the spiritual leader of the uptown Ohab Zedek in 1909. Gurock, *When Harlem Was Jewish*, 93, 117, 119.

144. Drachman, *Unfailing Light*, 358.

145. Ibid., 105.

146. Ibid., 400.

147. *La America* (June 18, 1915).

148. Author's compilation from List of Removals, boxes 6–12, IRO, AJHS.

149. Frank, *Exploring a Neighborhood*, 10.

150. David de Sola Pool to M. D. Gaon, c/o Gran Rabino Sabetay J. Djaen, Buenos Aires, undated letter written sometime shortly after February 25, 1929, box 4, folder "Correspondence, 1930–1936," Union of Sephardic Congregations, ASF.

151. Pool noted, "there are dozens of Hebrew teachers, particularly Palestinians, in this country who are virtually without work." David de Sola Pool to Isaac S. Emmanuel, November 22, 1928, box 4, folder "Correspondence, 1930–1936," Union of Sephardic Congregations, ASF, p. 2.

152. Ellen M. Umansky, *From Christian Science to Jewish Science: Spiritual Healing and America Jews* (New York: Oxford University Press, 2004), 144–47.

153. Minutes of the Committee of the Union of Sephardic Congregations, April 15, 1937, box 4, folder "Minutes, 1935–1943," Union of Sephardic Congregations, ASF, pp. 3–4; Papo, *Sephardim in Twentieth Century America*, 63.

154. "Earle to Address Hadassah Tonight," *New York Times* (October 18, 1936): D7.

155. Ben-Avi, "Of One Accent," 1. I was unable to find a causal connection.

156. Resolution dated May 31, 1939, box 4, folder "Sephardic Pronunciation, 1937–1940," Union of Sephardic Congregations, ASF. The resolution was sent to the Central Conference of American Rabbis, the Rabbinical Assembly of the Jewish Theological Seminary, the Rabbinical Council of America in New York, the Union of American Hebrew Con-

gregations in Cincinnati, the United Synagogue of America in New York, the Union of Orthodox Jewish Congregations of America in New York, and the Masada Youth Zionist Organization of America, affiliated with the Zionist Organization of America. The Teachers Institute of the Jewish Theological Seminary of America had attempted to introduce the Sephardic accent into its pedagogy but abandoned this experiment because most of its students and some of its faculty were not accustomed to this accent.

157. Minutes of the Union of Sephardic Congregations, May 11, 1938, box 4, folder "Minutes, 1935–1943," Union of Sephardic Congregations, ASF, p. 3.

158. Solomon Solis-Cohen to David de Sola Pool, May 14, 1937, box 4, folder "Sephardic Pronunciation, 1937–1940," Union of Sephardic Congregations, ASF.

159. Adler to Mendes, 1923, in Adler, *Selected Letters*, 2:77.

160. Cyrus Adler to David de Sola Pool, May 14, 1937, 1, box 4, folder "Sephardic Pronunciation, 1937–1940," Union of Sephardic Congregations, ASF. On his mastery of the Sephardic pronunciation, see Adler, *I Have Considered the Days*, 105.

161. Minutes of the Board of Directors of the Union of Sephardic Congregations, December 21, 1937, box 4, Union of Sephardic Congregations, ASF, p. 2; Mrs. Emanuel Halpern to David de Sola Pool, November 29, 1937, box 4, folder "Sephardic Pronunciation, 1937–1940," Union of Sephardic Congregations, ASF.

162. Z. Szajkowski, "The Alliance Israélite Universelle in the United States, 1860–1949," *PAJHS* 39:4 (June 1950): 406.

163. Ibid., 420–21, 437; "In Behalf of Jews," *Boston Daily Globe* (October 21, 1902): 7; "Nissim Behar Dead; Aged Philanthropist," *New York Times* (January 2, 1931): 16; Bigart, *A la mémoire de Nissim Behar*, 21; Lipsett, "Nissim Behar"; G. K., "Behar, Nissim," *Ha-Intsipklopedia HaIvrit Klalit, Yehudit, ve-Eretsisraelite* (Jerusalem and Tel Aviv: Hevra LaHotsa'at Entsiklopedia Yerushalayim, 1967), 8:718.

164. For example, Behar served on the advisory board of the Federation of Oriental Jews of America, organized in 1912. *American Jewish Year Book*, 1915–1916. On the term "padre de la kolonia" see "A la memoria del difunto senior Nessim Behar, zl," *La Vara* (April 26, 1935): 2.

165. Ben-Yehuda, *HaLohem HaMeushar*, 100. For only a short time, Ben-Yehuda had lived as an orthodox Jew in Palestine for the sake of furthering his revivalist dream (see p. 84).

166. Lipsett, "Nissim Behar"; "Urges Aid for Unemployed," *New York Times* (June 16, 1908): 8; "A Fight Coming on Immigration: Liberal League to Resist Restriction Plan of Order of American Mechanics," *New York Times* (June 21, 1908): 5; "To Try Steerage Conditions, Liberal Immigration League Head Will Take Trip on the Lorraine," *New York Times* (July 2, 1908): 9.

167. "Boston our Zion," *Boston Daily Globe* (December 4, 1904): 20; Szajkowski, "Alliance Israélite Universelle," 409–11.

168. Angel, *La America*, 134, 135; Szajkowski, "Alliance Israélite Universelle," 440–41.

169. Angel, *La America*, 34, 77.

170. For another example of his enchantment with "*mizrahiut*," see Ben-Yehuda, *HaLohem HaMeushar*, 46–47.

171. Harshav, *Language in Time of Revolution*, 160.

172. As quoted in ibid., 159.

173. Raymond Dayan, *He Died Alone in Tijuana* (Xlibris, 2002), 50.

174. "Hebrew Classes Open to All," *Victory Bulletin* 3:9 (February 1945): 7.

175. "News from the Community," *Victory Bulletin* 3:9 (February 1945): 8.

176. Syrian Hebrew plays an important role in the dialogue of Stanley Sultan's *Rabbi: A Tale of the Waning Year* (West Whately, MA: American Novelists' Cooperative Publications, 1977). Alas, the author does not include Latin-scripted transliterations.

177. Matalon, *Ha-Ivrit ha- mitnavenet be-Yisrael*, 47.

178. Sutton, *Magic Carpet*, 253–54; Matalon, *Ha-Ivrit ha- mitnavenet be-Yisrael*, 61, 65. See also Avraham Matalon, *The Hebrew Pronunciation in Its Struggle* [Mivta Ha-Ivri Be-Ma'avako] (Tel Aviv: Hadar, 1979), 186–87.

179. Sutton, *Magic Carpet*, 253–54.

180. Rabeeya, *Encyclopedia of Wisdom*, 93.

181. His profile can be found at Rabeeya, *Encyclopedia of Wisdom*, 143, 153, and his website, http://www.angelfire.com/ultra/drabeeya/ (accessed November 6, 2007). Rabeeya taught Hebrew in the "Arabic-Sephardic" accent, which he learned in Iraq. David Rabeeya, email correspondence to author, December 11, 2007.

182. Walter P. Zenner, *A Global Community: The Jews from Aleppo, Syria* (Detroit: Wayne State University Press, 2000), 147.

183. Sitton, *Sephardi Communities Today*, 355 (anecdote dates to 1972). As a comparison, it is noteworthy that Australia's Eastern Sephardi and Mizrahi community, originating in the late 1940s, has also been too small to influence the broader Jewish community. See Gale, *Sephardim of Sydney*, 148.

184. Hayyim Schauss, *The Lifetime of a Jew throughout the Ages of Jewish History* (New York: Union of American Hebrew Congregations, 1950), vii. For the reaction of an Iraqi-Egyptian Jew to this passage, see Wahba, "Benign Ignorance," 55–56.

185. The identical text is found in Ruth Gerber, "Hebrew as She Is Spoke," *Commentary* (November 1950): 466; Ruth Gerber, *Israel without Tears* (New York: Current Books, 1950), 31; and Ruth Gerber, *Israel Today: Land of Many Nations*, rev. ed. (New York: Hill and Wang, 1963 [1958]), 36.

186. Joan Comay, *Everyone's Guide to Israel* (New York: Doubleday, 1962), 69–70. As Comay points out (p. 5), most tourists to Israel were from the United States; it is therefore

probable that these travel guides had mainly an American audience in mind.

187. Peter Novick, *The Holocaust in American Life* (Boston: Houghton Mifflin, 1999), 149, citing Charles S. Leibman and Steven M. Cohen, *Two Worlds of Judaism: The Israeli and American Experiences* (New Haven, CT: Yale University Press, 1990), 83.

188. Saul Levin, *The Indo-European and Semitic Languages: An Exploration of Structural Similarities Related to Accent, Chiefly in Greek, Sanskrit, and Hebrew* (Albany: State University of New York Press, 1971), 87.

189. Alfred J. Kolatch, *The New Name Dictionary: Modern English and Hebrew Names* (Middle Village, NY: Jonathan David, 1994 [1989]), vii.

190. Fellman, *Revival of a Classical Tongue*, 98, 100.

191. See, for example, Beatrice J. Barwell, "Pronunciation of Hebrew" (letter to the editor), and Reverend Isaac Levy, "Pronunciation of Hebrew," *Jewish Chronicle* (July 30, 1948): 13.

192. L. Glinert, "Hebrew toward the Year 2000: From Symbol to Substance," in Alan Mintz, ed., *Hebrew in America: Perspectives and Prospects* (Detroit: Wayne State University Press, 1993), 246.

193. Preschel, "Hebrew," 473.

194. Abraham G. Duker, "Emerging Culture Patterns in American Jewish Life: The Psycho-Cultural Approach to the Study of Jewish Life in America," *PAJHS* 39:4 (June 1950): 362n. 17.

195. Simon Greenberg, "The Role of the Concept of K'lal Yisrael in Jewish Education," *Jewish Education* 32:3 (spring 1962): 139, citing Rabbi Max Routtenberg, *Temple Bnai Sholom Bulletin*, January 26, 1962.

196. Rabbi Dr. Barry Dov Schwartz, telephone interview with author, December 17, 2007.

197. Donin, *To Raise a Jewish Child*, 163.

198. Ibid., 162.

199. Tzvi Bisk and Moshe Dror, *Futurizing the Jews: Alternative Futures for Meaningful Jewish Existence in the 21st Century* (Westport, CT: Praeger, 2003), 21.

200. Horowitz, *Striking Roots*, 106. See also letters to the editor published in the *London Jewish Chronicle* during the 1930s and 1940s.

201. Donin, *To Raise a Jewish Child*, 162.

202. Harshav, *Language in Time of Revolution*, 163; Donin, *To Raise a Jewish Child*, 162.

203. On this axiom, see Raphael, *Judaism in America*, 129.

204. As Benjamin Harshav notes, "the Hebrew finally accepted as the basic language in Eretz-Israel is not Sephardi Hebrew at all, but rather the lowest common denominator between the two main dialects, Sephardi and Ashkenazi." Harshav, *Language in a Time of Revolution*, 163. See also Rabeeya, *Encyclopedia of Wisdom*, 93. In the 1960s, Israeli Hebrew was sometimes referred to as Ashke-Sephardic. Philip Birnbaum, *'Ivrit shotefet = Fluent Hebrew* (New York: Hebrew Publishing Company, 1966), 289.

205. I thank Sarah Bunin Benor for sharing with me the feedback of those who privately responded to her query.

206. Ben-Yehuda, *HaLohem HaMeushar*; Ben-Yehuda, *Nose Ha-Degel*; Ben-Avi, *Avi*.

207. On American Jewry's increasing orientation toward the diaspora and away from Israel, see Raphael, *Judaism in America*, 130–32; Caryn Aviv and David Shneer, *New Jews: The End of the Jewish Diaspora* (New York: New York University Press, 2005); and Rabeeya, *Encyclopedia of Wisdom*, 179.

208. The advertisement appeared in the November 12, 2007, issue of H-Judaic.

209. "About the *Encyclopedia of American Jewish History*," promotional advertisement. See also Jonah Cohen, "Integrating Education in Jewish Day Schools: Toward a Jewish Great Books Program," *Covenant—Global Jewish Magazine* 1:3 (October 2007). Cohen, chair of the history department at the Dr. Miriam and Sheldon G. Adelson School, the first Jewish high school in Las Vegas, Nevada, argues that Jewish day schools should introduce their students to the works of Jewish intellectuals and artists who have contributed to the "arts, sciences, law, medicine, finance, entrepreneurship, and the media."

210. Eliot E. Cohen, ed., *Commentary on the American Scene: Portraits of Jewish Life in America* (New York: Knopf, 1953), xxii. This quotation has been attributed to many others as well. For arguments that Jews are the most American of all the nation's groups, see Robert Ezra Park, *Race and Culture* (Glencoe, IL: Free Press, 1950); Nathan Glazer, *American Judaism* (Chicago: University of Chicago Press, 1989); Stephen Whitfield, "The Bourgeois Humanism of American Jews," *Judaism* 29:2 (spring 1980): 153–66; Henry L. Feingold, *A Midrash on American Jewish History* (Albany: State University of New York Press, 1982), 188–89; and Seymour Martin Lipset, "A Unique People in an Exceptional Country," *American Pluralism and the Jewish Community* (New Brunswick, NJ: Transaction Books, 1990). These citations come from the contributions of Seth A. Forman and Samuel Heilman to the January 29, 1999, issue of H-Judaic. For a recent treatment, see Jeremy Cohen and Richard I. Cohen, *The Jewish Contribution to Civilization: Reassessing an Idea* (Oxford, UK: Littman Library of Jewish Civilization, 2007).

NOTES TO CHAPTER 3

1. Henry Pereira Mendes to Alice Davis Menken, December 17, 1933, folder "Correspondence re: *On the Side of Mercy*," Alice Davis Menken Papers, AJHS, p. 2.

2. Angel, *La America*, 96–97, 101. See correspondence between Mendes and Moise Gadol in *La America* (December 12, 1913): 4 and (December 26, 1913): 2.

3. Stephen Birmingham, *The Grandees: America's Sephardic Elite* (Syracuse, NY: Syracuse University Press, 1997 [1971]).

4. Marc D. Angel, "'The Grandees': A Voice from Shearith Israel," 16–19, and Paula O. de Benardete, "A

Sephardic Woman's Point of View," 20–26, both in the Foundation for the Advancement of Sephardic Studies and Culture, ed., *Four Reviews on Stephen Birmingham's Book "The Grandees"* (New York: Foundation for the Advancement of Sephardic Studies and Culture, 1971). Birmingham's most serious historical distortions occur in his discussion of Eastern Sephardim. On this chapter, see especially David N. Barocas, "A Refutation of the 21st Chapter of 'The Grandees,'" in the same volume, 1–15, and Steven Shaw, untitled book review of *The Grandees*, in *International Migration Review* 7:2 (summer 1973): 211–12.

5. Meyer was a cousin of Emma Lazarus. For their biographies and literary contributions, see Diane Matza, "Tradition and History: Sephardic Contributions to American Literature," in Martin A. Cohen and Abraham J. Peck, eds., *Sephardim in the Americas: Studies in Culture and History*, 379–454 (Tuscaloosa: University of Alabama Press, 1993); 387–93. Meyer "started the movement to found" Barnard College, according to her sister, Maud Nathan, *Once Upon a Time and Today* (New York: Arno, 1974 [1933]), 23.

6. Cardozo was the nation's first Hispanic Supreme Court justice, but he has not been so recognized in the U.S. media. See 289n162.

7. Pool, *H. Pereira Mendes*, 16. The reference to dignity and decorum is to Mendes and his cousin Rev. Meldola de Sola of Montreal's Spanish and Portuguese congregation, but it may arguably apply to previous generations as well. At a public funeral in 1905 for Kasriel Sarahson, the Orthodox publisher of the Yiddish newspaper *Tageblat*, Mendes differed from all the Eastern European eulogists in that his object was not to reduce his audience to "tears and loud lamentations." To the broader Jewish community, the English-speaking Mendes (along with Rabbi Bernard Drachman and others) represented "modernizing Orthodox Judaism." Arthur Aryeh Goren, "Sacred and Secular: The Place of Public Funerals in the Immigrant Life of American Jews," *Jewish History* 8:1–2 (1994): 277.

8. Meyer Polonies was the donor. Dushkin, *Jewish Education in New York City*, 43, 129.

9. Raphael, *Judaism in America*, 43.

10. Unknown author to Jacob da Silva Solis, June 4, 1828, box 1, folder 1, Solis Family Papers, AJHS; undated letter fragment relating to the founding of the New Orleans Congregation and its founding officers, box 2, folder 12, Solis Family Papers, AJHS; Solomon Solis Cohen to Mr. Friedenwald, February 23, 1900, box 3, folder 12, Solis Family Papers, AJHS.

11. Israel Friedlaender, "The Problem of Jewish Education in America and the Bureau of Education of the Jewish Community of New York City," *Report of the Commissioner of Education for the Year Ended June 30, 1913*, vol. 1 (Washington, DC: Government Printing Office, 1914), 367.

12. Ashkenazim also outnumbered Western Sephardim in most indi-

vidual communities in what is today the United States. Baron, *Steeled by Adversity*, 45.

13. Meyer, *It's Been Fun*, 11.

14. George D. M. Peixotto to Elvira Nathan Solis, October 25, 1902, and November 21, 1902, box 5, Elvira Nathan Solis, folder "Peixotto Family: Correspondence re genealogy, 1902," Solis Family Papers, AJHS, pp. 1, 2, 4.

15. "Tracing the Ancestry of the Family of David Nunes Carvalho (on his Mother's side) Back to the first King of Portugal," box 5, folder 20, Jacob da Silva Solis-Cohen, Jr. (1890–1968), folder "Solomon Nunes Carvalho: Miscellaneous, 1903–1989," Solis Family Papers, AJHS. Only descent from the marquis is verified in Cecil Roth to Jacob da Solis-Cohen, Jr., June 4, 1927, box 5, folder 13, Jacob da Silva Solis-Cohen, Jr. (1890–1968), folder "genealogy: Cecil Roth: Family Research, Da Silva, Fonseca, Correspondence 1827–1951," Solis Family Papers, AJHS, p. 1.

16. Roth to Solis-Cohen, Jr., June 4, 1927, AJHS, p. 1.

17. Claire Carvalho Weiller of New Rochelle, NY, to Uncle Jack, August 25, n.d., box 6, folder 18, Jacob da Silva Solis (1780–1829): Wimington, Solis Family Papers, AJHS, p. 1.

18. Prominent examples are Meyer, *It's Been Fun*, and Nathan, *Once Upon a Time and Today*, esp. 48, 50, and 78. For the white Protestant counterpart of this custom, see Helen Howe, *The Gentle Americans: Biography of a Breed* (New York: Harper and Row, 1965), 80.

19. Angel, *La America*, 88–89.

20. Application for membership to the National Society of the Children of the American Revolution, Washington, D.C., box 2, folder 8, Alice D. Menken Papers, AJHS, p. 2. A Western Sephardic contemporary of Menken, Frances Nathan Wolff (b. 1856), had applied for membership in the Daughters of the American Revolution during World War I in order "to establish my hundred-percent American citizenship." Frances Nathan Wolff, *Four Generations: My Life and Memories of New York for Over Eighty Years* (New York: self-published, 1939), 130.

21. Schorsch, "Myth of Sephardic Supremacy," 49. The myth came full circle when Western Sephardim cited certain Ashkenazic authors influenced by this myth. For example, in her memoir *It's Been Fun* (p. 11), Annie Nathan Meyer alludes to German Jewish scholar Meyer Kayserling's characterization of Sephardim as "more than usually self-conscious; they considered themselves a superior class—the nobility of Jewry," by virtue of their "many sufferings, which they had endured for the sake of their faith." The myth of Sephardic supremacy receives broader treatment in chapter 4 of this volume.

22. Necrology of Mortimer Morange Menken, unpublished manuscript, [1930], New York County Lawyers Association, box 1, folder 5, Alice D. Menken Papers, AJHS.

23. Meyer, *It's Been Fun*, 109. Meyer's first encounter with anti-Semitism occurred when her family temporarily relocated to Wisconsin.

24. Ibid., 112.
25. Nathan, *Once Upon a Time and Today*, 31.
26. Meyer, *It's Been Fun*, 93.
27. Chroniclers of the past few decades have continued to use the terms "Old" and "New Sephardim." See, for example, Angel, *La America*, and Barocas, *History of the Broome & Allen Boys Association*, 2.
28. For example, Frances Nathan Wolff, who was married to Venezuelan-born Julius Reuben Wolff, lived to see four of her children marry non-Jews. Nathan (b. 1856 in New York City) was the thirteenth child of Benjamin and Emily Grace Nathan. Her tenuous ties to the Jewish religion, and her children's distance from Judaism, are alluded to throughout her memoir. Wolff, *Four Generations*, 1, 30, 64, 155–57.
29. David de Sola Pool, "The Numbering of the People" (1912), in Marc D. Angel, ed., *Rabbi David de Sola Pool: Selections from Six Decades of Sermons, Addresses and Writings*, 28–32 (New York: Leon Amiel/Union of Sephardic Congregations, 1980), 30–32; Solomon Solis Cohen, "The Sephardic Jews of America," address delivered at the celebration of the twenty-fifth anniversary of the installation of Rev. Dr. Henry Pereira Mendes as minister of the Congregation Shearith Israel of New York, *Menorah* (1903): 44; Moise S. Gadol, "Nuevo Movimiento por Talmud Torá en Uptown," *La America* (October 15, 1915): 6; Moise S. Gadol, "El Grande Skándalo en la Grande Sinagoga Portugeza," *La America* (October 17, 1924): 7; Benardete, *Hispanic Culture and Character of the Sephardic Jews*, 159.
30. The Catholicism of Sephardim's ancestors, though at odds with Protestantism, gave them familiarity with Christian concepts and conditioned them for cultural adaptation.
31. Johann Martin Boltzius, *Reliable answer to some submitted questions concerning the land Carolina in which answer, however, regard is also paid at the same time to the condition of the Colony of Georgia* (Rincon: Georgia Salzburger Society, 1957–1958 [1738]).
32. Marcus, *Colonial American Jew*, 3:1232.
33. Malcolm H. Stern, *Americans of Jewish Descent* (Cincinnati, OH: Hebrew Union College Press, 1960). The third, updated edition is entitled *First American Jewish Families: 600 Genealogies, 1654–1988* (Cincinnati, OH: Hebrew Union College Press, 1991).
34. Benardete, *Hispanic Culture and Character of the Sephardic Jews*, 137. This acculturation also occurred in the sister congregation of London, where Spanish and Portuguese had disappeared from schools, prayer books, sermons, and executive meetings by the mid-nineteenth century. On this point, Benardete quotes Reverend Beuno de Mesquita without attribution.
35. "Justice Cardozo, Sephardic Jew," AJHS website, http://www.ajhs.org/publications/chapters/chapter.cfm?documentID=261 (accessed June 28, 2007).
36. The quotation is from Solis Cohen, "Sephardic Jews of America," 45.

37. David de Sola Pool lectured to Eastern Sephardim in English, since he knew no Spanish. Congregation Shearith Israel leader Henry Hendricks, active in the Eastern Sephardic community during the early 1920s, likewise knew no Spanish (Angel, *La America*, 83). Rachel Nahon Toledano, prominent in the synagogue's Sisterhood, was a native of Morocco and fluent in modern Spanish. [Moise Gadol], "El Miting de la Sosietá de Damas de la Sinagoga Espaniola-Portugeza Shearít Israél," *La America* (February 16, 1912): 3; Angel, *La America*, 91.

38. David de Sola Pool, "The Use of Portuguese and Spanish in the Historic Shearith Israel Congregation in New York," in Izaak A. Langnas and Barton Sholod, eds., *Studies in Honor of M. J. Benardete (Essays in Hispanic and Sephardic Culture)*, 359–62 (New York: Las Americas, 1965), 361. See also Pool, "World of the Sephardim," 9; David de Sola Pool and Tamar de Sola Pool, *An Old Faith in the New World: Portrait of Shearith Israel, 1654–1954* (New York: Columbia University Press, 1955), 87–89.

39. Chapter 21, "'An Altogether Different Sort,'" in Birmingham's *The Grandees*, 330–40. Note how on p. 340 the author both misquotes and misrepresents the anecdote related by Annie Nathan Meyer in *It's Been Fun*, 9.

40. The differences between the Western and Eastern Sephardic rites are often only vaguely described in primary and secondary sources. Angel (*La America*, 90) notes that "the services at Shearith Israel ... were not conducted in the manner of services in Oriental countries," but he does not elaborate. Cyrus Adler observes that the prayer books of Istanbul (and Tunis) included "more Piyutim than exist in the prayer-book inherited from Amsterdam." Cyrus Adler, *Address of Dr. Cyrus Adler, Delivered at the Twentieth Annual Meeting of the Sisterhood of the Spanish and Portuguese Synagogue,* November 27, 1916, CSISA, p. 3 (unpaginated).

41. George White, *Statistics of the State of Georgia* (Savannah: W. Thorne Williams, 1849), 619–20. For more on this subject, see Mordecai Manuel Noah, *Discourse, Delivered at the Consecration of the Synagogue of* קייק שארית ישראל *in the City of New-York* (New York: C. S. Van Winkle, 1818), 46–47.

42. Harry Friedenwald to Cyrus Adler, July 20, 1906, box 1, folder "Correspondence with Harry Friedenwald," Cyrus Adler Papers, AJHS. The tradition of fetishizing the possessions of secret Jews was current during the time of Solomon Molcho, whose cloak and flag were preserved by subsequent generations as a martyr's relics and displayed in various museums in the twentieth century. See Manfred R. Lehmann, "An Historical Perspective of Moshiach," Manfred Lehmann website, http://www.manfredlehmann.com/sieg38.html (accessed June 28, 2007). By contrast, Congregation Shearith Israel tended to downplay the crypto-Jewish heritage of its religious leaders, perhaps so as not to cast doubts on these ancestors' commitment to Judaism. See, for example,

the oblique references to Rev. Henry Pereira Mendes's ancestors as "martyrs." Congregation Shearith Israel (corporate author), *To Henry Pereira Mendes, in celebration of his fifty years of service in the Congregation and in the Community* (New York: Congregation Shearith Israel, 1927). A genealogical tree in another source suggests that Mendes's ancestry most likely included Jews forcibly converted to Catholicism in Portugal. Pool, *H. Pereira Mendes*, illustration opposite p. 4.

43. The polemic was perhaps influenced by Isaac Abravanel's praise of Iberian Jewish exiles for honoring "our nation and our religion" rather than violating Jewish law by converting to Christianity. Isaac Abravanel, preface to his commentary on the Book of Kings, as cited in James A. Huie, *The History of the Jews* (Boston, 1844), 177.

44. Pool, "Numbering of the People," 31.

45. Ibid., and "The Oriental Jews," *Shearith Israel Bulletin* (March 1912): 6, CSISA. The unedited version of Pool's sermon is subtitled "The Congregation's Paramount Duty." It is available on microform at the New York Public Library under the title *The Numbering of the People: The Congregation's Paramount Duty* and was probably originally printed in pamphlet form. At the time, congregations Shearith Israel and Mikvé Israel of Philadelphia were the only existing houses of worship in America where Levantine Jews felt comfortable. Pool, "Immigration of Levantine Jews," 13.

The Hebrew accents of Western and Eastern Sephardim in fact differed significantly, as documented in chapter 2, note 56.

46. On the establishment of sisterhoods in America, see Barbara Welter, "The Feminization of American Religion, 1800–1860," in Mary S. Hartman and Lois Banner, eds., *Clio's Consciousness Raised: New Perspective in the History of Women*, 137–57 (New York: Octagon Books, 1976). On Jewish sisterhoods, see Karla Goldman, "The Ambivalence of Reform Judaism: Kaufmann Kohler and the Ideal Jewish Woman," *American Jewish History* 79 (summer 1990): 477–99; and Karla Goldman, *Beyond the Synagogue Gallery: Finding a Place for Women in American Judaism* (Cambridge, MA: Harvard University Press, 2000); and Jonathan D. Sarna, *A Great Awakening: The Transformation That Shaped Twentieth Century American Judaism and Its Implications for Today* (New York: Council for Initiatives in Jewish Education, 1995).

47. Pool, "Numbering of the People," 32.

48. Menken served as honorary president in 1935, on various Sisterhood committees, and on the Sisterhood's board of directors until her death in 1936. Minutes and Reports of Conferences of the Sisterhood of the Spanish and Portuguese Synagogue in the City of New York, 1933–1938, CSISA, p. 217.

49. Application for Membership, the Society of Colonial Dames XVII Century, box 5, folder "Papers Enter-

ing Granddaughter Marilyn M. Menken into the D.A.R.," Alice D. Menken Papers, AJHS.

50. Telegram, January 23, 1916, Scrapbook vol. 1, 1883–1919, Alice D. Menken Papers, AJHS.

51. "The Oriental Jews," 6.

52. Yaakov Kirschenbaum, "Activities of 'The Sisterhood and Spanish and Portuguese Synagogue' on the East Side," *Jewish Morning Journal* 25 (March 14, 1926): 7. I thank Daniella Har Paz for her assistance with the Yiddish translation.

53. Papo, *Sephardim in Twentieth Century America*, 58.

54. Kirschenbaum, "Activities of 'The Sisterhood and Spanish and Portuguese Synagogue.'"

55. Louis M. Hacker, "The Communal Life of the Sephardic Jews in New York City," *Jewish Social Service Quarterly* 3:2 (December 1926): 36–37.

56. Alice Davis Menken, *On the Side of Mercy: Problems in Social Readjustment* (New York: Covici Friede, 1933); Maurice Beck Hexter, *Life Size: An Autobiography* (West Kennebunk, ME: Phoenix, 1990), 11 (on Cincinnati's dance halls as recruitment grounds for young prostitutes). On Lower East Side dance halls as "questionably reputable," see also Frank, *Exploring a Neighborhood*, 26.

57. Angel, *La America*, 91. Another source indicates that the Settlement House moved in 1915 to temporary quarters on Grand Street and in 1916 to 133 Eldridge Street. Barocas, *History of the Broome & Allen Boys Association*, 8.

58. Undated pamphlet (c. 1916), Sisterhood of the Spanish and Portuguese Synagogue in the City of New York, box 1, folder 4, Alice D. Menken Papers, AJHS.

59. Menken, *On the Side of Mercy*, 13, 17–18. Menken states that this immigration was noticeable in large numbers from 1890 to 1910.

60. Kirschenbaum, "Activities of 'The Sisterhood and Spanish and Portuguese Synagogue.'"

61. The Sisterhood's Special Fund of the Oriental Relief Committee, for example, received a reimbursement of $16.93 from the United Hebrew Charities in 1916. Undated pamphlet (c. 1916), Alice D. Menken Papers, AJHS.

62. Nathan, *Once Upon a Time and Today*, 85.

63. Ibid., 94.

64. Alice Davis Menken, "Our Neighbor-Friends," 1921, no source cited, CSISA.

65. Menken, *On the Side of Mercy*, 18.

66. Papo, *Sephardim in Twentieth Century America*, 385n. 15, quoting "the professional staff of the United Hebrew Charities" and interviews that he conducted in 1937 and 1970.

67. On the importance of piano clubs in Sephardic and white elite circles of New York, see Meyer, *It's Been Fun*, 131. The piano was a symbol of upward mobility for many Lower East Side Jewish immigrants. See Jenna Joselit Weissman, *Getting Comfortable in New York: The American Jewish Home, 1880–1950* (New York: Jewish Museum, 1990), 45–69. Toledano headed the Social Service Division

of the Settlement House. Barocas, *History of the Broome & Allen Boys Association*, 8.

68. Gadol's report on this event appears in "El Miting de la Sosietá de Damas," 3. According to Gadol's report, it was Mr. Toledano who invited Turkinos to "come closer to them [Western Sephardim] and learn the true Spanish-Castilian," contrary to Angel's assertion that it was Mrs. Toledano (Angel, *La America,* 91).

69. Gadol, "El Miting de la Sosietá de Damas," 3.

70. Angel, *La America*, 91. As noted in the following section, learning Castilian could lead to lucrative positions in U.S. establishments doing business with Spanish-speaking countries. However, it is unclear whether Habib had this in mind.

71. Marc D. Angel also tends to elide the names of these two languages, a reflection of the usage in his sources and perhaps also of common practice in his native community of Seattle. See, for example, Angel, *La America*, 103.

72. "Sisterhood of the Spanish Synagogue Entertains Orientals," article dated 1914 (from the *Shearith Israel Bulletin*?), CSISA.

73. Maurice B. Hexter, "The Dawn of a Problem," *Jewish Charities* (January 1913): 2. Hexter notes that Ladino-speaking Jews "can with difficulty understand Spanish, unless they are especially educated." He also points out (p. 3) that the existing English classes in the night schools in Cincinnati would not help Eastern Sephardim since "the basis of instruction is Spanish instead of Ladino."

74. "Kursos Gratis de Lingua Kastiliana," *La Vara* (August 29, 1924): 9.

75. Moise Angel to Editor, "La Boz de Nuestros Lektores," *La Vara* (July 17, 1936): 9. *La Prensa* was New York's leading Spanish-language newspaper. Virginia E. Sánchez Korrol, *From Colonia to Community: The History of Puerto Ricans in New York City* (Berkeley: University of California Press, 1994), 70.

76. Moshe Azuz to Editor, "La Boz de Nuestros Lektores," *La Vara* (July 17, 1936): 9.

77. Chek Abrevaya to Editor, "La Boz de Nuestros Lektores," *La Vara* (July 24, 1936): 2.

78. As discussed in Henry V. Besso, "Benardete's Bibliography," in Izaak A. Langnas and Barton Sholod, eds., *Studies in Honor of M. J. Benardete (Essays in Hispanic and Sephardic Culture)* (New York: Las Americas, 1965), 464, 478.

79. Soyer, *Jewish Immigrant Associations*, 72–73, 229n. 82. Soyer also indicates that daytshmerish had a ritualistic function, no longer in demand by the 1920s as both Jewish and gentile fraternal associations moved away from ritualism.

80. The congregation first met in a rented hall on the south side of 110th Street, east of Park Avenue, and later established a synagogue on the south side of 112th Street between Lexington and Third avenues. All officials, except for the *shammash*, were volunteers. The congregation closed following the dispersal of its members to other parts of the city. Pool and Pool, *Old*

Faith in the New World, 443. Henry Pereira Mendes opened the synagogue's religious school in 1885. Congregation Shearith Israel, *To Henry Pereira Mendes,* 16; Pool, *H. Pereira Mendes,* 21.

81. See, for example, Albert J. Amateau, "'Sephardic Jews,'" *American Hebrew* (October 3, 1916): 792. Joseph A. de Benyunes may also have identified as Western Sephardic; he was from Gibraltar, where many Jews of recent Moroccan descent resided for centuries.

82. Perhaps, too, the concept of Maghrebi (which means "Western" in Arabic) would have contradicted an Eastern or Levantine identity.

83. [Moise Gadol], "El emportante raporto del Bureau Oriental," *La America* (January 5, 1912): 2; Angel, *La America,* 27.

84. Concerning this matter, the author of his obituary, likely Moise Gadol, wrote, "we will discuss that at a later point." *La America* (March 19, 1915).

85. Ibid.

86. *Scrap Book of the Sisterhood of the Spanish and Portuguese Synagogue,* from 1897, *Shearith Israel Sisterhood Fair Descriptive Catalogue of a Collection of Objects of Jewish Ceremonial,* n.d. (probably c. 1915), CSISA.

87. Grace Cohen Grossman with Richard Eighme Ahlborn, *Judaism at the Smithsonian: Cultural Politics as Cultural Model* (Washington, DC: Smithsonian Institution Press, 1997), 54. According to Cyrus Adler, the family was from Damascus, and Ephraim Benguiat, the elder of the family, was living in Boston by 1892. Adler, *I Have Considered the Days,* 174.

88. Pool, "Numbering of the People," 31.

89. Pool, "Immigration of Levantine Jews," 24.

90. "The Oriental Jews," 6.

91. Henry Pereira Mendes, "Letra a la Redaksión del Reverende Dr. H. Pereira Mendes," *La America* (December 26, 1913): 2. The letter was probably translated from the English. For a discussion of this letter, see Angel, *La America,* 96.

92. Pool, "Immigration of Levantine Jews."

93. Adler, *Address of Dr. Cyrus Adler,* 3.

94. "Orasiones Rosh A-Shaná i Yom Kipúr," *La America* (August 27, 1915): 1.

95. Pool and Pool, *Old Faith in the New World,* 118–19.

96. Papo, *Sephardim in Twentieth Century America,* 93.

97. I base this founding date on the fact that Joseph de A. Benyunes became involved with the *kolonia* in 1913. Amateau, "'Sephardic Jews,'" 792. On the founding of Berith Shalom, see Angel, *La America,* 35, 91, 95.

98. Moise S. Gadol, response to "Letra a la Redaksión," *La America* (December 26, 1913): 2; [Moise Soulam], "Postemas de Ham Avraham," *La Vara* (August 28, 1931): 8. See note 56.

99. Benyunes was an agent for Semtob R. Sequerra, a merchant of crude rubber, cocoa beans, and dried fruits, located in Lisbon. J. de A. Benyunes to David de Sola Pool, Feb-

ruary 1, 1916 (his business profile is printed on this letterhead), CSISA. He apparently arrived from London and is identified as the "ordained rabbi" of Berith Shalom, the congregation of the Settlement House. Barocas, *History of the Broome & Allen Boys Association*, 8, 9. Benyunes modestly claimed in 1913 that he was not a rabbi. Angel, *La America*, 95.

100. The daily morning and evening services averaged thirty men on weekdays and eighty men, women, and children on Saturdays. The High Holy Days attracted as many as two hundred worshipers, bringing the synagogue to its full capacity. Additional worshipers were constantly turned away for lack of space. Joseph de A. Benyunes, "The Oriental Sephardic Jews of New York," undated article (1910s), box 1, folder 4, Alice D. Menken Papers, AJHS; Barocas, "Refutation of the 21st Chapter of 'The Grandees,'" 7.

101. It seems unlikely that Benyunes would have conducted services according to the Eastern Sephardic rite. When he was not officiating (on nonholiday weekdays), perhaps the Eastern Sephardic rite was followed.

102. By-Laws of the Congregation Shearith Israel of New York, Article 1, Oriental Jews—Correspondence, 1912–1917, CSISA, p. 4. The Ladino reads, "las orasiones i seremonias ke serán selebradas en la sinagoga 86 Orchard St. serán siempre según el minhág sefaradí i en lashón a-kodesh i en ningún kazo no puedrá ser trokado" (transliteration mine).

103. "Sinagoga Espaniola i Portugeza, 86 Orchard St.," *La Bos del Pueblo* (January 26, 1917): 1. Ladino and English sermons were to be given twice monthly. "Sinagoga Espaniola i Portugeza," *La America* (January 12, 1917): 1.

104. Undated pamphlet (1921), box 1, folder 4, Alice D. Menken Papers, AJHS, p. 2 (unpaginated).

105. Benyunes, "Oriental Sephardic Jews of New York."

106. Shelomo Emanuel, "Al Onorado Públiko," *La America* (August 27, 1915): 1. The choir was a hallmark of Congregation Shearith Israel's synagogue service. According to Moise Gadol, this Talmud Torah had been taken over by Congregation Shearith Israel by 1914. Angel, *La America*, 97.

107. Shelomo Emanuel, "Yamím Noraím Están Serka," *La America* (July 24, 1914): 3.

108. Angel, *La America*, 90.

109. Moise S. Gadol, "Por los Judíos Sefaradím Amerikanos," *La America* (November 25, 1910): 4; Shimon S. Nessim, "Lo Ke Nuestro Editor Pensa," *La Luz* (October 23, 1921): 2.

110. [Moise S. Gadol], "Hanukát A-Bayit de la Maniefika Sinagoga Sefaradít Berít Shalom," *La America* (May 17, 1918): 2.

111. Mendes, "Letra a la Redaksión," 2. This letter appears in Ladino and was probably translated from the English.

112. Papo, *Sephardim in Twentieth Century America*, 307–8; Pool and Pool, *Old Faith in the New World*, 443–44.

113. Pool and Pool, *Old Faith in the New World*, 444.

114. "Una Konferensia Sefaradita," *La America* (May 25, 1917): 1.

115. Papo, *Sephardim in Twentieth Century America*, 307–8.

116. For a discussion of the tensions that led to secession, see Angel, *La America*, 99–105.

117. Mendes to Menken, December 17, 1933, Alice Davis Menken Papers, AJHS, p. 2.

118. The name change is noted in Minutes of the second meeting of the Board of Directors, January 30, 1912, Series I, File No. 1-4, YIVO microfilm, pp. 1–2. The standing committee for "Aid of Sephardi Jewish Immigrants" for 1912 was composed of John L. Bernstein, Isidore Hershfield, and Philip Hersch. Ibid., and Minutes of the third meeting of the Board of Directors, February 12, 1912, Series I, File No. 1-4, YIVO microfilm, pp. 1–2.

119. "Entrevista Enteresante," *La Bos del Pueblo* (April 14, 1916): 2. This interview with Joseph Gedalecia was serialized in the following additional issues: March 26, 1916: 2; March 31, 1916: 4; April 7, 1916: 2; and April 21, 1916: 2. Gedalecia did not mention Pool in this debate, only stating that the founders of this organization, Sephardim of both Western and Eastern origins, chose the term "Oriental" in order to differentiate Levantine Jews from Western Sephardim. According to the HIAS minutes, this occurred in January 1911: "A motion was made and carried that the new Bureau for the benefit of the Oriental immigrants shall be called 'Bureau for Sephardic Jewish Immigrants.'" HIAS Board of Directors Meeting—Minutes (microfilm available at YIVO), Minutes of the second meeting of the Board of Directors, January 30, 1912, 1.

120. Papo, *Sephardim in Twentieth Century America*, 52. Papo (p. 384n. 8) cites articles from *La America* and correspondence from Albert J. Amateau to him from the early 1970s.

121. Ibid., 54, citing HIAS, Minutes of the Board of Directors, January 24, 1914, and February 10 and 15, 1914.

122. Isidore Hershfield to David de Sola Pool, January 23, 1914, Oriental Jews—Correspondence, 1912–1917, CSISA. Albert J. Amateau maintained that "Levantine" was rejected because it suggested "one who is dishonest and sharp in business." Albert J. Amateau to Joseph M. Papo, June 2, 1971, 2 pages, Joseph M. Papo Papers, AJA, p. 1.

123. Corrections to Minutes of Board of Directors, January 13, 1914, Series I, No. 1-4A, YIVO microfilm, p. 2.

124. Leon Sanders to David de Sola Pool, February 25, 1914, Oriental Jews—Correspondence, 1912–1917, CSISA. During this period, there was great sensitivity to the implications of ethnic labels in New York's broader Jewish community. A move to change HIAS's name to the Jewish Immigration Society of America had been tabled just a few years earlier. Minutes of the fourteenth meeting of the Board of Directors, 1912–1913, Series I, File No. 1-5, YIVO microfilm, pp. 1–2.

125. Ben Avi, "Tribuna Libera," 3.
126. Reporter, "Una Deskusión Revelantricho," *La Bos del Pueblo* (March 17, 1916): 2.
127. "Entrevista Enteresante," *La Bos del Pueblo* (April 7, 1916): 2 and (April 14, 1916): 2. Two years earlier, however, Gedalecia had strongly advocated the term "Oriental" in a discussion with David de Sola Pool. Joseph Gedalecia, "Discussion," *Jewish Charities* 4:11 (June 1914): 29.
128. "Entrevista Enteresante," *La Bos del Pueblo* (March 26, 1916): 1 and (April 14, 1916): 2. Gedalecia specifically mentioned Levantine Jewish communities in Austria, France, Italy, Germany, and England. Gadol countered that Gedalecia objected to changing the organization's name to Federation of Sephardic Jews because the change would disqualify him from serving as president. Gadol repeatedly referred to Gedalecia as an Ashkenazic Jew. [Moise Gadol], "La Vieja Istoria Se Repita," *La America* (December 24, 1915): 6.
129. Ben-Sion Behar, "Sefaradím, Ma No Orientales," *El Progreso* (October 29, 1915): 2.
130. [Moise S. Gadol], "Hanukát A-Bayit de la Maniefika Sinagoga Sefaradít Berít Shalom," *La America* (May 17, 1918): 2.
131. Angel, "Sephardim of the United States," 101; Papo, *Sephardim in Twentieth Century America*, 54.
132. Pool, "Immigration of Levantine Jews."
133. Albert J. Amateau concurred when he wrote that "[t]he Shearith Israel crowd, continually referred to us as the Oriental Sephardim to distinguish them from themselves [sic] as the Spanish and Portuguese Sephardim." Albert J. Amateau to Joseph M. Papo, June 2, 1971, 2 pages, Joseph M. Papo Papers, AJA, p. 1.
134. Pool, "Immigration of Levantine Jews," 12. For Joseph Gedalecia's negative response to Pool's reasoning, see Gedalecia, "Discussion," 29. Gedalecia embraced the term "Oriental." Samuel M. Auerbach, an Ashkenazic Jew from the Levant, agreed that "Sephardic" referred solely to religious rite. "The Sephardic Jews of New York," *Hebrew Standard* (October 27, 1916): 11.
135. Members of eight congregations, most of them Eastern Sephardic, attended the meeting at which the union was established, but the leadership was composed largely of Western Sephardim. Papo, *Sephardim in Twentieth Century America*, 64; Pool and Pool, *Old Faith in the New World*, 385; "The Union of Sephardic Congregations," *Sephardic Bulletin* 1:7 (May 1929): 1; "Brevities," *Sephardic Bulletin* 1:6 (April 1929): 4.
136. Papo, *Sephardim in Twentieth Century America*, 63; Simon S. Nessim to Henry S. Hendricks, June 10, 1929, box 4, folder "Correspondence, 1930–1936," Union of Sephardic Congregations, ASF.
137. Congregation Shearith Israel (and probably other Western Sephardic congregations of North America) had previously used the Isaac Leeser edition, copies of which were few and far between by the 1940s, as well as "very badly worn and . . . inad-

equate." David de Sola Pool to Henry S. Hendricks, March 3, 1947, and David de Sola Pool to Ivan Salomon, June 17, 1943, box 5, folder "Festival Prayer Book, 1946–1949," Union of Sephardic Congregations, ASF. For a Leeser edition, see, for example, Isaac Leeser, ed., *Sidur Siftei Sadikim/ Service for the Fast Days According to the Sephardi Tradition* (Philadelphia, 5627 [1866/1867]). The Eastern Sephardic prayer books published by Joseph Schlesinger in Vienna (the most widely used Sephardic prayer books in the United States by the 1940s) and some published in Leghorn were no longer obtainable during World War II. The Moses Gaster edition from Great Britain was too costly. Pool to Salomon, June 17, 1943.

138. Minutes of the Meeting of the Union of Sephardic Congregations, December 16, 1935, box 4, folder "Minutes, 1935–1943," Union of Sephardic Congregations, ASF. Pool specifically referred to "a group of young men in the Castoria Society" who had organized "Junior reform services on Yom Kippur."

139. Papo, *Sephardim in Twentieth Century America*, 64; Pool and Pool, *Old Faith in the New World*, 86, 444; and the following, all in Union of Sephardic Congregations, ASF: David de Sola Pool to Myer Solis-Cohen, September 16, 1941, folder "Prayer Books, 1941–1942"; Pool to Salomon, June 17, 1943, 2; Minutes of meeting of Board of Directors of the Union of Sephardic Congregations, April 30, 1936, box 4, folder "Minutes, 1935–1943," p. 2; David de Sola Pool to Hardwig Peres of Memphis, May 12, 1927, box 4, folder "Maimon, Solomon, 1937–1945." For the distribution of the *Book of Prayers* throughout the world, see Pool, "World of the Sephardim," 6; and the following, all in Union of Sephardic Congregations, ASF: Minutes of the Committee of the Union of Sephardic Congregations, April 15, 1937, box 4, folder "Minutes, 1935–1943," p. 6; untitled booklet with alphabetized index tabs, box 5, folder "All Hebrew Edition of Daily and Sabbath Prayer Book: Sales, 1948"; David de Sola Pool to Henry S. Hendricks, Victory Tarry, Matthew J. Levy, Simon Nessim, and D. A. J. Cardozo, March 4, 1946, box 5, folder "Festival Prayer Book, 1946–1949"; orders for the Shelosh Regalim prayer book, December 11, 1945, November 9, 1945, and July 10, 1946, box 5, folder "Festival Prayer Book, 1946–1949."

140. David de Sola Pool, "Traditional Sephardic Prayer Book," *La Vara* (August 3, 1934): 8.

141. Ibid.

142. Ibid.

143. David de Sola Pool, ed. and trans., *Book of Prayers According to the Custom of the Spanish and Portuguese Jews*, 2nd ed. (New York: Union of Sephardic Congregations, 1997 [1941]), vi. The preface to his *Prayers for the New Year* also indicates that the "text ... includes prayers characteristic of the Oriental Sephardic traditions, thus making the book serviceable to the Sephardim of the Occident and the Orient." David de Sola Pool, ed. and trans., *Prayers*

for the New Year According to the Custom of the Spanish and Portuguese Jews (New York: Union of Sephardic Congregations, 1987 [1937]), xi.

144. Joe Elias, interview with author, September 18, 1997. Pool apparently consulted with Eastern Sephardic rabbis for each prayer book (daily and Sabbath, as well as holiday). In 1943, he contacted "Rev." Jacob Cabouli of the Bronx for guidance on Eastern Sephardic prayers for Pesach, Shavuot, and Sukkot. See David de Sola Pool to Jacob Cabouli, June 17, 1943, box 5, folder "Festival Prayer Book, 1946–1949," Union of Sephardic Congregations, ASF.

145. Joe Elias, interview with author, September 18, 1997.

146. David de Sola Pool to Nissim S. Saul, April 24, 1944, box 4, folder "Minutes, 1935–1943," Union of Sephardic Congregations, ASF, p. 1.

147. Nissim S. Saul to David de Sola Pool, April 17, 1944, box 4, folder "Minutes, 1935–1943," Union of Sephardic Congregations, ASF. In Saul's correspondence, he shows a prejudice against presumably Eastern Sephardic religious leaders (whom he refers to as "amateurs who are still singing Turkish melodies"). It is not always clear in this letter whether he is lamenting the dearth of Sephardic or Western Sephardic religious leaders. The context of the letter leads me to presume his Eastern (as opposed to Western) Sephardic origins.

148. Pool to Saul, April 24, 1944, 1.

149. Papo, *Sephardim in Twentieth Century America*, 63; Pool to Saul, April 24, 1944, 2.

150. For a recently released prayer book representing Jews from Arab lands, see Rabbi Eliezer Toledano, ed., *The Orot Sephardic Rosh HaShannah Mahazor* [sic] (Lakewood, NJ: Orot, 1996), xi. For a prayer book representing Jews from both the Balkans and Arab lands, see Rabbi Moises Benzaken and Earl Klein, eds., *Mahzor Ori Ve'yish'i: A Prayerbook for Rosh Hashanah According to the Oriental Sephardic Rite*, 4th ed. (Los Angeles: West Coast Torah Center, 1997), foreword (unpaginated).

151. See, for example, David J. Behar, comp., *Ladino Hymns for Rosh Hashanah and Yom Kippur* (Seattle: Congregation Ezra Bessaroth, 1993 [1963, 1971]); Isaac Azose, ed., *The Seattle Sephardic Community, Daily and Sabbath Siddur According to the Rhodes and Turkish Traditions (as practiced in Seattle, Washington, USA)* (Seattle: Sephardic Traditions Foundation, 2002); and Isaac Azose, ed., *The Seattle Sephardic Community Mahzor for the Shalosh Regalim According to the Rhodes and Turkish Traditions (as practiced in Seattle, Washington, USA)* (Seattle: Sephardic Traditions Foundation, 2007).

152. Papo, *Sephardim in Twentieth Century America*, 52. Papo explains (pp. 139–40) that the federation had no exact year of demise; leaders began discussing its ultimate failure in 1921. In 1913, Eastern Sephardim also founded the Oriental Jewish Community of New York (*Kolel*), which eclipsed around 1919. See ibid., 141–48.

153. Angel, *La America*, 82; Papo, *Sephardim in Twentieth Century*

America, 149–52. This is probably the same organization listed as the Sephardic Jewish Community of New York, which was incorporated on May 8, 1924, and dissolved by proclamation on October 15, 1952. Louis J. Lefkowitz to Joseph M. Papo, April 9, 1974, box "Sephardic organizations," Joseph M. Papo Papers, AJA. Located in the heart of Sephardic Harlem, it was active for nine years and eclipsed as a result of the Depression and the outmigration of its members from the neighborhood. Franco, "History of The Rhodes League of Brothers' Aid Society," 11.

154. Papo, *Sephardim in Twentieth Century America*, 153–68. The community began to falter as a result of the Great Depression, and in 1932, all affiliated societies voted for disaffiliation. The lifespan of the community stretched to eight years, but its complete liquidation was not official until 1947.

155. Papo, *Sephardim in Twentieth Century America*, 181. It was incorporated on August 8, 1941, and by 1974 had not been formally dissolved. Lefkowitz to Papo, April 9, 1974. Papo (p. 320) lists Emilie Levy as its president beginning in 1982, with no end date.

156. Mizrahi, *703 American Sephardim*, 7.

157. "We represent the heritage of all Sephardim from the Iberian Peninsula and the Balkans, to the Jews of North Africa and Muslim lands including Iraq, Iran, Syria, Turkey, Yemen, Ethiopia [*sic*] and Bukharian Jews." "About Us," American Sephardi Federation website, http://www.americansephardifederation.org/sub/about/default.asp (accessed July 6, 2007). Under "FAQs," the ASF, citing Marc D. Angel, more specifically defines Sephardic as "almost any Jew who is not Ashkenazi. Although there are wide cultural divergences within the Sephardic world, common liturgy and religious customs constitute underlying factors of unity." In recent years, however, the organization has also used the term "Sephardi and Mizrahi" in its programming. See, for example, the flier for the "Jews from Arab Countries" program, November 5, 2007, which reads, "Participate in the Launch of Sephardi-Mizrahi Heritage Week."

158. Judith Mizrahi, "Sources of Diversity in Sephardim," Ph.D. diss., New York University, 1987, xix. Note the problem with these national classifications, particularly "Greek" and "Egyptian." She defines this group as "peoples whose national group languages vary widely (Judeo-Spanish, Judeo-Greek, Judeo-Arabic, French, Spanish, Judeo-Italian, etc.), but whose basic liturgy, customs and life-style follow the Sephardic tradition" (p. 4).

159. Albert de Vidas to the Editor of *The Jewish Week*, August 16, 1992, box 9, Joseph M. Papo Papers, AJS.

160. Lea-Nora Kordova, a self-described Ashkenazic Jew married to an Israeli Sephardic Jew of Turkish origin (Edirne), describes the term "Sephardic" as "basically an Ashkenazic umbrella used to classify Jews who are not Ashkenazic." Lea-Nora Kordova, Annette Labovitz, and Eugene Labo-

vitz, *Our Story: The Jews of Sepharad: Celebrations and Stories* (New York: Coalition for the Advancement of Jewish Education, 1991), 1.

161. "Sefardíes," in Eduardo Weinfeld and Isaac Babani, eds., *Enciclopedia Judaica Castellana*, 10 vols. (México: Editorial Enciclopedia Judaica Castellana, 1951): 9:496.

162. Ibid., 9:516.

163. Mizrahi, *703 American Sephardim*, xiii. One survey of Sephardic Jews telescoped the genesis of Sephardic identity back to the Babylonian exile, many centuries before either Sephardic or Ashkenazic identity began to emerge. L. Gubbay, *Sephardim: Their Glorious Tradition from the Babylonian Exile to the Present Day* (London: Carnell, 1992).

164. Mizrahi, *703 American Sephardim*, 29, 175–78.

NOTES TO CHAPTER 4

1. Papo, *Sephardim in Twentieth Century America*, 43 (without attribution); William Isaac Thomas, *Old World Traits Transplanted* (Montclair, NJ: Patterson Smith, 1971 [1921]), 200. Thomas attributes the anecdote to "Rene Darmstadter, The Jewish Community (manuscript)," which I have not been able to locate. William Jay Gaynor (1848–1913) served as mayor of New York City from 1909 until his death. Robert F. Wesser, in Kenneth T. Jackson, ed., *The Encyclopedia of New York City* (New Haven, CT: Yale University Press; New York: New-York Historical Society, 1995), 455.

2. The concept was first developed in Aviva Ben-Ur, "Where Diasporas Met: Sephardi and Ashkenazi Jews in the City of New York—A Study in Intra-Ethnic Relations, 1880–1950," Ph.D. diss., Brandeis University, 1998.

3. Amiga Serena (pseudonym), "Penserios de Nieta," *Sephardic House Newsletter* 10:3 (fall 1996): 1, 5; and *Los Muestros* 24 (September 1996): 37–38.

4. Emiliana, "El Judío Espaniól en Amérika," *La America* (May 19, 1911): 2. See also Moise Gadol, "La Avla de Nuestro Editor en la Unión de Nuestras Ijas de la Greva," *La America* (January 31, 1913): 2. Another source states that Eastern Sephardim looked like Spaniards, Mexicans, and Italians. *El Progreso* (April 28, 1916).

5. [Moise Gadol], "El rolo del jurnal 'La Amerika,'" *La America* (December 29, 1911): 2. The men also indicated that Ashkenazim most often mistook them for gentile Greeks and Italians. The short-lived newspaper that Gadol says he launched in reaction was probably the evanescent *La Aguila*, the country's first Ladino newspaper. See Ben-Ur, "In Search of the Ladino Press."

6. [Moise Gadol], "Por La Lingua," *La America* (December 9, 1910): 1.

7. Max Aaron Luria, "Judeo-Spanish Dialects in New York City," in John D. Fitz-Gerald and Pauline Taylor, eds., *Todd Memorial Volume Philological Studies*, 2 vols. (New York: Columbia University Press, 1930), 2:7–16; Jack Glazier, "American Sephardim, Memory, and Representation of European Life," in Stacy N. Beckwith, ed., *Chart-*

ing Memory: Recalling Medieval Spain, 307–9 (New York: Garland, 2000), 310; Leon A. Ligier, "The Chicago and Los Angeles Sephardic Communities in Transition," *American Sephardi* 2:1–2 (1968): 80; Walter P. Zenner, "Chicago's Sephardim," *American Jewish History* 79:2 (1990): 233–34; Stern, *Sephardic Jewish Community of Los Angeles*, 98; Stern, "Ethnic Identity among the Sephardic Jews of Los Angeles," 143; Dash, "Sephardim in Seattle," 12; Marc D. Angel, "Sephardic Culture in America," in Abraham D. Lavender, ed., *A Coat of Many Colors: Jewish Subcommunities in the United States*, 277–80 (Westport, CT: Greenwood, 1977), 277; Angel, *La America*, 52–53; Papo, *Sephardim in Twentieth Century America*, 46–47; Glaser, "Greek Jews in Baltimore," 328; for Atlanta, Marcie Cohen Ferris, *Matzoh Ball Gumbo: Culinary Tales of the Jewish South* (Chapel Hill: University of North Carolina Press, 2005), 166; and for Syrian Jews, Sutton, *Magic Carpet*, 23.

8. Dahbany-Miraglia, "Analysis of Ethnic Identity among Yemenite Jews," 1, 6.

9. Glazier ("Indianapolis Sephardim," 31) argues that this parochialism was at play in the context of Indianapolis. In Latin America's immigrant Jewish communities, Eastern European Ashkenazim often assumed that Syrian Jews were gentile Arabs or Turks. Ignacio Klich, "Arab-Jewish Coexistence in 1900's Argentina: Overcoming Self-Imposed Amnesia," in Ignacio Klich and Jeffrey Lesser, eds., *Arab and Jewish Immigrants in Latin America: Images and Realities*, 1–37 (London: Frank Cass, 1998), 19–20.

10. The idea that Jews embody indelible, physical differences is older. See Sander Gilman, *The Jew's Body* (New York: Routledge, 1991).

11. On Eastern European Jewish immigrant to Central Europe, see Steven E. Aschheim, *Brothers and Strangers: The East European Jew in German and German Jewish Consciousness, 1800–1923* (Madison: University of Wisconsin Press, 1982); and Jack Wertheimer, *Unwelcome Strangers: East European Jews in Imperial Germany* (New York: Oxford University Press, 1987).

12. Sachar, *History of the Jews in America*, 125.

13. The term for non-Jew was also used polemically in the Zionist Organization of America, in which some Jews of Eastern European origin called other Jews "goyim." Cyrus Adler to Louis Marshall, 1921, in Cyrus Adler, *Selected Letters*, 2:36.

14. Glazier, "American Sephardim," 308. This was Morris Marcus Feuerlicht (1879–1959), rabbi of the Indianapolis Hebrew Congregation.

15. Adatto, "Sephardim and the Seattle Sephardic Community," 63. This was Rabbi Hirsch Genss, who arrived in Seattle in 1899.

16. Ben-Ur, "The Ladino (Judeo-Spanish) Press in the United States," 64–77.

17. [Moise Gadol], "Por La Lingua," *La America* (December 9, 1910): 1. For another example of *La America* used as proof of Jewishness, see [Moise Gadol], "La Nasión Judía

i nuestros ermanos de Turkía," *La America* (January 5, 1912): 3.

18. Moise Gadol, "La Avla de Nuestro Editor en la Unión de Nuestras Ijas de la Greva," *La America* (January 31, 1913): 2.

19. Glazier, "Indianapolis Sephardim"; Glazier, "American Sephardim," 309. Cohen was a World War II veteran and resided in Indianapolis until the 1950s. Monastir is today the city of Bitola in the Republic of Macedonia. Sephardim in Los Angeles also tended to identify as Sephardic and to reject the term "Jewish" as a self-referential. Stern, "Ethnic Identity among the Sephardic Jews of Los Angeles," 136.

20. This term has been used by Sephardim more often in oral testimony than in print. For published examples, see Maír José Benardete, "A Look into the Historical Significance of the Sephardim, Their History and Culture," in Foundation for the Advancement of Sephardic Studies and Culture, *Four Reviews on Stephen Birmingham's Book "The Grandees,"* 27–37 (New York: Foundation for the Advancement of Sephardic Studies and Culture, 1971), 35–36.

21. Sutton, *Magic Carpet*, 151; Marshall, *From Baghdad to Brooklyn*, 46; *Victory Bulletin* (Brooklyn, NY), 1942–1945, passim; and personal observation.

22. Linda Cohen, "Captain Silvera, Community, M.D. Doing Valiant Work in England," *Victory Bulletin* 3:2–3 (February-March 1944): 3.

23. Sutton, *Magic Carpet*, 151.

24. Dahbany-Miraglia, "Analysis of Ethnic Identity among Yemenite Jews," 179; Dahbany-Miraglia, "Acculturation and Assimilation: American Yemenite Jews," *Perspectives: Research, Instruction and Curriculum Development, a Journal of the Faculty, New York City Technical College, CUNY* 10 (1987–1988): 130; and Dahbany-Miraglia, "On the Outside Looking In: Reflections of a Natural Feminist," 3–5 (unpublished, unpaginated manuscript, courtesy of the author). For parallel examples in the State of Israel, see the aforementioned works by Dahbany-Miraglia; Morris B. Gross, "Exploration of the Differences in Pre-School Learning Readiness and Concomitant Differences in Certain Cultural Attitudes between Two Subcultural Jewish Groups," Ed.D. diss., Columbia University, 1966, 1; and Lev Hakak (trans. Dorothea Shefer-Vanson), *Stranger among Brothers* (Los Angeles: Ridgefield, 1984), 117–18. For an example of the term applied to an Eastern Sephardic Jew, see Jodi Varon, *Drawing to an Inside Straight: The Legacy of an Absent Father* (Columbia: University of Missouri Press, 2006), 52.

25. "Tribuna Libera: Lo Ke Nuestros Lektores Pensan: Porke No?" *La Bos del Pueblo* (May 26, 1916): 6. Clara's letter appears in Ladino translation only.

26. Angel, "Sephardim of the United States," 126–30; Cohen, "Sephardi Jews in the United States."

27. Adatto, "Sephardim and the Seattle Sephardic Community," 63, 64; Sitton, *Sephardi Communities Today*, 357.

28. Maurice Beck Hexter, "Discussion," *Jewish Charities* 4:11 (June 1914): 27. Hexter (1891–1990) was a social worker, director of the Federation of Jewish Charities in Milwaukee in 1914, and a member of the Jewish Agency Executive from 1929 to 1938. Cyrus Adler, *Selected Letters*, 2:177; Hexter, *Life Size*; biographical sketch available at the American Jewish Archives website, http://www.americanjewisharchives.org/aja/FindingAids/hexter.htm.

29. Hacker, "Communal Life of the Sephardic Jews," 33. Hacker (1899–1987) was a proponent of adult education and an economics professor and dean at Columbia University. Obituary, *New York Times* (March 24, 1987): B6.

30. Benardete, *Hispanic Culture and Character of the Sephardic Jews*, 168–69. My translation from Latin-scripted Ladino.

31. Sutton, *Magic Carpet*, 35.

32. Barocas, "Refutation of the 21st Chapter," 8. Barocas arrived in the United States at the age of thirteen in 1920. Barocas, *History of the Broome & Allen Boys Association*, 1.

33. Hank Halio, *Ladino Reveries: Tales of the Sephardic Experience in America* (New York: Foundation for the Advancement of Sephardic Studies and Culture, 1996), 32.

34. Most Muslims in the United States immigrated after 1965, and those of early America, numbering thousands or several thousand, were primarily Western African in origin and imported as slaves. See Michael A. Gomez, "Muslims in Early America," *Journal of Southern History* 60:4 (November 1994): 672, 674–75; and M. Arif Ghayur, "Muslims in the United States: Settlers and Visitors," *Annals of the American Academy of Political and Social Science* 454 (March 1981): 150, 152.

35. Advertisements for Cassorla's practice as a cantor and ritual circumciser appeared regularly in *La Vara* during the 1930s. He is the same Cassorla who met with David de Sola Pool to discuss a new Sephardic rite (see chapter 3 of this volume).

36. Joe Elias, interview with author, July 18, 1995.

37. Bortnick, *One Century*, 55. The bracketed word "houses," is Bortnick's. For another example of coethnic recognition failure, see ibid., 6.

38. As quoted in Thomas, *Old World Traits Transplanted*, 200, without attribution or date.

39. Druyan, "Early Contacts," 157–58.

40. Nitza Druyan, "Yemenite Jews on American Soil: Community Organizations and Constitutional Documents," in Daniel J. Elazar, Jonathan D. Sarna, and Rela G. Monson, eds., *A Double Bond: Constitutional Documents of American Jewry*, 93–100 (Lanham, MD: University Press of America, 1992); and Dina Dahbany-Miraglia, "American Yemenite Jews: Interethnic Strategies," in Walter P. Zenner, ed., *Persistence and Flexibility: Anthropological Perspectives on the American Jewish Experience*, 63–78 (Albany: State University of New York Press, 1988).

41. Dahbany-Miraglia, "American Yemenite Jews," 67. The skin color

and hair terminology is Dahbany-Miraglia's. For Yemeni Jews as a physiologically varied group often mistaken for gentile Hispanic and black in the United States, see Yael Arami, "A Synagogue of One's Own," in Loolwa Khazzoom, ed., *The Flying Camel: Essays on Identity by Women of North African and Middle Eastern Jewish Heritage*, 101–13 (New York: Seal, 2003), 104.

42. Marilyn Halter, *Between Race and Ethnicity: Cape Verdean American Immigrants, 1860–1965* (Urbana: University of Illinois Press, 1993), 7, 24, 150–51, 171.

43. Jerre Gerlando Mangione, *La Storia: Five Centuries of the Italian American Experience, 1492–1992* (New York: HarperCollins: 1992), 27, 33.

44. See, for example, [Moise Gadol], "La Nasión Judía i nuestros ermanos de Turkía," *La America* (January 5, 1912): 3; and [Moise Gadol], "El emportante raporto del Bureau Oriental," *La America* (January 12, 1912): 2.

45. The history of this organization and its official names (e.g., Hebrew Sheltering and Immigration Society) is rather convoluted. HIAS emerged from the union of several immigrant aid societies that preceded it. See Soyer, *Jewish Immigrant Associations*, 138–40.

46. The "Oriental Bureau" is first mentioned in Minutes of the Special Meeting of the Board of Directors, December 21, 1911, YIVO microfilm, p. 1.

47. Moise Gadol, "La Avla de Nuestro Editor en la Unión de Nuestras Ijas de la Greva," *La America* (January 31, 1913): 2.

48. Gadol was named secretary of the Oriental Bureau, and Jacob Farhi was to succeed him. Papo, *Sephardim in Twentieth Century America*, 48. Gadol once referred to Leon Sanders, president of HIAS, as the "author of the founding" of the Oriental Bureau, but he probably meant the official who approved of the idea. [Moise Gadol], "El prezidente de la grande sosietá de Proteksión i ayudo a los emigrantes judíos," *La America* (January 19, 1912): 1.

49. "Entrevista Enteresante," *La Bos del Pueblo* (April 14, 1916): 2.

50. Minutes of the Special Meeting of the Board of Directors, December 21, 1911, 2; [Moise Gadol], "El emportante raporto del Bureau Oriental," *La America* (January 19, 1912): 2. For a confirmation of my analysis regarding the responses of Jewish and non-Jewish organizations to Eastern Sephardim, see Bortnick, *One Century*, 75.

51. Papo, *Sephardim in Twentieth Century America*, 48.

52. The Oriental Bureau was apparently shut down in June, reopened the next month, and then closed again in September. *La America* (June 18, July 16, and September 8, 1915); *El Progreso* (October 24 and December 10, 1915).

53. See, for example, Isaac Azriel, "Letra de Elis Ailand," *La America* (June 11, 1915): 8; Isaac Azriel, "Komo fui delivrado de Elis Ailand," *La America* (June 25, 1915): 6; *La America* (November 12 and 19,

1915); and *El Progreso* (October 10 and November 5, 1915).

54. Robert Ouziel, 1951 eulogy for Joseph Isaac Cohen, as reprinted in Barocas, *History of the Broome & Allen Boys Association*, 17c.

55. Albert J. Amateau to Joseph M. Papo, March 18, 1976, Joseph M. Papo Papers, AJA, p. 2; Alcosser, "My Life's Memoirs," 48–49.

56. HIAS appointed as this representative one Samuel Bero (known in the Ladino press as "Stanley Berro") in 1912. Minutes of the Special Meeting of the Board of Directors, December 21, 1911, Series I, file no. 1-3a; Minutes of the third meeting of the Board of Directors, February 12, 1912, Series I, File no. 1-4, pp. 1–2; Minutes of the eleventh meeting of the Board of Directors, October 8, 1912, p. 3; all in YIVO microfilm.

57. Minutes of the Special Meeting of the Board of Directors, December 21, 1911; [Gadol], "El prezidente de la grande sosietá," 1; Goren, "Sacred and Secular," 269–305.

58. Minutes of the Special Meeting of the Board of Directors, December 21, 1911, 2.

59. As cited in Eli Lederhendler, *Jewish Responses to Modernity: New Voices in America and Eastern Europe* (New York: New York University Press, 1994), 121.

60. Sachar, *History of the Jews in America*, 125.

61. Ibid., 133.

62. Sutton, *Magic Carpet*, 22. See also Lucy Dawidowicz, "Louis Marshall's Yiddish Newspaper," in *Jewish Social Studies* 25:2 (April 1963): 103–32.

63. Gary Dean Best, "Jacob H. Schiff's Galveston Movement: An Experiment in Immigrant Deflection, 1907–1914," *American Jewish Archives* 30:1 (April 1978): 43–79; Bernard Marinbach, "The Galveston Movement," Ph.D. diss., Jewish Theological Seminary, 1976.

64. Glazier, *Dispersing the Ghetto*.

65. Between 1907 and 1913, 181 "Turks," many of them Ashkenazim, were removed to the interior, representing 0.005 percent of the total beneficiaries. *Thirteenth Annual Report of the Industrial Removal Office for the Year Nineteen Thirteen* (New York: Industrial Removal Office, 1914), box 1, folder 5: "Annual Reports," IRO, p. 14. Elsewhere, the figure for the total number of "Levantine Jews" removed to the interior in 1913 is 78. This smaller figure may exclude Ottoman-born Ashkenazim. Abraham Solomon, "Dr. David de Sola Pool on 'Immigration of Levantine Jews,'" *Jewish Charities* (June 1914): 126.

66. In 1912, "cheap illustrated American papers" cost one cent per copy, and a magazine cost ten cents. John Foster Carr, *Guide to the United States for the Jewish Immigrant: A Nearly Literal Translation of the Second Yiddish Edition*, 2nd ed. (New York: Connecticut Daughters of the American Revolution, 1912), 15.

67. John Foster Carr, *Committee of Patriotic Education Connecticut Daughters of the American Revolution Guide to the United States for the Immigrant Alien*, pamphlet, box 22 of 124, folder 39: "Daughters of the American Revolution," IRO, p. 4.

68. John Foster Carr to the American Jewish Committee, November 1912, box 22, folder 25, IRO.

69. Minutes of the Industrial Removal Committee, January 29, 1913, box 1, folder 3, marked I-3: "Removal Committee Minutes (1903–1917)," IRO. The constituents are actually referred to as the "Federation of Turkish Jews," a probable misnomer.

70. *Tenth Annual Report of the Industrial Removal Office for the Year Nineteen Hundred and Ten* (New York: Industrial Removal Office, 1911), 7.

71. Ibid.

72. Undated report, box 1, folder 3, marked I-3: "Removal Committee Minutes (1903–1917)," IRO.

73. Minutes of the Industrial Removal Committee, January 29, 1913.

74. Minutes, November 17, 1915, box 1, folder 3, marked I-3: "Removal Committee Minutes (1903–1917)," IRO, pp. 2–3.

75. Solomon, "Dr. David de Sola Pool on 'Immigration of Levantine Jews,'" 126.

76. Ibid. On Senior, see Hexter, *Life Size*, 15. For the IRO's efforts to transport non-Ashkenazic Jews to the interior, see Minutes of the Industrial Removal Committee, January 29, 1913. Albert J. Amateau worked for the IRO from 1911 to 1912 or 1913 (probably 1913) in this effort. Bortnick, *One Century*, vi, 66; Amateau to Papo, March 18, 1976, 3; Minutes of the Industrial Removal Committee, January 29, 1913.

77. *La America* (February 3, 1911). Gadol added that once his newspaper began publication, the Kehilla showed great interest and invited Eastern Sephardim to join.

78. Asher Levy to H. Pereira Mendes, December 9, 1912, CSISA; Asher Levy to H. Pereira Mendes, December 15, 1912, CSISA. Levy refers to the organization only as the "society" on Second Avenue at 21st Street. The only Jewish organization at that address in 1912 (besides the Jewish Agricultural Experiment Station) was the American Jewish Committee. See *American Jewish Year Book 5673* (Philadelphia: Jewish Publication Society of America, 1912), 217. Albert Amateau clarifies that the building at 356 Second Avenue (apparently later) housed a number of New York Jewish charities and communal organizations, including the Kehilla, the Placement Bureau for the Jewish Handicapped, the National Desertion Bureau, the Bureau for Jewish Education, the Bureau for the Jewish Blind, and the Society for the Welfare of the Jewish Deaf. Amateau to Papo, March 18, 1976, 3.

79. Hacker, "Communal Life of the Sephardic Jews," 32.

80. Ibid., 40.

81. Baron dates the founding of the FAZ to 1897, when under the presidency of Richard J. H. Gottheil a number of small Zionist groups banded together. In 1900, it enrolled eight thousand members. Baron, *Steeled by Adversity*, 393.

82. *La America* (May 7, 1915).

83. [Moise Gadol], "Agudá Sionít Sefaradít," *La America* (April 30, 1915): 1; and [Moise Gadol], "El Mit-

ing de la Agudá Sionít Sefaradít," *La America* (June 25, 1915): 5. The FAZ, whose elected officials were evenly divided between Central and Eastern European Jews, was organized in 1898 in New York by Eastern European Jewish intellectuals. Raider, *Emergence of American Zionism*, 13–14.

84. M.G. [Moise Gadol], "El Sionizmo Sefaradí de NuYork," *La America* (May 7, 1915): 8. See also *La America* (June 25, 1915), concerning a meeting with Louis Lipsky, during which Lipsky promised to financially support the cause of Zionism among American Sephardim.

85. [Moise Gadol], "Nada por Nuestros Sefaradím," *La America* (July 7, 1916): 3.

86. Ibid.

87. [Moise Gadol], "El Sionizmo i los Sefaradím," *La America* (December 2, 1921): 2.

88. [Moise Gadol], "Por el Sionizmo," *La America* (May 18, 1917): 3.

89. [Moise Gadol], "El Progreso de la 'Ivriá,'" *La America* (February 12 and 19, 1915): 2.

90. [Moise Gadol], "El Sionizmo Sefaradí en Amérika," *La America* (May 28, 1920): 2.

91. Gedalecia, fluent in Yiddish, may have claimed not to understand the language out of solidarity with Nessim Behar. Moise Gadol, fluent in Yiddish, was infuriated by the unfavorable remarks made about Eastern Sephardim. Nessim Behar to Moise Gadol, *La America* (March 8, 1912): 3; [Moise Gadol], "Sala de Pasatiempo enfrente nuestro puevlo," *La America* (March 15, 1912): 2.

92. Raider, *Emergence of American Zionism*, 126–28.

93. Ibid., 128.

94. Ricardo Djaen, "Sefardismo y Sionismo en el período de entreguerras (1918–1939): el caso de la Confederación Universal de los Judíos Sefaradim," *Sefárdica* (Buenos Aires) 17 (May 2008): 59–68.

95. For another example of this dynamic, see Papo, *Sephardim in Twentieth Century America*, 104 (an example from 1917).

96. Amateau to Papo, March 18, 1976, 4.

97. Adina Cimet, *Ashkenazi Jews in Mexico: Ideologies in the Structuring of a Community* (Albany: State University of New York Press, 1997).

98. Ibid., 178.

99. Ibid., 7, 9–10, 18–20, 131.

100. Leon Levy to Joe Halio, February 18, 1998, box 9, folder "Center for Jewish History—Accession, 1997–1998," ASF.

101. Caryn Aviv and David Shneer, *New Jews: The End of the Jewish Diaspora* (New York: New York University Press, 2005), 148–49. The interpretation of the ASF's initial exclusion as subethnic bias is mine. Fundraising letter to Dr. Raphael, Mr. Lerner, and Mr. Zukrow, March 27, 1998, series 2, subseries 2, box 9: "Administration," folder 2, Center for Jewish History, 1998, ASF; Board of Directors Meeting, November 1997, box 1, series 1, ASF.

102. See, for example, Houston Stewart Chamberlain, *Foundations of the Nineteenth Century* (New York: Howard Fertig, 1968 [1899]), 1:272–73.

103. [Moise Gadol], "Keshas por Nuestros Turkinos," *La America* (August 16, 1912): 2.

104. [Moise Gadol], "La Nasión Judía i nuestros ermanos de Turkía," *La America* (January 5, 1912): 3 ("los jidiós de Yerushalayim").

105. "La Fiesta de la Sosietá Hayim VeHesed Galipoli," *La America* (October 1, 1915): 2.

106. "Six Wed at Once to Allen Street's Joy," *The Sun* (May 26, 1913): 14.

107. Until the mass influx of Eastern European Jews after 1903, Jerusalem had the largest Jewish population of Palestine (some forty thousand Jews in the mid-1880s), who formed the majority (54 percent) of the city's general population by 1881. Fellman, *Revival of a Classical Tongue*, 27, 61.

108. Sutton, *Magic Carpet*, 15.

109. Tía Satula [pseudonym of Moise Soulam], "Palavras de Mujer," *El Progreso* (October 10, 1915): 3–4. In Yiddish, the term was apparently "Yerushalayim Yid." See Marion Golde, "Children of the Inquisition," *American Weekly Jewish News* (May 17, 1918): 11.

110. Joseph Saltiel to Editor, *El Progreso* (October 24, 1915): 3.

111. Albert J. Amateau, who was active in the *kolonia* when "Jerusalem Jew" was a current term, explains that though Levantine Jews were initially identified and respected as "authentic Eretz Yisrael Jews," they were later resented for their aggressive quests for charitable contributions and unsavory business tactics. Albert J. Amateau to Joseph M. Papo, June 7, 1976, Joseph M. Papo Papers, AJA, p. 2.

112. Walter P. Zenner, "The Meaning of 'Levantinization,'" *Alliance Review* 18:38 (winter 1964): 16.

113. Bargaining was also a tradition among Arabic-speaking Jewish immigrants. Joseph Sutton states that "nothing purchased in those days was not bargained for, on the East Side," most of the negotiation being executed by the husband or older children fluent in English. In contrast to the Ladino-speaking community, women in the Syrian Jewish community were generally not involved in this activity, a difference that Sutton attributes to traditional gender roles. Sutton, *Magic Carpet*, 30.

114. Soyer, *Jewish Immigrant Associations*, 49.

115. Melinda Given Guttman, *The Enigma of Anna O.: A Biography of Bertha Pappenheim* (Wickford, RI: Moyer Bell, 2001), 157.

116. See 208n68.

117. Emiliana, *La America* (May 19, 1911): 3.

118. Mary Frank, in John Foster Carr, ed., *Library Work with the Foreign Born; Exploring a Neighborhood: Our Jewish People from Eastern Europe and the Orient* (New York: Immigrant Publication Society, 1919), 11.

119. Varon, *Drawing to an Inside Straight*, 2.

120. Gloria Sananes Stein, *Marguerite: Journey of a Sephardic Woman* (Morgantown, PA: Masthof, 1997), 194 and (for year of immigration) 63.

121. Berlin (1880–1949), a.k.a. Meir Bar-Ilan, was a Mizrachi leader

and served as editor of *Haibri* from 1908 to 1912. See "Berlin, Meyer," *The Universal Jewish Encyclopedia* (New York: Ktav, 1969), 2:217–18; and Yishayahu Bernstein and Yosef Tirosh, eds., *MiVolozhin Ad Yerushalayim*, 3 vols. (Tel Aviv: ha-Ve'adah le-Hotsa'at Kitve ha-Rav Me'ir Bar-Ilan, 1971). On the Mizrachi (religious Zionist) movement, see Yitzchak Goldshlag and Louis Bernstein, "Mizrachi," *Encyclopedia Judaica* (Jerusalem: Keter, 1971), 12:175–80.

122. [Meyer Berlin], "Aheinu HaSefardim," *Haibri* 7:23 (June 22, 1917): 2.

123. Dash, "Sephardim in Seattle," 13, probably derived from Adatto, *Sephardim and the Seattle Sephardic Community*, 128–29.

124. Marc D. Angel, "Ruminations about Sephardic Identity," *Midstream* 18:3 (1972): 65; and Angel, "Sephardic Culture in America," 279–80.

125. David Porter, *Constantinople and its Environs: In a series of letters, exhibiting the actual state of the manners, customs, and habits of the Turks, Armenians, Jews and Greeks, as modified by the policy of Sultan Mohammed. By an American*, 2 vols. (New York, 1835), 2:167. See also Theophile Gautier, *Constantinople*, trans. Robert H. Gould (New York, 1875), 227–28.

126. James Finn, *Sephardim; or, The History of the Jews in Spain and Portugal* (London: J. G. F. & Rivington, 1841), ix. Finn was British Consul in Jerusalem. See James Finn, *Stirring Times; or, Records from Jerusalem Consular Chronicles of 1853 to 1856* (London, 1878).

127. Emiliana, "El Judío Espaniól en Amérika," 2.

128. Benardete, *Hispanic Culture and Character of the Sephardic Jews* (1st ed.), 140.

129. Ibid. (2nd ed.), 168–69. My translation from Latin-scripted Ladino; Benardete does not provide the specific citation in *La Vara*.

130. Harry S. Mazal, "The True Sephardim," *American Weekly Jewish News* (May 31, 1918): 18, probably referring to the Schinasi brothers. La Luz club, in existence from 1916 to 1918, organized English and Spanish classes for Eastern Sephardic youths and also planned to establish a gymnastics group and musical band. Angel, *La America*, 31.

131. Ben-Sion Behar, "Sefaradím, Ma No Orientales," *La America* (October 29, 1915): 2.

132. Maurice H. Harris, *History of the Mediaeval Jews: From the Moslem Conquest of Spain to the Discovery of America* (New York: Bloch, 1916), 359–60.

133. "Los Jidiós Sefaradím," *La Bos del Pueblo* (March 23, 1917): 3. The review of Harris's book appeared in the context of Samuel M. Auerbach's article, discussed later in the chapter.

134. Mary Wortley Montague, *The Letters and Works of Lady Mary Wortley Montague*, ed. Lord Wharncliffe, 3 vols. (London, 1837), 1:410–11.

135. Hacker, "Communal Life of the Sephardic Jews," 33; [Berlin], "Aheinu HaSefardim," 2.

136. Eastern Sephardic self-critique at public lectures organized by Ashkenazim stimulated similar responses. Moise Gadol commented on this phenomenon in the March 8, 1912, issue of *La America* (as cited in Angel, *La America*, 16).

137. [Moise Gadol], "Mi Samha LeTsar VeShofet Aleinu?! Ken Te Metió Por . . . . . . [*sic*] i Juzgador Sovre Nozotros?!" *La America* (June 11, 1915): 1.

138. Moise Gadol, "El Artíkulo Puvlikado en el Jurnal Idish 'Der Feder,' Kon Data Jueves 10 Jun, 1915" and "Nuestra Repuesta," *La America* (June 18, 1915): 5.

139. Moise Gadol, "Nuestra Repuesta," *La America* (June 18, 1915): 5.

140. [Moise Gadol], "Basta Piedrer Tiempo en Vazío," *La America* (October 22, 1915): 4.

141. Oscar Handlin, *Race and Nationality in American Life* (Boston: Little, Brown, 1957), 74.

142. Gadol, "Nuestra Repuesta," 5.

143. Papo, *Sephardim in Twentieth Century America*, 363. Marc D. Angel (*La America*, 23, 135) also incorrectly identifies Gedalecia as Ashkenazic. *El Progreso* (March 26, 1916, p. 2) does not specify his ethnicity but does identify him as a native of Constantinople, as were his parents, and notes that he arrived in America at the age of eleven. On the Oriental Progressive Society, see [Moise Gadol], "El emportante raporto del Bureau Oriental," *La America* (January 5, 1912): 2.

144. According to grandson David Gedalecia, Joseph Gedalecia's father may have been "of mixed Sephardic/Moslem heritage and his mother of mixed Swiss Catholic/French Huguenot [*sic*] heritage." Email correspondence to author, February 18, 2006. Albert J. Amateau once described Gedalecia as "half Ashkenazi and half Sephardi." Amateau to Papo, June 2, 1971, 1. Later, however, Amateau recalled that Gedalecia's father was a "descendant of a tribe of Chirkasian Jews (Sephardim) who had immigrated in a body from Batum in the South of Russia in the 1700's" and that his mother was a "Sephardic lady of Constantinople." Furthermore, Amateau claimed that Gedalecia "always considered himself a Sephardi." Albert J. Amateau to Joseph M. Papo, December 23, 1974, Joseph M. Papo Papers, AJA, p. 1. Still later, Amateau claimed that Gedalecia's father was "Donmé" and his mother "Sephardic." Albert J. Amateau, "The Sephardic Immigrant from Bulgaria: A Personal Profile of Moise Gadol," *American Jewish Archives* 42:1 (fall/winter 1990): 66.

145. Papo, *Sephardim in Twentieth Century America*, 363.

146. "Una Enteresante Entrevista," *El Progreso* (March 26, 1916): 2. Another source maintains that he arrived in 1887 at age eleven. *The Jewish Communal Register of New York City, 1917–1918* (New York: Lipshitz, 1918), 1339.

147. Soyer, *Jewish Immigrant Associations*, 123.

148. Ibid., 118, 123; Goren, *New York Jews*, 65, 69, 127, 215, 274, 283; *Jewish Communal Register*, 72, 373.

149. "Una Enformasión," *La Bos del Pueblo* (April 7, 1916): 1.

150. *Jewish Communal Register*, 1337–39; Soyer, *Jewish Immigrant Associations*, 118, 123.

151. His membership is mentioned in [Moise Gadol], "El emportante raporto del Bureau Oriental," *La America* (January 5, 1912): 2.

152. Samuel M. Auerbach to Editor, "Correspondence: The Sephardic Jews of New York," *Hebrew Standard* (October 27, 1916): 11. The primary sources that I have examined never specify Auerbach's ethnic background, but he was probably affiliated with Istanbul's Ashkenazic community. For Ashkenazim in what is today Turkey, see Erdal Frayman, Moshe Grosman, and Robert Schild, *A Hundred Year Old Synagogue in Yüksekkaldirim: Ashkenazi Jews* (Istanbul: Galata Ashkenazi Cultural Association, 2000); and Amado Bortnick, *One Century*, 6–7.

153. Samuel M. Auerbach, "The Levantine Jews," *Immigrants in America Review* 2:2 (July 1916): 47.

154. Maurice S. Nessim, "Los Sefaradím-Orientales-'Los Jidiós Levantinos,'" *La Bos del Pueblo* (August 18, 1916): 4.

155. "Jidiós Levantinos," *La Bos del Pueblo* (August 4, 1916): 5; "'The Levantine Jew,'" *La Bos del Pueblo* (July 28, 1916): 4, (August 22, 1916): 6, and (August 18, 1916): 5.

156. Maurice S. Nessim, "The Oriental Sephardim vs. 'The Levantine Jew,'" *La Bos del Pueblo* (August 25, 1916): 2.

157. Samuel M. Auerbach to Editor, "Correspondence: The Sephardic Jews of New York," *Hebrew Standard* (October 27, 1916): 11.

158. See, for example, Bula Klara (pseudonym for Moise Soulam?), "Krónika Popular," *El Kirbatch* (December 2, 1910): 4. In this installment, the columnist identifies Salonika in particular as a city where Jews hang up their laundry in public. See also *El Kirbatch* (March 3, 1911): 4, in which the columnist criticizes Salonika's Jews for their ostentation and rowdiness at weddings.

159. On "self-mystique," "ascribed identity," and the development of ethnic cultural symbols in America, see Sarna, "From Immigrants to Ethnics," esp. 372–73 and 375–76.

160. "Lo Negro es Siempre Kopiado," *La Bos del Pueblo* (October 6, 1916): 6.

161. Marion Golde, "Children of the Inquisition," *American Weekly Jewish News* (May 17, 1918): 2, 12.

162. Ibid., 2.

163. Ibid.

164. "De Nuevo Todos Semos [sic] Ridikularizados: Será Una Lesión Para Nozotros?—'La Boz del Pueblo' Protesta," *La Bos del Pueblo* (May 24, 1918): 1.

165. Maurice S. Nessim to Editor, "The Sephardic Jews of New York," *American Weekly Jewish News* (May 24, 1918): 18.

166. Harry S. Mazal, "The True Sephardim," and Ralph Pardo, "The True Sephardim," *American Weekly Jewish News* (May 31, 1918): 18.

167. Sefaradí to Joseph Kotovski, "Otra Letra Avierta a Senior Kotovski (Marion Golde)," *La Bos del Pueblo* (June 14, 1918): 3.

168. León Yafo to Joseph Kotovski, "A La Atansión de Sr. Kotovski!" *La Bos del Pueblo* (June 7, 1918): 3.

169. See, for example, Hacker, "Communal Life of the Sephardic Jews."

170. Soyer, *Jewish Immigrant Associations*, 76.

171. Shemuél A. Moshe, "Basta el Skándalo," and Maurice S. Nessim, "Nota de el Editor," *La Bos del Pueblo* (June 28, 1918): 1.

172. Nessim, "Nota de el Editor."

173. Jonathan D. Sarna, "The History of the Jewish Press in North America," in *The North American Jewish Press* (Waltham, MA: Brandeis University Press, [1995]), 5.

174. My analysis of the reluctance of Ashkenazic organizations to assist Eastern Sephardim and Mizrahim does not necessarily apply to every situation, nor does it preclude other perspectives. Albert Amateau, for example, underscores Ashkenazic incivility but also concedes that Ashkenazim "had their own problems" and that "Sephardic Jews were too proud to go and ask for help." Bortnick, *One Century*, 74–75.

175. Franco, "History of The Rhodes League of Brothers' Aid Society," 4–5.

176. *Forty-Second Anniversary Dinner in Honor of Mr. Victor Alhadeff Sponsored by Filo Center, Inc.*, September 26, 1959, 3 (anniversary album, unpaginated).

177. J. Farhi to Editor, "Korespondensia de la Sivdad," *La America* (April 28, 1911): 1.

178. Angel, *La America*, 140.

179. Papo, *Sephardim in Twentieth Century America*, 44.

180. [Moise Gadol], "La Presa Judía i Nuestro Jurnal," *La America* (February 3, 1911): 3.

181. Papo, *Sephardim in Twentieth Century America*, 44.

182. My translation from a photostat of the greeting card (Papo, *Sephardim in Twentieth Century America*, 45).

183. Angel, *La America*, 23.

184. Papo, *Sephardim in Twentieth Century America*, 47–48.

185. Soyer, *Jewish Immigrant Associations*, 123. Soyer does not mention if any of these calls for recruitment were published in Ladino, Arabic, or Greek.

186. Angel, *La America*, 133.

187. Drachman, *Unfailing Light*, 358. See my comments in chapters 3 and 5 about the comprehensibility of Spanish among Ladino speakers.

188. Ibid.

189. Papo, *Sephardim in Twentieth Century America*, 45–46. For more information on Drachman's activities with Levantine Jewish immigrants, see P[hilip] Cowen, "The New Sefardic Immigration," *Mikve Israel Record* 4:2 (November 1913); and P[hilip] Cowen and David de Sola Pool, "Correspondence about Sefardic Immigration," 4:3 *Mikve Israel Record* (December 1913): 3.

190. "Farmasia Espaniola," *La America* (July 7, 1916): 3. The Latin-letter spelling of his last name is specified in an advertisement for "Food Tonic Jelol," *La America* (November 10, 1916): 6.

191. *La America* (February 5, 1915): 4.

192. Max Schurman, "Tribuna Libera," *La Bos del Pueblo* (November 26, 1915): 3. Given the flawlessness of the Ladino, this letter was probably translated from the English.

193. Franco, "History of The Rhodes League of Brothers' Aid Society," 19. The society at first supported non-Jewish wives and dependents of members for burial, though not in the society's cemetery (ibid., 20). Most, if not all, Eastern Sephardic mutual-aid societies did not accept non-Jewish members or Jews married to gentiles.

194. Albert Franco, "A Brief History of Abravanel Lodge No. 1116, F. & A.M.," 1964 (date is identified in "1981 Bicentennial Questionnaire by the Grand Historian"), Grand Lodge Library.

195. Revised Constitution and By-Laws of the Chios Brotherhood Society Inc., undated (1967 or 1968; dates are mentioned on p. 2), photocopy in author's possession, pp. 2, 4. On the Abravanel lodge, see chapter 5 of this volume.

196. Angel, "Sephardim of the United States," 128; Cohen, "Sephardi Jews in the United States," 151–60.

197. Marianne R. Sanua, "From the Pages of the Victory Bulletin: The Syrian Jews of Brooklyn during World War II," *YIVO Annual* 19 (1990): 283–330; Sutton, *Magic Carpet*.

198. Sitton, *Sephardi Communities Today*, 336 (visit of 1962).

199. Sutton, *Aleppo Chronicles*, 84.

200. Zev Chafets, "The Sy Empire," *New York Times* (October 14, 2007): 83.

201. Franco, "Historical Survey of the United Sephardim of Brooklyn," 7; Sitton, *Sephardi Communities Today*, 330, 340–41.

202. Sitton, *Sephardi Communities Today*, 337 (information gathered during a 1962 visit).

203. Marshall, *From Baghdad to Brooklyn*, 86.

204. Such close contact, according to one source, seldom occurred in Argentina. The 1947 appointment of Amram Blum as rabbi of the Aleppan community in Buenos Aires was cited in 1963 as "a rare instance." Sitton, *Sephardi Communities Today*, 308. Blum's fall from grace is recounted in Chafets, "Sy Empire," 83.

205. Saporta, *My Life in Retrospect*, 223.

206. Leonard Gold to David de Sola Pool, December 8, 1949, box 5, folder "Ladino, 1949," Union of Sephardic Congregations, ASF.

207. Kaye/Kantrowitz, *Colors of Jews*, ix–x, 16.

208. Wahba, "Benign Ignorance," 51, 53 (quotation marks in original).

209. Stern, "Ethnic Identity among the Sephardic Jews of Los Angeles," 143, citing a 1974 issue of the newsletter the *Young Sephardic Voice*, published by the Sephardic Federation's youth division.

210. Sanchez, "Wrestling with the Angel of Identity," 17. See also Tobin, Tobin, and Rubin, *In Every Tongue*; Kaye/Kantrowitz, *Color of Jews*.

211. Sanchez, "Wresting with the Angel of Identity," 21.

212. Sachar, *History of the Jews in America*, 337–40.

213. Alexander M. Dushkin, however, indicates that by 1919–1920,

"the Kehillah had disappeared form the horizon of Jewish life." Dushkin, *Living Bridges*, 23.

214. Alice Davis Menken's response to David de Sola Pool's Report on the Berith Shalom Congregation, November, 1922, CSISA, p. 2. Heading reads, "To the Board of Trustees, Congregation Shearith Israel."

215. Mrs. Mortimer M. Menken, comp. and ed., *Report of the Probation Committee of the Sisterhood of the Spanish and Portuguese Synagogue in the City of New York* (New York, 1915), box 1, folder 4, Alice D. Menken Papers, AJHS, p. 3 (unpaginated). Between 1911 and 1926, only one arraigned woman was Eastern Sephardic. Report of Alice Davis Menken to Martha B. Bruere, December 7, 1926, CSISA, p. 1.

216. Melvin Konner, *Unsettled: An Anthropology of the Jews* (New York: Penguin, 2003), 220. On the frequent association of "exotic" with "peculiar," see Ken Blady, *Jewish Communities in Exotic Places* (Northvale, NJ: Jason Aronson, 2000), xii.

217. Blady, *Jewish Communities*.

218. Ibid., xv

219. Ibid., xvi. Michael Pollak, who wrote the preface to *Jewish Communities*, also refers to the customs of some of these communities as anathema to "'normative' rabbinic-Jewish values." Consider, too, Pollak's description of "cave-dwellers from the mountain escarpments above the Sahara sporting feathered tufts that looked like mohawks, golden earrings, and peot (earlocks)." Hasidic Jews are noticeably absent from this description.

220. George Lenczowski, *The Middle East in World Affairs*, 4th ed. (Ithaca, NY: Cornell University Press, 1980 [1952]), 415. His religious identity is surmised from obituaries; the memorial mass for Lenczowski (1915–2000) took place in a Roman Catholic church. For the reaction of an erstwhile high school student of Iraqi origin to this passage, see Lital Levy, "How the Camel Found Its Wings," in Loolwa Khazzoom, ed., *The Flying Camel: Essays on Identity by Women of North African and Middle Eastern Jewish Heritage* (New York: Seal Press, 2003), 179–80.

221. Birmingham, *The Grandees*, 330–40. Ironically, many Eastern Sephardic immigrants, particularly those of Salonika, experienced America as technologically backward and ugly. See, for example, Glazier, "American Sephardim," 318; and Saporta, *My Life in Retrospect*, 156.

222. Western Sephardim also evoked this paradigm when urging Eastern Sephardim to "progress." But such exhortations were, perforce, also implicitly self-referential. See, for example, Henry Pereira Mendes to H. Shircas, Director of Clubs, "From a Most Esteemed Friend," *Neighborhood Chronicle* (April 1921): 1–2.

223. This unconscious attitude was especially pronounced during preparations for 1992 as a year commemorating the Expulsion of Jews from Spain. In the United States, the emphasis was on the Jews in the Iberian Peninsula from Visigoth rule until 1492. Jewish pedagogues were encouraged to "make the lives and creativity of

these [Golden Age Spanish] Jewish 'heroes' part and parcel of the Jewish school curriculum." One would never learn from these exhortations that Sephardim continued to exist and to shape Jewish history after 1492. Alvin I. Schiff, "Educational Readiness for 1991: Sepharad 92," *Jewish Education* 59:1 (spring-summer 1991): 2.

224. On this function of stereotypes, see Celia S. Heller, "The Emerging Consciousness of the Ethnic Problem among the Jews of Israel," in Michael Curtis and Mordecai Chertoff, eds., *Israel: Social Structure and Change*, 313–32 (New Brunswick, NJ: Transaction Books, 1973), 320. These extreme and contradictory representations are also characteristic of ethnic stereotypes more broadly. See the discussion of "Jews," "Chinese," "Italians," and the "Irishman" as targets of nineteenth-century "American ambivalence" in Louise A. Mayo, *The Ambivalent Image: Nineteenth-Century America's Perception of the Jews* (Madison, NJ: Fairleigh Dickinson University Press, 1988), 184.

225. Some of these observations are inspired by Lev Hakak, "The Image of Sephardim in the Modern Hebrew Short Story," in Issachar Ben-Ami, ed., *The Sephardi and Oriental Jewish Heritage: Studies*, 297–310 (Jerusalem: Magnes, 1982), esp. 298.

226. Ivan G. Marcus, "Beyond the Sephardic Mystique," *Orim* 1 (1985): 38.

227. David Biale, "Challenging the Boundaries," *AJS Perspectives* (fall/winter 2003): 11–12. Jacob Katz argued in the 1950s that socially, all traditional Jewish communities are generally alike, and the striking differences between them are attributable to variant processes of modernization. Jacob Katz, "Traditional Society and Modern Society," in Shlomo Deshen and Walter P. Zenner, eds., *Jewish Societies in the Middle East: Community, Culture and Authority* (Lanham, MD: University Press of America, 1982), 35–47.

228. Wahba, "Benign Ignorance," 54.

229. Lida, "Vanishing Sephardim," 1047.

NOTES TO CHAPTER 5

1. Germán Rueda, *La emigración contemporánea de españoles a Estados Unidos, 1820–1950—De "Dons" a "Misters"* (Madrid: MAPFRE, 1993), 26. Rueda documented fifty-eight Spanish immigrants to the United States who listed "Turkey" as their country of last residence for the years 1899–1921, 1923–30, 1932, 1944, and 1945. Most of these immigrants arrived between 1904 and 1914 (p. 276). On the Ladino language, see Tracy K. Harris, *Death of a Language: The History of Judeo-Spanish* (Newark: University of Delaware Press; London: Associated University Presses, 1994).

2. L. H. Gann and Peter J. Duignan, *The Hispanics in the United States: A History* (Boulder, CO: Westview/Hoover Institution on War, Revolution and Peace, 1986), 28.

3. The U.S. Census currently defines "Hispanics" as people who

originate from Spanish-speaking countries or regions. Hispanics are understood as an ethnic group and may belong to any race. U.S. government agencies began to use the term "Hispanic" in 1970. The term as an ethnic indicator grew more entrenched in the mainstream beginning in 1980, when, for the first time, a question on the U.S. Census asked respondents to indicate whether they were of "Spanish/Hispanic origin or descent." Suzanne Oboler, *Ethnic Labels, Latino Lives: Identity and the Politics of (Re)Presentation in the United States* (Minneapolis: University of Minnesota Press, 1995), vii, xiii; "Hispanic American," Wikipedia, http://en.wikipedia.org/wiki/Hispanic_American#History_of_the_term_.22Hispanic.22 (accessed February 15, 2008).

4. Frank, *Exploring a Neighborhood*, 11.

5. Drachman, *Unfailing Light*, 358.

6. Esther Tuvi to Editor, *La Vara* (April 26, 1935): 7.

7. Antonio Quilis, "Causas de desaparición de formas dialectales," in I. Hassan, ed., *Actas del primer simposio de estudios sefardíes*, 225–32 (Madrid: Consejo Superior de Investigationes Científicas, Instituto Arias Montano, 1990, [1964]), 232. Quilis writes, "después del vínculo de la sangre nada une tanto como el idioma." On the importance of language in fostering ethnic identity, see also Jack Glazier and Arthur W. Helweg, *Ethnicity in Michigan: Issues and People* (East Lansing: Michigan State University Press, 2001), 4–5.

8. Dwight Bolinger, *Aspects of Language*, 2nd ed. (New York: Harcourt Brace Jovanovich, 1975), 84, 92. On the importance of language in social organization and cultural expression, see Joseph Harold Greenberg, *A New Invitation to Linguistics* (Garden City, NY: Anchor, 1977), 84.

9. Compare the similar dynamics in the use of dialects in Southern Britain, as discussed in Bolinger, *Aspects of Language*, 591.

10. Ben Rampton, *Crossing: Language and Ethnicity among Adolescents* (London: Longman, 1995).

11. Dahbany-Miraglia, "Analysis of Ethnic Identity among Yemenite Jews," 12.

12. Katya Gibel Azoulay, *Black, Jewish, and Interracial: It's Not the Color of Your Skin, but the Race of Your Kin, and Other Myths of Identity* (Durham, NC: Duke University Press, 1997), 18, 25.

13. Bernardo Vega, *Memorias de Bernardo Vega: Contribución a la Historia de la Comunidad Puertorriqueña en Nueva York,* ed. César Andreu Iglesias (Puerto Rico: Ediciones Huracán, 1977), 49, 192–93; Joseph P. Fitzpatrick, "Puerto Ricans," in Stephan Thernstrom, ed., *Harvard Encyclopedia of American Ethnic Groups* (Cambridge, MA: Belknap Press of Harvard University Press, 1980), 858–67. Gurock (*When Harlem Was Jewish*, 150, 195–96n. 35) indicates that Puerto Ricans emigrated en masse to East Harlem in the late 1920s and that Harlem's Jewish community numbered one hundred thousand in the 1910s, representing the

largest ethnic group of the neighborhood (p. 1). The geographic boundaries of Harlem were variably defined over the years. Gurock (p. 6) defines Harlem, a part of New York's Twelfth Ward, as a region extending "north of 96th Street to the Harlem River on the East Side and north of Central Park at 110th Street to 145th Street and east of Morningside Park and St. Nicholas Park on the West Side." "El Barrio" extends from 98th to 117th streets, between Lenox and Second avenues. Ramón Colón, *Carlos Tapia: A Puerto Rican Hero in New York* (New York: Vantage, 1976), 79. "Boricua" or "Borincua," derived from the Taino name for the island, denotes a Puerto Rican or a person of Puerto Rican descent. "Borinquen" denotes Puerto Rico.

14. Vega, *Memorias de Bernardo Vega*, 46–47.

15. Moise Gadol identified ten Eastern Sephardic restaurants on Christie, Rivington, and Allen streets in 1912. [Moise Gadol], "El emportante raporto del Bureau Oriental," *La America* (January 5, 1912): 2. By 1919, Allen Street was known not only for its "oriental and 'kosher' restaurants" but also as a red-light district. Frank, *Exploring a Neighborhood*, 8.

16. The first Judeo-Spanish exiles, recently baptized Christians returning to Judaism, arrived in the Ottoman Empire as a result of the forced conversions in Spain in 1391.

17. In the nineteenth and early twentieth centuries, most Ladino speakers interviewed by scholars were not aware that they spoke a Spanish or Romance language and considered their native tongue simply a Jewish language. Tracy Kay Harris, "The Prognosis for Judeo-Spanish: Its Description, Present Status, Survival and Decline, with Implications for the Study of Language Death in General," Ph.D. diss., Georgetown University, 1979, 138. Ladino songs do not truly represent medieval traditions since most musical texts have not survived and their melodies transformed over time. Judith R. Cohen, "'We've Always Sung It That Way': Re/Appropriation of Medieval Spanish Jewish Culture in a Galician Town," in Stacy N. Beckwith, ed., *Charting Memory: Recalling Medieval Spain*, 1–34 (New York: Garland, 2000), 17.

18. [Moise Gadol], "Basta Piedrer Tiempo en Vazío," *La America* (October 22, 1915): 4.

19. Bula Satula (pseudonym of Moise Soulam), "Postemas de Mujer," *La Vara* (October 16, 1931): 8.

20. Jeffrey Gurock specifically applies these observations to Eastern European Jews migrating from the Lower East Side to Harlem after 1903. Gurock, *When Harlem Was Jewish*, 27–28, 30. The same probably holds true for Eastern Sephardim, though their mass immigration began later.

21. *La America* (April 28, 1911).

22. Neighborhood migration has been documented in a variety of sources. According to one estimate, the Ladino-speaking population of the Lower East Side in 1925 was probably as large as that of Harlem. "Levantine Jews in America," *The Interpreter*, 6.

Another source indicates that most of New York's Sephardim, and especially those from Salonika, lived in Harlem (around 116th Street) in 1925. By the time Albert Daniel Saporta returned to New York in 1938, the Bronx was the preferred place of residence for Sephardim. Saporta, *My Life in Retrospect*, 159, 169, 183, 215. The Filo Center, a social and cultural organization founded by Eastern Sephardim of Harlem in 1918, was forced to close its beautifully furnished headquarters on 118th Street in 1925 because the majority of its members had moved to the Bronx, with others settling in Brooklyn and Long Island. *Forty-Second Anniversary Dinner in Honor of Mr. Victor Alhadeff*, 3. In 1927, there were reportedly twenty thousand Sephardic Jews living in Harlem and another twenty thousand on the Lower East Side. *Souvenir Programme First Annual Ball of the Sephardic Jewish Community of New York*, 4. By 1931, Moise Soulam reported that few Sephardim remained in Harlem and that it was no longer a "little Jerusalem." Bula Satula (pseudonym of Moise Soulam), "Postemas de Mujer," *La Vara* (October 16, 1931): 8. Similarly, the Ashkenazic population of Harlem began to decline in the early 1920s and by 1930 no longer had a visibly Jewish enclave. Most of Harlem's Ashkenazim migrated to the West Side, Washington Heights, the Bronx, and Brooklyn. Gurock, *When Harlem Was Jewish*, 146–47, 154. By 1944 some five thousand Eastern Sephardim lived in the Bronx, most of them having arrived within the previous ten years. Cohen, "Sephardic Jews in the Bronx," 6.

23. Max Aaron Luria, "Judeo-Spanish Dialects in New York City," in John D. Fitz-Gerald and Pauline Taylor, eds., *Todd Memorial Volumes Philological Studies*, 2:7–16 (New York: Columbia University Press, 1930), 2:7.

24. El Paladar ("The Palate"), located at 42 Rivington Street, was owned by Avraham Gormezano and Yosef Saltiel. Behor bar Liya and Yakov Cohen owned La Estrella ("The Star") at 72 Rivington Street. *La America* (November 5, 1915); *La Vara* (October 17, 1924). Saltiel may be the same "Yosef Shaltiel" advertised as the cook of the Eastern Sephardic Café and Restaurant owned by Nissim Moise and Shemuél Florentine, both of Salonika, at 184 Chrystie Street. *La America* (January 15, 1915); *El Progreso* (November 5, 1915). El Amaneser, first owned by Dan Meir Aroeste and then by Ovadiah Farash and Yosef Rousso, at 105–107 Eldridge Street, was advertised as a strictly kosher restaurant serving "Oriental"-style food. *La Vara* (January 29, 1932): 7 and (August 5, 1932): 8.

25. La Vida Orientala, operating in the 1910s and '20s, was located at 16 East 116 Street. Levy's English-language business card identifies the establishment as "The Oriental Life in America: Oriental Restaurant and Turkish Coffee," located at 1393–95 Fifth Avenue, between 114 and 115 streets. Constantinopla, which changed ownership a few times,

variably advertised its location at 184 Chrystie Street and 165 Eldridge Street. Business cards of Hayim D. Levy in Hebrew-scripted Ladino and English; Denah Levy Lida, interview with author, April 2, 1999; *La America* (January 1, 1915 and March 12, 1915). Both cards are in the possession of Denah Lida, to whom I am grateful for sharing both personal testimony and family heirlooms. For examples of food and food establishments as ethnic intensifiers, see Hasia Diner, *Hungering for America: Italian, Irish, and Jewish Foodways in the Age of Migration* (Cambridge, MA: Harvard University Press).

26. *La America* (January 1, 1915); *La America* (February 5, 1915).

27. Benardete, *Hispanic Culture and Character of the Sephardic Jews* (1st ed.), 113–14, 144; and Maír José Benardete, "Cultural Erosion among the Hispano-Levantine Jews," in *Homenaje a Millás-Villacrosa*, 2 vols., 1:125–53 (Barcelona: Consejo Superior de Investigaciones Científicas, 1954), 1:146; Angel, *La America*, 9; Henry V. Besso to M. J. Benardete, April 21, 1936, Henry V. Besso archives; Marion Golde (pseudonym of Joseph Kotovski), "Children of the Inquisition," *American Weekly Jewish News* (May 17, 1918): 2.

28. The tradition to which Benardete refers of reading Ladino newspapers aloud in the cafés of Vienna, Salonika, Izmir, and Istanbul was imported to New York. Benardete, *Hispanic Character and Culture of the Sephardic Jews* (1st ed.), 117. S. Gabai and Bar David of the Kosher Cosmopolitan Restaurant of 25 Rivington Street invited their clientele to "eat well, cleanly and inexpensively," while Nissim Moise and Shemuél Florentine, originally of Salonika and owners of Cafe and Restaurant Constantinopla of 184 Chrystie Street, advertised "cleanliness, cleanliness, and cleanliness." *La America* (January 15 and August 13, 1915). Dan Meir Aroeste, proprietor of El Amaneser, insisted that no other downtown restaurant was as spacious and clean as his. Advertisement for El Amaneser, *La Vara* (January 29, 1932): 7. On Eastern Sephardic cafés as an escape from frigid tenement rooms, see Angel, *La America*, 9.

29. Benardete, *Hispanic Culture and Character of the Sephardic Jews* (1st ed.), 144.

30. Angel, *La America*, 9, 20–21; Hacker, "Communal Life of the Sephardic Jews"; Aviva Ben-Ur, "*Nuestra Kolonia*: A Report on the Sephardic Community of the Lower East Side as Conveyed through the Judeo-Spanish Press, 1910–1925," researched and prepared under the direction of Dr. Jane S. Gerber for the Komunidad Project of the Lower East Side Tenement Museum, 1995.

31. For food establishments as ethnic performance, see Shalom Staub, "The Near East Restaurant: A Study of the Spatial Manifestation of the Folklore of Ethnicity," *New York Folklore* 7:1–2 (1981): 116; Stephen Stern, "Ethnic Folklore and the Folklore of Ethnicity," *Western Folklore* 36 (1977): 7–32; and Barbara Kirshenblatt-Gimblett, "Studying Immigrant

and Ethnic Folklore," in Richard M. Dorson, ed., *Handbook of American Folklore* (Bloomington: Indiana University Press, 1983).

32. Douglas Martin, "Salvator Altchek, 'the $5 Doctor' of Brooklyn, Dies at 92," *New York Times* (September 15, 2002).

33. Stella Altchek Shapiro, interview with author, September 15, 2005.

34. Jose A. (Babby) Quintero, ed., *Who's Who: A Biographical Directory and Reference Book of and for the Spanish-Speaking Community of New York* (New York: self-published, 1964), 10, 85. The Spanish title is *Quién es quién: Un directorio biográfico y de referencias de y para la comunidad de habla española de Nueva York*.

35. Colón, *Carlos Tapia*, 10.

36. Nathan Glazer and Daniel Patrick Moynihan, *Beyond the Melting Pot: Negroes, Puerto Ricans, Jews, Italians, and Irish of New York City* (Cambridge, MA: MIT Press and Harvard University Press, 1963), 145; Alcosser, "My Life's Memoirs," 153 (anecdote dated to 1954). These Spanish speakers told Alcosser that they did not wish to learn English because "after they save [sic] sufficient amount of money they would return to their country of their origin, and live like kings, with maids to serve them, and to my years association with them this was their concensus [sic] of opinion."

37. Chammou, "Migration and Adjustment," 99, 100, 102n. 7, 178.

38. Alice Davis Menken, "Report on Conference Members from Board of Directors of Sisterhood," CSISA. Moise Soulam also indicated that Sephardim had moved to the Bronx because Puerto Ricans and their churches were taking over the once Jewish neighborhood of Harlem. Bula Satula (pseudonym of Moise Soulam), "Postemas de Mujer," *La Vara* (November 16, 1934): 5. "Dr. H. Goldstein" is probably Rabbi Dr. Herbert S. Goldstein, who received his first ordination from a New York Orthodox rabbi and his second from the Jewish Theological Seminary of New York. Goldstein established the Institutional Synagogue in Harlem in 1917, pioneering the concept of the "Jewish Center" or "synagogue center," which served both the social and religious needs of disaffected uptown Jewish youths. These centers included a sanctuary, study and social halls, and a gymnasium, assembled together in an Orthodox environment that was appealing to U.S. Jews. The founders of these institutions were mainly Orthodox rabbis trained at the Jewish Theological Seminary who served the Jewish youth. Gurock, *When Harlem Was Jewish*, 116, 131–36. This view that Sephardim fled the neighborhood due to a Puerto Rican influx should be considered cautiously. Gurock (p. 167) argues that Ashkenazic Jews who abandoned Harlem were not reacting to a mass influx of African Americans but rather were in search of better housing and that this motivation may also apply to other out-migrating groups as well. The Sephardic exodus from Harlem to the Bronx had begun by the 1920s. Menken, "Report on Conference Members from Board of Directors of Sisterhood."

39. Bula Satula (pseudonym of Moise Soulam), "Postemas de Mujer," *La Vara* (May 17, 1929): 10, (July 26, 1929): 10, (August 23, 1929): 10, (January 3, 1930): 10, (January 24, 1930): 10, (May 30, 1930): 10, (August 29, 1930): 10, (September 28, 1934): 5. See also Ham Moshón (pseudonym of Moise Soulam), "Postemas de Ham Moshón," *La Vara* (April 20, 1934): 8.

40. Henry Pereira Mendes to Alice Davis Menken, December 17, 1933, Alice D. Menken Papers, AJHS, p. 3.

41. Bula Satula, "Postemas de Mujer," *La Vara* (July 26, 1929): 10, (January 3, 1930): 10, (January 10, 1930): 10. See also Ham Moshón, "Postemas de Ham Moshón," *La Vara* (April 20, 1934): 8.

42. Bula Satula, "Postemas de Mujer," *La Vara* (May 30, 1930): 10.

43. Bula Satula, "Postemas de Mujer," *La Vara* (October 16, 1931): 8.

44. Mendes to Menken, December 17, 1933, 3.

45. Bula Satula, "Postemas de Mujer," *La Vara* (May 30, 1930): 10.

46. Such physical descriptions never acknowledge the diversity of skin shades in each ethnic community, or the role of (subjective) perception in assessing skin shade.

47. Vega, *Memorias de Bernardo Vega*, passim.

48. Bula Satula, "Postemas de Mujer," *La Vara* (May 17, 1929): 10, (May 25, 1929): 10, (May 31, 1929): 10, (October 18, 1929): 10, (January 15, 1932): 8, (January 22, 1932): 8, (January 29, 1932): 8, (December 16, 1932): 8, (November 16, 1934): 5.

On the link between prostitution and eras of depression in the United States, see, for example, Maimie Pinzer, *The Maimie Papers: Letters from an Ex-Prostitute* (New York: Feminist Press, 1997). For an earlier, rather oblique reference to prostitution in New York's Eastern Sephardic community, see [Moise Gadol], "Sala de Pasatiempo enfrente nuestro puevlo," *La America* (March 15, 1912): 2.

49. Bula Satula, "Postemas de Mujer," *La Vara* (November 30, 1928): 10. For a translation of and commentary on the installment, see Aviva Ben-Ur, "'We Speak and Write This Language against Our Will': Jews, Hispanics, and the Dilemma of Ladino-Speaking Sephardim in Early 20th Century New York," *American Jewish Archives* 50:1–2 (1998): 131–42.

50. On the concept of neither black nor white, see James R. Barrett and David Roediger, "Inbetween Peoples: Race, Nationality and the 'New Immigrant' Working Class," *Journal of American Ethnic History* 16:3 (spring 1997): 3–44; and Karen Brodkin, *How Jews Became White Folks and What That Says about Race in America* (New Brunswick, NJ: Rutgers University Press, 1999), esp. 60.

51. Jesús Colón, "Nuestras señoritas latinas," in Edwin Karli Padilla Aponte, ed., *"Lo Que el Pueblo Me Dice,"* 17–19 (Houston: Arte Público, 2001), 18.

52. Joaquín Colón López, *Pioneros puertorriqueños en Nueva York, 1917–1947* (Houston: Arte Público, 2002), 25–29, 246–47.

53. Jesús Colón, "Los Judíos y Nosotros," in Edwin Karli Padilla Aponte, *"Lo Que el Pueblo Me Dice,"* 114–15 (Houston: Arte Público, 2001), 114.

54. Jesús Colón, "Quiénes son los Judíos?" in Edwin Karli Padilla Aponte, *"Lo Que el Pueblo Me Dice,"* 53–56 (Houston: Arte Público, 2001), 56. Contrary to Colón's testimony, Bernardo Vega maintained that cross-cultural tolerance was particular to Catholic Puerto Ricans, who brought with them a "racial tolerance . . . foreign to the prevailing mode of interaction" in the continental U.S. Vega, *Memoirs of Bernardo Vega*, xiii.

55. Vega, *Memoirs of Bernardo Vega*, 91.

56. Similarly, Mexicans in California were initially categorized as white based on the social class of Mexican landowning elites, but the courts categorized working-class Mexicans as Native Americans and thus deprived them of citizenship and civil rights. By the 1930s, census takers assumed Mexicans to be nonwhite unless an individual was known to be white, but by 1940, this group was again presumed to be white. See Tomás Almaguer, *Racial Fault Lines: The Historical Origins of White Supremacy in California* (Berkeley: University of California Press, 1994), 56; and George Sanchez, *Becoming Mexican American: Ethnicity, Culture and Identity in Chicano Los Angeles, 1900–1945* (New York: Oxford University Press, 1993), 258. The federal racial and ethnicity classification system since 1977 lists Hispanics as an ethnic group rather than a race, while those of European and Middle Eastern descent are classified as white. Thus, Hispanics are still not completely white (which they were in the 1960 census), since they may belong to any race, whether white or black. See Lawrence Wright, "Annals of Politics: One Drop of Blood," *New Yorker* (July 25, 1994): 50–51; and Soheir A. Morsy, "Beyond the Honorary 'White' Classifications of Egyptians: Societal Identity in Historical Context," in Gregory Steven and Roger Sanjek, eds., *Race* (New Brunswick, NJ: Rutgers University Press, 1994), 175–98.

57. Max Aaron Luria, "A Study of the Monastir Dialect of Judeo-Spanish Based on Oral Material Collected in Monastir, Yugo-Slavia," *Revue Hispanique* 79:176 (1930): 323–24, 331.

58. This area included the neighborhood from the intersection of Cherry Street and Franklin D. Roosevelt Drive in the east, to Canal Street and southward. Rueda, *La emigración contemporánea*, 85, 87.

59. Their neighborhood in East Manhattan extended from Christopher Street to West 23rd Street. Rueda, *La emigración contemporánea*, 87. Little Spain is usually identified with West 14th Street. See Morton Marks, *Brooklyn's Hispanic Communities* (Brooklyn: Brooklyn Historical Society, 1989); and Patricia Fieldsteel, "'Feliz Navidad,' The Pope's Nose and Cowboy Cactus," *The Villager* 75:32 (December 28–January 3, 2005). According to another source, by the 1920s some twenty thousand Spaniards dwelled in New York, many in the Spanish quarter located between

Seventh and Eighth avenues, around 14th to 23rd streets. By 1917 "little Spain" had been recently inhabited by "swarthy Latins of South America." Ernestine Rose, *Bridging the Gulf: Work with the Russian Jews and Other Newcomers* (New York: Immigrant Publication Society, 1917), 7.

60. Rueda, *La emigración contemporánea*, 89–90.

61. A small contingent of Spaniards, mostly stevedores, did dwell on the Lower East Side in between the Greek and Syrian quarters. "New York City and the Spanish," unidentified article published in 1924, Old and Sold website, www.oldandsold.com/articles06/new-york-city-65.shtml (accessed June 15, 2007).

62. Maír José Benardete, "¿Quiénes Son los Sefardíes?" *España Libre* (June 9, 1944).

63. Benardete called this an "artificial rehispanization of the Hispano-Levantines" and believed that this would reverse the "complete obliteration" of Ladino dialects among Sephardim. Benardete, *Hispanic Culture and Character of the Sephardic Jews* (1st ed.), 71. Benardete's attitude toward Ladino, no doubt partly conditioned by his elementary education in the Alliance Israélite Universelle school (p. 169), was in consonance with early-twentieth-century Spaniards who took part in the philo-Sephardic movement.

64. In a typewritten address, for example, Besso wrote, "las obras de Maimonides caen *basho* tres clasificasiones distintas" (italics added). Unpublished address, "Maimonides, Su epoca, su vida, y su obra," Henry V. Besso collection, ASF, p. 10. Similarly, Ovadia de Benardete used words like "handrajo" (Ladino for "rag") in letters to her husband. I thank Diego Benardete for sharing this letter with me and for confirming her professional affiliation in a March 20, 2007, interview. A recent example of Ladino retention occurs in the 1996 film *The Birdcage*, in which Hank Azaria plays a Guatemalan immigrant in the United States. Toward the beginning of the film, Azaria's supposed Spanish exclamation comes out as Ladino ("Ah, Dió!" instead of "¡Ay, Diós!"). Azaria was born in 1964 in Queens to a Ladino-speaking family with roots in Salonika.

65. Ángel Pulido, *Españoles sin patria y la raza sefardí* (Madrid: E. Teodoro, 1905). The modern movement had begun as early as the nineteenth century and at one point involved plans for a Muslim repatriation, part of a vision to return Spain to its glory days as the "España de las tres castas" (Spain of the three races).

66. Benardete, *Hispanic Culture and Character of the Sephardic Jews* (1st ed.), 162n. 4.

67. The first reference that I have found to this campaign is [Moise Gadol], "La Espania i los Judíos," *La America* (August 16, 1912): 2.

68. Mary Brown Sumner, "The Ladino Speakers," *The Survey* 30:4 (April 26, 1913): 137.

69. Joseph Gedalecia, "Spain and the Jews," *American Hebrew* (July 2, 1915): 7.

70. Ibid.

71. Ibid.

72. "Spain and the Jews," *American Hebrew* (June 25, 1915): 193.

73. Gedalecia, "Spain and the Jews."

74. [Moise Gadol], *La America* (June 25, 1915).

75. Ibid. See Gadol's related idea that Western Sephardim in the United States had progressively forgotten their "native" Spanish language due to unpleasant historical memories. [Moise Gadol], "El Importante Raporto del Buro Oriental," *La America* (December 29, 1911): 2.

76. Denah Levy Lida, interview with author, April 2, 1999.

77. Gadol attributed its failure in Turkey, Bulgaria, Serbia, and Romania to both bitter historical memories and Jewish nationalism. [Moise Gadol], "La Espania i los Judíos," *La America* (August 16, 1912): 2.

78. Benardete, *Hispanic Culture and Character of the Sephardic Jews* (1st ed.), 14 (the phrase is Benardete's). Elsewhere, he referred to the "new movement . . . on behalf of the Spanish Jews." Maír Jose Benardete, "Cansinos-Asséns," in Horatio Smith, ed., *Columbia Dictionary of Modern European Literature* (New York: Columbia University Press, 1947), 137.

79. Benardete, *Hispanic Culture and Character of the Sephardic Jews* (1st ed.), 14.

80. Pulido was apparently aware of his "Hebraic" origins. G., "The New Era for Jews in Spain: An Interview with Eduardo Zamcois," *American Hebrew* 101:4 (June 1, 1917): 101. I was unable to identify "G." among the journal's staff. For the nickname "'apóstol' de los sefardíes," see Besso, "Los Sefardíes y el Idioma Castellano," 191.

81. Benardete, "Cansinos-Assens"; and Benardete, *Hispanic Culture and Character of the Sephardic Jews* (1st ed.), 156. Compare Adolfo de Castro, who in his preface to *Historia de los judíos en España* (1847) indicates that he does not have Jewish ancestry.

82. James D. Fernández, "Longfellow's Law: The Place of Latin American and Spain in U.S. Hispanism, circa 1915," in Brad Epps and Luis Fernández Cifuentes, eds., *Spain beyond Spain: Modernity, Literary History, and National Identity*, 49–69 (Lewisburg, PA: Bucknell University Press, 2005), 51. For a slightly different version of this article, see James D. Fernández, "Longfellow's Law: The Place of Latin American and Spain in U.S. Hispanism, circa 1915," in Richard L. Kagan, ed., *Spain in America: The Origins of Hispanism in the United States*, 122–41 (Urbana: University of Illinois Press, 2002). (All subsequent references are to the 2005 version.)

83. Federico de Onís, *España en América: estudios, ensayos y discursos sobre temas españoles e hispanoamericanos* (Río Piedras, PR: Universidad de Puerto Rico, 1955), 729. On the explosion of Spanish studies in colleges and schools beginning in 1916, see also Federico de Onís, "El Español en los Estados Unidos," *Hispania* 3:5 (1920): 276; Lawrence Wilkins, "On the Threshold," *Hispania* 1 (1917): 4–5; Lawrence Wilkins, "The President's Address," *Hispania* 2:1

(February 1919): 38–40; and Lawrence Wilkins, "President's Address," *Hispania* 4:1 (February 1921): 31–32.

84. Onís, *España en América*, 9.

85. Rueda, *La emigración contemporánea*, 91. I have not been able to ascertain Onís's precise place of residence in Manhattan. Onís also maintained a residence in Newburgh, New York, which may have been a summer house. Barton Sholod, telephone interview with author, March 26, 2007. Susana Redondo de Feldman, Onís's secretary and later director of the Hispanic Institute, reports that Onís was sometimes seen to favor Spanish America and Sephardim over Spain. Susana Redondo de Feldman, telephone interview with author, June 1999.

86. In 1940, Onís initiated the official name change to Hispanic Institute in the United States. He found that the original name was often misinterpreted as referring only to Spain or to the local Spanish community. Federico de Onís to Frank D. Fackenthal, October 23, 1940, 2 pages, Hispanic Institute.

87. *Bulletin of the Spanish Institute in the United States* 1 (January 1931): 2. The establishment of the institute was a joint effort by the Institute of International Education, the American Association of Teachers of Spain, the Junta para Ampliación de Estudios, and several Spanish and American universities. Onís, *España en América*, 8–9.

88. As mentioned earlier, this name change was apparently initiated in 1940. Onís to Fackenthal, October 23, 1940.

89. Onís, *España en América*, 729.

90. Ibid., 728.

91. Castro's revolutionary works on Spanish historiography include *España en su historia: cristianos, moros y judíos* (Buenos Aires: Editorial Losada, 1948).

92. Onís, *España en América*, 8.

93. Edith Helman, "Early Interest in Spanish in New England (1815–1835)," *Hispania* 29:3 (1946): 340; as discussed in Fernández, "Longfellow's Law," 51.

94. Fernández, "Longfellow's Law," 60–61. Fernández (p. 60) defines "Hispanidad" as an "affirmation of essential Hispanic values shared by Spain and Latin America." The term, which developed after the Spanish-American War of 1898, reaffirmed Latin America's links to Spain. By contrast, "Pan-Americanism" emphasized the unity of purpose and destiny among American nations.

95. Besso, "Los Sefardíes y el Idioma Castellano," 176; Onís, *España en América*, 103.

96. The Sephardic Section was also called the Sección de Estudios Sefardíes (Section of Sephardic Studies). I have not been able to pinpoint the precise year of the section's founding. Henry V. Besso indicates that the Instituto de las Españas was concerned with the "aproximación hispano-sefardí" since 1930 and that he met Federico de Onís around 1931. Besso, "Los Sefardíes y el Idioma Castellano," 176. Maír José Benardete is first mentioned as director of the Sephardic Section in a list of officers, *RHM* 2:1 (October 1935), first page of the unpaginated blue pages appearing before p. 1, and

the first descriptive reference to the Sephardic Section appears in *RHM* 2:4 (July 1936): 371. The heading reads "Sección de Estudios Sefarditas" and announces the formation of a dramatic group whose first performance in April of that year, "El castigo de Ataliau," translated to Ladino, achieved "extraordinary success." However, a former student indicates that Benardete had served as director of the Sephardic Section since the late 1920s. George Christopoulos, "Biography and Career," in Izaak A. Langnas and Barton Sholod, eds., *Studies in Honor of M. J. Benardete (Essays in Hispanic and Sephardic Culture)* (New York: Las Americas, 1965), 14.

97. Benardete, *Hispanic Culture and Character of the Sephardic Jews* (1st ed.), 23.

98. As mentioned in note 96, the first reference I have found to Benardete's directorship of "Estudios sefarditas" appears in *RHM* 2:1 (October 1935), list of officers.

99. Samuel Armistead and Joseph H. Silverman, eds., *Judeo-Spanish Ballads from New York: Collected by José Maír Benardete* (Berkeley: University of California Press, 1981), 7, 11; Maír José Benardete, "Los romances Judeo-españoles en Nueva York," M.A. thesis, Columbia University, 1923.

100. Benardete, *Hispanic Culture and Character of the Sephardic Jews* (1st ed.), 14.

101. In Luria's acknowledgments, he thanked Onís "for generous assistance and advice while the study was being prepared and for his painstaking care and invaluable criticism in reading the manuscript in final form." Luria, "Study of the Monastir Dialect," 334.

102. The informants were Mentesh Amiras, Elvira Ben David, Ishak Sustiel, and Maria Vivas of Salonika, and Clara Turiel of Rhodes. Israel J. Katz, "The Sacred and Secular Musical Traditions of the Sephardic Jews in the United States," in Martin A. Cohen and Abraham J. Peck, eds., *Sephardim in the Americas: Studies in Culture and History,* 331–56 (Tuscaloosa: University of Alabama Press, 1993), 336, without attribution. For Moroccan recordings by Onís, see Samuel Armistead and Joseph H. Silverman, eds., *Romances judeo-españoles de Tánger recogidos por Zarita Nahón* (Madrid: Cátedra-Seminario Menéndez Pidal, 1977); and Samuel Armistead and Israel J. Katz, "Judeo-Spanish Folk Poetry from Morocco (The Boas-Nahón Collection)," *Yearbook of the International Folk Music Council* 11 (1979): 59–75.

103. Besso, "Los Sefardíes y el Idioma Castellano," 176.

104. *Bulletin of the Spanish Institute in the United States* 1 (January 1931): 9; Zarita Nahón, "Spagnioli of Tangier," M.A. thesis, Columbia University, 1912.

105. The state of the field began to improve in the 1940s. See Yitzhak Baer and Abraham A. Neuman, *The Jews in Spain: Their Social, Political and Cultural Life during the Middle Ages* (Philadelphia: Jewish Publication Society of America, 1942); *Toldot ha-Yehudim bi-Sefarad ha-Notsrit* (Tel Aviv: Am Oved, 1944). Before then,

there were José Amador de los Ríos, *Historia social, política y religiosa de los Judíos de España*, 3 vols. (Madrid: Imprenta de Fortanet, 1876); Heinrich Graetz, *Geschichte der Juden von den ältesten Zeiten bis zur Gegenwart*, 11 vols. (Leipzig: O. Leiner, 1897–1911), translated as *History of the Jews*, 6 vols. (Philadelphia: Jewish Publication Society of America, 1891–1898).

106. Benardete, "Los romances Judeo-españoles en Nueva York"; and Benardete, *Hispanic Culture and Character of the Sephardic Jews*, 11–12.

107. Armistead and Silverman, *Judeo-Spanish Ballads from New York*, 7, 11; Benardete, "Los romances judeo-españoles en Nueva York."

108. Besso, "Benardete's Bibliography"; Moise Angel to Editor, "La Boz de Nuestros Lektores," and Moshe Azuz to Editor, *La Vara* (July 17, 1936): 9; Chek Abrevaya to Editor, "La Boz de Nuestros Lektores," *La Vara* (July 24, 1936): 2.

109. The dissertation was completed in 1953 and appeared as *Hispanic Culture and Character of the Sephardic Jews* (1st ed.).

110. The earliest evidence that I have regarding the starting date of his directorial position is the first issue of *RHM*, inaugurated in 1934, which carries a listing of the Hispanic Institute's officers. For the years of his career as professor and director of the Sephardic Section, see "Mair J. Benardete, 93, Spanish Professor, Dies," *New York Times* (April 19, 1989): B7; and the Hispanic Institute's list of officers in *RHM* 31:1–4 (January–

October 1965). Private correspondence implies that he began as director in 1934. Henry V. Besso to Maír José Benardete, February 29, 1936, Henry V. Besso collection, ASF, pp. 9–10.

111. Benardete, *Hispanic Culture and Character of the Sephardic Jews* (1st ed.), 120n. 16; Michael Molho, *Le Meam-Loez: Encylopédie populaire du séphardisme Levantine* (Salonica, 1945).

112. Besso, "Benardete's Bibliography," 461.

113. Ibid., 462.

114. *Bulletin of the Spanish Institute in the United States* 12 (July 1934): 112.

115. Besso, "Benardete's Bibliography," 462.

116. *Bulletin of the Spanish Institute in the United States* 12 (July 1934): 112. "Señorita Abolafia" is identified as Jennie Abolafia in a typewritten, undated transcript by Henry V. Besso (c. 1980), p. 2, from the archives of the Henry V. Besso family, to whom I am grateful for permitting me access to their precious collection.

117. The institute's *ex libris* label, reading "Sangre de Hispania Fecunda," also emphasized racial ties. Adhered to the inside cover of Aubrey F. G. Bell, *Gaspar Corrêa* (Oxford: Oxford University Press/Humphrey Milford, 1924), in the author's possession.

118. *Bulletin of the Spanish Institute in the United States* 1 (January 1931): 17; Celia and Dinah Hakim, interview with author, June 11, 2000. The Hakim sisters were able to identify from performance photographs

several members as young Ladino-speakers from New York. Besso identifies as active in the Sephardic Section the following "Sephardic students": Rachel Nahoum, Robert Nassi, Henry V. Besso, Jennie Abolafia, Paula Ovadia (Benardete), Joseph H. Kattan, Maurice Molho, Albert Matarasso, Professor Abraham Yahuda, "and a couple of others whose names I cannot recall." Some of the "young men and young women" in this list were "either students at Columbia University, or students of Prof. Benardete either at Hunter College or Brooklyn College." Typewritten, undated transcript by Henry V. Besso (c. 1980), archives of the Henry V. Besso family, p. 2.

119. Eastern Sephardic writers helped to perpetuate this distortion. Historian Joseph Néhama concluded that sixteenth-century Salonikan Jews spoke a Spanish "free of admixtures and in general rather pure," evidently basing himself on the Spanish used by former crypto-Jews who settled in the Ottoman Empire. As noted, without attribution, in Benardete, *Hispanic Culture and Character of the Sephardic Jews* (1st ed.), 56.

120. Fernández, "Longfellow's Law," 60–61.

121. In 1931, *El Ermanado*, a publication of New York's Sephardic Jewish Brotherhood of America, appeared on the subscription list. *Bulletin of the Spanish Institute in the United States* 1 (January 1931): 10.

122. Miguel Asín Palacios, "El Islam Cristianizado: Estudio de Sufismo' a través de las obras de Abenarabi de Murcia" (Madrid: Editorial Plutarco, 1931), as cited in *Bulletin of the Spanish Institute in the United States* 1 (January 1931): 5.

123. "Información Cultural: La Misión del Instituto de las Españas Expuso su Director Sr. de Onis," *La Prensa* (October 14, 1936).

124. As noted earlier, most Muslims in the United States immigrated after 1965, and those of early America, numbering thousands or several thousand, were primarily Western African in origin and imported as slaves.

125. *Bulletin of the Spanish Institute in the United States* 1 (January 1931): 5.

126. I have identified a handful of Levantine Jews who carried out major projects on their own heritage at Columbia University prior to the 1940s. Among them is the aforementioned Zarita Nahón, a Columbia University graduate student from Tangier, who, under the guidance of Professor Franz Boas of the Anthropology Department, pursued a study of Haketía (North African Judeo-Spanish). Columbia University's library catalog lists the M.A. thesis as "Spagnioli of Tangier" (1912). As mentioned earlier, Nahón enlisted her sister, Simy (Suzanne) Nahón de Toledano, to perform a number of ballads and songs that she had collected, which were recorded in 1930 under Boas's supervision and which represent the first "scientific attempt in the United States to make field recordings of Judeo-Spanish songs." Armistead and Silverman, *Romances judeo-españoles de Tánger recogidos por Zarita*

Nahón. Following the Nahón sisters was Robert J. Nassi, who undertook an M.A. thesis on a converso playwright. Nassi is cited on p. 2 of a typewritten, undated transcript by Henry V. Besso (c. 1980) from the archives of the Henry V. Besso family. Nassi's thesis is preserved in Columbia University's library under the title "Traditional Lore in El Siglo Pitagórico y Vida de Don Gregorio Guadaña" (1934 [1935]). The work—which does not focus on Jewish themes—deals with the life and literary output of Antonio Enríquez Gómez, the son of a converted Portuguese Jew who fled to France and Amsterdam, where he openly returned to his ancestral faith. Besso's aforementioned 1935 M.A. thesis, "Dramatic Literature of the Spanish and Portuguese Jews of Amsterdam, Holland, in the 17th and 18th Centuries," should be considered even though it dealt with Western, not Eastern, Sephardim.

127. Denah Lida, untitled essay in author's possession, 21 pages; Denah Levy, "El sefardí de Nueva York: observaciones sobre el judeo-español de Esmirna," master's thesis, Columbia University, 1944. She concluded her doctoral studies in Mexico with "El sefardí esmiriano de Nueva York," Ph.D. diss., Universidad Nacional Autónoma de México, 1952.

128. Denah Levy Lida, interview with author, April 2, 1999.

129. Ibid.

130. "El Centenario de Maimónides Festejado Solemnemente en la Casa de las Españas," *La Prensa* (April 1, 1935).

131. Benardete, *Hispanic Culture and Character of the Sephardic Jews* (1st ed.), 190. Among those who responded enthusiastically to Spain's interest in Eastern Sephardim are Rabbi Abraham Danon (1857–1925), *Sa vie et ses oeuvres* (Paris: Imprimerie H. Elias, 1925), and Bejarano (first name not given), both of whom contributed articles to scholarly journals and undertook studies of their own history and heritage. Baruch Camhi of Yugoslavia was the pupil of Ramón Menéndez Pidal in Madrid and published some of his linguistic studies in *Revista de Filología Española*, as did Palestinian-born A. S. Yahuda. Likewise, Romanian-born Mosco Galimir established in Vienna the first Casa Sefardita (with a peak of 1,450 members), devoted to the propagation of Sephardic culture and language. Benardete, *Hispanic Culture and Character of the Sephardic Jews* (1st ed.), 163n. (m).

132. Angel, "Sephardim in the United States"; Cohen, "Sephardi Jews in the United States."

133. Frances León Quintana, "Spaniards," in Stephan Thernstrom, ed., *Harvard Encyclopedia of American Ethnic Groups*, 948–50 (Cambridge, MA: Harvard University Press, 1980), 950. Ramón Menéndez Pidal (1869–1968), a visiting professor at Columbia University from 1937 to 1938, was among those who left Spain at that time. He attended at least one Sephardic Section event, his presence being duly noted by *La Prensa*, New York's most important Spanish-language newspaper. "Los sefarditas

españoles conservaron las costumbres y usos tradicionales," *La Prensa* (April 13, 1938); Sánchez Korrol, *From Colonia to Community*, 70.

134. Rueda, *La emigración contemporánea*, 223, 231–33, 236, 237. The Atlantic City chapter is first mentioned in *RHM* 4:1 (October 1937): 183. The chapters of Newark, New Jersey, and Omaha, Nebraska, are first listed in a list of officers, *RHM* 3:1 (October 1936), first unpaginated blue page before p. 1. The Florida branch opened on December 29, 1933, not in 1935 as Rueda indicates. The Florida chapter is first mentioned in A. J. Hanna, "Sección de Florida" (extract of official announcement), *RHM* 1:1 (October 1934): 76; and the Texas chapter, whose center was located at St. Edward's University, in *RHM* 7:3–4 (October 1941): 370.

135. I have perused all issues of *RHM* through the 1960s and have verified that only one affiliate outside New York sponsored Sephardic-related events. In 1935, the New Orleans section at Newcomb College sponsored a lecture on Maimonides's life and invited representatives of the "various Hebraic groups of the city." *RHM* 1:4 (July 1935): 315. In the same issue a "cantiga Sefardita" was published (p. 316), along with a portrait by (Spanish painter Juan Eugenio?) Mingorance (b. 1900) of "Hebrews in synagogue" (p. 318). The following year the section sponsored a lecture at Tulane University on Spinoza and his philosophy. *RHM* 2:4 (July 1936): 374. The activities of the various Hispanic Institute branches tapered off or ceased entirely during World War II and were never again announced in *RHM*.

136. Veladas de los Lunes announcement card, Beraha Safira, canciones sefardíes, March 6, 1950, Hispanic Institute, Columbia University. The last Sephardic-related announcement card that I was able to locate dates to December 16, 1968.

137. The list of the Hispanic Institute's officers, including Benardete as director of the Sephardic Section, appears for the last time in *RHM* 34 (1968). Benardete is last listed among the institute's "colaboradores" in *RHM* 35:1–2 (January-April 1969), where the collaborators' names appear on the table of contents page. By the following year (*RHM* 36:1–2 [1970–1971]) no Hispanic Institute officials are listed, and only a list of editors and advisory editors appears. This suggests that by 1970 the institute had officially ceased to function as a multifaceted cultural and intellectual center. Its name continues on largely through the *RHM*, the journal that Federico de Onís founded in 1920.

138. Besso, "Los Sefardíes y el Idioma Castellano," 176.

139. Benardete, *Hispanic Culture and Character of the Sephardic Jews* (1st ed.), 12–13; Besso, "Benardete's Bibliography," 462.

140. William J. McGill to Henry V. Besso, April 5, 1971, folder "RHM (old) Correspondencia," Hispanic Institute archives. When I first visited the archives in the year 2000, I found them wasting away in a dungeon-like

basement, in complete disarray and gathering thick layers of dust.

141. Here I consider not only audience members at the institute's performances but also readers of *La Vara*, which so carefully chronicled and commented on the activities of the Hispanic Institute.

142. The 1882 Chinese Exclusion Act, enacted by the Senate and House of Representatives, barred the "coming of Chinese laborers to the United States" for the following ten years. This act was reissued in 1902 and in 1904 "without modification, limitation, or condition." See the text of the two acts at the Ancestors in the Americas website, http://www.cetel.org/1882_exclusion.html and http://www.cetel.org/1904_extension.html (accessed July 14, 2006). The fact that polygamy at that time was legally practiced among Muslims in the Ottoman Empire (and outlawed in the United States) may have also been a reason to identify as Spanish. The mistaking of an Ottoman Jew for a Muslim at Ellis Island could result in deportation, as mentioned in Papo, *Sephardim in Twentieth Century America*, 22–23, without attribution. As we have seen, both Eastern and Western Sephardim worried that U.S. authorities would confuse Eastern Sephardim and Mizrahim with "Orientals."

143. "La Fraternidad, 387," *Masonic Standard* (New York) 1:5 (May 14, 1898): 1, and 10:49 (December 9, 1905): 1. The eight founders included six Cubans, one Colombian, and one Frenchman. One Hundredth Anniversary Celebration program, 1955, La Fraternidad lodge, p. 16 (unpaginated).

144. Baron, *Steeled by Adversity*, 324. Baron writes that particularly after 1900, "Even Freemasons now refused membership to Jews; as a result, Jews formed their own lodges."

145. Microfilm of membership list, La Fraternidad archives. This list does not appear to be comprehensive but gives some indication as to the proportion of Eastern Sephardic brothers.

146. One Hundredth Anniversary Celebration program, 1955, 18–19.

147. Ibid., 53–56 (my tally is based on Sephardic names and recognized Sephardic personalities).

148. One Hundredth Anniversary Celebration program, 1955, 15. Brothers Eli and Salomon Contente, as we have seen, arrived in the United States from Izmir in 1904 to participate in the World's Fair in St. Louis. They successfully petitioned Theodore Roosevelt to allow them to remain in the country and then settled in New York, where they worked as executives and foremen for the Schinasi brothers in the cigarette industry. Amateau, "Turkish-Jewish Pioneers in the US."

149. La Fraternidad membership book, 1951, 20. Salomón Emanuel may be the same man identified as "Shelomo Emanuel," president of the Ahavath Shalom of Monastir Society in 1912, who was involved in the founding of the Federation of Oriental Jews of America. Angel, *La America*, 62. Alternatively, this may be Solomon Emanuel, who arrived in the United States from Jerusalem in 1904 to

participate in the World's Fair in St. Louis. He, too, successfully petitioned Theodore Roosevelt to remain in the country and then settled in New York, where he worked as an insurance broker. Amateau, "Turkish-Jewish Pioneers in the US."

150. La Fraternidad newsletter, March 11, 1933, 4; December 8, 1934, 3; January 12, 1935, 4; and April 9, 1939, 4. Torres joined La Fraternidad in 1921. La Fraternidad membership booklet, 1951, 18.

151. Microfilm of membership list, La Fraternidad archives; Manuel Marina to Dominick C. Grippo, December 26, 1977, La Fraternidad archives. As in the case of most Sephardic masons, Nahum's birthplace is listed as "Turkey." Nahum died on May 21, 1981. La Fraternidad newsletter, June 12, 1981, 2.

152. On this membership depletion see "La Fraternidad No. 387," *Masonic Standard* 10:49 (December 9, 1905): 1.

153. There is evidence that depletion of membership stimulated recruitment efforts. During the Depression, for example, the lodge's secretary issued a special financial report and suggested that new candidates be inducted in order to offset the lodge's deficit. Of 278 brothers, only 19 in 1935 were members in good standing. Inserted circular, La Fraternidad newsletter, January 12, 1935. The circular, authored by Roger Noy, is addressed to Ramon Mosteiro.

154. This theme is explored in Michal Friedman, "Recovering 'Jewish Spain': Sephardic Studies in the Span-

ish Political and Cultural Landscape (1848–1940)," Ph.D. dissertation in progress, Columbia University.

155. Advertisement for Masonic Life Association, *Masonic Standard* 17:37 (September 14, 1912): 9.

156. Lenny Lubitz, interview with author (also including Barry Cohen, Howard Danon, and Máximo Dextre), August 17, 2000.

157. Maria Vassilikou, "Greeks and Jews in Salonika and Odessa: Inter-ethnic Relations in Cosmopolitan Port Cities," in David Cesarani, ed., *Port Jews: Jewish Communities in Cosmopolitan Maritime Trading Centres, 1550–1950*, 155–72 (London: Frank Cass, 2002), 162. Daniel Saporta, a Salonikan businessman, was a member of the "Veritas" lodge of the Grand Orient de France, which took up the cause of the prevention of cruelty to animals. Saporta, *My Life in Retrospect*, 31.

158. On the persecution of Freemasons in Latin America, Spain, and the erstwhile Spanish colony of Cuba, see "La Fraternidad, 387," *Masonic Standard* (New York) 1:5 (May 14, 1898): 1; and "La Fraternidades from All the World," *Masonic Standard* 20:45 (November 6, 1915): 3. On Masonic opposition to the Church's teachings about Jews as Christ killers, see "The Black Christmas of 1905," *Masonic Standard* 10:49 (December 9, 1905): 1.

159. One Hundredth Anniversary Celebration program, 1955, 18.

160. As suggested in ibid., 17, 19.

161. "La Fraternidades from All the World," 3.

162. Brazilian-born Spanish historian Américo Castro (1885–1972) published revolutionary works on Spanish historiography, including *España en su historia*. The attitude that Jewishness and Hispanicity are not compatible endures today. The national radio program *Latino U.S.A.* contacted the author in September 2005 for a story on President Bush's nomination of a Hispanic Supreme Court justice. Alex Avila, who conducted the interview, wondered if Sephardim could be considered Hispanic, and if so, could Benjamin Cardozo be considered the first Hispanic Supreme Court justice?

163. "Locha Masónica Sefaradít," *La Vara* (January 1, 1932): 3.

164. "1981 Bicentennial Questionnaire by the Grand Historian," 1979, La Fraternidad, Grand Lodge of New York archives, p. 2. This information was retrieved from the Book of Grand Lodge, p. 15.

165. Later generations of Abravanel brothers remembered the founders as "mostly" Sephardim. Undated newsletter from Abravanel lodge, announcing next meeting of January 20, 1988, Grand Lodge of New York archives, p. 3.

166. Dispensation, dated June 1932, to constitute a new lodge and to install its officers, reprinted in undated Abravanel newsletter, announcing installation of Mark Adler on June 3, 1998, Grand Lodge of New York archives, p. 4.

167. La Fraternidad newsletter, November 9, 1957, Grand Lodge of New York archives, p. 3. I was unable to ascertain Louis Opal's birth date.

168. Franco, "Brief History of Abravanel Lodge," Grand Lodge Library. The first meeting to discuss the possibility of a Sephardic lodge convened on November 22, 1930. Barry Cohen, telephone interview with author, July 12, 2007.

169. "1981 Bicentennial Questionnaire by the Grand Historian," 2. The Pythian Temple was built in 1926–1927 at 135 West 70th Street in New York City "for the local chapter of the Knights of Pythias, a fraternal order founded in 1864." "The Pythian," Tom Fletcher's New York Architecture website, http://www.nyc-architecture.com/UWS/UWS009.htm (accessed June 11, 2007). The synagogue is located at 8 West 70th Street.

170. Barry Cohen, interview with author (also including Howard Danon, Lenny Lubitz, and Máximo Dextre), August 2000. Cohen indicated that he chose to join the Abravanel lodge rather than La Fraternidad because he did not speak Spanish.

171. La Fraternidad newsletter, November 9, 1957, 3.

172. "La Fraternidad, 387," *Masonic Standard* 1:5 (May 14, 1898): 1. Two subsequent offshoots of La Fraternidad, in order of founding, were the Abravanel lodge and Pan American lodge. Lenny Lubitz, telephone interview with author, June 6, 2007.

173. Baron, *Steeled by Adversity*, 350–51.

174. Barry Cohen, recalling his childhood conversations with Abravanel member Victor Nahoum, in interview with author, August 2000;

Barry Cohen, telephone interview with author, July 12, 2007.

175. La Fraternidad newsletter, January 12, 1935, Grand Lodge of New York archives, p. 2.

176. Undated newsletter from Abravanel lodge, announcing next meeting of January 20, 1988, Grand Lodge of New York archives, p. 3. The identification of the Gabo's use comes from Lenny Lubitz, email correspondence to author, June 11, 2007, and Barry Cohen, telephone interview with author, June 12, 2007.

177. Announcement of 88oth Stated Communication, February 18, 1987, Grand Lodge of New York archives, p. 2.

178. Undated newsletter from Abravanel lodge, announcing next meeting of January 20, 1988, 3.

179. La Fraternidad newsletter, November 9, 1957, Grand Lodge of New York archives, p. 3.

180. La Fraternidad newsletter, March 11, 1933, 4; circular of Installation of Officers of La Fraternidad Lodge, December 16, 1933; circular for El Sol de la Fraternidad Gran Velada Artística y Baile, March 31, 1934, 2; La Fraternidad newsletters of December 8, 1934, 3; January 12, 1935, 4; April 9, 1939, 4; and December 24, 1941, 3; program for ceremony extending Honorary Membership in honor of M. W. William Frederick Strang, October 2, 1943, 1; La Fraternidad membership booklet, 1951, 2 (unpaginated); One Hundredth Anniversary Celebration program, 1955, 9, 28; La Fraternidad newsletters of November 9, 1957, 4; November 5, 1960, 4; and June 17, 1961, 4; La Fraternidad invitation to Annual Convention, March 27, 1965, 3, 4; and La Fraternidad invitation to the Presentation Ceremony of Right Worshipful Herman Mondzak, February 24, 1968, 4; all in Grand Lodge of New York archives.

181. Record Book honoring Isidore Saba Mevorah, 1949, Henry V. Besso archives, unpaginated; undated newsletter from Abravanel lodge, announcing next meeting of January 20, 1988, 3. According to the Record Book, in 1949 the club enrolled about 110 members (p. 46). By the same year, Arabic-speaking Jews native to the Middle East with probably no Iberian ancestry were also considered as Sephardim (p. 13).

182. Barry Cohen, Howard Danon, Lenny Lubitz, and Máximo Dextre, interview with author, August 17, 2000.

183. In 1935, for the sake of "progress," the editors of *La Vara* introduced an English section. "Dos palavras por el tokamiento de nuestra kavesera," *La Vara* (April 19, 1935): 1. By comparison, the Yiddish daily *Tageblatt* had an "English Department" (English page) since at least 1902. See Arthur Aryeh Goren, "Sacred and Secular: The Place of Public Funerals in the Immigrant Life of American Jews," *Jewish History* 8:1–2 (1944): 276.

184. On language attrition as a factor in the erosion of ethnic identity, see Glazier and Helweg, *Ethnicity in Michigan*, 4–5.

185. The phenomenon came to national attention in 1988, when Na-

tional Public Radio debuted the first of three programs called "The Hidden Jews of New Mexico." The other two, directed by Nan Rubin and produced by Benjamin Shapiro, were broadcast in 1992 and 1995. Stanley Hordes served as consulting historian.

186. Martin A. Cohen, *The Martyr: The Story of a Secret Jew and the Mexican Inquisition in the Sixteenth Century* (Philadelphia: Jewish Publication Society of America, 1973).

187. S. Schwartz, *Os christãos novos em Portugal no século XX* (1925); *Menorah Journal* 12 (1926): 138–49, 283–97; Fréderic Brenner, *Marranes* (Paris: Éditions de la Différence, 1991).

188. Judith S. Neulander, "The New Mexican Crypto-Jewish Canon: Choosing to Be 'Chosen' in Millennial Tradition," *Journal of Jewish Folklore and Ethnology Review* 18:1–2 (1996): 21.

189. See Hordes, *To the End of the Earth*; and my review in *American Jewish History* 93:2 (2007): 264–68.

190. Barbara Ferry and Debbie Nathan, "Mistaken Identity? The Case of New Mexico's 'Hidden Jews,'" *Atlantic Monthly* (December 2000): 85–96; "The Society for Crypto-Judaic Studies," Abraham D. Lavender website, http://www.fiu.edu/~lavender/SCJS%20for%20adl%20website%201-13-04.htm.

191. Judith Neulander, "Crypto-Jews of the Southwest: An Imagined Community," *Jewish Folklore and Ethnology Review* 16:1 (1994): 64–68, borrowing the term from Benedict Richard O'Gorman Anderson, *Imagined Communities: Reflections on the Origin and Spread of Nationalism* (London: Verso, 1983).

192. Ferry and Nathan, "Mistaken Identity?" 94.

193. Margaret Ramirez, "Renewing a Jewish Heritage," *Los Angeles Times* (September 20, 1999): A15.

194. Seymour Drescher, "Jews and New Christians in the Atlantic Slave Trade," in Paolo Bernardini and Norman Fiering, eds., *The Jews and the Expansion of Europe to the West*, 439–70 (New York: Berghahn, 2001), 455.

195. See, for example, Janet Liebman Jacobs, "The Spiritual Self-in-Relation: Empathy and the Construction of Spirituality among Modern Descendants of the Spanish Crypto-Jews," *Journal for the Scientific Study of Religion* 39:1 (March 2000): 53–63; and Janet Liebman Jacobs, *Hidden Heritage: The Legacy of the Crypto-Jews* (Berkeley: University of California Press, 2002), 12.

196. Hordes himself affirms this in *To the End of the Earth*, xi, 244, 245.

197. An extensive example of a historian's reliance on social scientific work to build a historical argument is Hordes, *To the End of the Earth*.

198. Hayyim J. Angel, ed., *Seeking Good, Speaking Peace: Collected Essays of Rabbi Marc D. Angel* (Hoboken, NJ: Ktav, 1994), 275–78.

199. Ramirez, "Renewing a Jewish Heritage," A15. Similarly, a congregation composed of Orthodox immigrants from Iraq, Yemen, Tunisia, and Morocco and located "on the margins of Dallas's mainstream Jewish community" seems to welcome self-proclaimed crypto-Jewish

descendants. Liebman Jacobs, *Hidden Heritage*, 108–9.

200. Steven Almond, "Hispanics Rediscover Jewish Identity," *New Mexico Magazine* (June 1991): 29.

201. Many claimants of crypto-Jewish heritage do not consider themselves Mexican, even though their families had resided for generations in what is today Mexico. Gloria Golden, *Remnants of Crypto-Jews among Hispanic Americans* (Mountain View, CA: Floricanto, 2005), 13–14, 62, 69, 97, 106, 117–18, 184.

202. On self-identified crypto-Jews who participated in the Chicano civil-rights movement, see Liebman Jacobs, *Hidden Heritage*, 145–46. An example of those who reject the prestige claim appears in Golden, *Remnants of Crypto-Jews*, 195.

203. Angel, *Seeking Good, Speaking Peace*, 276.

204. Mica Rosenberg, "Crypto Jews: New Mexican Hispanics Claim a Hidden Jewish Past," *New Voices: National Jewish Student Magazine* (March 2003): 11–13; author's visit to the group's conclusion of Sabbath celebration, November 2004.

205. Benardete, *Hispanic Culture and Character of the Sephardic Jews* (1st ed.), 156.

206. Ibid., 158, without attribution.

207. The extent of interethnic relations has varied according to Mizrahi subethnic group. Dina Dahbany-Miraglia ("Analysis of Ethnic Identity among Yemenite Jews," 199), for example, maintains that interactions between Yemeni Jews and gentile Arabs in the United States were minimal.

208. Sutton, *Magic Carpet*, 11, 17, 35.

209. Ibid., 11.

210. Ibid., 35.

211. This information is derived from their February 13, 1921, ship manifest, available at ellisisland.org. Many other Jewish individuals and families bearing the surname "Esses" and listed on various ship manifests from 1903 to the early 1920s were listed as "Hebrew."

212. See, for example, the entry for Orslan Kassin, December 9, 1922, line 1.

213. *Victory Bulletin* 3:9 (April 1945): 4.

214. "Girls Junior League Swell [sic] Coffers of National War Fund," *Victory Bulletin* 2:3 (November 1943): 1. The film was screened in Bradley Beach, New Jersey.

215. For similar events, see "Syrian Picture Shown for Army Welfare," *Victory Bulletin* 3:2–3 (February-March 1944): 1; "Soldiers of Bensonhurst to Get Gift Packages," *Victory Bulletin* 3:4 (April 1944): 6; "Girls' Junior League Gala Dance Hits $1500," *Victory Bulletin* 3:6 (July 1944): 1; "Girls Junior League to Present Syrian 'Aida' for Red Cross Benefit," *Victory Bulletin* 3:11 (June 1945): 3.

216. "Pvt. Beyda Meets a Royal Sheik," *Victory Bulletin* 3:2–3 (February-March 1944): 5.

217. Sutton, *Magic Carpet*, 148.

218. Ibid., 55–57.

219. R. W. Apple, "Haddad-Farbstein Campaign Draws Attention to Syrian Jews," *New York Times* (June 1, 1964): 21.

220. Herbert Hadad, "My Family Reunion: A Middle-East Dream Fulfilled," *Northeastern University Magazine* (January 1994): 31–32.

221. Herbert Hadad, "Both Jewish and Arabic," *New York Times* (August 3, 1985): 23.

222. Apple, "Haddad-Farbstein Campaign." Newspapermen who were Haddad's colleagues when he reported for the *New York Post* claimed that "he usually described himself simply as an Arab."

223. Ibid. Haddad's political opposition was Leonard Farbstein.

224. Shohat, "Reflections of an Arab Jew," 117. See also Kyla Wazana Tompkins, "Home Is Where You Make It," in Loolwa Khazzoom, ed., *The Flying Camel: Essays on Identity by Women of North African and Middle Eastern Jewish Heritage*, 131–40 (New York: Seal, 2003), 138.

225. Consider, for example, the activities of IVRI-NASAWI (New Association of Sephardi/Mizrahi Artists and Writers International), cofounded in 1996 by Jordan Elgrably; and Mervat F. Hatem, "The Invisible American Half: Arab American Hybridity and Feminist Discourses in the 1990s," esp. notes 1 and 3, available online at http://www.haussite.net/haus.o/SCRIPT/txt2001/01/hatem_n_X.HTML. Author and religious leader David Rabeeya, of Iraqi origin, unambiguously identifies as an Arab Jew (see, e.g., Rabeeya, *Journey of an Arab-Jew*).

226. An investigation of these relations should be placed within a transnational context. One example is the close cultural and political cooperation of Eastern Sephardi and Mizrahi Jews with their non-Jewish Arab neighbors in 1960s Argentina (see Sitton, *Sephardi Communities Today*, 322–24).

227. Ruppin, *Soziologie der Juden*, 2:131. Another estimate, half a million in 1903, comes from Ángel Pulido y Fernández, *Los israelitas españoles y el idioma castellano* (Barcelona: Riopiedras, 1992 [1904]).

228. Edwin Black, "Hispanics and Jews: A Hopeful New Alliance," *Jewish Monthly* (May 1986): 12–19; Peter Beinart, "New Bedfellows," *New Republic* (August 11 and 18, 1997): 22–26. Interestingly, the Jewish identity of some self-proclaimed crypto-Jews in the United States is unwittingly or unconsciously Ashkenazic. Liebman Jacobs, *Hidden Heritage*, 141–42, 144–45.

229. See, for example, Liebman Jacobs's recollections of her 1950s Sunday-school education in *Hidden Heritage*, 2.

230. Neulander, "Crypto-Jews of the Southwest"; Golden, *Remnants of Crypto-Jews*, 26, 36, 41, 54, 62, 82, 87, 90, 96, 97, 98, 99, 100, 132, 157, 158, 164, 170, 190, 193, 196, 199, 201. Consider, too, incorrect information about Jewish names, naming traditions, and Spanish etymology (in Golden, *Remnants of Crypto-Jews*, 38–39, 50, 131, 132, 184, 196, 199).

231. Golden, *Remnants of Crypto-Jews*, 44. Some have (presumably Catholic) Irish ancestry (pp. 120, 174), and others embrace Protestantism or Messianic Judaism (e.g., pp. 86, 88, 128, 135). The apparent ignorance of Spanish displayed by many Ash-

kenazic mediators of modern crypto-Judaism may help to explain the lack of appreciation for these southwestern populations (e.g., p. 160).

232. Ibid., 135. Consider also the following testimony (p. 34): "It doesn't feel important that I find out if I'm Jewish. I'm interested in genealogy and interested in the truth."

233. Ibid., 13.

234. Ibid., back cover blurbs by Elana Harris (managing editor of *B'nai B'rith Magazine*) and Norman Simms (coordinating editor of *Mentalités/Mentalities*).

235. Golden, *Remnants of Crypto-Jews*, passim.

236. Pauline Kollontai, "Messianic Jews and Jewish Identity," *Journal of Modern Jewish Studies* 3:2 (July 2004): 195–205.

237. Golden, *Remnants of Crypto-Jews*, 45, 48, 53, 60, 69, 83, 195, 196, 203; Hordes, *To the End of the Earth*, passim.

238. Sarna, *American Judaism*, 356–74; Jonathan D. Sarna, "The Secret of Jewish Continuity," *Commentary* 98:4 (October 1994): 55–58.

239. Novick, *Holocaust in American Life*, 190.

240. Jacob Rader Marcus, ed., *The Jew in the American World: A Source Book* (Detroit: Wayne State University Press, 1996), 615; Novick, *Holocaust in American Life*, 190.

241. Novick, *Holocaust in American Life*, esp. 184–90.

242. Others report that non-Jews were the first to ascribe to these interviewees a Jewish identity. See, for example, Golden, *Remnants of Crypto-Jews*, 27, 31–32, 40, 42, 112, 139, 141, 167, 187, 201.

243. See, for example, Liebman Jacobs, *Hidden Heritage*, 26–28, 134, 137–39. In reality, Judaism was a legal religion in Spain and Portugal until 1492 and 1497, respectively, and the Inquisition targeted not Jews but rather heretics or "bad Christians." Indeed, most of that institution's victims in the sixteenth century were suspected Protestants of non-Jewish descent.

244. For an article on the recent openness of the mainstream Jewish community to nonwhite Jews, see Debra Nussbaum Cohen, "Finding Their Voice," *Jewish Week* (December 6, 2002).

NOTES TO CHAPTER 6

1. Tom W. Smith, *Jewish Distinctiveness in America: A Statistical Portrait* (New York: American Jewish Committee, 2005), viii.

2. Ibid., 55.

3. Ibid., 287. See also Tom W. Smith, *Intergroup Relations in a Diverse America: Data from the 2000 General Survey* (New York: American Jewish Committee, 2001).

4. Barry Kosmin to Hal Lewis, December 14, 1998; Hal M. Lewis to Barry A. Kosmin, Director of Research, Council of Jewish Federations, New York, December 20, 1988; Hal M. Lewis to Steven Huberman, Jewish Federation of Greater Los Angeles, January 3, 1989; Hal Lewis to Michael Novick, Executive Director of the Jewish Federation of Greater

Seattle, January 9, 1989; all in box 9, folder "ADM, Demographic Study, 1986–1989," ASF.

5. Lisa Aslan, "'Oh, So That's Why You Look So Exotic!': Musings of an Iraqi-Persian Jewess," *New Voices* (December 2005).

6. Julie Iny, "Ashkenazi Eyes," in Loolwa Khazzoom, ed., *The Flying Camel: Essays on Identity by Women of North African and Middle Eastern Jewish Heritage,* 81–100 (New York: Seal, 2003), 83.

7. Levy, "How the Camel Found Its Wings," 179.

8. Marc D. Angel, "Building Sephardic House," undated flier (c. 1998), author's private collection.

9. Rachel Amado Bortnick, "Ladinokomunita's (Rachel Amado Bortnick) review of Flor de Serena's concert in San Diego," weblog of Vanessa Paloma, http://vanessapaloma.blogspot.com/2007/07/ladinokomunitas-rachel-amado-bortnick.html (accessed September 7, 2007). The original Ladino reads, "siempre remarko ke kuando ay konserto de kantes en Yiddish i en Ebreo, lo yaman 'Jewish Music,' ma kuando es en Ladino, es 'Sephardic Music.'"

10. Sanchez, "Wrestling with the Angel of Identity," 17. See also Tobin, Tobin, and Rubin, *In Every Tongue*; Kaye/Kantrowitz, *Colors of Jews*.

11. Khazzoom, introduction to *Flying Camel*, xv.

12. Regarding the question "Is the Jew white?" American Jewish historiography has tacitly equated Jewish identity with *ashkenaziut* and has thereby reinforced the whiteness of that identity. For examples, see Brodkin, *How Jews Became White Folks,* and Goldstein, *Price of Whiteness*. For an exception, see the works of Katya Gibel Azoulay.

13. For a discussion of ethnic identity among American Jews, see Sergio della Pergola, "Socio-demographic Aspects and Types of Identity of Sephardic and Ashkenazic Jews in the United States in 1990," in Michel Abitbol, Galit Hasan-Rokem, and Yom Tov Assis, eds., *Hispano-Jewish Civilization after 1492* [in Hebrew] (Jerusalem: Misgav Yerushalayim, 1997), 105–35.

14. Egon Mayer, Barry Kosmin, and Ariela Keysar, *American Jewish Identity Survey 2001* (New York: Center for Cultural Judaism, 2003), 53.

15. Ibid., 9.

16. Gale, *Sephardim of Sydney*, 26.

17. Ibid., 59.

18. Ibid., 49.

19. Ibid., 60–61.

20. Malcolm Gladwell, *The Tipping Point: How Little Things Can Make a Big Difference* (Boston: Little, Brown, 2000), 12.

21. A recent study (Tobin, Tobin, and Rubin, *In Every Tongue*, 20–21) argues that "diverse Jews," including Sephardim and Mizrahim, constitute at least 20 percent of the broader community. However, these authors do not discuss the issue of impact.

Index

Aaroni, Avraham, 231n70
Aboab, Imanuel, 14
Abolafia, Jennie, 168, 283n116, 283n118
Abravanel family, 128
Abravanel, Isaac, 129, 176, 246n43
Abravanel No.1116 (Sephardic Masonic lodge), 142, 174, 176, 177, 269n195, 289n165, 289n170, 289n172, 289n174
Abravanel Square Club, 177, 290n181
Abrevaya, Chek, 92
accomplishment, myth of, 51
acculturation, 42–46, 85–86, 91–93, 177–178, 244n30, 245n34, 290n183, 290n184
adamiyeh, 114
Adatto, Albert, 36
Adler, Cyrus, 66, 67, 73, 95, 216n35, 221n101, 228n26, 229n40, 233n100, 245n40, 249n87
Africa, African, 99, 146, 167, 259n34. *See also* North Africa
African Americans, 8, 39, 116, 151, 157, 188, 276n38. See also *shvartze/shvartze khaye*
African American Vernacular English, 151
African-Caribbean, 151
Agudat Achim Oriental Society of New York, 43
Aguila, La, 256n5
Akademiya LaLashon HaIvrit. *See* Hebrew Language Academy
Albuquerque, 180, 181

Alcosser, Leon, 118, 276n36
Aleppo, 43, 74, 75, 102, 127, 182, 183, 184, 210n63, 223n138, 269n204. *See also* Syria
Alexandria, Egypt, 28
Algeria, 43, 55, 228n33
Algranate, Behor, 38
Alliance Israélite Universelle, 34, 56, 67, 73, 74, 137, 229n40, 236n141, 279n63
Altchek, David, 155
Altchek, Emanuel, 155
Altchek, Salvatore, 155
Altchek, Victor, vii, 155
Alva, Ya'akov, 23
Amado, Raphael S., 173
Amateau, Albert J., 1, 24, 30, 49, 115, 118, 124, 216n36, 218n50, 251n120, 251n122, 252n133, 262n76, 262n78, 264n111, 266n144, 268n174
America, La, 9, 23, 28, 29, 31, 95, 97, 99, 108, 111 (illustration), 126, 130, 135, 140, 141, 153, 161, 205n42, 251n120, 257n17, 262n77
American Israelite, 119
American Jewish Committee, 105, 120, 122, 188, 262n78
American Jewish community, 2, 3, 4, 8, 189, 190, 192
American Jewish Historical Society, ix, 125
American Jewish historiography, 2–3, 5, 7, 8, 79, 145–148, 187, 192, 200n9, 204n31

297

American Jewish Identity Survey, 190
American Sephardi Federation (ASF), 3, 4, 35, 46, 105, 107, 125–126, 188, 189, 263n101
American Society of Sephardic Studies, 3
Americans of Jewish Descent, 86
American Union of Roumanian Jews, 135
American Weekly Jewish News, 131, 137, 138
Amerikaner, Der, 118
Amharic, 105
Amiras, Mentesh, 282n102
Amsterdam, 14, 84, 87, 102, 200n8, 245n40, 284n126
Anatolian Peninsula. *See* Turkey
Andalusia, 152
Angel, Marc D. (Rabbi Dr.), x, 100, 130, 180, 189, 205n42, 245n40, 248n68, 248n71, 255n157, 266n143
Angel, Moise, 92
Anglo-America, 103, 173, 178
Anglo-British, 151
anti-Semitism, 31, 157–158, 173, 181, 186, 288n158
Antwerp, 13, 87
Arab: as ethnic identity, 7, 19, 20, 44, 46, 104, 107, 114, 115, 157, 182, 183, 184, 189, 191, 192, 222n120, 254n150, 255n157, 257n9, 292n207, 293n222, 293n226; Jew, 293n225
Arabian Peninsula, 89, 215n14
Arabic, 16, 17, 20, 43, 52, 53, 55, 58, 95, 100, 105, 112, 120, 121, 125, 144, 147, 152, 169, 184, 193, 205n42, 229n44, 249n82, 264n113, 268n185, 290n181. *See also* Judeo-Arabic
Arabs, 8

Aragon, 152
Aramaic, 16, 52, 152, 213n120
Argentina, 156, 269n204, 293n226. *See also* Buenos Aires
Armenia(n), 48, 175, 216n38
Aroeste, Dan Meir, 274n24, 275n28
Ascher, Alfred, 1
Ascher, Gloria, vii, 1, 199n3
Asia, 99, 146, 167. *See also* Central Asia
Asian, 100, 119, 188, 224n158
Asian Americans, 8
Asians, 133
Ashkenazim, 14, 17, 22, 23, 24, 34, 63, 82, 83, 89, 97, 99, 101, 104, 106, 107, 108–149, 155, 156, 157, 160, 166, 170, 171, 179, 185, 187, 188, 189, 191, 194, 203n19, 227n21, 229n44, 235n124, 242–243n12, 243n21, 252n128, 255–256n160, 256n163, 256n5, 266n136, 266n143, 268n174, 273–274n22, 276n38, 293n228, 293–294n231, 295n12. *See also* Eastern European Ashkenazim; Central European Ashkenazim
Ashkenazim born in the Ottoman Empire, 21, 29, 30, 34, 43, 49, 100–101, 105, 106, 132, 133–135, 226n7, 252n128, 252n134, 261n65, 266n144, 267n152
Association for the Protection of Jewish Immigrants in Philadelphia, 33
Astoria, 159
Atlanta, 7, 109
Atlantic City, 171, 286n134
Atlas mountains, 105
Auerbach, Samuel M., 30, 48–49, 135, 136, 137, 252n134, 265n133, 267n152
Austin, Texas, 171
Australia, 181, 221n100, 239n183

Austria, 15, 16, 128, 252n128
    Austria-Hungary, 16
auto-da-fe, 13, 91, 160
Averne (Long Island), 62
Avin, Elijah, 54
Aviv, Caryn, 126
Azaria, Hank, 279n64
Azoulay, Katya Gibel, 151
Azriel, Isaac, 23, 25, 213–214n1
Azuz, Moshe, 92

Balkan Jews, 93, 143, 144
Balkans, 18, 85, 104, 118, 152, 194, 254n150, 255n157
Baltimore, 47, 109, 221n99
Barcelona, 161
Bar David (first name not given), 275n28
Bar-Ilan, Meir. *See* Berlin, Meyer
bar Liya, Behor, 274n24
Barnard College, 82, 242n5
Barocas, David N., 177, 218n50, 259n32
Baron, Salo Wittmayer, 42, 167, 193
Basel, 235n122
Basque, 186
Bayezid II (Sultan), 14
Behar, Ben-Zion, 68, 99, 131
Behar, Nessim, 55–57, 73, 74, 123, 227n23, 229n39, 229n40, 238n164, 263n91
Bejarano (first name not given), 285n131
Belgian Congo. *See* Elisabethville
Belinfante, Randall, ix, 219–220n80
Belmonte, Portugal, 179
Benardete, Diego, vii, 279n64
Benardete, Maír José, 41, 44, 45, 92, 131, 159, 162, 166, 167, 168, 169, 171, 172, 244n34, 265n129, 275n28, 279n63, 280n78, 281–282n96, 282n98, 283n110, 286n137

Benardete, Paula Ovadia de, 159, 279n64, 283–284n118
Ben-Avi, Ittamar, 58, 59, 69, 70, 72, 141, 225n162, 230n55, 236n135, 236n137, 236–237n141
Ben-Avi (pseudonym?), 225n162
Ben David, Elvira, 282n102
Benderly, Samson, 62, 232n78, 232n83
Ben-Eliahu, Aharon, 123
Benei Romania (b'nai Roma). See Romaniote Jews
Benezra, Aharon, 96
Benforado, Mathilde, 216n30
Benguiat, Hadji Ephraim, 29, 94, 216n35, 249n87
Ben-Gurion, David, 69
Bennun, Alfred, 50
Benoliel, David Z., 94
Benor, Sarah Bunin, ix, 51, 79, 225n1, 240n205
Bensonhurst, 143
Benveniste, Art, vii, x
Ben-Yehuda, Ben-Avi. *See* Ben-Avi
Ben-Yehuda, Ben-Zion. *See* Ben-Avi
Ben-Yehuda, Eliezer, 55–57, 58, 60, 65, 67, 69, 71, 72, 73, 74, 79, 141, 225n162, 227n19, 228n33, 229n41, 238n165
Ben-Yehuda, Hemda, 236n137
Benyunes, Joseph de A., 48, 91, 96, 249n81, 249n97, 249–250n99, 250n101
Ben-Zvi, Yitschak, 69
Berber, 105
Berith Shalom (a.k.a. Synagogue House), 96, 97, 100, 249n97, 249–250n99
Berlin, Meyer, 129, 131, 264–265n121
Bero (or Berro), Samuel, 261n56
Besso, Henry V., 159, 166, 167, 168, 172, 279n64, 281–282n96, 283n116, 283–284n118

Beyda, David A., 183
Biale, David, 148
Bible, 54, 75, 127, 130, 207n63, 230–231n58, 232n78
Birmingham, Stephen, 81, 241–242n4, 245n39
Bitola. *See* Monastir
blacks. *See* African Americans
Blum, Amram, 269n204
Board of Delegates of American Israelites, 42
Board of Jewish Education (New York), 53
Boas, Franz, 167, 284–285n126
Bonomo, Albert J., 29
Bordeaux, 14
Bortnick, Rachel Amado, 189, 259n37
Bos del Pueblo, La, 96, 112–113, 135, 136, 137, 138, 139
Boston, vii, 9, 47, 54, 62, 74, 216n35, 227–228n25, 249n87
Bouskila, Daniel, 180
Bradley Beach, New Jersey, 292n214
Brandeis University, 3
Brazil, 14, 82, 165, 200n8, 289n162
British, 188, 211n106
Bronx, 1, 41, 153, 156, 157, 159, 254n144, 273–274n22, 276n38
Brooklyn, 37, 41, 45, 46, 75, 143, 144, 153, 155, 159, 176, 182, 183, 196, 224n145, 273–274n22
Brooklyn College, 159, 167, 172, 283–284n118
Bryn Mawr College, 76
Bucharest, 102
Bueno de Mesquita, Rev., 245n34
Buenos Aires, 102, 182, 269n204
Bukhara, 46
Bukharian Jews, 105, 219–220n80, 255n157
Bulgaria, 38, 56, 68, 217n44, 280n77

Bulgarian, 100, 205n42
Bureau for Sephardic Jewish Immigrants, 98
Bureau of Immigration, 47
Bureau of Industries and Immigration, 135
Bureau of Jewish Education, 142, 262n78
Bureau of Jewish Social Research, 113, 122
Butler, Nicholas Murray, 162, 165

Cabouli, Jacob, 254n144
cafés, 137, 152, 153, 154, 221n91, 273n15, 274n24, 274–275n25, 275n28, 275–276n31
Cahan, Abraham, 146
Cairo, 102, 184
Calgary, Canada, 63, 78
California, 278n56
Camhi, Baruch, 285n131
Camhi, Ovadia, 106
Camp Arverne, 232n78
Canada, 63, 64, 78, 101, 219–220n80
Canary Islands, 177
Cansinos-Asséns, Rafael, 161, 166, 182
Cape Verdean, 116
Cardozo, Rev., 104
Cardozo, Benjamin Nathan, 82, 85, 86, 242n6, 289n162
Caribbean, 81, 151, 152, 153. *See also* Curaçao; Jamaica; Suriname
Carlinger, Jacob, 135
Carr, John Foster, 120, 121
Cartagena (present-day Colombia), 178
Carvajal the Younger, Luis de, 179
Casa Hispánica, 164, 172
Casa Sefardita, Vienna, 285n131
Cassorla, David Eliyahu, 103, 115, 259n35

Castle Garden, 47
Castoria. *See* Kastoria
Castro, Américo, 165, 281n91, 289n162
Catalan, 52
Catholicism/Catholic, 116, 151, 152, 157, 175, 176, 177, 180, 181, 182, 186, 187, 244n30, 245n42, 266n144, 270n220, 273n16, 278n54, 293-294n231
"Caucasoid," 47
Center for Jewish History, 46, 125-126
Central Asia, 18, 104, 107, 213n120, 266n144
Central Europe, 257n11
Central European Ashkenazim (a.k.a. Germanic Jews, *Yahudim*), 15, 18, 26, 41-42, 59, 66, 82, 92, 93, 95, 105, 109, 110, 117, 119, 120, 122, 128, 146, 160, 166, 177, 190, 243n21, 262-263n83
Central Sephardic Jewish Community of America, 104, 105, 255n155
Cervantes, Miguel de, 168, 171
Chelsea, Massachusetts, 61
Chicago, 7, 61, 62, 109, 171, 172
Chicano/Chicana, 22, 179, 292n202
China, 22, 225n163
Chinese, as nationality or ethnicity, 98, 125, 224n155, 224n158, 225n163
Chinese Exclusion Act, 48, 133, 173, 224n158, 287n142
Chios Brotherhood Society, 143
Christian, Christians, Christianity, 12, 14, 30, 183, 184, 187, 243n18, 244n30, 246n43, 293-294n231, 294n243
Cimet, Adina, 125
Cincinnati, vii, 7, 248n73
circumcision, 114-115

Cleveland, Ohio, 145
Coen, Samuel, 29
coethnic recognition failure, 1-2, 26-27, 33, 35, 45, 108-110, 112-114, 116, 117, 126, 137, 140, 144-145, 184-185, 189, 191, 257n9, 257-258n17, 258n24, 259n37, 259n40, 259-260n41. *See also* passing
Cohen, Barry, vii, 289n170
Cohen, Ben, 112, 258n19
Cohen, Efraim, 58
Cohen, Eliot, 80
Cohen, Hayyim, 37, 143
Cohen, Joseph Isaac (Ellis Island volunteer), 118
Cohen, Joshua, 27
Cohen, Mark R., 19
Cohen, Yakov, 274n24
Cohn-Reiss, Ephraim, 229n46, 235n113
Colombia, Colombian, 178, 287n143
Colón, Jesús, 157, 158, 278n54
Columbia University, 161, 162, 164, 165, 166, 167, 169, 171, 172, 173, 259n29, 283-284n118, 284-285n126, 285-286n133
Columbus, South Carolina, 87
Comay, Joan, 239-240n186
Committee on Oriental Jewish Immigrants, 98, 100
Committee on Sephardic Jewish Immigrants, 98, 100
Congregation Adat Yeshua (Albuquerque, New Mexico), vii, 181
Congregation Mikveh Israel (Philadelphia), 82, 103, 104, 228n26, 246n45
Congregation Ohab Zedek, 237n143
Congregation Peace and Brotherhood of Monastir, 141
Congregation Shangaray Chasset (New Orleans), 82, 242n10

Congregation Shearith Israel (a.k.a. Spanish and Portuguese Synagogue), 14, 29, 84, 85, 86, 87, 91, 93, 94, 95, 96, 97, 98, 100, 104, 142, 156, 176, 180, 237n143, 245n37, 245–246n42, 246n45, 250n106, 252n133, 252–253n137
Congregation Shearith Israel (Montreal), 103, 242n7
Congregation Shomre Emunah, 237n143
Congregation Zichron Ephraim, 237n143
Constantinople. *See* Istanbul
Contente, Eli I., 174, 287n148
Contente, Solomón, 174, 287n148
conversion, forced, 12, 13
conversos, 11–13, 207n58
corporate exclusion, 117–118, 120–126, 140, 189, 190, 263n101
Corré, Alan D., 212n115
Count of Villa Real and Marquis of Monterrey, 83
Creole, 151
Crespo, Manuel, 175
cristianos nuevos. *See conversos*
crypto-Jews, 13, 14, 22, 86, 87, 161–162, 178–180, 182, 245–246n42, 284n119, 294n243; of the U.S. Southwest, 178–182, 185, 273–274n16, 290–291n185, 291–292n199, 292n200, 292n202, 293n228, 294n230–231
Cuba, 118, 119, 174, 175, 288n158
Cuban, 155, 173, 176, 287n143
Curaçao, 102

Dahbany-Miraglia, Dina, ix, 9, 109, 151, 206n48, 215n19, 259–260n41, 292–293n207
Dallas, 291–292n199

Damascus, 94, 183, 218n54, 223n138, 249n87
Danon, Abraham (Rabbi), 285n131
Danube, 159
Dardanelles, 38, 167
Darmstadter, Rene, 256n1
Daughters of the American Revolutions, 243n20
David, House of, 11, 83, 126, 127
Davidman, Lynn, 4
Dayan, Raymond, 75
"daytshmerish," 92, 93, 248n79
DeFunis, Marco, vii, 49–50
Delitzsch, Franz, 208n68, 264n116
Depression, the, 157, 176, 254–255n153, 255n154; economic depression, 277n48, 288n153
Deshen, Shlomo, 5
Detroit, Michigan, 55
"diverse Jews," 8, 189, 295n21. *See also* population statistics
Djaen, Ricardo, vii, 124
Donmeh (Donmé), 266n144
Drachman, Bernard, 70–71, 142, 151, 237n143, 242n7
Drescher, Seymour, 180
Dushkin, Alexander M., 53, 232n83

East Asians, 48
Eastern European, 188, 190
Eastern European Ashkenazim, 1, 6, 26, 34, 41–42, 54, 59, 60, 62, 63, 66, 73, 74, 82, 85, 88, 89, 92, 96, 103, 108, 109, 110, 112, 117, 119, 120, 122, 124, 133, 146, 147, 177, 183, 190, 191, 235n124, 242n7, 257n9, 257n11, 257n13, 262n83, 264n107, 264n113, 273n20. *See also* Ashkenazim born in the Ottoman Empire

Eastern Sephardic Jews, vii, 1, 2, 5; definition, 6, 8, 9, 16, 18, 19, 20, 21, 23–50, 59, 68, 70, 76, 77, 80, 81–149, 161, 189, 193–196, 200–201n9, 200n12, 212n115, 215n19, 219–220n80, 221n91, 221n99, 221n100, 224n155, 224n157, 230n56, 234n111, 236n136, 236n137, 236n138, 236–237n141, 237n142, 239n183, 81, 241–242n4, 244n27, 245n37, 248n73, 249n97, 250n101, 251n119, 252n133, 252n135, 252–253n137, 253–254n143, 254n144, 254n147, 254n152, 255–256n160, 256n163, 258n19, 258n24, 261n65, 262n76, 265n130, 266n136, 266n144, 268n174, 268n187, 269n193, 270n215, 270n221, 270n222, 273n16, 273n20, 273–274n22, 275n28, 276n38, 277n48, 280n78, 281n85, 283–284n118, 284n119, 284–285n126, 285n131, 287n142, 287n145, 287n147, 289n165, 293n226, 295n21
Edirne, 218n51
Educational Alliance, 69, 118, 123
Egypt, 43, 45, 191, 215n14; Egyptians, 183. *See also* Alexandria; Cairo
Egyptian Jews, 105, 145, 239n184, 255n158
Elazar, Daniel, 213n126
Elgrably, Jordan, 293n225
Elias, Joe, vii, 103, 115
Elisabethville, Belgian Congo, 102
Elkin, Judith Laikin, 18
Ellis Island, 1, 23, 25–26, 28, 32, 47, 111, 117, 118, 119, 121, 124, 183, 214n2, 214n6, 214n9, 214n10, 287n142

Emanuel, Mazal, 70, 237n142
Emmanuel, Salomon (a.k.a. Salomón Emanuel and Shelomo Emanuel?), 173, 176, 287–288n149
Encyclopedia of American Jewish History, 80
English, 29, 61, 64, 70, 71, 96, 101, 103, 120, 122, 124, 133, 136, 138, 140, 148, 237n143, 242n7, 245n37, 248n73, 249n91, 250n103, 250n111, 264n113, 265n130; Indian, 151, 166, 269n192, 276n36, 290n183
Enlightenment, 18
Ermanado, El, 284n121
"Espanols," 100. *See also* terminology
Esses family, 182, 293n211
Estrugo, José M., 10, 206n53
Ethiopia, 46, 105, 255n157
ethnicity, 47, 50; definition, 38–39, 151, 158, 187, 188, 190, 221n99, 224n161, 225n165, 266n143, 267n158, 271–272n3, 272n7, 275–276n31, 278n56, 290n184, 295n13
Europe, 85, 99, 100, 104, 184, 188; European, 278n56. *See also* Central Europe; Eastern European; Western Europe
Expulsion (of the Jews from Spain), 13, 84, 87, 150, 152, 161, 169, 175, 226n7, 270–271n223

"The Fallen Sephardi," (popular image and historiographical paradigm), 129–132, 170
Farash, Murray, 24
Farash, Ovadiah, 274n24
Farbstein, Leonard, 293n223
Farhi, J., 140, 260n48
Farsi, 105

Feder, Der, 132
Federation of American Zionists (FAZ), 68, 69, 122–124, 262n81
Federation of Galician and Bucovinean Jews, 135
Federation of Oriental Jews, 43, 44, 98, 99, 105, 115, 117–118, 120, 121, 133, 134, 160, 223n134, 238n164, 254n152, 287–288n149
Federation of Sephardic Societies, 98, 105. *See also* Federation of Oriental Jews
Federation of Turkish Jews, 262n69. *See also* Federation of Oriental Jews
Fellman, Jack, 57, 229n39
Ferdinand (King of Spain), 13, 150
Fernández, James D., 281n94
Feuerlicht, Rabbi Morris Marcus, 110, 257n14
Fiddler on the Roof, 3
Filo Center (Harlem), 140
Finn, James, 130, 265n126
Flatbush, 75, 196
Florentine, Shemuél, 274n24, 275n28
Florida, 171, 200–201n9, 286n134
Florida International University, 3
food, 2, 108, 154, 170, 274–275n25, 275–276n31. *See also* cafés
Forverts, 146
Foundation for the Advancement of Sephardi Studies and Culture (FASSC), 202n18
France, 34, 104, 191, 252n128, 284–285n126
Frank, Mary, 71, 128, 151
La Fraternidad No. 387 (Spanish-speaking Masonic lodge), 173–174, 177, 287n143, 287n145, 287n148, 287–288n149, 288n150, 288n153, 289n170, 289n172

Freidenreich, Harriet Pass, 232–233n88
French: ethnicity or nationality, 188, 266n144, 287n143; as language, 16, 23, 49, 56, 70, 152, 236–237n141, 255n158
French-in-French (a.k.a. the Berlitz method), 56
Friedman, Levy, 160

Gabai, S., 275n28
Gadol, Moise, 29, 30, 38, 48, 68, 69, 71, 90, 99, 100, 109, 111, 117, 123, 126, 132, 133, 134, 135, 140, 141, 145, 160, 161, 169, 205n42, 248n68, 249n84, 250n106, 252n128, 260n48, 262n77, 263n91, 266n136, 273n15, 280n75, 280n77
Galdós, Benito Pérez, 161
Gale, Naomi, 191, 221n100
Galician Federation, 135
Galician Jews, 128
Galicia, Spain, 152
Galimir, Mosco, 285n131
Galveston, Texas, 120
Galway, 116
Gaster, Moses, 252–253n137
Gaynor, William Jay (Mayor of New York), 108, 256n1
Gedalecia, David, viii, 134, 213n127, 225n163, 266n144
Gedalecia, Edmond, 134 (illustration)
Gedalecia, Joseph, 30, 34, 43, 44, 48, 49, 99, 100, 115, 120, 121, 122, 123, 132, 133, 134 (illustration), 135, 137, 160, 169, 251n119, 252n127, 252n128, 252n134, 263n91, 266n143, 266n144
Gedalecia, Sarah Levy, 134 (illustration)
Genss, Hirsch (Rabbi), 67, 111, 257n15
Georgian, 105

Georgian Jews, 57
Gerber, Ruth, 76
German: as ethnicity or nationality, 44, 188, 190; as language, 23, 64, 70, 92, 93, 105, 110, 134
Germany, 16, 59, 252n128
Gerstein, Louis C. (Rabbi Dr.), 104
Gertner, L., 234n103
Gibraltar, 93, 94, 96, 102, 249n81
Gitlitz, David, 180
Glasgow, 65
Gold, Leonard, 145
Golde, Marion. *See* Kotovski, Joseph
Golden, Gloria, 186
Golden, Sam, 110 (illustration)
"Golden Age" Spain, 12, 18, 84, 100, 126, 128, 129, 131, 132, 147, 168, 170, 173, 208n68, 270–271n223, 279n65
Goldstein, Herbert S., 156, 276n38
Goldstein, Israel, 66, 67
Goldstein, Samuel, 135
Gómez, Antonio Enríquez, 284–285n126
Gormezano, Avraham, 274n24
Gottheil, Richard J. H., 262n81
Graetz, Heinrich, 53, 71
Granada, Spain, 169
Grandees, The (Birmingham), 81
"grandezza," 18
Gratz, Rebecca, 82
Gratz College, 67
Great Britain, 234n103, 252n128, 252–253n137, 265n126, 272n7
Greece, 16, 21, 27, 28, 30, 31, 32, 33, 34, 42, 49, 89, 107, 196, 215n14. *See also* Salonika
Greek: as ethnicity or nationality, 44, 49, 100, 108, 170, 175, 221n99, 255n158, 256n5, 279n61; as language, 16, 20, 44, 95, 100, 120, 121, 125, 152, 161, 193, 204n36, 213n121, 223n131, 268n185

Greek Jews. *See* Romaniote Jews
Greenberg, William, 144
Greyno, A., 63
Guatemalan, 279n64
Guiat, Ben, 29
Gurock, Jeffrey, 272–273n13, 273n20, 276n38
Guyana, 116
Györ, Hungary, 63

Habib, Jacques, 174, 176
Habib, Pinhas, 90, 91, 93, 97, 248n70
Hacker, Louis M., 114, 122, 259n29
Hadassah, 72, 73
Hadad, Herbert, 184
Haddad, Charles, 184
Haddad, William F., 184, 293n222, 293n223
Hakak, Lev, ix, 271n225
Haketía (North African Judeo-Spanish), 284–285n126
Hakim, Celia, vii, 283–284n118
Hakim, Dinah, vii, 163 (illustration), 283–284n118
Ha-Lapid: The Journal of the Society for Crypto-Judaic Studies, 179
Halevi, Judah, 12, 128, 168
Haley, Alex, 3
Halio, Hank, 114
Halutzei Hamizrah (a.k.a. *Histadrut Hatze'irim Ha-sefaradim*), 106
Hamburg, 52
Harlem, 27, 37, 61, 97, 139, 140, 142, 152, 153, 155, 157, 159, 166, 169, 237n143, 254–255n153, 272–273n13, 273n20, 273–274n22, 274–275n25, 276n38
Har Paz, Daniella, 247n52
Harris, Maurice Henry, 18, 131, 211n106
Harshav, Benjamin, 74, 229–230n47, 231n64, 240n204

Harvard University, 66
Hasidic, 67, 101, 144, 270n219
Hassid, Jacob, 177
Hausdorff, Hayim, 142
Hebrew: as ethnicity, 33, 47, 48, 141, 183, 280n80; as language, 11, 12, 16, 22, 23, 33, 51–80, 70, 71, 90, 92, 96, 101, 103, 110, 115, 123–124, 143, 150, 151, 152, 153, 161, 168, 169, 189, 206n56, 210n95, 219n70, 229n42, 232n78, 234n109, 235n119, 235n122, 235n124, 236n138, 236–237n141, 237n151, 239n181, 240n204; script, 230n49, 231n64, 233n93, 233–234n100, 286n135, 292n211. See also Hebrew pronunciation
Hebrew Benevolent Society of Baltimore, 34
Hebrew Immigrant Aid Society. See HIAS
Hebrew-in-Hebrew (*ha-shitah ha-tivit, ivrit be-ivrit*), 53, 56, 57, 60, 61, 64, 73, 74, 227n23, 231n66, 236n136
Hebrew Language Academy (a.k.a. *Akademiya LaLashon HaIvrit*), 58
Hebrew Language Council (a.k.a. *Va'ad HaLashon HaIvrit*), 58, 59
Hebrew pronunciation, 51–80, 95, 235n124, 240n204; Arabic-inflected, 51, 58, 74–76, 144, 227n19, 227n21, 228n33, 233–234n100, 239n176, 239n181; Ashkenazic, 51, 53, 54, 58, 59, 61, 62, 63, 64, 76, 77, 78, 123–124, 227n21, 228n26, 228n33; Sephardic, 51, 55, 58, 59 (definition), 64, 114, 123–124, 226n9, 227n22, 228n26, 229–230n47, 230n56, 231n64, 231–232n74, 232n78, 232n83, 234n107, 234n108, 237–238n156, 238n160, 240n204, 246n45; Spanish, 230n52; Yemenite, 53
Hebrew schools, 51, 54, 55, 58, 60, 61, 63, 89, 96, 101, 189, 227–228n25, 229n40, 229n46, 231n70, 233n99, 235n113, 241n209, 245n34, 248–249n80, 250n106
Hecht, Rabbi Abraham, 144
Helman, Edith, 165
Hendel-Sebestyen, Giselle, vii
Hendricks, Henry, 245n37
Herschfield, Isidore, 98
Herut. See *Irgun Tsvai Leumi*
Hevra Ozer Dalim Sefaradita Orientala, 94
Hexter, Maurice B., 113, 248n73, 259n28
HIAS (Hebrew Immigrant Aid Society), 23, 26, 27, 28, 33, 98, 100, 117, 118, 119, 120, 124, 125, 141, 215n18, 215n19, 224n155, 251n119, 252n124, 260n45, 260n48, 261n56
Hindi, 116
Hindu, 100, 116
Hispania. See Spain
Hispanic as ethnic identity, 7, 19, 22, 49–50, 92, 106, 116, 131, 148–149, 150–182, 184–187, 188, 190, 192, 224n145, 242n6, 289n162
Hispanic Institute (a.k.a. Instituto Hispánico), 162, 164, 165, 166, 167, 168, 169, 171, 172, 173, 280n85, 281n86, 281n87, 281–282n96, 283n110, 286n135, 286n137, 286–287n140, 287n141
Hispanics, 7, 22, 93, 259–260n41, 271–272n3, 278n56
Hispanic Studies, 163, 280–281n83
"Hispanidad," 281n94
Hispano, 22, 179
Histadrut Hatze'irim Ha-sefaradim. See *Halutzei Hamizrah*

H-Judaic listserve, 51
Holland. *See* Netherlands
Holocaust, 3, 17, 103, 186–187, 237n142
Hobsbawm, Eric, 38
Hordes, Stanley, 22, 179–180, 290–291n185
Horowitz, Aron, 63, 64, 78
housing covenants, 116
Huguenot, 266n144
Hungary, 63
Hunter College, 167, 169, 283–284n118
Huntington, Archer Milton, 165
Hurwich, Louis, 62, 228n26, 235n124
Husik, Isaac, 67

Iberian Peninsula, 10, 11, 12, 13, 20, 39, 52, 55, 87, 127, 128, 152, 153, 165, 169, 181, 185, 209–210n93, 255n157, 270–271n223
illiteracy, 23
Illiowizi, Henry, 67
image of non-Ashkenazic Jews, 4, 271n224
Immigrant Publication Society, 121
Immigrants in America Review, 135
Immigration, 220n87, 257n9; to the Ottoman Empire, 14–15, 209n77; to Palestine, 227n21, 264n107; reasons for, 30–32, 217n45, 218n50; restrictive, 25–26, 214n3, 216n35, 216n37, 42; to the U.S.A., 1, 9, 14, 23–38, 47, 109, 110, 115, 116, 118, 119–121, 124, 134–135, 150, 154, 160, 172, 177, 234n111, 247n59, 247–248n67, 266n143, 266n146, 271n1
impact (as a historiographical paradigm), 51, 76, 79, 80, 191
"inbetween people," 157, 158, 277n50
"incomplete allowance," 125
India, 46, 102, 189, 191
Indian (Asian), 48, 116, 151
Indianapolis, 7, 54, 109, 110, 257n9, 258n19
Industrial Commission on Immigration, 47
Industrial Removal Office (IRO), 71, 120, 121, 122, 124, 262n76
influence, as a historiographical paradigm. *See* impact
Inquisition, 10, 13, 84, 87, 137, 160, 169, 175, 178, 179, 180, 187, 294n243
Institute for Jewish and Community Research (Los Angeles), 8
Instituto de las Españas en los Estados Unidos (Institute of the Spains in the United States). *See* Hispanic Institute
Instituto Hispánico. *See* Hispanic Institute
intermarriage, 112, 113, 114, 156, 171, 176, 219n78,
International Ladies' Garment Workers' Union (ILGWU), 155
Intramarriage, 37, 113, 114, 142, 143, 171, 219n78
Iny, Julie, 189
Ioannina, 17, 21, 22, 41, 102, 206n49
Iran. *See* Persia
Iraq, 191, 213n124, 215n14, 239n181, 255n157, 291–292n199, 293n225
Iraqi Jews, 105, 145, 189, 219–220n80, 239n184, 270n220
Ireland, 234n103
Irgun Tsvai Leumi, 232n79
Irish, 188, 293–294n231
Isaac Elchanan Theological Seminary in New York, 42

Isabella (Queen of Spain), 13, 150
Israel: as State, 50, 53, 59, 64, 65, 75, 76, 77, 79, 106, 144, 147, 174, 225n2, 231–232n74, 236n138, 239–240n186, 258n24; as tribe, 52
Israeli, 79, 230–231n58, 255–256n160
Istanbul, 16, 29, 40, 43, 56, 99, 133, 135, 218n51, 220n83, 221n101, 245n40, 266n143, 267n152, 275n28
Italian: as ethnicity, 49, 113, 117, 156, 188, 256n5; as language, 16, 108, 120, 152
Italy, 104, 252n128. See also Rome
IVRI-NASAWI (New Association of Sephardi/Mizrahi Artists and Writers International), 293n225
Ivriya, 68, 123, 235n122
Izmir, 1, 29, 38, 42, 94, 216n30, 218n51, 275n28, 287n148

Jacobson, Janet Liebman, 22
Jaffa, 58, 229n42, 235n122
Jamaica, 102
Janina. See Ioannina
Japanese, as ethnicity or nationality, 98, 100, 224n55
Jerusalem, 10, 11, 46, 56, 58, 73, 102, 115, 126, 127, 142, 144, 158, 235n122, 264n107, 265n126, 287–288n149
"Jerusalem Jews," 126–127, 264n109, 264n111
Jesus Christ, 181, 186, 288n158
Jewish (as ethnic identity), 7
Jewish Bureau of Education, 61
Jewish Immigration Bulletin, 137
Jewish Theological Seminary of America, 42, 53, 276n38
Jews' College, London, 58
"Jews of color," 145, 189, 294n244
Johannesburg, 64, 65

Johns Hopkins University, 234n100
Judah (tribe or kingdom of), 11, 52, 83, 127, 147
"JWs" (a.k.a. "J-Dubs"), 112
judaïsme sepharadi, Le, 106
Judeo-Arabic, 54, 56, 116, 206n51, 255n158
Judeo-German. See Yiddish
Judeo-Greek, 206n51, 255n158
Judeo-Italian, 255n158
Judeo-Spanish. See Ladino

Kahan, Rabbi, 104
Kahn, José Máximo (a.k.a. Medina Azara), 182
Kamen, Henry, 209n77
Kamenetz, Bruce, 4
Kamhi, Sarah Baruh, 23, 24, 25, 214n4
Kanellos, Nicolás, 148
Kassin, David, 75
Kassin, Joseph, 144
Kassin, Sol, 75
Kastoria, 40, 253n138
Kattan, Joseph H., 163 (illustration), 283–284n118
Katz, Jacob, 271n227
Kaye-Kantrowitz, Melanie, 145
Kayserling, Moritz, 18, 53, 243n21
Keane, A. H. See *The World's People*
Kehilla, 41, 69, 122, 134, 141, 145, 262n78, 269–270n213
Khazoom, Loolwa, 190
Kolatch, Alfred J., 77
Kordova, Lea-Nora, 255–256n160
Kotovski, Joseph (a.k.a. Marion Golde), 137–139

ladinar, 17
Ladino (a.k.a. Judeo-Spanish), 17, 18, 20, 25, 27, 33, 40, 43, 45, 54, 56, 59, 70, 71, 86, 88, 90, 91, 92, 93,

Index   309

95, 96, 99, 100, 102, 105, 107, 108, 112, 113, 119, 120, 121, 126, 131, 132, 133, 134, 136, 137, 140, 141, 142, 148, 150, 152, 153, 157, 158, 159, 160, 161, 166, 167, 168, 169, 170, 171, 172, 173, 175, 176, 178, 182, 185, 186, 193, 200n8, 210n94, 219–220n80, 248n73, 250n102, 250n103, 250n111, 255n158, 258n25, 259n30, 264n113, 265n129, 268n185, 268n187, 269n192, 271n1, 273n17, 279n63, 279n64, 284n118, 284n119, 295n9. *See also* press
Ladinokomunita, 189
"Ladinos," 100. *See also* terminology
La Guardia, Fiorello, 214n2
Land of Israel (a.k.a. Palestine), 11, 43, 51, 52, 53, 55, 56, 57, 58, 60, 61, 62, 63, 64, 65, 66, 67, 68, 69, 71, 72, 74, 77, 79, 83, 106, 109, 116, 123, 161, 173, 175, 228n26, 228n33, 229n44, 229n46, 232n79, 232n83, 235n113, 235n122, 236n137, 238n165, 264n107, 285n131; Palestinian Jews, 237n151
Landsmanschaften, 41, 92
Langh, Philip A., 129, 131
Larchmont, New York, 28, 216n30
Las Vegas, Nevada, 241n209
Latin America, 109, 180, 185, 189, 257n9, 288n158
Latinos, 8, 22, 185. *See also* Hispanics
"Latino U.S.A.," 289n162
Lavender, Abraham, 4
Lazarus, Emma, 82, 242n5
Lebanon, 46, 215n14
Leeser, Isaac, 66, 234n108, 252–253n137
Leghorn, 11, 252–253n137

Lenczowski, George, 270n220
Leo Baeck Institute, 125
Lerner, Gerda, 39
"Levantine Jews." *See* Eastern Sephardic Jews; terminology
Levi, Avraham Nessim, 38
Levi de Barrios, Daniel, 11
Levin, S., 233n95
Levy, Albert D., 110 (illustration)
Levy, Asher, 43, 122
Levy, Avigdor, 15
Levy, Emilie (née de Vidas), 255n155
Levy, Hayim D. (father of Denah Levy Lida), 153, 169, 274–275n25
Levy, Lital, 189, 270n220
Lida, Denah, viii, 148, 161, 169, 170, 274–275n25, 285n127
Ligier, Leon, 217n44
Lima, 178
Lipsky, Louis, 68, 69, 123, 141, 263n84
Lisbon, 84, 249–250n99
liturgy, 81–82, 86–87, 89, 93–97, 100–104
Lodz, 130
London, 14, 65, 72, 87, 102, 244n34, 249–250n99
London, Meir, 142
Long Island, 41, 216n30, 273–274n22
López, Joaquín Colón, 157
Lorca, Francisco García, 162
Los Angeles, vii, 7, 9, 10, 104, 109, 144, 145, 152, 155, 171, 180, 206n53, 220–221n88, 258n19
Lower East Side, 25, 36, 38, 40, 48, 61, 71, 95, 96, 97, 108, 114, 118, 126, 127, 129, 136, 138, 142, 152, 153, 155, 159, 166, 176, 213n121, 247n56, 247n57, 247n66, 264n113, 272–273n13, 273n20, 273–274n22, 274n24, 274–275n25, 275n28, 279n61

Lubavitch, 144
Lubitz, Lenny, viii, 174, 290n176
Luria, Max A., 40, 153, 158, 166, 168, 282n101
Lyons family, 87

Macedonia, Republic of, 23, 258n19
Madrid, 161, 162, 168, 182, 285n131
Magnes, Judah, 69
Magnesia, Greece, 29
Maghrebi. See North Africans
Maimon, Solomon (Rabbi), viii, 76, 103, 171
Maimonides, Moses, 12, 52, 128, 167, 279n64, 286n135
Malacovsky, Zvi, 231n66
Malamud, Bernard, 5
Manisa, 28
Marans, Rabbi Arnold B., 144
Marcus, Ivan, 148
Marcus, Joel, 4
marginalization, 4–5, 6–9, 80
Margoshes, Smauel, 135
Marmara, 36
Marquis of Turin, 83
Marrakesh. See Mogador
Marranos, 13. See also crypto-Jews
Marshall, Jack, 213n124
Martínez, Elmer, 181
Marxism, 136
Mashadi Jews, 219–220n80. See also Persian of Farsi-speaking Jews
maskilim (Jewish enlighteners), 52
Masons and Masonic lodges, 173–178, 181, 287n144, 288n157, 288n158, 289n168, 289n172. See also Abravanel family; La Fraternidad No. 387
Matalon, Avraham, 75, 230n56, 230–231n58
Matarasso, Albert, 114, 131, 163 (illustration), 283–284n118

Mathews, Jill, 4
Mayorkas family, 29
Mazal, Harry S., 131
McDonald, Jason, 39
McGill, William J., 172
MeAm Lo'ez, 167
Medina Azara. See Kahn, José Máximo
Medina, Samuel de (Rabbi), 226n7
megorashim, 20
Meldola de Sola, Rev., 242n7
Mendelssohn, Moses, 52
Menéndez Pidal, Ramón, 161, 285n131, 285–286n133
Menéndez y Pelayo, Marcelino, 161
Mendes, Henry Pereira (Rabbi Dr.), 81, 88, 95, 97, 98, 156, 237n143, 242n7, 245–246n42, 248–249n80, 249n91
Menken, Alice Davis, 84, 88, 89, 90, 146, 246n48, 247n59
Menken, Marilyn Marise, 84
Menken, Mortimer Morange, 84
Mesajero, El, 37, 220–221n88
Mesopotamia, 43
Messianic Jews, Messianic Judaism, 181, 186, 293–294n231
mestizo, 125, 181
Meyer, Annie Nathan, 82, 83, 84, 85, 81, 242n5, 243n21, 243–244n23, 245n39
Meyuhas, Yosef, 57
Mexican American, 22
Mexicans, 49, 278n56, 292n200
Mexico, 125, 178, 285n127
Miami, 7, 9
Middle East, 18, 20, 21, 55, 83, 85, 95, 101, 109, 118, 128, 146, 153, 154, 155, 183, 184, 189, 205n43, 217n42, 290n181; Middle Easterners, 278n56; Middle Eastern Jews, 93

Milas, 1, 199
Milman, Henry Hart, 209n77
Milwaukee, 259n28
Minneapolis, 67
"minority within a minority," 6, 204n35
Minsk, 67
mixed-race, 8
Mizrahi, Judith, 106
mizrahi (as a term), 20–21, 22, 255n157
Mizrahi Jews, 2, 3, 4, 5; definition: 6, 8, 9, 10, 17, 19, 20–21, 26, 35, 42–50, 79, 80, 89, 90, 93, 100, 101, 104, 105, 106, 107, 109, 112, 117, 122, 124, 125, 126, 147, 182, 184, 188, 189, 190, 191, 192, 193–196, 201n12, 203n19, 212n115, 215n19, 221n100, 225n2, 236n138, 239n183, 261n65, 262n76, 264n113, 268n174, 284–285n126, 287n142, 290n181, 292n207, 293n226, 295n21. *See also* Arabic; Farsi; Yemeni Jews
Mogador (now Essaouira), 102
Moise, Nissim, 274–275n24, 275n28
Molcho, Solomon, 245–246n42
Molho, Maurice, 283–284n118
Molho, Michael, 167
Monastir, 23, 40, 41, 102, 103, 112, 115, 118, 126, 141, 144, 158, 166, 222n105, 258n19, 287–288n149
Monis, Judah, 66, 234n107
Montague, Lady Mary Wortley, 132
Montefiore Sephardic Synagogue. *See* Moses Montefiore Congregation
Montgomery, Alabama, 7
Montreal, 102, 242n7
Morais, Sabato, 233–234n100
Moreschi (a.k.a. Moors), 20
Moroccan Jews, 93, 94, 105, 161, 213n126, 249n81, 291–292n199

Morocco, 19, 29, 43, 46, 55, 67, 94, 163, 215n14, 245n37; Moroccan, 282n102. *See also* Mogador; Tangier
Moses Montefiore Congregation (a.k.a. Montefiore Sephardic Synagogue), 93, 248–249n80
Mouradjian, Ida, 216n38
multiculturalism, Jewish, 8. *See also* "diverse Jews"; "Jews of color"
Muslim/Muslims, 11, 12, 19, 30, 49, 87, 114, 115, 131, 132, 169, 175, 176, 183, 184, 196, 255n157, 259n34, 266n144, 279n65, 284n124, 287n142
musta'rabim, mustarabi, mista'arvim, 20

Nachmi, Isaac, 28
Nachmi, Sultana, 28
Nahón, Zarita, 284–285n126
Nahón de Toledano, Simy (Suzanne), 166, 284–285n126
Nahoum, Rachel, 283–284n118
Nahum (Nahoum), Victor, 174, 288n151, 289–290n174
Najour, George, 47
Nassi, Robert, 163 (illustration), 283–284n118, 284–285n126
Nathan family, 244n28
Nathan, Maud, 85, 89, 90, 242n5
National Conference on Jewish Charities, 122
nationality, 33, 47
National Jewish Population Survey, 188
National Opinion Research Center, 188
National Society for Crypto-Judaic Studies, 179
National Society of the Children of the American Revolution, 84
National University of Ireland, Galway, 116

312 Index

Native American, 8, 10, 125, 179, 181, 186, 188, 278n56
natural method, of Hebrew instruction. *See* Hebrew-in-Hebrew
Navarre, 15
Navarro Tomás, Tomás, 162, 170
Nazi, 47, 158
Nebraska, 286n134
Nebuchadnezzar, 11
Néhama, Joseph, 41, 284n119
Neighborhood House. *See* Settlement House
Nessim, Maurice, 136, 137, 138, 139
Nessim, Simon S., 33
Netherlands, 104
Neulander, Judith, 179, 181
Neumann, Sundel Hirsch, 54
Nevada, 241n209
Newark, New Jersey, 171, 286n134
New Brunswick, New Jersey, 7
Newburgh, New York, 281n85
New Christians, 13, 14, 83, 86, 87, 181, 273n16
Newcomb College, 286n135
New Jersey, 286n134, 292n214
New Mexico, 171, 179, 180, 181
New Orleans, 171, 242n10, 286n135
Newport, Rhode Island, 82
"New Sephardim." *See* Eastern Sephardic Jews
New Spain (present-day Mexico), 178, 179
New York, vii, 1, 7, 9, 36–38, 40, 41, 54, 69, 71, 73, 74, 75, 82, 85, 88, 93, 97, 102, 105, 106, 109, 111, 115, 119, 129, 137, 143, 144, 145, 146, 150, 152, 155, 158, 159, 160, 166, 167, 172, 174, 182, 189, 193–196, 202n18, 205n42, 206n50, 219–220n80, 235n124, 236n137, 262–263n83, 273–274n22, 275n28, 277n48, 278–279n59, 281n85, 283–284n118, 286n135, 287n148, 287–288n149
New York (Jewish) Federation, 122, 124
New York State Department of Labor, 135
Nieuw Amsterdam (present-day New York), 14, 81
"nigger," "nigger beast," 112
Noah, Mordecai Manuel, 82, 87
North Africa, 18, 20, 22, 93, 94, 167, 183, 189, 230–231n58, 255n157
North Africans (a.k.a. Maghrebis), 19, 57, 93, 94, 176, 249n82
North America, 81, 163, 194, 252–253n137
North American Civic League for Immigrants, 118
Novick, Peter, 186–187
Nunes, Dr. Samuel, 86
Nunez, Zipporah, 87

Odessa, 58, 118
"Old Sephardim." *See* Western Sephardic Jews
Omaha, 171, 286n134
Onís, Federico de, 162, 163 (illustration), 164, 165, 166, 169, 171, 172, 281n85, 281n86, 282n101, 282n102, 286n137
On the Side of Mercy (Menken), 90
Opal, Louis J., 174, 176, 177, 289n167
oral testimony, vii–viii, 9, 49–50
Oran, Algeria, 94
Order B'rith Abraham (Masonic lodge), 177
Order of Sons of Benjamin (Masonic lodge), 177
Oriental Bureau (a.k.a. Committee on Oriental Hebrews), 27, 28, 31, 33, 98, 111, 117, 118, 120, 125, 260n46, 260n48, 260n52

Oriental Employment Bureau, 89
Oriental Jewish Community of New York (Kolel), 254n152
"Oriental Jews." *See* terminology
Oriental Progressive Society/Club (La Sosietá Progresiva Oriental), 29, 34, 44, 133–134, 135, 266n143
Ostjuden, 110
"other Jews," 10, 206n52
Ott, Rabbi Jacob, 144
Ottoman Empire, 10, 16, 19, 20, 21, 39, 43, 66, 69, 74, 87, 94, 97, 127, 128, 129, 131, 140, 147, 150, 152, 154, 155, 160, 161, 165, 166, 167, 171, 173, 177, 193, 273n16, 284n119, 287n142; Ottoman Jews, 287n142. *See also* Land of Israel
Ovadiah, Nissim J. (Rabbi Dr.), 70, 104, 237n142

Palestine. *See* Land of Israel
"Pan-Americanism," 165, 281n94
Panjabi, 151
Papo, Joseph M., viii, x, 98, 100, 105, 133, 205n42, 254n152
Pappenheim, Bertha, 128
Pardo, Aharón, 23
Parfitt, Tudor V., 57
Paris, 34, 40, 49, 53, 55, 73, 104, 105 passing, 34, 49, 108–116, 259n40, 259–260n41. *See also* coethnic recognition failure
Pasternak, Leo, 91
Patai, Raphael, 63
Patras, 1
Peixotto, George D. M., 83
Persia (a.k.a. Iran), 15, 46, 104, 105, 107, 213n120, 255n157
Persian or Farsi-speaking Jews, 2, 35, 36, 213n120, 219–220n80. *See also* Mizrahi Jews
Peru, 178

Pest, Hungary, 63
Philadelphia, 47, 66, 73, 82, 102, 228n26
Poland, 15, 63, 207n58
Polish, 120, 129, 146, 157, 188, 227n21
Pollack, Michael, 22, 270n219
Polonies Talmud Torah, 82. *See also* Yeshibat Minhat Areb
Pool, David de Sola (Rabbi Dr.), 33, 71, 72, 73, 88, 94, 95, 98, 100, 101, 102, 103, 104, 107, 122, 146, 230n56, 245n37, 251n119, 252n127, 252n134, 253–254n143, 254n144, 259n35
Pool, Tamar de Sola (née Hirschensohn), 72, 73
population statistics: for "diverse Jews," 8; for Jewish immigrants to Ottoman Empire, 209n77; for Jewish migration to and from Greece and Turkey to U.S., 32–34, 218n58, 218n59, 219n69; for Ladino speakers, 210–211n101, 102, 293n227; for U.S. Sephardi and Mizrahi Jews in Israel, 225n2; for U.S. Sephardi and Mizrahi Jews in the U.S.A., 3, 33–36, 193–196, 203n19, 205n41, 219–220n80
Portland, Oregon, vii, 9, 179
Portugal, 11, 13, 14, 15, 83, 84, 152, 178, 179, 180, 196, 208n71, 245–246n42, 294n243
Portuguese: as ethnicity or nationality, 86, 87, 116, 181, 252n133; as language, 16, 18, 59, 86, 148, 152, 169, 180, 226n5, 245n34; Portuguese Jews, 284–285n126
Potok, Chaim, 5
Prensa, La, 92, 248n75, 285n131
press: Arabic-Jewish, 206n50; American Hebrew, 9; Anglo-American,

9, 38, 139, 146, 157, 185; Anglo-American Jewish, 9, 94, 111, 138, 139, 141, 146, 160, 185; Greek-Jewish, 206n50; Hebrew, 55, 129, 206n50; Ladino, 9, 15, 36, 45, 68, 70, 108, 109, 111, 112, 118, 134, 135, 138, 139, 140, 142, 145, 148, 151, 154, 159, 206n50, 209n88, 256n5, 262n77, 275n28; Spanish-American, 92, 160; Yiddish, 9, 38, 45, 92, 135, 242n7. *See also individual newspapers by name*
Progreso, El, 99, 142, 266n143
prostitution, 146, 156, 157, 270n215, 272–273n13, 277n48
Protestant. *See* Christian, Christians, Christianity
Provence, 15
Puerto Rican, 152, 153, 156, 157, 158, 272–273n13, 276n38, 278n54; Puerto Rico, 163
Pulido Fernández, Ángel, 159, 161, 166, 280n80

Queens, New York, 279n64

Rabeeya, David, viii, 4, 76, 239n181, 293n225
race, 33, 47-50; definition, 38, 158, 183, 188, 190, 271–272n3, 277n46, 278n56. *See also* ethnicity; nationality
racism, 4, 39, 112, 116, 156, 157, 179, 181, 182, 186, 258n24, 259–260n41, 278n54, 278n56. *See also* anti-Semitism
Raisin, Max, 41
Rampton, Ben, 151
Recife, Brazil, 82
Recovering the U.S. Hispanic Literary Heritage program, 148

Redondo de Feldman, Susana, vii–viii, 281n85
religious denominations (Jewish), 4
Reuben, Shlomo, 24
restaurants. *See* cafés
Rhode Island, 82
Rhodes, 36, 41, 53, 102, 104, 140, 144, 166, 282n102
Rhodesia. *See* Salisbury
Rhodes League of Brothers Aid Society, 140, 142
Richmond, Virginia, 66
Río, A. del, 162
Rio de Janeiro, 102
rite. *See* liturgy
Rochester, New York, 23
Rockville Centre, New York, 78
Roditi, Edouard, 5
Rodosto, 36
Rodrigue, Aron, 14
Rollins College, 171
Romanian Federation, 135
Romania, Romanian, 34, 50, 280n77, 285n131
Romaniote Jews, 2, 3; definition, 6, 8, 9, 10, 14, 17, 19, 21, 35, 42–43, 46, 100, 101, 105, 126, 193, 204n36, 213n121, 221n99, 223n131. *See also* Greek
Romans, 12
romansas (a.k.a. Ladino ballads), 153, 166, 284–285n126, 286n135
Rome, 104
Roosevelt, Theodore, 288n148, 287–288n149
Roots (Haley), 3
Rosett, Louis, 140
Roth, Cecil, 83
Roth, Norman, 4
Roth, Philip, 5
Rousso, Yosef, 274n24

Index 315

Rubin, Nan, 290n185
Rueda, Germán, 150, 173, 271n1
Russia, 15, 16, 55, 72, 227–228n25
Russian: as language, 64, 233n95; as nationality: 78, 228n33, 231n66
Russian Jews, 128, 133
Russian-Polish Federation, 135
Rustow, Marina, 5
Rutgers State University, 50

Safira, Beraha, 172
Saklad, Abraham Isaac, 227–228n25
Salisbury, Rhodesia, 102
Salonika, 16, 23, 30, 36, 38, 40, 102, 129, 144, 155, 159, 166, 174, 182, 220n83, 226n7, 230n56, 267n158, 270n221, 273–274n22, 274n24, 275n28, 279n64, 282n102, 284n119, 288n157
Saltiel (Shaltiel?), Joseph, 127–128, 274n24
Saltiel, Marguerite, 129
Sanders, Louis, 118, 119, 260n48
San Francisco, 7, 171
Santana, Tomas, 177
Sanua, Marianne, 199n1
Saphir, Yaakov, 53
Saporta, Albert Daniel, 144–145, 218–219n60, 273–274n22, 288n157
Saposnik, Arieh Bruce, 64
Sarahson, Kasriel, 242n7
Sarna, Jonathan D., ix, 42, 45, 139
Saul, Nissim S., 104, 254n147
Scandinavian, 188
Schauss, Hayyim, 76
Schenectady, New York, 61
Schiff, Jacob, 120
Schinasi (or Schinazi) family, 28, 29, 49, 94, 216n30, 265n130, 287n148
Schlesinger, Joseph, 252–253n137
Schurman, Max, 142

Schwartz, Barry Dov, viii, 78, 240n196
Seattle, vii, 7, 9, 36, 37, 49, 53, 67, 76, 103, 104, 109, 110, 113, 129, 130, 144, 205n41, 220–221n88, 248n71
Sefarad. See Portugal; Spain
Sección Sefardí. *See* Sephardic Section
Seixas, Benjamin Mendez, 84
Seixas, Gershom Mendes, 86
Seixas, Isaac Mendez, 84
Selengut, Charles, 4
Semel, Bernard, 135
Semopolos, Behor, 161
Senior, Max, 122
Sephardic Bureau, 98
Sephardic Community of New York, 105
Sephardic Federation, 99
Sephardic Home for the Aged, vii, 37, 40
Sephardic House, 3, 189
Sephardic (Jewish) Brotherhood of America (formerly Salonician [Salonikan] Brotherhood), 21, 23–24, 44
Sephardic Jewish Community of New York, 105, 254–255n153
"Sephardic" Jews. *See* Eastern Sephardic Jews; Mizrahi Jews; Romaniote Jews; Western Sephardic Jews
Sephardic Section (of the Hispanic Institute), 162, 163, 166, 168, 169, 171, 172, 177, 281–282n96, 282n98, 285–286n133, 286n137
Sephardic supremacy myth, 17, 243n21
Sephardic Temple of Cedarhurst, Long Island, 144
Sephardic Temple Tifereth Israel (Los Angeles), 180, 206n53

(Sephardic) Zionist Maccabee Society, 70
Sephardic Zionist Union. *See* Zionist Sepharadim Society of New York
Sephardim for Yeshua, viii, 181
Sephiha, Haim Vidal, 19
Sequerra, Semtob R., 249–250n99
Serbia, 23, 280n77
Serbians, 100
Serels, M. Mitchell, 4
Settlement House (a.k.a. Neighborhood House), 89, 91, 95, 247n57, 249–250n99
Shalom, Shaya, 182
Shapiro, Benjamin, 290–291n185
Shapiro, Stella Altchek, viii, 276n33
Shasha, David, 4
Shneer, David, 126
Shohat, Ella, 184
Sholem Aleichem, 64
shvartze/shvartze khaye, 112
Siegelstein, Pierre, 135
Silvera, E., 43
Sisterhood. *See* Spanish and Portuguese Sisterhood
Sitt, Ezra, 30
Sitton, David, 46
Six-Day War, 77
Skopje, 23
social group, non-Ashkenazim as a, 20, 40, 104, 107, 222n100
socialism, 113, 135, 136
Society of Union and Peace (La Sosieté Unión i Pas), 29, 93
Solis, Jacob da Silva, 82
Solis, Jacob da Silva, Jr., 83
Solis family, 83
Soulam, Moise B., vii, 27, 31, 110 (illustration), 127, 128, 156, 273–274n22, 276n38
South Africa, 64, 65
South America, 81, 116, 160, 278–279n59, 281n85

Soyer, Daniel, 248n79
"Spagnualis" (Spaniolís), 100. *See also* terminology
Spain, 10, 11, 12, 13, 15, 19, 29, 50, 52, 84, 94, 130, 131, 137, 142, 147, 148, 150, 152, 158, 160–169, 171, 173–176, 178, 182, 185, 196, 206n56, 207n62, 279n65, 281n85, 281n86, 285n131, 285–286n133, 288n158, 294n243; "little Spain," 278–279n59
Spanish: as ethnicity or nationality, 44, 49, 86, 94, 150–153, 158–178, 185–186, 159, 164, 175, 176, 182, 252n133, 271n1, 278–279n59, 279n61, 279n63, 287n142, 289n162; as language (a.k.a. Castilian), 1, 18, 48, 49, 52, 70, 71, 86, 87, 88, 90, 91, 92, 93, 102, 108, 113, 125, 142, 148, 150, 151, 152, 159, 160, 163, 165, 168, 169, 170, 175, 177, 180, 183, 185, 245n34, 245n37, 248n68, 248n70, 248n73, 248n75, 255n158, 265n130, 268n187, 273n17, 276n36, 279n64, 280n75, 284n119, 285n131, 289n170, 293n230, 293–294n231
Spanish and Portuguese Sisterhood, 88, 89, 90, 91, 95, 96, 245n37, 246n48, 247n61
Spanish and Portuguese Synagogue. *See* Congregation Shearith Israel
Spanish Civil War, 171
Spanish "Golden Age." *See* "Golden Age" Spain
Spanish historiography, 282–283n105
Spanish History Museum (Albuquerque), 180
Special Committee on Oriental Jews, 89
Spinoza, Baruch, 286n135

SS *California*, 119
SS *Majestic*, 23
SS *Santa Maria*, 1
SS *Vasilefs Constantinos*, 23
Stampfer, Joshua, 179
Stanford University, 3
Stein, Sarah Abrevaya, 5
Stern, Malcolm, 86
St. Louis, Missouri, 61, 287n148, 287–288n149
Straus, Oscar, 160
Sudan, 46
Sultan, Stanley, 239n176
Sumner, Mary Brown, 160
Suriname, 102
Sustiel, Ishac, 282n102
Sutton, Joseph A. D., x, 9, 30, 112, 114, 127, 143, 183, 205n42, 212n114, 264n113
Swiss, 266n144
"S.Y.," 46, 112
Sydney, Australia, 191
Synagogue House. *See* Berith Shalom
Syria, 255n157; Syrian, 279n61. *See also* Aleppo; Damascus
Syrian Division of the Zionist Organization of America, 45
Syrian Jews, 9, 10, 19, 21–22, 30, 36, 43, 45, 46, 47, 74, 75, 89, 102, 105, 107, 112, 114, 127, 143, 144, 182, 183, 194–196, 205n42, 204–205n47, 219n78, 219–220n80, 223n138, 224n145, 257n9, 264n113

Tageblat (*Tageblatt*), 242n7, 290n183
Talmud, 52, 61, 116
Tangier, 284–285n126
Tel Aviv, 40
terminology: for Ashkenazic Jews, 110, 112, 187, 251n124, 257n13, 258n20; for Iberian-origin peoples, 22, 164; for the language of Eastern Sephardic Jews, 210n94; for non-Ashkenazic Jews, 18–22, 43, 47–50, 98–101, 105–107, 112, 182–183, 212n114, 224n155, 244n27, 249n82, 250n111, 251n119, 251n122, 252n128, 252n134, 255n157, 255n158, 256n163, 258n19; for non-Jewish Turks, 223n121; for Puerto Rico and Puerto Ricans, 272–273n13
Tetuan, 67
Texas, 286n134
"tipping point," 191
Toledano, Rachel Nahon, 90, 91, 93, 97, 245n37, 248n68
Toledo, 206n56
Torres, Albert J., 110 (illustration), 174, 288n150
Toshavim, 20
Touro, Isaac, 82
Touro, Judah, 82
Tripoli, 43
Tsemakh, Shlomo, 227n21
Tshashnikov (Russian journalist), 228n33
Tulane University, 286n135
Tunis, 245n40
Tunisia, 43, 55, 291–292n199
Turiel, Clara, 282n102
Turkey, 18, 27, 29, 32, 33, 34, 42, 43, 46, 47, 48, 49, 89, 94, 100, 107, 120, 126, 130, 131, 152, 194, 196, 199, 215n14, 218n58, 218n59, 230n56, 255n157, 267n152, 271n1, 280n77
Turkish: as ethnicity or nationality, 100, 108, 112, 131, 138, 154, 170, 193, 194, 254n147, 255–256n160, 257n9, 261n65; as language, 16, 23, 45; Turkish Jews, 105, 143
Tuvi, Esther, 151

Unamuno, Miguel de, 165, 168
Union and Peace Society. *See* Society of Union and Peace
Union of American Hebrew Congregations, 42
Union of Orthodox Synagogues of America (Union of Orthodox Jewish Congregations of America), 70, 141–142
Union of Sephardic Congregations (USC), 72, 101, 103
Union of Sephardic Jewish Organizations, 104
United Hebrew Charities, 26, 34, 90, 247n61, 247n66
United Kingdom, 65, 77, 81, 131. *See also* Anglo-British
United Sephardim of Brooklyn, 144
La Universal of Brooklyn (Masonic lodge), 176
University of Breslau, 53, 71
University of California at Los Angeles, 3
University of Cincinnati, 167
University of Salamanca, 162
University of Washington (Law School), 3, 49
U.S. Civil Rights Act of 1964, 50
U.S. Federal Court of Appeals, 50
Va'ad HaLashon HaIvri. See Hebrew Language Council
Valensi family, 29
Vara, La, 24, 27, 40, 44, 92, 109, 110 (illustration), 151, 156, 171, 174, 204n39, 259n35, 265n129, 287n141, 290n183
Varon, Benjamin, 129
Vega, Bernardo, 152, 153, 155, 156, 278n54
Vega, Lope de, 163, 168
Venezuela, 244n28

Venice, 15
Victory Bulletin, 45
Vidas, Albert de, 105, 106
Vidin, Bulgaria, 217n44
Vienna, 233n95, 236–237n141, 253n137, 275n28, 286n131
Vilna, 130
Vivas, Maria, 282n102

Wahab, Mohammed Abdul, 183
Wahba, Rachel, 5, 145, 148
Warsaw, 64
Washington, 160, 171
Washington Heights, New York, 273–274n22
Weiller, Claire Carvalho, 83
Weinman, Louis, 143
Weinreich, Uriel, 17
Wessely, Naftali Herz, 52
Westchester, New York, 82
Western Europe, 81
Western Sephardic Jews, 2, 3; definition, 6, 8, 13, 14, 18, 19, 20, 21, 29, 59, 66, 73, 78, 79, 81–107, 122, 203n19, 224n157, 228n26, 242–243n12, 243n20, 243n21, 244n27, 248n68, 249n81, 251n119, 252n135, 252–253n137, 253–254n143, 254n147, 256n163, 270n222, 280n75, 284–285n126, 287n142, 295n21
West Indian. *See* Caribbean
Wharton, Edith, 83
white (as racial identity), 157, 188, 190, 191, 243n18, 278n56, 295n12
White, Irving, 62, 64
Williamsburg, 114, 182, 194
Winter Park, 171
Wisconsin, 243n23
Wise, Isaac Mayer, 119
Wissenschaft des Judentums, 18

Wolf, Simon, 47
Wolff, Frances Nathan, 243n20, 244n28
Wolff, Julius Reuben, 244n28
women activists, 88, 90, 91, 93, 111, 146, 155
Work's Progress Administration, 41
World, The, 48
World Federation of Sephardic Organizations, 106
World's Fair, 29, 216n36, 287n148, 287–288n149
World's People, The (Keane), 47
World War I, 27–28, 62, 69, 71, 106, 118, 127, 141, 153, 163, 165, 215n27, 216n38, 235n124, 243n20
World War II, 37, 45, 103, 112, 143, 144, 148, 171, 183, 187, 253n137, 258n19, 287n135

Yafo, León, 139
Yahuda, A. S., 284n118, 285n131
Yahudim, 110
Yellin, David, 57, 229n41, 231n74
Yemeni Jews, 9, 32, 39, 46, 109, 112, 115, 116, 146, 151, 194, 196, 206n48, 215n19, 219–220n80, 236n138, 255n157, 259–260n41, 291–292n199, 292n207
Yeshibat Minhat Areb, 82

Yeshiva University, 1, 103
Yeshiva University Museum, 125
Yidishe Tagblatt, Der, 141
Yiddish, 1, 17, 18, 26, 29, 33, 43, 45, 48, 52, 54, 56, 61, 62, 92, 93, 105, 108, 109, 111, 113, 114, 115, 119, 120, 121, 122, 123, 124, 133, 134, 140, 141, 145, 189, 219n70, 233n95, 263n91, 264n109, 290n183
"Yiddishim," 112
YIVO, 125
Young Turk revolution, 30
Yugoslavia, 63, 285n131

Zagreb, 63
Zenner, Walter, ix, 4, 128
Zionism, 10, 58, 62, 63, 64, 65, 68, 69, 70, 71, 106, 122–124, 126, 141–142, 161, 189, 191, 262n81, 263n84, 264–265n121
Zionist Congress, 233n93, 233n95, 235n122
Zionist Federation, 234n103
Zionist Organization of America (formerly Federation of American Zionists), 45
Zionist Sepharadim Society of New York (*Aguda Sionít Sefaradít* or Sephardic Zionist Union), 68, 70, 71, 123, 141–142

About the Author

AVIVA BEN-UR is Associate Professor in the Department of Judaic and Near Eastern Studies at the University of Massachusetts Amherst. She is the author of several articles on the Jewish community of Suriname, including "A Matriarchal Matter: Slavery, Conversion, and Upward Mobility in Colonial Suriname," in Richard Kagan and Philip Morgan, eds., *Atlantic Diasporas: Jews, Conversos, and Crypto-Jews in the Age of Mercantalism, 1500–1800* (Baltimore: Johns Hopkins University Press, 2008).

www.ingramcontent.com/pod-product-compliance
Lightning Source LLC
Chambersburg PA
CBHW032027290426
44110CB00012B/704